THE RESPONSIBILITY OF THE PRESS

Also edited by Gerald Gross

PUBLISHERS ON PUBLISHING

EDITORS ON EDITING

MASTERPIECES OF MURDER:
AN EDMUND PEARSON TRUE CRIME READER

THE RESPONSIBILITY

OF THE PRESS

Edited by Gerald Gross

FLEET PUBLISHING CORPORATION

New York

To the Memory of My Mother

Contents

■

[vii

Foreword—and Last Word

■

The *foreword* is a curious literary device that has the magical property of going two opposite places at the same time. For the reader about to plunge into the theme of the book, it points ahead——suggesting what he will find. For the editor at the end of a long, stimulating and enormously complex project, it points back toward the inception of the work——reminding him what he had hoped to include for the reader's information and understanding.

Since editors are the servants of readers, let us look ahead first. In the over thirty pieces in *The Responsibility of the Press,* I have attempted to encompass the widest possible range of ethical and moral issues relating to the Press' struggle to attain and adhere to higher standards of responsibility. Academics, critics and working newsmen discuss a multitude of problems facing the American Press today. No two agree on exactly what the problems are, much less on how to solve them. The result, I hope, is not confusion but excitement, the continuing excitement of a profession that never stops seeking fresh answers to both old problems and new.

I have tried to be as comprehensive, inclusive and yet selective as possible——a juggler's task which, in terms of the craft of the anthologist, means keeping many issues up in the air at the same time. My hope is that the work will be of value to the practicing newsman or broadcaster, the journalism undergraduate, the academic community and last, but equally important, the interested

[xi

layman who is concerned with the qualitative value of mass communications in America.

As a frame of reference, a background, I have kept the issues mostly contemporary. Dealing with such an extraordinarily broad topic as *The Responsibility of the Press* tempts one to go back to man's first attempts at written communication to do justice to the theme. However one volume was the project at hand, not a basic reference library of, say, one thousand volumes.

Inevitably there will be those disappointed not to find their favorite piece on the subject (favorite and most important of course!). Inevitably there will be those who will suggest that the anthology is too weighted in one direction and feather-light in another (depending on the specialty of the particular reader). All these criticisms I accept beforehand, as must all anthologists. In my defense I can only plead a shameless indulgence in my own taste and adherence to my conception of what this book should——and should not——encompass. Like a lively and well-edited general magazine, I hope that there is something in this book for everyone.

Anthologies are made, not born. A plan exists in the editor's mind. Contours are established defining the length and breadth and depth of the material to be sought. How far back should the topic be taken? Should the book be edited for controversy or comprehensiveness? Is the anthology for the specialist or the general reader? Will all the material the editor wants to include be made available to him?

These are just a few of the many problems and considerations arising out of the compilation of this volume. One might start with rigid preconceptions about the final appearance of the anthology, but ultimately the editor is at the mercy of the material itself. The material shapes the book.

Some anthologies have to be padded to simulate thoroughness. Such was not the problem here. Instead it was necessary to be ruthlessly selective. The happy situation was such that there was a flood of material available about every conceivable aspect of the responsibility of the Press. The majority of the material was of a high level of seriousness in the exploration of the many problems besetting the American Press.

It is my hope that the discussions of the problems in attaining and adhering to higher standards of responsibility to be found in this book will open a national dialogue on the issue in professional and academic centers of influence. Constant self-searching and self-criticism must be addressed to such questions as: What kinds of responsibility are there? How does one achieve them? Where have we failed? In what manner can standards be maintained and further elevated?

That there are so many questions unanswered, methods debated and problems examined indicates the strength of the American Press today. It is no complacent fat cat, arrogant in its power, condescending to the creator of that power——the public. Shortcomings, outright failures, unfulfilled hopes and ill-conceived goals: all of these are spurs that goad the Press on to seek success with renewed vigor and revitalized conscience. The Press today is in a state of vibrant awareness of its increased responsibilities in an increasingly complex world.

If some insight into the nature of the Press' responsibility today is afforded by this book then it fulfills the intent of its purpose. My introductory comments suggest no superficial answers to basic problems of conscience, morals and ethics. They are written merely to raise the questions, indicate one or more possible approaches to their solution and, in general, ventilate the whole issue of responsibility so that fresh winds of change may caress it with new wisdom and new hope for improvement.

THE RESPONSIBILITY OF THE PRESS

1 A Free and Responsible Press: Report of the Commission on Freedom of the Press

■

First published in 1947, the Report has taken on, during these almost twenty years, increasing importance. The measures it suggested for self-criticism, self-evaluation and self-reform on behalf of the Press are still hotly debated.

Admitting the vital roles the government and the public can——and do——play in the Press' never-ending climb toward higher and higher standards of responsibility, the Commission put the emphasis on the maintaining of this responsibility squarely on the Press itself.

No contemporary work on the theme of this anthology can truly call itself comprehensive without inclusion of the several suggestions made by the Commission. They are indeed keystones in modern thinking on the entire question of ethics and responsibility.

THE PRINCIPAL AIM of this section of our report is not to recommend more governmental action but to clarify the role of government in relation to mass communication.

1. *We recommend that the constitutional guarantees of the freedom of the press be recognized as including the radio and motion pictures.*

In view of the approaching advent of the broadcast facsimile newspaper and the development of the newsreel and the documentary film, constitutional safeguards for the radio and the motion picture are needed more than ever. We believe that such regulation of these media as is desirable can and should be conducted within the limitations which the federal and state constitutions now place upon the regulation of newspapers and books.[1]

In the case of motion pictures this recommendation would not abolish state boards of review; it would require them to operate within the First Amendment as interpreted by the Supreme Court.

In the case of radio this recommendation would give constitutional support to the prohibition against censorship in the Communications Act. It would not prevent the Federal Communications Commission from denying a license on the ground that the applicant was unprepared to serve the public interest, convenience, and necessity. Nor would it prevent the Commission from considering, in connection with an application for renewal, whether the applicant had kept the promises he made when the license was granted and had actually served the public interest, convenience, and necessity. This recommendation is intended to strengthen the prohibition against censorship, not to guarantee licensees a perpetual franchise regardless of their performance. The air belongs to the public, not to the radio industry.

2. *We recommend that government facilitate new ventures in the communications industry, that it foster the introduction of new techniques, that it maintain competition among large units through the antitrust laws, but that those laws be sparingly used to break up such units, and that, where concentration is necessary in communications, the government endeavor to see to it that the public gets the benefit of such concentration.*

We accept the fact that some concentration must exist in the communications industry if the country is to have the service it needs. People need variety and diversity in mass communication; they must also have service, a quantity and quality of information and discussion which can often be supplied only by large units.

---

[1] The new constitution of Missouri protects "freedom of expression by whatever means."

The possibilities of evil inherent in concentration can be minimized by seeing to it that no artificial obstructions impede the creation and development of new units. In the communications industry it is difficult to start new units because of the large investment required and because of the control of the existing units over the means of distribution.

Little can be done by government or any other agency to reduce the cost of entering the industry except to adjust governmental charges, such as tax laws and postal rates, to facilitate new enterprises, and to prevent established interests from obstructing the introduction of new techniques. Tax laws and postal rates should be restudied with a view to discovering whether they do not discriminate against new, small businesses and in favor of large, well-established ones.

As for new techniques, an invention like FM radio offers the possibility of greatly increasing quantity and diversity in broadcasting. The cost of the equipment is low, and the number of frequencies large. We believe that the Federal Communications Commission should fully exploit the opportunity now before it and should prevent any greater concentration in FM radio than the service requires.

Government can stop the attempt by existing units of the press to monopolize distribution outlets. The types of governmental action called for range from police protection and city ordinances which would make it possible for new newspapers and magazines to get on the newsstands to antitrust suits against motion picture companies which monopolize theaters. The main function of government in relation to the communications industry is to keep the channels open, and this means, in part, facilitating in every way short of subsidy the creation of new units in the industry.

The Commission believes that there should be active competition in the communications industry. It inclines to the view that the issue of the size of the units competing is not one which can best be dealt with by law. The antitrust laws can be invoked to maintain competition among large units and to prevent the exclusion of any unit from facilities which ought to be open to all; their use to force the breaking-up of large units seems to us undesirable.

Though there can be no question that the antitrust laws apply to the communications industry, we would point out that these laws are extremely vague. They can be very dangerous to the freedom and the effectiveness of the press. They can be used to limit voices in opposition and to hinder the processes of public education.

Since the Commission looks principally to the units of the press itself to take joint action to provide the diversity, quantity, and quality of information and discussion which a free society requires, it would not care to see such action blocked by the mistaken application of the antitrust laws. Honest efforts to raise standards, such as we suggest elsewhere in this chapter, should not be thwarted, even though they result in higher costs.

Since the need for service is the justification for concentration, the government should see to it that, where concentration exists, the service is rendered; it should see to it that the public gets the benefit of the concentration. For example, the Federal Communications Commission should explore the possibilities of requiring the radio networks to increase the number of their affiliated stations and of using clear-channel licenses as a means of serving all the less populous regions of the country. The extension of radio service of the quality supplied by the networks and the maintenance and multiplication of local stations are of the first importance. There are only two ways of obtaining these results: they can be achieved by the acceptance of responsibility by the industry, or they can be achieved by government ownership. We prefer the former.

3. *As an alternative to the present remedy for libel, we recommend legislation by which the injured party might obtain a retraction or a restatement of the facts by the offender or an opportunity to reply.*

The only legal method by which a person injured by false statements in the press may vindicate his reputation is a civil action for damages. The remedy is expensive, difficult, and encumbered with technicalities. Many injured persons hesitate to sue because of the "shadow of racketeering and blackmail which hangs over libel plaintiffs."[2]

---

[2] Riesman, in *Columbia Law Review,* XLII, 1282, 1314–40. For a description of this remedy as well as for a more comprehensive discussion of the relation of government to the press, see the report to the Commission of one of its members, Zechariah Chafee, Jr., entitled *Government and Mass Communications,* to be published by the University of Chicago Press.

The proposed remedy should operate quickly while the issue is before the public. It should lead to an increase in the practice, now common among the responsible members of the press, of voluntarily correcting misstatements. It ought to diminish lying in the press.

We are opposed to the group libel laws now under discussion in several states. We believe that an action for libel should be a civil suit brought by a person who can show that he, as an individual, was damaged by a false statement about him. We fear that, if an individual may sue or initiate a criminal prosecution, because a group he belongs to has been criticized falsely, the law might be used to suppress legitimate public controversy.

The Commission has given extensive consideration to numerous suggested methods of reducing lying in the press by law. We insist that, morally considered, the freedom of the press is a conditional right ——conditional on the honesty and responsibility of writer, broadcaster, or publisher. A man who lies, intentionally or carelessly, is not morally entitled to claim the protection of the First Amendment. The remedy for press lying, however, must go deeper than the law can go. We are reluctant to suggest governmental interference with the freedom of the press; we see many difficulties of enforcement; we do not find in the present situation justification for stronger legislation than that which we here propose.

4. *We recommend the repeal of legislation prohibiting expressions in favor of revolutionary changes in our institutions where there is no clear and present danger that violence will result from the expressions.*

The Supreme Court has held that expressions urging the overthrow of the government by force are within the protection of the First Amendment unless there is a clear and present danger that these expressions will lead to violence. We believe that this sound principle is violated by the peacetime sedition clauses of the Alien Registration Act of 1940 and by the various state syndicalism acts which make it a crime to advocate the overthrow of the government by force, irrespective of the probable effect of the statements. The really dangerous persons within the scope of these laws can be reached by the conspiracy statutes and the general criminal law. As applied to other persons, which is most likely to be the case, these laws are of dubious constitutionality and unwise. Yet only a few of the agitators who are prosecuted can succeed in getting before the Supreme Court. Consequently, so long as this legislation remains on the statute-books, its intimidating effect is capable of stifling political and economic discussion. These acts ought to be repealed.

5. *We recommend that the government, through the media of mass communication, inform the public of the facts with respect to its policies and of the purposes underlying those policies and that, to the extent that private agencies of mass communication are unable or unwilling to supply such media to the government, the government itself may employ media of its own.*

We also recommend that, where the private agencies of mass communication are unable or unwilling to supply information about this country to a particular foreign country or countries, the government employ mass communication media of its own to supplement this deficiency.

We should not think it worth while to make these recommendations if it were not for the fact that in recent years there have been increasingly strident charges that the government is exceeding its proper functions and wasting the taxpayers' money when it undertakes to inform the people in regard to its program or to supplement and correct the picture of this country which the press has projected to other parts of the world or which results from misinformation or lack of information.

Doubtless some governmental officers have used their publicity departments for personal or partisan aggrandizement. But this evil is subject to correction by normal democratic processes and does not compare with the danger that the people of this country and other countries may, in the absence of official information and discussion, remain unenlightened on vital issues.

In addition to supplying information at home and abroad, the government has special obligations in international communications, which are elaborated in *Peoples Speaking to Peoples:* to use its influence to reduce press rates all over the world; to obtain equal access to the news for all; to break down barriers to the free flow of information; and to collaborate with the United Nations in promoting the widest dissemination of news and discussion by all the techniques which become available.

What Can Be Done by the Press

The recommendations we have made for action by government, though they are minimal, could be reduced still further in the domestic field, at least, by the action of the press itself. Existing units of the press could abstain from attempts to monopolize distribution outlets; they could insist that new techniques be made available and freely used; the press could of its own motion make it a rule that a person injured by a false statement should have an opportunity to reply. We believe that these changes are bound to come through legislation if they do not come through the action of the press and that it would be the part of wisdom for the press to take these measures on its own initiative.

The communications industry in the United States is and, in the opinion of the Commission, should remain a private business. But it is a business affected with a public interest. The Commission does not believe that it should be regulated by government like other businesses affected with a public interest, such as railroads and telephone companies. The Commission hopes that the press itself will recognize its public responsibility and obviate governmental action to enforce it.

It may be argued that the variety, quantity, and quality of information and discussion which we expect from the press cannot be purveyed at a profit and that a business which cannot operate at a profit cannot last under a system of private enterprise. It has been said that, if the press is to continue as a private business, it can succeed only as other retailers succeed, that is, by giving the customers what they want. On this theory the test of public service is financial success. On this theory, too, the press is bound by what it believes to be the interests and tastes of the mass audience; these interests and tastes are discovered by finding out what the mass audience will buy. On this theory, if the press tries to rise higher than the interests and tastes of the mass audience as they are revealed at the newsstands or at the box office, it will be driven into bankruptcy, and its existence as a private business will be at an end.

We have weighed the evidence carefully and do not accept this theory. As the example of many ventures in the communications industry shows, good practice in the interest of public enlightenment is good business as well. The agencies of mass communication are not serving static wants. Year by year they are building and transforming the interests of the public. They have an obligation to elevate rather than to degrade them.

The gist of the recommendations in this section of our report is that the press itself should assume the responsibility of providing the variety, quantity, and quality of information and discussion which the country needs. This seems to us largely a question of the way in which the press looks at itself. We suggest that the press look upon itself as performing a public service of a professional kind. Whatever may be thought of the conduct of individual members of the older, established professions, like law and medicine, each of these professions as a whole accepts a responsibility for the service rendered by the profession as a whole, and there are some things which a truly professional man will not do for money.

1. *We recommend that the agencies of mass communication accept the responsibilities of common carriers of information and discussion.*

Those agencies of mass communication which have achieved a dominant position in their areas can exert an influence over the minds of their audience too powerful to be disregarded. We do not wish to break up these agencies, because to do so would break up the service they can render. We do not wish to have them owned or controlled by government. They must therefore themselves be hospitable to ideas and attitudes different from their own, and they must present them to the public as meriting its attention. In no other way can the danger to the mind of democracy which is inherent in the present concentration be avoided.

2. *We recommend that the agencies of mass communication assume the responsibility of financing new, experimental activities in their fields.*

Here we have in mind activities of high literary, artistic, or intellectual quality which do not give promise of immediate financial return but which may offer long-term rewards. Only in a few metropolitan areas can the citizen easily gain access to a wide variety of motion pictures and radio programs. Elsewhere discriminating, serious minorities are prisoners of the estimate of mass taste made by the

industry. Motion pictures, radio programs, newspapers, and magazines aimed at these minorities may not make money at the beginning. They require a considerable investment. They do not attract
capital seeking quick profits. Nonprofit institutions can do something
in this field, but they should not be expected to do the whole job. The
responsibility of the industry for diversity and quality means that it
should finance ventures of this kind from the profits of its other
business.

3. *We recommend that the members of the press engage in
vigorous mutual criticism.*

Professional standards are not likely to be achieved as long as the
mistakes and errors, the frauds and crimes, committed by units of the
press are passed over in silence by other members of the profession.
As we indicated in chapter 5, the formal organization of the press
into a profession, with power in the organization to deprive an erring
member of his livelihood, is unlikely and perhaps undesirable. We
have repeatedly evidenced our desire that the power of government
should not be invoked to punish the aberrations of the press. If the
press is to be accountable——and it must be if it is to remain
free——its members must discipline one another by the only means
they have available, namely, public criticism.

4. *We recommend that the press use every means that can be
devised to increase the competence, independence, and effectiveness
of its staff.*

The quality of the press depends in large part upon the capacity
and independence of the working members in the lower ranks. At the
present time their wages and prestige are low and their tenure precarious. Adequate compensation, adequate recognition, and adequate
contracts seem to us an indispensable prerequisite to the development
of a professional personnel.

Elsewhere in this chapter we shall refer to education for journalism. Here we would merely indicate that the press can do a good deal
to improve the quality of its staff by promoting an intelligent educational program, both for young people and for men and women who
are already at work in the field. The type of educational experience
provided for working journalists by the Nieman Fellowships at Har-

vard seems to us to deserve extension, if not through private philanthropy, then with the financial assistance of the press itself.

5. *We recommend that the radio industry take control of its programs and that it treat advertising as it is treated by the best newspapers.*

Radio cannot become a responsible agency of communication as long as its programming is controlled by the advertisers. No newspaper would call itself respectable if its editorial columns were dominated by its advertisers and if it published advertising, information, and discussion so mixed together that the reader could not tell them apart. The importance and validity of this recommendation seem to us so obvious as not to require argument. Radio is one of the most powerful means of communication known to man. With the advent of facsimile and television, it will become more powerful still. The public should not be forced to continue to take its radio fare from the manufacturers of soap, cosmetics, cigarettes, soft drinks, and packaged foods.

WHAT CAN BE DONE BY THE PUBLIC

The people of this country are the purchasers of the products of the press. The effectiveness of buyers' boycotts, even of very little ones, has been amply demonstrated. Many of these boycotts are the wrong kind for the wrong purposes; they are the work of pressure groups seeking to protect themselves from justifiable criticism or to gain some special advantage. The success of their efforts indicates what a revolt of the American people against the service given them by the press might accomplish.

We are not in favor of a revolt and hope that less drastic means of improving the press may be employed. We cannot tell what direction a revolt might take; it might lead to government control or to the emasculation of the First Amendment. We want the press to be free, and a revolt against the press conducted for the purpose of giving the country a truly free press might end in less freedom than we have today.

What is needed, first of all, is recognition by the American people of the vital importance of the press in the present world crisis. We have the impression that the American people do not realize what has happened to them. They are not aware that the communications revolution has occurred. They do not appreciate the tremendous power which the new instruments and the new organization of the press place in the hands of a few men. They have not yet understood how far the performance of the press falls short of the requirements of a free society in the world today. The principal object of our report is to make these points clear.

If these points are clear, what can the people do about them? They have, or they can create, agencies which can be used to supplement the press, to propose standards for its emulation, and to hold it to its accountability.

1. *We recommend that nonprofit institutions help supply the variety, quantity, and quality of press service required by the American people.*

We have indicated our belief that the agencies of mass communication have a responsibility to the public like that of educational institutions. We now wish to add that educational institutions have a responsibility to the public to use the instruments employed by the agencies of mass communications. The radio, the motion picture, television, and facsimile broadcasting are most powerful means of molding the minds of men. That is why we worry about their exclusive appropriation by agencies engaged in the pursuit of profit. Not that educational institutions are free from financial problems and the pressures associated with them. But the nonprofit corporation does not exist for the purpose of making profits. It is peculiarly able to enlist the co-operation of all who are interested in the cultural development of the country. Hence it can render those services which commercial enterprise cannot offer on a profit-making basis.

It can restore an element of diversity to the information and discussion reaching the public by organizing the demand for good things and by putting out good things itself. A chain of libraries, schools, colleges, and universities, together with the various religious organizations, could establish the documentary film in mass communication. A chain of educational FM stations could put before the public the best thought of America and could make many present radio programs look as silly as they are.

The business of organizing demand requires nothing but realization of the importance of the opportunity and co-operation, to which educational institutions are notoriously averse. The business of putting out good things requires in addition a determined effort to acquire the professional skill that is needed if the efforts of nonprofit corporations are not to be scorned as the work of second-rate amateurs.

We cannot believe that nonprofit institutions will continue to fail to grasp the opportunity they have before them. It has always been clear that education is a process which goes on through the whole of life. It has always been clear that, as working hours diminished and leisure increased, a responsibility devolved upon educators to help people make wise use of their leisure. Now a new urgency is added to this duty. The world seems on the brink of suicide, and the ultimate catastrophe can be avoided only if the adult citizens of today can learn how to live together in peace. It will not be enough to educate the rising generation; the time is too short. The educators have the enormous task of trying to make the peoples of the earth intelligent now. It is fortunate that, as their task has grown greater and more pressing, technology has given them new instruments of incredible range and power.

2. *We recommend the creation of academic-professional centers of advanced study, research, and publication in the field of communications. We recommend further that existing schools of journalism exploit the total resources of their universities to the end that their students may obtain the broadest and most liberal training.*

The importance of the field of communications does not seem to us to have been adequately recognized by the educational institutions of the country. We doubt that new professional or technical training schools should be established in this area. We do see, however, a need for centers of investigation, graduate study, and critical publication. These are, in fact, so important that without them it is unlikely that the professional practices and attitudes which we recommend to the press can ever become characteristic of the communications industry.

Preparation for work in the press seems to us to require the best possible general education. It is important that students who enter schools of journalism should not be deprived of liberal education because they have made up their minds that they want to work on the press. Few schools of journalism can develop a liberal curriculum within their own faculties. It is therefore imperative that they associate themselves as closely as possible with other departments and schools of their universities.

3. *We recommend the establishment of a new and independent agency to appraise and report annually upon the performance of the press.*

The public makes itself felt by the press at the present time chiefly through pressure groups. These groups are quite as likely to have bad influence as good. In this field we cannot turn to government as the representative of the people as a whole, and we would not do so if we could. Yet it seems to us clear that some agency which reflects the ambitions of the American people for its press should exist for the purpose of comparing the accomplishments of the press with the aspirations which the people have for it. Such an agency would also educate the people as to aspirations which they ought to have for the press.

The Commission suggests that such a body be independent of government and of the press; that it be created by gifts; and that it be given a ten-year trial, at the end of which an audit of its achievement could determine anew the institutional form best adapted to its purposes.

The activities of such an agency would include:

1. Continuing efforts, through conference with practitioners and analysis by its staff, to help the press define workable standards of performance, a task on which our Commission has attempted a beginning.

2. Pointing out the inadequacy of press service in certain areas and the trend toward concentration in others, to the end that local communities and the press itself may organize to supply service where it is lacking or to provide alternative service where the drift toward monopoly seems dangerous.

3. Inquiries in areas where minority groups are excluded from reasonable access to the channels of communication.

4. Inquiries abroad regarding the picture of American life pre-

sented by the American press; and co-operation with agencies in other countries and with international agencies engaged in analysis of communication across national borders.

5. Investigation of instances of press lying, with particular reference to persistent misrepresentation of the data required for judging public issues.

6. Periodic appraisal of the tendencies and characteristics of the various branches of the communications industry.

7. Continuous appraisal of governmental action affecting communications.

8. Encouragement of the establishment of centers of advanced study, research, and criticism in the field of communications at universities.

9. Encouragement of projects which give hope of meeting the needs of special audiences.

10. The widest possible publicity and public discussion on all the foregoing.

The above recommendations taken together give some indication of methods by which the press may become accountable and hence remain free. We believe that if they are carried out, press performance will be brought much closer to the five ideal demands of society for the communication of news and ideas which were set forth in the second chapter: (1) a truthful, comprehensive, and intelligent account of the day's events in a context which gives them meaning; (2) a forum for the exchange of comment and criticism; (3) the projection of a representative picture of the constituent groups in the society; (4) the presentation and clarification of the goals and values of the society; (5) full access to the day's intelligence.

Plainly, each of these five ideals will be served by more than one of our recommendations. Instead of stating those relationships in detail, we think that it will be more helpful to point out how the various recommendations will supplement each other in remedying some aspects of the press as it now exists which have constantly disturbed the members of the Commission during our investigation.

The failure of radio to reach all citizens adequately can be relieved through the licensing policy of the F.C.C., while the international coverage of American news and opinions can be extended by various measures proposed in *Peoples Speaking to Peoples*.

Deliberate falsifications and reckless misstatements of fact will be lessened by a new legal remedy compelling the publication of a retraction or reply and, even more, by the assumption of a greater responsibility for accuracy on the part of the press, by the readiness of newspapers and other agencies of communication to criticize one another for gross departures from truthfulness, and by periodic appraisals of press accuracy issuing from a body of citizens.

The inclination of the press to adapt most of its output to the supposed desires of the largest possible number of consumers and the resulting trends toward sensationalism and meaninglessness can be reduced by similar periodical appraisals from citizens and by the initiation of new activities for the benefit of specialized audiences on the part of the press itself as well as nonprofit institutions. In the case of radio, the quality of output can be improved through organizations of listeners in the communities and through the determination of the industry to take control of its programs out of the hands of the advertisers and their agents.

The greatest difficulty in preserving free communications in a technical society arises from the concentration of power within the instruments of communication. The most conspicuous example of this is in the ownership of instrumentalities, but the concentration also exists in the power of advertisers, of labor organizations, of organized pressure groups——all capable of impairing the free interchange of news and ideas. The danger is that the entire function of communications will fall under the control of fewer and fewer persons.

Among the consequences of this concentration, the output of the press reflects the bias of owners and denies adequate expression to important elements in communities.

In order to counteract the evil effects of concentration, we have urged that newspapers and other agencies of mass communication regard themselves as common carriers of information and discussion, that the entry of new units into the field be facilitated, and that the government prevent monopolistic control of outlets by the sources of production.

Finally, members of the Commission were disturbed by finding that many able reporters and editorial writers displayed frustration—— the feeling that they were not allowed to do the kind of work which their professional ideals demanded, that they were unable to give the service which the community needs from the press. A continuation of this disturbing situation will prevent the press from discharging its responsibilities toward society. As remedies we have urged the press to use every means that can be devised to increase the competence and independence of the staff, and we have urged universities and schools of journalism to train existing or potential members of the press in the exercise of judgment on public affairs. In many different ways the rank and file of the press can be developed into a genuine profession.

The outside forces of law and public opinion can in various ways check bad aspects of press performance, but good press performance can come only from the human beings who operate the instrumentalities of communication.

We believe that our recommendations, taken together, give some indication of methods by which the press may become accountable and, hence, remain free. The urgent and perplexing issues which confront our country, the new dangers which encompass our free society, the new fatefulness attaching to every step in foreign policy and to what the press publishes about it, mean that the preservation of democracy and perhaps of civilization may now depend upon a free and responsible press. Such a press we must have if we would have progress and peace.

ROBERT M. HUTCHINS	ARCHIBALD MACLEISH
ZECHARIAH CHAFEE, JR.	CHARLES E. MERRIAM
JOHN M. CLARK	REINHOLD NIEBUHR
JOHN DICKINSON	ROBERT REDFIELD
WILLIAM E. HOCKING	BEARDSLEY RUML
HAROLD D. LASSWELL	ARTHUR M. SCHLESINGER

GEORGE N. SHUSTER

THEODORE PETERSON

2 Social Responsibility——Theory and Practice

■

In the following thoughtful and stimulating essay on the New Ethic of Journalism, Mr. Peterson charts the historical and social course of changing concepts of Press responsibilities——from the Libertarian idea of little or no social responsibilities to the public, to the contemporary premise that the Press' freedom entails a basic responsibility to the public to provide it with sound, intelligent journalism. Going on to more sophisticated realms, Mr. Peterson urges that the newspaper-buying public has its responsibility as well——to be informed, to read the papers and to keep its mind open and its opinions soundly based.

Mr. Peterson's delineation of this changing ethic——and the interrelation between the social responsibilities of Press and public——is developed against the fascinating background of the societal configurations that generate evolving and differing moral criteria. No one seriously interested in the philosophical bases of contemporary journalism can come away from the article with anything but a fresher, more insightful understanding of this seldom discussed facet of Press responsibility.

Theodore Peterson is Dean of the College of Journalism and Communications of the University of Illinois, Urbana, Illinois. This article was given originally as the keynote talk at a communications forum *sponsored by the School of Journalism at Pennsylvania State University.*

ONE DAY IN JULY, 1959, a reporter-photographer for the *Gazette and Daily* at York, Pennsylvania, covered the drowning of four little boys who had walked beyond their depths in the Susquehanna River. He was told their parents did not want pictures taken, but he decided to take them anyway. Volunteer firepolicemen and a state trooper ordered him to leave. Spectators threatened to beat him up, even to kill him. The mother of three of the victims, rising from the body of one of her sons, held up her surviving two-year-old and cried, "Why don't you take a picture of him? He's all I have left." Moments later, as the photographer afterward described the events, he was attacked and slugged by fire officials, who tore away his gadget bag, threw his camera to the ground, and deliberately ruined part of his film. But the photographer left with some of the pictures he was assigned to bring back.

Even a month later he was sure that his decision to get the pictures regardless of personal sympathies was the correct one, but he was troubled enough to write a full page for *Editor & Publisher* (August 15, 1959) asking other newsmen what they thought.

Whether or not the photographer made a morally correct decision, the incident can be instructive for at least three reasons.

First, it underscores the obvious point that the newsman on the job is often confronted with moral decisions, which he must make quickly and under pressure.

Second, it raises many of the questions to be considered in any discussion of responsibility of the press. Here, for example, was a potential conflict between a private interest (the parents' desire for privacy) and a public interest (the newspaper's desire to inform its readers); in this instance, was the public interest served by intruding on so private a moment of grief? Here was a question of good taste; should a newspaper run photographs of the shrouded bodies on the riverbank or a mother caught in a moment of naked anguish? Here was a question of news emphasis; should not a newspaper cover important issues with all of the aggressiveness and energy which it demonstrates on covering tragedies and trivia? Here was the question of who should make decisions involving ethics; should the newsman on the job, a hired man operating under orders, or the editor who assigns him? Here was the question of what principles one should apply in making such a decision. And here again, I cannot resist adding, was an instance in which the press thought that it could resolve an essentially ethical problem by expediency; for the reporter concluded that he could have avoided all of the trouble if he had used an unobtrusive 35 mm camera instead of his bulky black box.

Third, the incident is important because the photographer was apparently so concerned about his decision that he sought the opinions of others in his craft. To me that regard for ethics seems a distinctly twentieth-century phenomenon, for throughout most of its history, the press has not been conspicuously concerned about the right way of behaving. True, from time to time over the years, some practitioners have struggled with the ethical problems of their calling. But for the most part, publishers of the past seem to have assumed that the very existence of the press assured the public welfare.

The libertarian theory of the press, which grew out of the Enlightenment, encouraged the notion that no matter how the press performed, its performance was *per se* in the ultimate public interest. That libertarian theory has guided the press through most of its existence since the last years of the eighteenth century, and it is still largely the one governing attitudes about what the American press should be and do. However, there are indications that traditional libertarian theory is yielding to a new theory, an emerging theory which is being grafted onto the old, a theory of social responsibility.

In this short space, I would like to review traditional libertarian theory, note the emergence of social responsibility theory, and comment briefly on some of the implications this new theory holds for the press.

In summary, my pitch is this: Freedom of the press, as originally conceived, was essentially a negative freedom which implied no standards of performance or responsibility. In the nineteenth century, publishers themselves began to take a new view of freedom. More and more, especially in the twentieth century, they came to see freedom as imposing upon them certain responsibilities for its exercise. As a result, traditional libertarian theory is giving way to a new theory, social responsibility, which will probably play an ever-important part in shaping our attitudes towards press performance.

As important as this change is, however, newsmen should not become complacent; for despite their public professions of social responsibility, they still revert to some of the doubtful principles of libertarian theory in deciding many of the ethical problems which confront them.

I

The professional attitudes that a reporter for the Buffalo *Courier-Express* and the writer for *Pravda* hold toward their craft have been shaped in part, whether they realize it or not, by the assumptions of their societies. So are their public's expectations of the functions of the press. For the ideas that any society holds about what the press should be and do arise from the way in which that society has answered certain basic questions: What is the nature of man? What is the ideal relationship between man and the state? What is the nature of truth?

Both our theory of the press and our theory of democratic government rest upon the answers we have come up with to those questions. We have taken our answers from a number of theorists of the seventeenth and eighteenth centuries whose ideas added up to the libertarian philosophy.

Behind this philosophy was the Newtonian idea that the universe is a vast perpetual motion machine, going on timelessly according to certain laws of nature. The Creator had set man down into this rationally planned universe and then withdrawn. But man could work out his own salvation because his Creator had given him reason. Applying that reason, man could discover the timeless laws of nature which govern the universe and bring his institutions into harmony with them. By so doing, he could build the good society.

All men, those early thinkers also believed, are born with certain natural rights. To enjoy those rights to their fullest, men formed governments, their badge of lost innocence. Before men first got together to establish governments, the libertarians thought, men lived free and equal in a state of nature. In such circumstances, they held their rights precariously; there was ever the danger that the strong bullies among them might take away their liberty and their property. So men by common consent formed governments to protect their property and to make sure that their natural rights were not curtailed.

The best way the government could assure men of their rights was by leaving the individual as free as possible. Hence, according to the libertarians, the best government was that which governed least. If the government betrayed the liberties of the people or failed to protect private property, the whole deal was off; government was at an end, and the people had the right and duty to establish order anew.

Those early libertarians, who had long seen church or state hoard truth as its monopoly, argued that truth does not derive from any temporal authority, but from man's intellect. Men can find truth by using reason; he is not to be directed or led to it. By feeding his free mind from the open marketplace of ideas, man can discover the all-embracing truths which unify the universe and everything in it.

The libertarians, then, had their answers to the basic questions mentioned earlier. What is the nature of man? Man is a perfectible creature of reason, born free, who wishes to know truth and be governed by it. What is the ideal relationship between man and the state? The state should interfere as little as possible in the affairs of its citizens. What is the nature of truth? Truth is the key to understanding the laws of nature and the good society. It is not the proud possession of the few, but the property of all men if they will but use their reason to find it.

From those same answers came our traditional libertarian theory of the press. Under it the press was to have only wide and scattered boundaries to its freedom——laws against obscenity and libel, mild laws against sedition. Virtually everything the press carried served the cause of truth. If what it carried was false, men would reject it; if what it carried was true, men would accept it. More often, of course, man would find some truth amidst falsehood, some falsehood amidst truth. But as long as he had free access to all information and ideas, he would eventually find the truth he sought. The system carried its own built-in correctives against those who would lie and distort and suppress. For although some men might find it profitable to lie, other men might find it profitable to expose them. And over all was that most powerful safeguard of all——men's rationality.

For several reasons, the libertarians held no truck with censorship before publication. For one thing, censorship violates man's natural right of free expression. For another thing, censorship provides those in power the means to retain their power and to deprive citizens of their freedom. For still another thing, it might temporarily hinder the quest for truth by weighting the balance in favor of one cause or another. Moreover, censorship implies a fear of ideas——a fear unwarranted, given man's rationality and his desire to know the truth.

Libel laws, however, were acceptable. On the one hand, they protect the individual from unjustified defamation. On the other hand, they allow the press to make its contribution to the market-place of ideas even if it later must answer for indiscretions.

Traditional libertarian theory gave the press arguments for justifying the publication of almost anything it wished. Any interference was an interference with its natural right of free expression and with the search for truth. Furthermore, the theory provided the press with a rationalization for giving the public what it wants. What seems more in accord with the libertarian tradition than the often-made remark that readers vote with their coins every time the editor brings out a new edition?

Over the years, as libertarian theory evolved, theorists and practitioners alike ascribed six social functions to the press. Most of these functions have firm roots in theory, although the last one or two were merely grafted on:

1. *Enlightening the public.* The press should be a major source of the information which man needs to form his own opinions and should keep him in touch with the opinions and ideas of others.

2. *Servicing the political system.* Under a system of popular government, citizens should know how the business of government is conducted on their behalf. They should be aware of the important problems and issues. The press is an important means of providing them with the information and ideas they need.

3. *Safeguarding personal liberties.* The press should keep a close watch on government, that ever-dangerous foe of freedom, and sound the alarm whenever the citizens' rights are infringed.

4. *Making a profit.* The press, to be free, should be beholden to no single individual or group. Hence it should earn its way in the marketplace.

5. *Providing entertainment.* Almost from its beginning, the press has entertained as well as edified. Few persons have questioned entertainment as a legitimate function, although some have been disturbed by what they regard as the emphasis given it.

6. *Servicing the economic system.* Through advertising, the press can contribute to a dynamic and expanding economy by bringing together the buyers and sellers of goods and services. It can also serve the economy by carrying much of the information on which the decisions of business are based.

II

Just how did publishers interpret their freedom under libertarian theory? Charles Beard, the historian, once put the matter this way:

> In its origin freedom of the press had little or nothing to do with truth-telling. In fact most of the early newspapers established in the United States after the adoption of the Constitution were partisan sheets devoted to savage attacks on party opponents. If we are to take George Washington's own statement at face value, it was scurrilous abuse by the press which drove him into retirement at the end of his second term. Freedom of the press means the right to be just or unjust, partisan or nonpartisan, true or false, in news column and editorial column.

Since publishers have always been pious in their public utterances, one finds few early publishers candidly saying just what freedom meant to them. Few were as forthright——or as impolitic——as the publisher who remarked, "A newspaper is a private enterprise owing nothing whatever to the public, which grants it no franchise. It is therefore affected with no public interest. It is emphatically the property of the owner, who is selling a manufactured product at his own risk. . . ."

Yet as Americans settled down to life under their new Constitution, publishers by their performance demonstrated their apparent conviction that freedom carried no responsibilities. For roughly the first third of the nineteenth century——a period which Frank Luther Mott has called The Dark Ages of Partisan Journalism——the press was a vicious weapon of political warfare, supported by political parties and factions. The lies, the calumnies, the distortions, the plagiarisms which abounded in it moved a number of observers to bitter comment. Thomas Jefferson, who had more than a normal amount of tolerance for the frailties of the press, said in 1802:

> It is a melancholy truth, that a suppression of the press could not more completely deprive the nation of its benefits, than is done by its aban-

doned prostitution to falsehood. Nothing can now be believed which is seen in a newspaper. Truth itself becomes suspicious by being put into that polluted vehicle.

Indeed, so lacking in principle was the press that even newspaper-men themselves remarked on it. Here is John Ward Fenno, an old newspaperman himself, speaking in 1799:

The American newspapers are the most base, false, servile and venal publications, that ever polluted the fountains of society——their editors the most ignorant, mercenary, and vulgar automatons that ever were moved by the continually rusting wires of sordid mercantile avarice. . . .

By comparison, the description by Alexis de Tocqueville, who visited America in 1831, is a model of restraint: "The characteristics of the American journalist consist in an open and coarse appeal to his readers; he abandons principle to assail the characters of individuals, to track them into private life and disclose all their weaknesses and vices."

Irresponsible newspapers with partisan financial support had their heyday in the first third of the nineteenth century, although the official party paper lingered until the last years of the century.

But as partisan papers faded, there was born another kind of journalism which also has had periods of irresponsibility. In the 1830s, when Ben Day, James Gordon Bennett and others took advantage of rising technology and increasing urbanization to bring out penny papers, the newspaper began its big change from a class to a mass audience. The press switched its major emphasis from politics to human interest, crime, sex, trivia and hoaxes. By aiming at the masses instead of the select few, the newspaper became "democ-ratized."

And that democratization, even today, carries with it the perennial danger of irresponsibility. For while no one would deny the good that has resulted from the press' becoming available to the many instead of the few, the concomitant quest for a wide audience at times has led to a debasement of content and a callous disregard for public welfare. One time was in the late years of the nineteenth century when William Randolph Hearst came out of the West to challenge Joseph Pulitzer's comfortable hold on New York. Their vicious battle for circulation brought about the period of yellow journalism, a journalism of screaming scare-heads, faked news, pilfered pictures and cynical championship of the underdog; a jingoistic journalism which probably touched off the Spanish-American War; a journalism which faded, temporarily, only with the First World War. A second time was in the frenetic 1920s, those free-wheeling days of tabloid journalism when New Yorkers nicknamed the *Graphic* the *Pornographic,* when the height of journalistic enterprise was a photographer's smuggling a camera into the death-house to get a full-page picture of Ruth Snyder struggling against the bonds of the electric chair as the current surged through her, when Bernarr Macfadden's idea of a good front page was a picture of a convict electrocuted at Sing Sing under the stark head "Roasted Alive," when editor Emile Gauvreau's only half-hearted worry about the $12,000,000 in libel suits hanging over him was that the business office might deduct it from his salary, when the editor of one New York paper told his reporters to "bear in mind that from now on it is a waste of time to write a story that cannot stand up under a sensational head."

III

Meanwhile, however, some newspapermen were preaching a different kind of journalism. In the mid-nineteenth century, there were such men as Horace Greeley, who thought that the newspaper should ignore the trivialities of the penny press and the political bondage of the partisan press. The newspaper should not be politically neutral, but neither should it owe allegiance to any political party or faction. Rather it should furnish political leadership by setting the public good above duty to party. At mid-century, too, there were men such as Henry Raymond of the New York *Times,* who thought that the newspaper should be free of party but not of principle, that it should give the readers the broadest possible editorial coverage, and that it should actively promote the community welfare. Later in the century there were men such as William Rockhill Nelson of the Kansas City *Star,* who saw the newspaper as an aggressive force for civic betterment.

In all of this there were traces of a growing sense of social responsibility, for the publishers were acknowledging that a newspaper had some duty to the public.

In the new century, the professions of public responsibility became more numerous and more explicit. In 1904 Joseph Pulitzer, that noble old lion, blind and no longer stalking the pulp-paper jungle, took nearly forty pages of the *North American Review* to defend his proposal for the creation of a college of journalism. But his article was more than a plea that education for journalism be given academic sanctity. It was his call that the press should put public duty above duty to the counting-room. "Commercialism," he said, "has a legitimate place in a newspaper, namely, in the business office. . . . But commercialism, which is proper in the business office, becomes a degradation and a danger when it invades the editorial rooms. Once let the publisher come to regard the press as exclusively a commercial business and there is an end of its moral power." He had a clear idea of the sort of men needed to staff the nation's press. They were to be courageous and moral men who would resign rather than sacrifice their principles to any business interest, men who, if they could not keep a newspaper from degrading itself, at least would not be a party to the degradation. They were to give the newspaper its ideals; and, as Pulitzer put it, "without high ethical ideals a newspaper not only is stripped of its splendid possibilities for public service, but may become a positive danger to the community."

Let me mention just two twentieth-century developments which strike me as underscoring the point that American publishers have come to hold a different attitude toward press freedom than formerly.

One was the voluntary adoption of media codes as standards of performance——the Canons of Journalism of the ASNE in 1923, the production code of the movie industry in 1930, the radio broadcasters' code in 1937, and the television code in 1952. By the very fact of adopting those codes, the media have linked freedom with responsibility. True, those codes may have little binding force. One may argue that their standards are inadequate. Some of them probably were inaugurated to forestall government intervention. Grant all of that; yet every one of the codes explicitly acknowledges the media's duty to perform in the public interest, however variously that interest is defined.

Moreover, apart from the Canons of Journalism, those codes reflect a break with traditional libertarian theory in other ways. Three of them——those for movies, radio and television——regard man not as the creature of reason that libertarian theory saw him, but as essentially immature and susceptible to moral corruption. Hence ethical performance for those media seems to consist less in informing than in promoting public morals.

Second is the relatively recent campaign to gain access to information because of "the public's right to know." Social responsibility is implicit in that campaign, in which the press pictures itself as an organ of the people, working to gain access on their behalf. In another significant respect the campaign departs from traditional theory, which was basically negative. Libertarians assumed that, granted freedom, some people would talk, some would listen. But traditional theory, being negative, provided no lever for prying open the lips of persons who would not talk, since it was inconceivable that they would not. Indeed, it is hard to read into our negative Constitutional guarantee of free speech——"Congress shall make no law"——any means for forcing the mute to speak.

Publishers today, then, seem to agree with Grove Patterson, who in 1955 defined the social responsibilities of the American newspaper (the term was his own) as making certain that the people shall know; providing interpretation; including views representative of the people as a whole, not just those of special interests; and rising standards of American journalism.

Editors and publishers are not the only ones with a hand in fashioning the social responsibility theory. In its most complete and coherent form, the theory has been stated in several books issued in the mid-1940s by the Commission on Freedom of the Press headed by Robert M. Hutchins. The Commission's basic report said little that has not been said before or since by publishers themselves, although they might not agree with all of the logical extensions of the Commission's ideas.

Few newsmen would really disagree with the Commission's requirements of the press: to provide "a truthful, comprehensive, and intelligent account of the day's events in a context which gives them meaning"; to serve as "a forum for the exchange of comment and criticism"; to give "a representative picture of the constituent groups in society"; to help in "the presentation and clarification of the goals and values of society"; and to provide "full access to the day's intelligence." In fact, Grove Patterson in the talk just mentioned gave those as the social responsibilities of the press, although he expressed them somewhat differently.

Practitioners even seem to agree with social responsibility theory in some of its philosophical breaks with libertarian theory, among them these:

1. The negative freedom of libertarian theory is inadequate to modern society. (The attempts of the press to gain free access to information reflect this view.)

2. Freedom carries with it responsibility. (The various media codes of performance reflect this view.)

3. Man is not a wholly rational creature; he is not so much irrational as lethargic, and his reluctance to use his reason makes him ready prey for special pleaders. (The various media codes except the Canons also reflect this view. And so does the great bulk of advertising that all of the media carry.)

So far social responsibility is still more theory than practice. But it is by no means all theory: In a good many places, it has spilled into practice.

Across the Atlantic, in Britain, where many of our ideas about press freedom sprang from, social responsibility theory has been reflected in the activities of the General Council of the Press, an unofficial arbiter between press and public which grew out of recommendations by the Royal Commission on the Press in 1949. With a nudge from Parliament, professional organizations of journalists, newspaper trade associations and unions set up the Press Council in 1953. The Council has resisted the generosity of some members of Parliament who would give it statutory powers or the means of enforcing its decisions.

Complaints of press performance have come to the Council from a variety of sources: the Chairman of the Metropolitan Mayors Association, the Town Clerk of Poole, the Educational Institute of Scotland, the General Secretary of the Peace Pledge Union, a member of the German War Graves Commission, the National Association of Retail Furnishers, the Torquay Trades Council, the Hull Vigilance Association, even the Royal Household.

The alleged offenses have fallen into such broad categories as errors or poor taste in content, invasions of privacy, and violations of professional ethics. Specifically, the Council has investigated such charges as that an editor closed discussion in his letters column without publishing a reply from the party attacked, the newspapers published too many details when an eleven-year-old girl was criminally assaulted, that the press had tempted employees of the Royal Household to break contracts forbidding them to give information to or write for the press, that newspapers had said conductresses had threatened to strike when in fact they had said they would resign and——inevitably, perhaps——that a public official was misquoted.

Although the Council has not tried to write a general code of ethics, it has hoped that each decision would help guide its judgment in later cases. Digesting its decisions, as J. Edward Gerald has done in *Journalism Quarterly* (Summer, 1959), one gets an idea of the ethical attitudes expressed by the Council. Few American newsmen would disagree, in the abstract, with some of the positions the Council has taken:

1. An editor may end a running series of letters on a given topic whenever he likes, but he should not arbitrarily deprive those with a material interest of the right to state their case.

2. The press should not omit criticism of an individual officeholder on the grounds that it will damage the prestige and usefulness of the office.

3. If a newspaper misstates the facts and potential sufferers call the error to the attention of the editor, he should run a frank correction and apology where those who read the original are likely to see it.

4. The press should pay no heed to a city council's protest that news about juvenile gangs will harm business.

IV

What caused publishers——and operators of the new electronic media——to view their freedom differently? Probably several interrelated forces were at work. Let us mention just a few.

First was industrial and technological change which hit the press, as it did the nation, with the force of revolution in the nineteenth century. Joseph Pulitzer, as the new century opened, looked back in awe on all of the changes in journalism that had taken place in the 70 years of his lifetime. And indeed those 70 years had brought greater changes than the previous 350 after Caxton had introduced printing to England.

From sidelines of printers, newspapers became large, mass-production enterprises. So long as papers were simply adjuncts of printing establishments, one could not expect their proprietors to be concerned with professional ideals and responsibilities. In the 1830s, de Tocqueville had wondered if newspapers would ever be able to attract men of any caliber because the large number of them meant that most were marginal operations. But as newspapers became businesses unto their own, and profitable ones, despite the lachrymose cries of publishers, they became increasingly able to attract men of talent, education and principle.

Cut loose from the support of political factions, the mass-produced newspaper sought its keep in the marketplace. Meeting the wants and needs of its consumers became as important to the newspaper as it was to, say, General Motors or General Foods. To put the matter somewhat cynically, some public responsibility became good business. But there was more to it all than just profit; the newspaper no doubt shared in the increased sense of social responsibility assumed by big business generally as it moved from the slogan "the public be damned" to the operating principle "the consumer is king."

Moreover, the media had felt the chill blast of public criticism—criticism which grew sharper and more prolific (if not necessarily more informed) in the twentieth century.

Coupled with criticism was the dark threat of government intervention. The media have been in a situation not entirely unlike that of the public utility companies, which were among the pioneers in public relations because they were private enterprises operating under public franchise. Just as the public utilities saw that satisfying their public was one way of preserving their private character, so the media no doubt saw that its freedom rests on self-correction of its worst abuses. The direct threat of government regulation was clearly behind the adoption of some media codes of performance, although not behind that of the Canons of Journalism. The black cloud of government restriction does seem to hang over every one-newspaper town, however. Either it or an awareness of public duty heightened by lack of competition has made publishers in one-newspaper communities especially prone to speak of their social responsibilities.

Second, some changes in the intellectual environment carried implications for social responsibility theory. Libertarian theory set well with the scheme of things as eighteenth-century thinkers saw it. But modern thought has torn apart their tidy package. Darwin and Einstein have cast doubts on the concept of natural rights and on the picture of a mechanistic, timeless, static universe, as has modern physics. Freud and his followers have undermined faith in man's pure rationality. Most modern nations, in theory and in practice, have largely repudiated *laissez-faire* economics. And even newsmen themselves have found the negative freedom of traditional theory at times inadequate in modern society.

V

From all that I have said so far, we should see that the press today is operating not only in a different environment from that of a century ago, but also under a different conception of freedom. The final shape that social responsibility theory will take is still to be evolved and remains in large measure up to the press itself. Reviewing the history of the past century, newsmen may feel either helpless or complacent ——helpless because press performance has been determined to large degree by the nature of the system, which itself has been shaped by social, economic and cultural forces outside of their direct control; complacent because they have had an important part in shaping social responsibility theory. They should feel neither. On the one hand, while the nature of the system in part governs the performance of the press, men still have a good deal to say about the nature of the system; on the other hand, social responsibility is still more theory than fact, and newsmen still have much work to do in molding its future form.

One of the greatest deeds that the press could perform, I think, is helping its readers to accept an idea that the press has already accepted——that responsibility goes with freedom. If the press links responsibility with freedom to publish, then should not the reader link responsibility with freedom to read and listen? In short, does the citizen in a democratic society have the right to be misinformed, ill-informed or uninformed? The press has begun to see its own responsibilities, but it has done precious little to make readers see theirs.

Before it can, the press must get rid of its curious notion, shared by the public, that what it sells is a commodity like detergents, depilatories and dog biscuits. There is a vast difference between the products of the AP and the A & P, and newsmen really know there is, even if they and the public sometimes talk as if there isn't. Consumer choice is one of the blessings of the supermarket, and if a customer wants to stock his wire pushcart with pretzels and beer instead of proteins, milk and leafy green vegetables, his dietary eccentricities are no concern of the merchant. But the diet of the reader is of concern to editor and publisher. They should be far less quick than at present to keep their shelves of beer and pretzels filled with a superabundance of items, because that is where the traffic is, and far more prone to move their nourishing foods.

When the issue is survival, the citizen, however he may grumble, accepts certain obligations such as bearing arms or producing them. Even for the smooth operation of a peacetime democratic society, the citizen accepts certain duties which he may not like, such as serving on juries and paying taxes. When the issue is both survival and the smooth functioning of a democratic society, the citizen certainly should be as obliged to be informed as the press is to inform him. He has the duty to study the facts, unsettling as they may be; weigh ideas which do not necessarily match his own, disturbing as that may be; and put his basic assumptions up for challenge, impossible as that may seem. The press is accepting only half of its responsibility if it does not help him to realize that he must.

Since the uncomplicated time of Ben Day, editors have been justifying whatever they have found profitable on the grounds that the readers want it. All too often, some of them have rationalized part of their content on the shaky grounds of public interest. Editors may say that in their heavy coverage of crime and trivia they are simply reporting the seamier and brighter sides of society, something readers have a right to know. They may say that in running pictures of mangled corpses in crumpled cars their civic-minded intent is to reduce highway fatalities (although I have seen no evidence that fear is a deterrent to those bent on getting killed). And presumably they would say that in informing their readers of the every bowel movement of an ailing President they were practicing reporting in depth. What God lets happen they are proud to publish in the public interest, although it is amazing how many things God lets happen that they overlook.

In all of this there is a big difference, I submit, between public interest and public curiosity. If the intent behind much of what the press carries is really public interest, then there seems something wrong, not so much with the subjects themselves as with the editorial approach.

Social responsibility theory puts strong faith in the conscience of every newsman. It expects him, in following it, to do duty not only to himself but to society as well. On his everyday assignments, he cannot dodge an ethical decision on the grounds that the boss, not he, edits the paper; for that is a little as if Polly Adler's piano player should say that what goes on in the other rooms of the establishment doesn't concern him, that his dedication is to Bach.

3   The Warren Commission Report on the Role of the Press in the Assassination of President John F. Kennedy

■

The Warren Commission's factual, dispassionate and conclusive report on the Press' activity during the tragic three days of the President's murder remains the basic work of record, despite an endless flood of critical, interpretive and suppositious writing on the subject since that event.

Basic and enduring issues concerning the responsibility of the Press were raised as a result of the President's death and they are pursued in the Warren Commission Report. Was Lee Harvey Oswald "convicted" by the Press before he had a chance to defend himself? If he had lived, would the Press have, by reason of its enormous publicity, accusations and guesses about his guilt, deprived him of a rational milieu in which he would have received a fair trial? Did the swarm of newsmen surrounding the alleged assassin in the basement of the Dallas police station jeopardize his safety and therefore facilitate Jack Ruby's opportunity to kill Oswald?

For many the events surrounding the death of President Kennedy leave many issues unresolved. Similarly, the role of the Press on that terrible occasion——whether it lived up to or abused its responsibilities——remains a question of continuing controversy.

ACTIVITY OF NEWSMEN

Within an hour of Oswald's arrival at the police department on November 22, it became known to newsmen that he was a possible suspect in the slaying of President Kennedy as well as in the murder of Patrolman Tippit. At least as early as 3:26 P.M. a television report carried this information. Reporters and cameramen flooded into the building and congregated in the corridor of the third floor, joining those few who had been present when Oswald first arrived.

On the Third Floor

Felix McKnight, editor of the Dallas *Times-Herald,* who handled press arrangements for the President's visit, estimated that within 24 hours of the assassination more than 300 representatives of news media were in Dallas, including correspondents from foreign newspapers and press associations. District Attorney Henry M. Wade thought that the crowd in the third floor hallway itself may have numbered as many as 300. Most estimates, including those based on examination of video tapes, place upwards of 100 newsmen and cameramen in the third floor corridor of the police department by the evening of November 22.

In the words of an FBI agent who was present, the conditions at the police station were "not too much unlike Grand Central Station at rush hour, maybe like the Yankee Stadium during the World Series games. . . ." In the lobby of the third floor, television cameramen set up two large cameras and floodlights in strategic positions that gave them a sweep of the corridor in either direction. Technicians stretched their television cables into and out of offices, running some of them out of the windows of a deputy chief's office and down the side of the building. Men with newsreel cameras, still cameras, and microphones, more mobile than the television cameramen, moved back and forth seeking information and opportunities for interviews. Newsmen wandered into the offices of other bureaus located on the third floor, sat on desks, and used police telephones; indeed, one reporter admits hiding a telephone behind a desk so that he would have exclusive access to it if something developed.

By the time Chief Curry returned to the building in the middle of the afternoon from Love Field where he had escorted President Johnson from Parkland Hospital, he found that "there was just pandemonium on the third floor." The news representatives, he testified:

. . . were jammed into the north hall of the third floor, which are the offices of the criminal investigation division. The television trucks, there were several of them around the city hall. I went into my administrative offices, I saw cables coming through the administrative assistant office and through the deputy chief of traffic through his office, and running through the hall they had a live TV set up on the third floor, and it was a bedlam of confusion.

According to Special Agent Winston G. Lawson of the Secret Service:

At least by 6 or 7 o'clock . . . [the reporters and cameramen] were quite in evidence up and down the corridors, cameras on the tripods, the sound equipment, people with still cameras, motion picture-type hand cameras, all kinds of people with tape recorders, and they were trying to interview people, anybody that belonged in police headquarters that might know anything about Oswald. . . .

The corridor became so jammed that policemen and newsmen had to push and shove if they wanted to get through, stepping over cables, wires, and tripods. The crowd in the hallway was so dense that District Attorney Wade found it a "strain to get the door open" to get into the homicide office. According to Lawson, "You had to literally fight your way through the people to get up and down the corridor." A witness who was escorted into the homicide offices on Saturday afternoon related that he

tried to get by the reporters, stepping over television cables and you couldn't hardly get by, they would grab you and wanted to know what you were doing down here, even with the detectives one in front and one behind you.

The television cameras continued to record the scene on the third floor as some of the newsmen kept vigil through the night.

Such police efforts as there were to control the newsmen were unavailing. Capt. Glen D. King, administrative assistant to Chief Curry, witnessed efforts to clear an aisle through the hallway, but related that "this was a constant battle because of the number of newsmen who were there. They would move back into the aisleway that had been cleared. They interfered with the movement of people who had to be there." According to one detective, "they would be asked to stand back and stay back but it wouldn't do much good, and they would push forward and you had to hold them off physically." The detective recalled that on one occasion when he was escorting a witness through the corridor he "stopped . . . and looked down and there was a joker had a camera stuck between . . . [his] legs taking pictures. . . . " Forrest V. Sorrels of the Secret Service had the impression that the "press and the television people just . . . took over."

Police control over the access of other than newsmen to the third floor was of limited but increasing effectiveness after Oswald's arrival at the police department. Initially no steps were taken to exclude unauthorized persons from the third floor corridor, but late Friday afternoon Assistant Chief Charles Batchelor stationed guards at the elevators and the stairway to prevent the admission of such persons. He also directed the records room in the basement to issue passes, after verification by the bureaus involved, to people who had legitimate business on the third floor. Throughout the three days of Oswald's detention, the police were obliged to continue normal business in all five bureaus located along the third floor hallway. Thus many persons——relatives of prisoners, complainants, witnesses——had occasion to visit police offices on the third floor on business unrelated to the investigation of the assassination.

Newsmen seeking admission to the third floor were required to identify themselves by their personal press cards; however, the department did not follow its usual procedure of checking the authenticity of press credentials. Captain King felt that this would have been impossible in light of "the atmosphere that existed over there, the tremendous pressures that existed, the fact that telephones were ringing constantly, that there were droves of people in there . . . the fact that the method by which you positively identify someone . . . it's not easy."

Police officers on the third floor testified that they carefully checked all persons for credentials, and most newsmen indicated that after Batchelor imposed security they were required to identify themselves by their press cards. Special Agent Sorrels of the Secret

Service stated that he was requested to present credentials on some of his visits to the third floor. However, other newsmen apparently went unchallenged during the entire period before Oswald was killed, although some of them were wearing press badges on their lapels and some may have been known to the police officers.

According to some reporters and policemen, people who appeared to be unauthorized were present on the third floor after security procedures were instituted, and video tapes seem to confirm their observations. Jack Ruby was present on the third floor on Friday night. Assistant Chief of Police N. T. Fisher testified that even on Saturday "anybody could come up with a plausible reason for going to one of the third floor bureaus and was able to get in."

Oswald and the Press

When the police car bringing Oswald from the Texas Theatre drove into the basement of police headquarters at about 2 P.M. on Friday, some reporters and cameramen, principally from local papers and stations, were already on hand. The policemen formed a wedge around Oswald and conducted him to the elevator, but several newsmen crowded into the elevator with Oswald and the police. When the elevator stopped at the third floor, the cameramen ran ahead down the corridor, and then turned around and backed up, taking pictures of Oswald as he was escorted toward the homicide and robbery bureau office. According to one escorting officer, some six or seven reporters followed the police into the bureau office.

From Friday afternoon, when Oswald arrived in the building, until Sunday, newspaper reporters and television cameras focused their attention on the homicide office. In full view and within arm's length of the assembled newsmen, Oswald traversed the 20 feet of corridor between the homicide office and the locked door leading to the jail elevator at least 15 times after his initial arrival. The jail elevator, sealed off from public use, took him to his fifth-floor cell and to the assembly room in the basement for lineups and the Friday night news conference.

On most occasions, Oswald's escort of three to six detectives and policemen had to push their way through the newsmen who sought to surround them. Although the Dallas press normally did not take pictures of a prisoner without first obtaining permission of the police, who generally asked the prisoner, this practice was not followed by any of the newsmen with Oswald. Generally when Oswald appeared the newsmen turned their cameras on him, thrust microphones at his face, and shouted questions at him. Sometimes he answered. Reporters in the forefront of the throng would repeat his answers for the benefit of those behind them who could not hear. On Saturday, however, in response to police admonitions, the reporters exercised more restraint and shouted fewer questions at Oswald when he passed through the corridor.

Oswald's most prolonged exposure occurred at the midnight press conference on Friday night. In response to demands of newsmen, District Attorney Wade, after consulting with Chief Curry and Captain Fritz, had announced shortly before midnight that Oswald would appear at a press conference in the basement assembly room. An estimated 70 to 100 people, including Jack Ruby, and other unauthorized persons, crowded into the small downstairs room. No identification was required. The room was so packed that Deputy Chief M. W. Stevenson and Captain Fritz who came down to the basement after the crowd had assembled could not get in and were forced to remain in the doorway.

Oswald was brought into the room shortly after midnight. Curry had instructed policemen not to permit newsmen to touch Oswald or get close to him, but no steps were taken to shield Oswald from the crowd. Captain Fritz had asked that Oswald be placed on the platform used for lineups so that he could be more easily removed "if anything happened." Chief Curry, however, insisted that Oswald stand on the floor in front of the stage, where he was also in front of the one-way nylon-cloth screen customarily used to prevent a suspect from seeing those present in the room. This was done because cameramen had told Curry that their cameras would not photograph well through the screen.

Curry had instructed the reporters that they were not to "ask any questions and try to interview . . . [Oswald] in any way," but when he was brought into the room, "immediately they began to shoot questions at him and shove microphones into his face." It was difficult to hear Oswald's answers above the uproar. Cameramen stood on the tables to take pictures and others pushed forward to get close-ups. The noise and confusion mounted as reporters shouted at each other to get out of the way and camermen made frantic efforts to get into position for pictures. After Oswald had been in the room only a few minutes, Chief Curry intervened and directed that Oswald be taken back to the jail because, he testified, the newsmen "tried to overrun him."

THE ABORTIVE TRANSFER

In Dallas, after a person is charged with a felony, the county sheriff ordinarily takes custody of the prisoner and assumes responsibility for his safekeeping. Normally, the Dallas Police Department notifies the sheriff when a prisoner has been charged with a felony and the sheriff dispatches his deputies to transport the accused to the county jail. This is usually done within a few hours after the complaint has been filed. In cases of unusual importance, however, the Dallas city police sometimes transport the prisoners to the county jail.

The decision to move Oswald to the county jail on Sunday morning was reached by Chief Curry the preceding evening. Sometime after 7:30 Saturday evening, according to Assistant Chief Batchelor, two reporters told him that they wanted to go out to dinner but that "they didn't want to miss anything if we were going to move the prisoner." Curry came upon them at that point and told the two newsmen that if they returned by 10 o'clock in the morning, they wouldn't "miss anything." A little later, after checking with Captain Fritz, Curry made a similar announcement to the assembled reporters. Curry reported the making of his decision to move Oswald as follows:

Then, I talked to Fritz about when he thought he would transfer the prisoner, and he didn't think it was a good idea to transfer him at night because of the fact you couldn't see, and if anybody tried to cause them any trouble, they needed to see who they were and where it was coming from and so forth, and he suggested that we wait until daylight, so this was normal procedure, I mean, for Fritz to determine when he is going to transfer his prisoners, so I told him "Okay." I asked him, I said, "What time do you think you will be ready tomorrow?" And he didn't know exactly and I said, "Do you think about 10 o'clock," and he said, "I believe so," and then is when I went out and told the newspaper people . . . "I believe if you are back here by 10 o'clock you will be back in time to observe anything you care to observe."

During the night, between 2:30 and 3 A.M., the local office of the FBI and the sheriff's office received telephone calls from an unidentified man who warned that a committee had decided "to kill the man that killed the President." Shortly after, an FBI agent notified the Dallas police of the anonymous threat. The police department and ultimately Chief Curry were informed of both threats.

Immediately after his arrival at the building on Sunday morning between 8:30 and 8:45 A.M., Curry spoke by telephone with Sheriff J. E. Decker about the transfer. When Decker indicated that he would leave to Curry the decision on whether the sheriff's office or the police would move Oswald, Curry decided that the police would handle it because "we had so much involved here, we were the ones that were investigating the case and we had the officers set up downstairs to handle it."

After talking with Decker, Curry began to discuss plans for the transfer. With the threats against Oswald in mind, Curry suggested to Batchelor and Deputy Chief Stevenson that Oswald be transported to the county jail in an armored truck, to which they agreed. While Batchelor made arrangements to have an armored truck brought to the building, Curry and Stevenson tentatively agreed on the route the armored truck would follow from the building to the county jail.

Curry decided that Oswald would leave the building via the basement. He stated later that he reached this decision shortly after his arrival at the police building Sunday morning, when members of the press had already begun to gather in the basement. There is no evidence that anyone opposed this decision. Two members of the Dallas police did suggest to Captain Fritz that Oswald be taken from the building by another exit, leaving the press "waiting in the basement and on Commerce Street, and we could be to the county jail before anyone knew what was taking place." However, Fritz said that he did not think Curry would agree to such a plan because he had promised that Oswald would be transferred at a time when newsmen could take pictures. Forrest Sorrels also suggested to Fritz that Oswald be moved at an unannounced time when no one was around, but Fritz again responded that Curry "wanted to go along with the press and not try to put anything over on them."

Preliminary arrangements to obtain additional personnel to assist with the transfer were begun Saturday evening. On Saturday night, the police reserves were requested to provide eight to ten men on Sunday, and additional reservists were sought in the morning. Capt. C. E. Talbert, who was in charge of the patrol division for the city of Dallas on the morning of November 24, retained a small number of policemen in the building when he took charge that morning and later ordered other patrolmen from several districts to report to the basement. At about 9 A.M. Deputy Chief Stevenson instructed all detectives within the building to remain for the transfer. Sheriff Decker testified that his men were ready to receive Oswald at the county jail from the early hours of Sunday morning.

With the patrolmen and reserve policemen available to him, Captain Talbert, on his own initiative, undertook to secure the basement of the police department building. He placed policemen outside the building at the top of the Commerce Street ramp to keep all spectators on the opposite side of Commerce Street. Later, Talbert directed that patrolmen be assigned to all street intersections the transfer vehicle would cross along the route to the county jail. His most significant security precautions, however, were steps designed to exclude unauthorized persons from the basement area.

The spacious basement of the Police and Courts Building contains, among other things, the jail office and the police garage. The jail office, into which the jail elevator opens, is situated on the west side of an auto ramp cutting across the length of the basement from Main Street, on the north side of the building, to Commerce Street, on the south side. From the foot of this ramp, on the east side, midway through the basement, a decline runs down a short distance to the L-shaped police garage. In addition to the auto ramp, five doors to the garage provide access to the basement from the Police and Courts Building on the west side of the garage and the attached Municipal Building on the east. Three of these five doors provide access to three elevators opening into the garage, two for passengers near the central part of the garage and one for service at the east end of the garage. A fourth door near the passenger elevator opens into the municipal building; the fifth door, at the Commerce Street side of the garage, opens into a sub-basement that is connected with both buildings.

Shortly after 9 o'clock Sunday morning, policemen cleared the basement of all but police personnel. Guards were stationed at the top of the Main and Commerce Streets auto ramps leading down into the basement, at each of the five doorways into the garage, and at the double doors leading to the public hallway adjacent to the jail office. Then, Sgt. Patrick T. Dean, acting under instructions from Talbert,

THE WARREN COMMISSION REPORT

directed 14 men in a search of the garage. Maintenance workers were directed to leave the area. The searchers examined the rafters, tops of air conditioning ducts, and every closet and room opening off the garage. They searched the interior and trunk compartment of automobiles parked in the garage. The two passenger elevators in the central part of the garage were not in service and the doors were shut and locked; the service elevator was moved to the first floor, and the operator was instructed not to return it to the basement.

Despite the thoroughness with which the search was conducted, there still existed one and perhaps two weak points in controlling access to the garage. Testimony did not resolve positively whether or not the stairway door near the public elevators was locked both from the inside and outside as was necessary to secure it effectively. And although guards were stationed near the double doors, the hallway near the jail office was accessible to people from inside the Police and Courts Building without the necessity of presenting identification. Until seconds before Oswald was shot, newsmen hurrying to photograph Oswald were able to run without challenge through those doors into the basement.

After the search had been completed, the police allowed news representatives to reenter the basement area and gather along the entrance to the garage on the east side of the ramp. Later, the police permitted the newsmen to stand in front of the railing on the east side of the ramp leading to Main Street. The policemen deployed by Talbert and Dean had instructions to allow no one but identified news media representatives into the basement. As before, the police accepted any credentials that appeared authentic, though some officers did make special efforts to check for pictures and other forms of corroborating identification. Many newsmen reported that they were checked on more than one occasion while they waited in the basement. A small number did not recall that their credentials were ever checked.

Shortly after his arrival on Sunday morning, Chief Curry issued instructions to keep reporters and cameramen out of the jail office and to keep television equipment behind the railing separating the basement auto ramp from the garage. Curry observed that in other respects Captain Talbert appeared to have security measures in hand and allowed him to proceed on his own initiative. Batchelor and

Stevenson checked progress in the basement during the course of the morning, and the officials were generally satisfied with the steps Talbert had taken.

At about 11 A.M., Deputy Chief Stevenson requested that Capt. O. A. Jones of the forgery bureau bring all available detectives from the third floor offices to the basement. Jones instructed the detectives who accompanied him to the basement to line the walls on either side of the passageway cleared for the transfer party. According to Detective T. D. McMillon,

. . . Captain Jones explained to us that, when they brought the prisoner out, that he wanted two lines formed and we were to keep these two lines formed, you know, a barrier on either side of them, kind of an aisle . . . for them to walk through, and when they came down this aisle, we were to keep this line intact and move along with them until the man was placed in the car.

With Assistant Chief Batchelor's permission, Jones removed photographers who had gathered once again in the basement jail office. Jones recalled that he instructed all newsmen along the Main Street ramp to remain behind an imaginary line extending from the southeast corner of the jail office to the railing on the east side of the ramp; other officers recalled that Jones directed the newsmen to move away from the foot of the Main Street ramp and to line up against the east railing. In any event, newsmen were allowed to congregate along the foot of the ramp after Batchelor observed that there was insufficient room along the east of the ramp to permit all the news representatives to see Oswald as he was brought out.

By the time Oswald reached the basement, 40 to 50 newsmen and 70 to 75 police officers were assembled there. Three television cameras stood along the railing and most of the newsmen were congregated in that area and at the top of the adjacent decline leading into the garage. A group of newsmen and police officers, best estimated at about 20, stood strung across the bottom of the Main Street ramp. Along the south wall of the passageway outside the jail office door were about eight detectives, and three detectives lined the north wall. Two officers stood in front of the double doors leading into the passageway from the corridor next to the jail office.

Beginning Saturday night, the public had been kept informed of the approximate time of the transfer. At approximately 10:20 A.M. Curry told a press conference that Oswald would be moved in an armored truck and gave a general description of other security precautions. Apparently no newsmen were informed of the transfer route, however, and the route was not disclosed to the driver of the armored truck until the truck arrived at the Commerce Street exit at about 11:07 A.M. When they learned of its arrival, many of the remaining newsmen who had waited on the third floor descended to the basement. Shortly after, newsmen may have had another indication that the transfer was imminent if they caught a glimpse through the glass windows of Oswald putting on a sweater in Captain Fritz' office.

Because the driver feared that the truck might stall if it had to start from the bottom of the ramp and because the overhead clearance appeared to be inadequate, Assistant Chief Batchelor had it backed only into the entranceway at the top of the ramp. Batchelor and others then inspected the inside of the truck.

When Chief Curry learned that the truck had arrived, he informed Captain Fritz that security controls were in effect and inquired how long the questioning of Oswald would continue. At this point, Fritz learned for the first time of the plan to convey Oswald by armored truck and immediately expressed his disapproval. He urged the use of an unmarked police car driven by a police officer, pointing out that this would be better from the standpoint of both speed and maneuverability. Curry agreed to Fritz' plan; the armored truck would be used as a decoy. They decided that the armored truck would leave the ramp first, followed by a car which would contain only security officers. A police car bearing Oswald would follow. After proceeding one block, the car with Oswald would turn off and proceed directly to the county jail; the armored truck would follow a lead car to the jail along the previously agreed upon and more circuitous route.

Captain Fritz instructed Detectives C. W. Brown and C. N. Dhority and a third detective to proceed to the garage and move the followup car and the transfer car into place on the auto ramp. He told Lt. Rio S. Pierce to obtain another automobile from the basement and take up a lead position on Commerce Street. Deputy Chief Stevenson went back to the basement to inform Batchelor and Jones of the change in plans. Oswald was given his sweater, and then his right hand was handcuffed to the left hand of Detective J. R. Leavelle. Detective T. L. Baker called the jail office to check on security precautions in the basement and notify officials that the prisoner was being brought down.

On arriving in the basement, Pierce asked Sgts. James A. Putnam and Billy Joe Maxey to accompany him in the lead car. Since the armored truck was blocking the Commerce Street ramp, it would be necessary to drive out the Main Street ramp and circle the block to Commerce Street. Maxey sat on the back seat of Pierce's car, and Putnam helped clear a path through reporters on the ramp so that Pierce could drive up toward Main Street. When the car passed by the reporters at about 11:20 A.M., Putnam entered the car on the right front side. Pierce drove to the top of the Main Street ramp and slowed momentarily as Patrolman Roy E. Vaughn stepped from his position at the top of the ramp toward the street to watch for traffic. After Pierce's car left the garage area, Brown drove another police car out of the garage, moved part way up the Commerce Street ramp, and began to back down into position to receive Oswald. Dhority also proceeded to drive the followup car into position ahead of Brown.

As Pierce's car started up the ramp at about 11:20 A.M., Oswald, accompanied by Captain Fritz and four detectives, arrived at the jail office. Cameramen in the hallway of the basement took pictures of Oswald through the interior glass windows of the jail office as he was led through the office to the exit. Some of these cameramen then ran through the double doors near the jail office and squeezed into the line which had formed across the Main Street ramp. Still others remained just inside the double doors or proceeded through the double doors after Oswald and his escort emerged from the jail office.

When Fritz came to the jail office door, he asked if everything was ready, and a detective standing in the passageway answered yes. Someone shouted, "Here he comes!"; additional spotlights were turned on in the basement, and the din increased. A detective stepped from the jail office and proceeded toward the transfer car. Seconds later Fritz and then Oswald, with Detective Leavelle at his right, Detective L. C. Graves at his left, and Detective L. D. Montgomery at his rear, came through the door. Fritz walked to Brown's car, which had not yet backed fully into position; Oswald followed a few feet behind. Newsmen near the double door moved forward after him. Though movie films and video tapes indicate that the front line of newsmen along the Main Street ramp remained fairly stationary, it was the impression of many who were close to the scene that with Oswald's appearance the crowd surged forward. According to Detective Montgomery, who was walking directly behind Oswald, "as soon

as we came out this door . . . this bunch here just moved in on us."
To Detective B. H. Combest, standing on the Commerce Street side
of the passageway from the jail office door, it appeared that

Almost the whole line of people pushed forward when Oswald started to
leave the jail office, the door, the hall—— all the newsmen were poking
their sound mikes across to him and asking questions, and they were
everyone sticking their flashbulbs up and around and over him and in his
face.

After Oswald had moved about 10 feet from the door of the jail
office, Jack Ruby passed between a newsman and a detective at the
edge of the straining crowd on the Main Street ramp. With his right
hand extended and holding a .38 caliber revolver, Ruby stepped
quickly forward and fired a single fatal bullet into Oswald's abdomen.

ADEQUACY OF SECURITY PRECAUTIONS

The shooting of Lee Harvey Oswald obviously resulted from the
failure of the security precautions which the Dallas Police Department had taken to protect their prisoner. In assessing the causes of
the security failure, the Commission has not overlooked the extraordinary circumstances which prevailed during the days that the attention of the world was turned on Dallas. Confronted with a unique
situation, the Dallas police took special security measures to insure
Oswald's safety. Unfortunately these did not include adequate control
of the great crowd of newsmen that inundated the police department
building.

The Dallas police had in custody a man whose alleged act had
brought upon him immediate and universal opprobrium. There were
many possible reasons why people might have attempted to kill him if
given the opportunity. Concerned that there might be an attempt on
Oswald's life, FBI Director J. Edgar Hoover sent a message to Chief
Curry on November 22 through Special Agent Manning C. Clements
of the FBI's Dallas office, urging that Oswald be afforded the utmost
security. Curry does not recall receiving the message.

Although the presence of a great mass of press representatives
created an extraordinary security problem in the building, the police
department pursued its normal policy of admitting the press. That
policy, set forth in General Order No. 81 of the Dallas Police Department, provided,

. . . that members of this Department render every assistance, except such as obviously may seriously hinder or delay the proper functioning of the Department, to the accredited members of the official news-gathering agencies and this includes newspaper, television cameramen and news-reel photographers.

In a letter to all members of the police department, dated February 7, 1963, Chief Curry explained the general order, in part, as follows:

The General Order covering this subject is not merely permissive. It does not state that the Officer may, if he so chooses, assist the press. It rather places on him a responsibility to lend active assistance.

*　　　　*　　　　*

. . . as a Department we deal with public affairs. It is the right of the public to know about these affairs, and one of the most accurate and useful avenues we have of supplying this information is through the newspapers and radio and television stations.

Implied in the General Order is a prohibition for the Officer to improperly attempt to interfere with the news media representative, who is functioning in his capacity as such. Such activity on the part of any Police Officer is regarded by the press as an infringement of rights, and the Department shares this view.

Under this policy, news representatives ordinarily had access to the Police and Courts Building. The first newsmen to arrive on Friday afternoon were admitted in accordance with the policy; others who came later simply followed behind them. Shortly after Oswald arrived, Captain King granted permission to bring television cameras to the third floor. By the time the unwieldy proportions of the crowd of newsmen became apparent, it had already become well entrenched on the third floor. No one suggested reversing the department's policy expressed in General Order No. 81. Chief Curry testified that at no time did he consider clearing the crowd from the building; he "saw no particular harm in allowing the media to observe the prisoner." Captain King later stated candidly that he simply became "accustomed to the idea of them being out there."

The general policy of the Dallas police recognized that the rule of full cooperation did not apply when it might jeopardize an investigation. In retrospect, most members of the department believed that the general rule allowing admittance of the press to the police quarters should not have been followed after the assassination. Few, if any, thought this at the time. By failing to exclude the press from the building on Friday and Saturday, the Dallas police made it possible for the uncontrolled crowd to nearly surround Oswald on the frequent occasions that he moved through the third floor corridor. The decision to allow newsmen to observe the transfer on Sunday followed naturally the policy established during these first two days of Oswald's detention.

The reporters and cameramen descended upon the third floor of the Police and Courts Building in such numbers that the pressroom on the third floor proved wholly inadequate. Rather than the "two or three or maybe a half dozen reporters" who normally appeared to cover local police stories, the police were faced with upward of 100. Bringing with them cameras, microphones, cables, and spotlights, the newsmen inevitably spilled over into areas where they interfered with the transaction of police business and the maintenance of security.

Aside from numbers, the gathering of reporters presented a problem because most of them were representatives of the national and foreign press, rather than the local press. These newsmen carried individual press cards rather than identification cards issued by the Dallas police. Therefore, it was impossible for the police to verify quickly the identity of this great number of unfamiliar people who appeared almost simultaneously. Because of the close physical proximity of the milling mass of insistent newsmen to the prisoner, the failure to authenticate press credentials subjected the prisoner to a serious security risk.

Although steps were taken on Friday afternoon to insure that persons seeking entry to the third floor were there for a legitimate purpose, reasons could be fabricated. Moreover, because of the large crowd, it was easier for unauthorized persons to slip by those guarding the entrances. Jack Ruby, for one, was able to gain entry to the third-floor corridor on Friday night.

The third-floor corridor provided the only passageway between the homicide and robbery bureau and the jail elevator. No thought seems to have been given, however, to the possibility of questioning Oswald on some other floor. Moreover, Oswald's most extended exposure to the press, at the Friday evening press conference, was unrelated to any phase of the investigation and was motivated primarily by the desire to satisfy the demands of the news media to see the prisoner.

The risks attendant upon this appearance were emphasized by the presence of unauthorized persons, including Jack Ruby, at the press conference in the basement assembly room.

Although Oswald was repeatedly exposed to possible assaults on Friday and Saturday, he met his death on Sunday, when police took the most extensive security precautions. The assembly of more than 70 police officers, some of them armed with tear gas, and the contemplated use of an armored truck, appear to have been designed primarily to repel an attempt of a mob to seize the prisoner. Chief Curry's own testimony indicated that such a focus resulted not from any appraisal of the varied risks to Oswald's life but came about in response to the telephone threat Sunday morning that a hundred men were going to attack Oswald.

A more balanced appraisal would have given thought to protection against any attack. For example, the acceptance of inadequate press credentials posed a clear avenue for a one-man assault. The likelihood of an unauthorized person obtaining entry by such means is confirmed not alone by the fact that Jack Ruby managed to get by a guard at one entrance. Several newsmen related that their credentials were not checked as they entered the basement Sunday morning. Seconds before Oswald was shot, the double doors from the hallway next to the jail office afforded a means of entry to the basement without presentation of credentials earlier demanded of newsmen.

The swarm of newspeople in the basement also substantially limited the ability of the police to detect an unauthorized person once he had entered the basement. While Jack Ruby might have been easily spotted if only police officers had been in the basement, he remained apparently unnoticed in the crowd of newsmen until he lunged forward toward Oswald. The near-blinding television and motion picture lights which were allowed to shine upon the escort party further increased the difficulty of observing unusual movements in the basement.

Moreover, by making public the plans for the transfer, the police attracted to the city jail many persons who otherwise might not have learned of the move until it had been completed. This group included the onlookers gathered on Commerce Street and a few people on Main Street. Also, continuous television and radio coverage of the activities in the basement might have resulted in compromise of the transfer operation.

These risks to Oswald's safety, growing in part out of adherence to the general policy of the police department, were also accepted for other reasons. Many members of the police department believed that the extraordinary public attention aroused by the tragic death of President Kennedy obliged them to make special efforts to accommodate the press. Captain King carefully articulated one reason why the newsmen were permitted

. . . to remain in the hallways, . . . to view the investigation and to keep in constant touch with progress of the investigation.

*   *   *

We realized that if we arrested a suspect, that if we brought him into the police station and then conducted all of our investigations behind closed doors, that if we gave no reports on the progress of our investigation and did not permit the newsmen to see the suspect——if we excluded them from it——we would leave ourselves open not only to criticisms that we were fabricating a suspect and were attempting to pin something on someone, but even more importantly, we would cause people to lose faith in our fairness and, through losing faith in our fairness, to lose faith to a certain extent in the processes of law.

We felt it was mandatory that as many people knew about it as possible. We knew, too, that if we did exclude the newsmen, we would be leaving ourselves open to a charge that we were using improper action, duress, physical abuse, all of these things.

While Oswald was in custody, the Dallas police kept the press informed about the treatment Oswald was receiving. The public could have been assured that the prisoner was not mistreated and that his rights were fully respected by the police, without each one of hundreds of cameramen and reporters being permitted to satisfy himself that the police had not abused the prisoner. This result could have been accomplished by obtaining reports from members of the family who visited him, or by a committee of the bar or other substantial citizens of the community. When it became known on Saturday that Oswald did not have an attorney, the president of the Dallas Bar Association visited him to inquire whether he wished assistance in obtaining counsel.

Moreover, the right of the public to know does not give the press license to interfere with the efficient operation of law-enforcement agencies. Permitting the press to remain on the third floor of the building served no valid purpose that could not have been met if the press had been excluded from the third floor, as it was from the fourth and fifth floors, and informed of developments either through press releases or at press conferences elsewhere in the building.

Having failed to exclude the mass of the press from the basement during the transfer of Oswald, the police department's security measures could not be completely effective. Despite the pressures that prevailed, planning and coordination of security arrangements could have been more thorough and precise. No single member of the Dallas Police Department ever assumed full responsibility for the details of Oswald's transfer. Chief Curry participated in some of the planning, but he felt that primary authority for the transfer should be Fritz', since Fritz had charge of the investigation. According to Chief Curry,

Fritz and I, I think, discussed this briefly, the possibility of getting that prisoner out of the city hall during the night hours and by another route and slipping him to the jail, but actually Fritz was not too much in favor of this and I more or less left this up to Fritz as to when and how this transfer would be made, because he has in the past transferred many of his prisoners to the county jail and I felt that since it was his responsibility, the prisoner was, to let him decide when and how he wanted to transfer this prisoner.

Fritz, on the other hand, felt that Curry was directing the transfer arrangements: "I was transferring him like the chief told me to transfer him." When Capt. W. B. Frazier notified Fritz by telephone early Sunday morning about the threats to Oswald's life, Fritz replied that Curry should be notified, since he was handling the transfer. When urged to modify the transfer plans to avoid the press, as he later testified he would have preferred to do, Fritz declined on the ground that Curry had already decided to the contrary. Hence, if the recollection of both officials is accurate, the basic decision to move Oswald at an announced time and in the presence of the news media was never carefully thought through by either man. Curry and Fritz had agreed Saturday evening that Oswald should not be moved at night, but their discussion apparently went little further.

Perhaps the members of the Dallas Police Department were, as many testified, accustomed to working together so that formal instructions were sometimes unnecessary. On the other hand, it is clear, at least in retrospect, that this particular occasion demanded more than the usual informal unspoken understandings. The evidence indicates that no member of the department at any time considered fully the implications of moving Oswald through the basement. Nor did any single official or group of officials coordinate and direct where the transfer vehicle would be stationed to accept Oswald, where the press would stand, and the number and positioning of police officers in the basement. Captain Jones indicated that there were to be two solid lines of policemen from the jail office door to the transfer vehicle, but lines were formed only along the walls of the areaway between the jail office door and the ramp. The newsmen were not kept east of the auto ramp where a railing would have separated them from Oswald. No strong ranks of policemen were ever placed in front of the newsmen once they were allowed to gather in the area of the Main Street ramp. Many policemen in the basement did not know the function they were supposed to perform. No instructions were given that certain policemen should watch the crowd rather than Oswald. Apparently no one gave any thought to the blinding effect of television and other camera lights upon the escort party.

Largely on his own initiative, Captain Talbert undertook to secure the basement, with only minimal coordination with those responsible for and familiar with the route Oswald would take through the basement. Several officials recalled that Lt. Woodrow Wiggins was directed to clear the basement jail office, but Wiggins testified that he received no such assignment. In any event, less than 20 minutes before the transfer, Captain Jones observed newsmen in the jail office and had them removed. But no official removed news personnel from the corridor beside the jail office; indeed, cameramen took pictures through the glass windows of the jail office as Oswald walked through it toward the basement, and then approached to within 20 feet of Oswald from the rear at the same time that Jack Ruby moved toward Oswald from the front.

A clear example of the inadequacy of coordination was the last-minute change in plans to transfer Oswald in an unmarked police car rather than by armored truck. The plan to use an armored vehicle was adopted without informing Fritz. When Fritz was told of the arrangement shortly after 11 o'clock, he objected, and hurried steps were taken to modify the arrangements. Fritz was then prematurely informed that the basement arrangements were complete. When Oswald and the escorting detectives entered the basement, the transfer car had not yet been backed into position, nor had the policemen been arranged to block the newsmen's access to Oswald's path. If the transfer car had been carefully positioned between the press and Oswald, Ruby might have been kept several yards from his victim and possibly without a clear view of him. Detective Leavelle, who accompanied Oswald into the basement, testified:

. . . I was surprised when I walked to the door and the car was not in the spot it should have been, but I could see it was in back, and backing into position, but had it been in position where we were told it would be, that would have eliminated a lot of the area in which anyone would have access to him, because it would have been blocked by the car. In fact, if the car had been sitting where we were told it was going to be, see——it would have been sitting directly upon the spot where Ruby was standing when he fired the shot.

Captain Jones described the confusion with which Oswald's entry into the basement was in fact received:

Then the change——going to put two cars up there. There is no reason why that back car can't get all the way back to the jail office. The original plan would be that the line of officers would be from the jail door to the vehicle. Then they say, "Here he comes." . . . It is too late to get the people out of the way of the car and form the line. I am aware that Oswald is already coming because of the furor, so, I was trying to keep everybody out of the way and keep the way clear and I heard a shot.

Therefore, regardless of whether the press should have been allowed to witness the transfer, security measures in the basement for Oswald's protection could and should have been better organized and more thorough. These additional deficiencies were directly related to the decision to admit newsmen to the basement. The Commission concludes that the failure of the police to remove Oswald secretly or to control the crowd in the basement at the time of the transfer were the major causes of the security breakdown which led to Oswald's death.

NEWS COVERAGE AND POLICE POLICY

Consistent with its policy of allowing news representatives to remain within the working quarters of the Police and Courts Building, the police department made every effort to keep the press fully informed about the progress of the investigation. As a result, from Friday afternoon until after the killing of Oswald on Sunday, the press was able to publicize virtually all of the information about the case which had been gathered until that time. In the process, a great deal of misinformation was disseminated to a worldwide audience.

As administrative assistant to Chief Curry, Captain King also handled departmental press relations and issued press releases. According to King, it was "the responsibility of each member of the department to furnish to the press information on incidents in which they, themselves, were involved, except on matters which involved . . . personnel policies of the department, or . . . unless it would obviously interfere with an investigation underway." In Oswald's case, Chief Curry released most of the information to the press. He and Assistant Chief Batchelor agreed on Friday that Curry would make all announcements to the press. However, there is no evidence that this decision was ever communicated to the rest of the police force. The chief consequence appears to have been that Batchelor refrained from making statements to the news media during this period.

Most of the information was disclosed through informal oral statements or answers to questions at impromptu and clamorous press conferences in the third floor corridor. Written press releases were not employed. The ambulatory press conference became a familiar sight during these days. Whenever Curry or other officials appeared in the hallway, newsmen surrounded them, asking questions and requesting statements. Usually the officials complied.

Curry appeared in interviews on television and radio at least a dozen times during November 22–24. He did not attend any of the interrogations of Oswald in Captain Fritz' office except at the beginning and toward the end of Sunday morning's session; he received his information through Captain Fritz and other sources. Nevertheless, in sessions with the newsmen on Friday and Saturday he gave detailed information on the progress of the case against Oswald. Recorded statements of television and radio interviews with Curry and other officials in Dallas during November 22–24 have been transcribed and included in the record compiled by the Commission. An example of these interviews is the following transcript of remarks made by Curry to newsmen on Saturday:

Q. Chief Curry, I understand you have some new information in this case. Could you relate what that is?

A. Yes, we've just been informed by the Federal Bureau of Investigation, that they, the FBI, have the order letter from a mail order house, and the order was sent to their laboratory in Washington and the writing on this order was compared with known samples of our suspect, Oswald's handwriting and found to be the same.

Q. This order was for the rifle?

A. This order was for the rifle to a mail order house in Chicago. It was [inaudible]. The return address was to Dallas, Texas, to the post office box under the name of A. Hidell, H-I-D-E-double L. This is the post office box of our suspect. This gun was mailed parcel post March 20, 1963. I understand he left Dallas shortly after this and didn't come back until I think about two months ago.

Q. Do you know again on what date this rifle was ordered and are you able to link it definitely as the rifle which you confiscated at the School Book Depository?

A. That we have not done so far. If the FBI has been able to do it I have not been informed of it yet. We do know that this man ordered a rifle of the type that was used in the assassination of the President from this mail order house in Chicago and the FBI has definitely identified the writing as that of our suspect.

Q. On another subject——I understand you have photographs of the suspect, Oswald, with a rifle like that used. Could you describe that picture?

A. This is the picture of Oswald standing facing a camera with a rifle in his hand which is very similar to the rifle that we have in our possession. He also had a pistol strapped on his hip. He was holding two papers in his hand, with one of them seemed to be *The Worker* and the other says "Be Militant"——I don't know whether that was headlines or the name of the paper.

Q. How much did the gun cost from the mail order house?

A. I understand the gun was advertised for $12.78, I believe.

Q. Have you received any results on the ballistics test conducted on the gun and on Oswald?

A. They're going to be favorable. I don't have a formal report yet.

Q. But you are sure at this time they will be favorable?

A. Yes.

Q. Do you feel now that you have the case completely wrapped up, or are you continuing?

A. We will continue as long as there is a shred of evidence to be gathered. We have a strong case at this time.

Q. I believe you said earlier this afternoon that you have a new development which does wrap up the case——the first time you said the case definitely is secure. Is that correct?

A. That was this morning. This additional evidence just makes a stronger case.

Q. But this is not the same evidence you were referring to then?

A. No, that's true.

Q. Would you be willing to say what that evidence was?

A. No, sir. I don't wish to reveal it. It might jeopardize our case.

Commentator: Thank you very much Chief Jesse Curry of the Dallas Police Department.

Although Captain Fritz permitted himself to be interviewed by the news media less frequently than did Chief Curry, he nevertheless answered questions and ventured opinions about the progress of the investigation. On Saturday he told reporters that he was convinced beyond a doubt that Oswald had killed the President. He discussed some of the evidence in the case, especially the rifle, but his contribution to the knowledge of the reporters was small compared with that of Chief Curry.

Many other members of the police department, including high officials, detectives, and patrolmen, were also interviewed by news representatives during these days. Some of these men had participated in specific aspects of the case, such as the capture of Oswald at the Texas Theatre and the search for evidence at the Texas School Book Depository Building. Few, if any, seemed reluctant to submit to questions and to being televised. It seemed to District Attorney Wade that the newsmen "just followed everybody everywhere they went . . . they interviewed some of your patrolmen . . . on the corner . . . they were interviewing anybody."

Wade himself also made several statements to the press. He visited police headquarters twice on Friday, twice on Saturday, and twice on Sunday. On most of these occasions he was interviewed by the press and appeared on television. After Oswald had appeared before the press on Friday night, Wade held an impromptu conference with reporters in the overflowing assembly room. Wade told the press on Saturday that he would not reveal any evidence because it might prejudice the selection of a jury. On other occasions, however, he mentioned some items of evidence and expressed his opinions regarding Oswald's guilt. He told the press on Friday night that Oswald's wife had told the police that her husband had a rifle in the garage at the house in Irving and that it was missing the morning of the assassination. On one occasion he repeated the error that the murder rifle had been a Mauser. Another time, he stated his belief that Oswald had prepared for the assassination months in advance, including what he would tell the police. He also said that Oswald had practiced with the rifle to improve his marksmanship.

The running commentary on the investigation by the police inevitably carried with it the disclosure of many details that proved to be erroneous. In their efforts to keep the public abreast of the investigation, the police reported hearsay items and unverified leads; further investigation proved many of these to be incorrect or inaccurate. For example, the rifle found on the sixth floor of the Texas School Book Depository Building was initially identified as a Mauser 7.65 rather than a Mannlicher-Carcano 6.5 because a deputy constable who was one of the first to see it thought it looked like a Mauser. He neither handled the weapon nor saw it at close range.

Police sources were also responsible for the mistaken notion that the chicken bones found on the sixth floor were the remains of Oswald's lunch. They had in fact been left by another employee who ate his lunch there at least 15 minutes before the assassination. Curry repeated the erroneous report that a Negro had picked up Oswald near the scene of the assassination and driven him across town. It was also reported that the map found in Oswald's room contained a marked route of the Presidential motorcade when it actually contained markings of places where Oswald may have applied for jobs, including, of course, the Texas School Book Depository.

Concern about the effects of the unlimited disclosures was being voiced by Saturday morning. According to District Attorney Wade, he received calls from lawyers in Dallas and elsewhere expressing concern about providing an attorney for Oswald and about the amount of information being given to the press by the police and the district attorney. Curry continued to answer questions on television and radio during the remainder of the day and Sunday morning.

FBI Director J. Edgar Hoover became concerned because "almost as soon as . . . [FBI laboratory reports] would reach the Dallas Police Department, the chief of police or one of the representatives of the department would go on TV or radio and relate findings of the FBI, giving information such as the identification of the gun and other items of physical evidence." On Sunday, after Oswald was shot,

Hoover dispatched a personal message to Curry requesting him "not to go on the air any more until this case . . . [is] resolved." Hoover testified later that Curry agreed not to make any more statements.

The shooting of Oswald shocked the Dallas police, and after the interviews that immediately followed the shooting they were disposed to remain silent. Chief Curry made only more more television appearance after the shooting. At 1:30 P.M., he descended to the assembly room where, tersely and grimly, he announced Oswald's death. He refused to answer any of the questions shouted at him by the persistent reporters, concluding the conference in less than a minute.

District Attorney Wade also held one more press conference. Before doing so on Sunday evening, he returned once more to the police station and held a meeting with "all the brass" except Curry. Wade told them that "people are saying . . . you had the wrong man and you all were the one who killed him or let him out here to have him killed intentionally." Wade told the police that "somebody ought to go out in television and lay out the evidence that you had on Oswald, and tell them everything." He sat down and listed from memory items of evidence in the case against Oswald. According to Wade, Chief Curry refused to make any statements because he had told an FBI inspector that he would say no more. The police refused to furnish Wade with additional details of the case.

Wade nonetheless proceeded to hold a lengthy formal press conference that evening, in which he attempted to list all of the evidence that had been accumulated at that point tending to establish Oswald as the assassin of President Kennedy. Unfortunately, at that time, as he subsequently testified, he lacked a thorough grasp of the evidence and made a number of errors. He stated that Oswald had told a woman on a bus that the President had been killed, an error apparently caused by the bus driver having confused Oswald with another passenger who was on the bus after Oswald had left. Wade also repeated the error about Oswald's having a map marked with the route of the motorcade. He told reporters that Oswald's description and name "went out by the police to look for him." The police never mentioned Oswald's name in their broadcast descriptions before his arrest.

Wade was innocent of one error imputed to him since November 24. The published transcript of part of the press conference furnished to newspapers by the Associated Press represented Wade as having identified the cab driver who took Oswald to North Beckley Avenue after the shooting as one named "Darryl Click." The transcript as it appeared in the New York *Times* and the Washington *Post* of November 26, reads:

A. [Wade] A lady. He then——the bus, he asked the bus driver to stop, got off at a stop, caught a taxicab driver, Darryl Click. I don't have his exact place——and went to his home in Oak Cliff, changed his clothes hurriedly, and left.

The correct transcript of the press conference, taken from an audio tape supplied by station WBAP, Fort Worth, is as follows:

A. [Wade] A lady. He then——the bus, he asked the bus driver to stop, got off at a stop, caught a taxicab driver.
Q. Where?
A. In Oak Cliff. I don't have the exact place——and went to his home in Oak Cliff, changed his clothes hurriedly and left.

In this manner, a section of Dallas, "Oak Cliff," became a non-existent taxicab driver, "Darryl Click." Wade did not mention the cab driver by name at any time. In transcribing the conference from the sound tape, a stenographer apparently made an error that might have become permanently imbedded in the literature of the event but for the preservation and use of an original sound tape.

Though many of the inaccuracies were subsequently corrected by the police and are negated by findings of the Commission included elsewhere in this report, the publicizing of unchecked information provided much of the basis for the myths and rumors that came into being soon after the President's death. The erroneous disclosures became the basis for distorted reconstructions and interpretations of the assassination. The necessity for the Dallas authorities to correct themselves or to be corrected by other sources gave rise not only to criticism of the police department's competence but also to doubts regarding the veracity of the police. Skeptics sought to cast doubt on much of the correct evidence later developed and to find support for their own theories in these early police statements.

The immediate disclosure of information by the police created a further risk of injuring innocent citizens by unfavorable publicity. This was the unfortunate experience of Joe R. Molina, a Dallas-born Navy veteran who had been employed by the Texas School Book

Depository since 1947 and on November 22, 1963, held the position of credit manager. Apparently because of Molina's employment at the Depository and his membership in a veterans' organization, the American G.I. Forum, that the Dallas police considered possibly subversive, Dallas policemen searched Molina's home with his permission, at about 1:30 A.M., Saturday, November 23. During the day Molina was intermittently interrogated at police headquarters for six or seven hours, chiefly about his membership in the American G.I. Forum and also about Oswald. He was never arrested, charged, or held in custody.

While Molina was being questioned, officials of the police department made statements or answered questions that provided the basis for television reports about Molina during the day. These reports spoke of a "second suspect being picked up," insinuated that the Dallas police had reason to suspect another person who worked in the Texas School Book Depository, stated that the suspect had been arrested and his home searched, and mentioned that Molina may have been identified by the U.S. Department of Justice as a possible subversive.

No evidence was ever presented to link Molina with Oswald except as a fellow employee of the Texas School Book Depository. According to Molina, he had never spoken to Oswald. The FBI notified the Commission that Molina had never been the subject of an investigation by it and that it had never given any information about Molina to the Dallas police concerning any alleged subversive activities by him. The Dallas police explained in a statement to the FBI that they had never had a file on Molina, but that they did have one on the American G.I. Forum.

Molina lost his job in December. He felt that he was being discharged because of the unfavorable publicity he had received, but officials of the Depository claimed that automation was the reason. Molina testified that he had difficulty in finding another position, until finally, with the help of a fellow church member, he secured a position at a lower salary than his previous one.

If Oswald had been tried for his murders of November 22, the effects of the news policy pursued by the Dallas authorities would have proven harmful both to the prosecution and the defense. The misinformation reported after the shootings might have been used by the defense to cast doubt on the reliability of the State's entire case.

Though each inaccuracy can be explained without great difficulty, the number and variety of misstatements issued by the police shortly after the assassination would have greatly assisted a skillful defense attorney attempting to influence the attitudes of jurors.

A fundamental objection to the news policy pursued by the Dallas police, however, is the extent to which it endangered Oswald's constitutional right to a trial by an impartial jury. Because of the nature of the crime, the widespread attention which it necessarily received, and the intense public feelings which it aroused, it would have been a most difficult task to select an unprejudiced jury, either in Dallas or elsewhere. But the difficulty was markedly increased by the divulgence of the specific items of evidence with which the police linked Oswald to the two killings. The disclosure of evidence encouraged the public, from which a jury would ultimately be impaneled, to prejudge the very questions that would be raised at trial.

Moreover, rules of law might have prevented the prosecution from presenting portions of this evidence to the jury. For example, though expressly recognizing that Oswald's wife could not be compelled to testify against him, District Attorney Wade revealed to the nation that Marina Oswald had affirmed her husband's ownership of a rifle like that found on the sixth floor of the Texas School Book Depository. Curry stated that Oswald had refused to take a lie detector test, although such a statement would have been inadmissible in a trial. The exclusion of such evidence, however, would have been meaningless if jurors were already familiar with the same facts from previous television or newspaper reports. Wade might have influenced prospective jurors by his mistaken statement that the paraffin test showed that Oswald had fired a gun. The tests merely showed that he had nitrate traces on his hands, which did not necessarily mean that he had fired either a rifle or a pistol.

The disclosure of evidence was seriously aggravated by the statements of numerous responsible officials that they were certain of Oswald's guilt. Captain Fritz said that the case against Oswald was "cinched." Curry reported on Saturday that "we are sure of our case." Curry announced that he considered Oswald sane, and Wade told the public that he would ask for the death penalty.

The American Bar Association declared in December, 1963, that "widespread publicizing of Oswald's alleged guilt, involving statements by officials and public disclosures of the details of 'evidence,' would have made it extremely difficult to impanel an unprejudiced jury and afford the accused a fair trial." Local bar associations expressed similar feelings. The Commission agrees that Lee Harvey Oswald's opportunity for a trial by 12 jurors free of preconception as to his guilt or innocence would have been seriously jeopardized by the premature disclosure and weighing of the evidence against him.

The problem of disclosure of information and its effect on trials is, of course, further complicated by the independent activities of the press in developing information on its own from sources other than law enforcement agencies. Had the police not released the specific items of evidence against Oswald, it is still possible that the other information presented on television and in the newspapers, chiefly of a biographical nature, would itself have had a prejudicial effect on the public.

In explanation of the news policy adopted by the Dallas authorities, Chief Curry observed that "it seemed like there was a great demand by the general public to know what was going on." In a prepared statement, Captain King wrote:

At that time we felt a necessity for permitting the newsmen as much latitude as possible. We realized the magnitude of the incident the newsmen were there to cover. We realized that not only the nation but the world would be greatly interested in what occurred in Dallas. We believed that we had an obligation to make as widely known as possible everything we could regarding the investigation of the assassination and the manner in which we undertook that investigation.

The Commission recognizes that the people of the United States, and indeed the world, had a deep-felt interest in learning of the events surrounding the death of President Kennedy, including the development of the investigation in Dallas. An informed public provided the ultimate guarantee that adequate steps would be taken to apprehend those responsible for the assassination and that all necessary precautions would be taken to protect the national security. It was therefore proper and desirable that the public know which agencies were participating in the investigation and the rate at which their work was progressing. The public was also entitled to know that Lee Harvey Oswald had been apprehended and that the State had gathered sufficient evidence to arraign him for the murders of the President and Patrolman Tippit, that he was being held pending action of the grand jury, that the investigation was continuing, and that the law enforcement agencies had discovered no evidence which tended to show that any other person was involved in either slaying.

However, neither the press nor the public had a right to be contemporaneously informed by the police or prosecuting authorities of the details of the evidence being accumulated against Oswald. Undoubtedly the public was interested in these disclosures, but its curiosity should not have been satisfied at the expense of the accused's right to a trial by an impartial jury. The courtroom, not the newspaper or television screen, is the appropriate forum in our system for the trial of a man accused of a crime.

If the evidence in the possession of the authorities had not been disclosed, it is true that the public would not have been in a position to assess the adequacy of the investigation or to apply pressures for further official undertakings. But a major consequence of the hasty and at times inaccurate divulgence of evidence after the assassination was simply to give rise to groundless rumors and public confusion. Moreover, without learning the details of the case, the public could have been informed by the responsible authority of the general scope of the investigation and the extent to which State and Federal agencies were assisting in the police work.

RESPONSIBILITY OF NEWS MEDIA

While appreciating the heavy and unique pressures with which the Dallas Police Department was confronted by reason of the assassination of President Kennedy, primary responsibility for having failed to control the press and to check the flow of undigested evidence to the public must be borne by the police department. It was the only agency that could have established orderly and sound operating procedures to control the multitude of newsmen gathered in the police building after the assassination.

The Commission believes, however, that a part of the responsibility for the unfortunate circumstances following the President's death must be borne by the news media. The crowd of newsmen generally failed to respond properly to the demands of the police. Frequently without permission, news representatives used police offices on the third floor, tying up facilities and interfering with normal police operations. Police efforts to preserve order and to clear passageways in the corridor were usually unsuccessful. On Friday night the reporters completely ignored Curry's injunction against asking Oswald questions in the assembly room and crowding in on him. On Sunday morning, the newsmen were instructed to direct no questions at Oswald; nevertheless, several reporters shouted questions at him when he appeared in the basement.

Moreover, by constantly pursuing public officials, the news representatives placed an insistent pressure upon them to disclose information. And this pressure was not without effect, since the police attitude toward the press was affected by the desire to maintain satisfactory relations with the news representatives and to create a favorable image of themselves. Chief Curry frankly told the Commission that,

I didn't order them out of the building, which if I had it to do over I would. In the past like I say, we had always maintained very good relations with our press, and they had always respected us. . . .

Curry refused Fritz' request to put Oswald behind the screen in the assembly room at the Friday night press conference because this might have hindered the taking of pictures. Curry's subordinates had the impression that an unannounced transfer of Oswald to the county jail was unacceptable because Curry did not want to disappoint the newsmen; he had promised that they could witness the transfer. It seemed clear enough that any attempt to exclude the press from the building or to place limits on the information disclosed to them would have been resented and disputed by the newsmen, who were constantly and aggressively demanding all possible information about anything related to the assassination.

Although the Commission has found no corroboration in the video and audio tapes, police officials recall that one or two representatives of the press reinforced their demands to see Oswald by suggesting that the police had been guilty of brutalizing him. They intimated that unless they were given the opportunity to see him, these suggestions would be passed on to the public. Captain King testified that he had been told that,

A short time after Oswald's arrest one newsman held up a photograph and said, "This is what the man charged with the assassination of the President looks like. Or at least this is what he did look like. We don't know what he looks like after an hour in the custody of the Dallas Police Department."

City Manager Elgin Crull stated that when he visited Chief Curry in his office on the morning of November 23, Curry told him that he "felt it was necessary to cooperate with the news media representatives, in order to avoid being accused of using Gestapo tactics in connection with the handling of Oswald." Crull agreed with Curry. The Commission deems any such veiled threats to be absolutely without justification.

The general disorder in the Police and Courts Building during November 22–24 reveals a regrettable lack of self-discipline by the newsmen. The Commission believes that the news media, as well as the police authorities, who failed to impose conditions more in keeping with the orderly process of justice, must share responsibility for the failure of law enforcement which occurred in connection with the death of Oswald. On previous occasions, public bodies have voiced the need for the exercise of self-restraint by the news media in periods when the demand for information must be tempered by other fundamental requirements of our society.

At its annual meeting in Washington in April 1964, the American Society of Newspaper Editors discussed the role of the press in Dallas immediately after President Kennedy's assassination. The discussion revealed the strong misgivings among the editors themselves about the role that the press had played and their desire that the press display more self-discipline and adhere to higher standards of conduct in the future. To prevent a recurrence of the unfortunate events which followed the assassination, however, more than general concern will be needed. The promulgation of a code of professional conduct governing representatives of all news media would be welcome evidence that the press had profited by the lesson of Dallas.

The burden of insuring that appropriate action is taken to establish ethical standards of conduct for the news media must also be borne, however, by State and local governments, by the bar, and ultimately by the public. The experience in Dallas during Novermber 22–24 is a dramatic affirmation of the need for steps to bring about a proper balance between the right of the public to be kept informed and the right of the individual to a fair and impartial trial.

ROY A. ROBERTS

4   The Responsibility of Newspapers

■

Forward-looking, immune to the sentimentality of gazing backward in nostalgia, hard-nosed when it comes to rational, level-headed criticism of the duties of the Press to the Public——these are just a few of the outstanding characteristics of Mr. Roberts' comments contained in the following article. Perhaps the quintessence of his attitude toward the nature of the responsibility of the Press is Mr. Roberts' firm belief that newspapers must never avoid their obligations by putting themselves above criticism——either self-generated or from outside sources; or to put it another way, there is nothing so unholy as a sacrosanct Press.

The Responsibility of Newspapers, the seventh annual William Allen White Memorial Lecture, was given by Mr. Roberts on February 10, 1956, when he was the President of the Kansas City Star. His comments appear here in a somewhat abridged format.

THIS I BELIEVE FIRMLY: Newspapers today are incomparably better, more useful than the newspapers of the past, even in that era of great publishing giants which some think back to as the golden days. It's all relative. The country, our mode of living, our problems, our horizon of interests, have changed violently and newspapers have changed with them. They should. We have largely passed from personal journalism to impersonal. We have become more objective. We cover the world today as we used to cover our community or even our state.

Yet, curiously, newspapers do a good job of selling everything but themselves. As press agents for newspapers, newspapers do a terrible job. By and large, newspapers today are more responsive to their obligations to reader and community than ever before. Something of the glamour and personality of the past may be lost as newspapers have become with the times sizeable business operations. Just go back and read the newspapers of 25 years ago. Then scan those of today. Draw your own judgment. There is only one answer. Our horizons of news coverage now are global so the comparison itself may be unfair. The field of entertainment is more varied, the appeal broader. If the same test is applied 25 years hence, we of today will suffer in comparison. That's progress. Newspapers have met the challenge of a growing, changing world and still represent, in spite of rate increases, forced by economic pressures, the greatest bargain that comes into the house. That, despite the amazing development of television.

Soul searching, self-criticism is always in order, even accepting the premise that newspapers are better today than ever before. To start with——the press services——and they are the backbone of bringing world news, as well as national, to your home——have expanded not only in coverage, but in intelligence in handling and interpreting what it is all about. You can't have real truth in news without such inter-pretation. Just mechanical transmission of barebone facts won't do the job. Accepting the principles of giving the background, as well as the barebone facts, is the greatest single advance in press services, even more than the miracle story of the expansion of wire service to the far nooks and corners of the globe.

I intend no invidious comparison with the other press services when I refer to the Associated Press. It's only because I sat so many years on the AP board and saw it function. The smallest complaint of one-sided presentation of the news from the smallest publisher re-ceives almost incredible study and attention. With membership com-posed of every conceivable faith and thinking, political, economic and otherwise, the service has to be objective. Of course, there will be slips and mistakes. But how few! Right there you have a buffer against unfair presentation of the news. Consider what a percentage of columns each day originate with press services, especially on national coverage. That's just item one on why newspapers are better today, because press services are better, more interpretative with background fill-in, with the entire world girded with wires and reporters.

Let's move to the editorial page. From personal to impersonal journalism, something was lost. But I believe we are coming out of the doldrums even there. Too often, editorial pages in the past were a catch-all for over-age writers you couldn't find any other place for. The trend today——and this goes even for smaller papers——is for building younger, better-informed editorial staffs, distinct from the news staff. The editorial pages are reflecting the opening of the doors of the ivory tower. The change is not universal, but it's coming. You sense, especially, too much of an inclination to abdicate editorial function to columnists and commentators. Let me make it clear I am not against columnists and commentators, *per se.* There are good and bad ones, as there are capable and wooden editors. Let me ask one question: Why should a publisher or an editor, large or small, apply different standards of responsibility to a columnist or a commentator than he does to his own staff? We let the special writers carry on personal vendettas with each other, bounce the truth and fact about by innuendo, without applying the same tests of accuracy you insist on for your own staff and writers. The uneasy conscience reflected by the palliative explanation above a column "that it does not necessarily represent the views of the newspaper" is the most supine apology imaginable. To make it completely irresponsible you should add you are not vouching for its truth or accuracy.

In this day of increasing one-newspaper towns, the public is entitled not just to news, but diverse viewpoints of how it is evaluated. But, certainly, your own editorial policy ought to be vigorous enough so your readers won't be shocked and don't need to be told that you are printing something just to give the other side. Print it if you think it is fair comment or criticism, not scurrilous or irresponsible. You don't have to label it. There is one columnist——I won't mention his name——who has long been a good friend of mine. He comes up with something unusual every now or then. I have never let him in the *Star* and he knows why. He mangles English and good taste and good usage. That's his business and lots of folks like it. That's their business. But, I can't see making your own staff adhere strictly to principles of good writing and usage and letting an outsider, just because he has a name, chew up good writing. Instead of abdicating so much to the columnists and commentators, wouldn't it be healthier if more publishers wrote signed columns from time to time? Specifically, I have in mind such regular stints as Jack Knight turns out for the Knight newspapers. There are others, but too few. I have been on both sides, editorial and business. I know the problem of the publisher. I recognize he has his hands full, particularly lately in the complicated and costly years of operation. Ultimate responsibility, after all, rests in ownership. More publishers and owners should write powerful editorials, as well as powerful checks.

So the new staffs have changed and kept pace with the growing world. The day of the hardboiled, old-fashioned reporter out to get his scoop at any cost may be passing. Possibly, there may be too much reliance in some quarters on the ticker and the press agent or public relations releases, all of which makes for loss of initiative. By and large, the news staffs of today are better prepared for their job. That job is infinitely more difficult than it was decades ago——in the so-called good old days of old-fashioned reporters, old-fashioned at least to the extent of long hours and lots of glamour and mighty little pay. The good reporter of today has to have more technical training and background to do a good job. Staffs are evolving into specialists along some line. It all makes for better written, more intelligent news presentation, more substance. Today's newspapers reflect the change.

So by the major tests the newspaper of today has met the challenge of the changing years. Yet, where do we stand today before our final judges, the public and our readers? As a profession we haven't done a good job of putting our own story over. We have sold everything else except the great contribution newspapers have made to national and local well-being. Newspapers have been too much on the defensive, too apologetic, if you please. You can hardly go to a newspaper meeting or hear a speech on newspapers without much of the oratory turning around the dangers of losing the cherished freedom. We convert each other, who don't need conversion, but we certainly haven't gotten over to the public what we're driving at or concerned about. Somehow, the notion prevails that newspapers are asking some special license or freedoms or privilege not accorded to anyone else. Still lacking is full recognition that the right of the public to know is the very basis of a free democratic system.

It is my firm conviction that freedom of the press will be preserved as long as newspapers deserve it——no longer.

Likewise freedom of the press encompasses responsibility of newspapers. The two are indivisible.

Clarify the atmosphere by stressing more our responsibility; dissipate the notion that newspapers seek to set themselves up as a special class licensed under the free speech and free press amendment guarantees, to some privilege not enjoyed by others.

If the public once understands it is its own right to know that is at stake, that the very foundations of a free democracy are involved, then there will be no question of the issue. Remember, a good newspaper doing its duty will never win a popularity contest. It may be respected. But popular, no.

There is another newspaper trend that makes responsibility of the newspaper a more impelling topic than ever. There is no good served in backing away from it. That is the continuing erosion in the newspaper field. The number of dailies, year by year, has diminished. The cities and towns with only one newspaper or a single newspaper ownership have steadily increased. Whether it is healthy from a national standpoint or not, there it is. There it will be. Whether you like it or not, the sheer force of economic pressures is making it so. All the theorists on earth can't change such a picture except by reversal of the pressures that produced it. Costs——labor, distribution, sky-rocketing newsprint, once a cheap and plentiful commodity, and taxes——have been the big factors. Already in the average smaller town or even fair-sized city, competing newspapers are becoming as extinct as the Washington handpress. I am not passing judgment on the trend, just stating the fact.

I do say with conviction that by and large most newspapers have accepted the responsibilities that go along with a one-newspaper town or ownership. All is not to the bad. The medium-class city newspaper is incomparably better in every way than the papers used to be when two or three were struggling to make ends meet. In that field has been the greatest improvement in newspapers anywhere. Even in the larger cities, scan the lists of those cities with one newspaper and you find some of the best and strongest newspapers. It is curious, maybe, but often there you find more consecration and devotion to civic and community building than in the few remaining cities with fiercely competing papers, striving for circulation and supremacy. For the most part, the rule has been to give the reader more service, more coverage and a better package and certainly more objective presentation of the news. Whatever disadvantages of the one-newspaper town, the increased ability to serve is inescapable and beyond argument. Whether something in editorial vigor has been lost in the process might be questioned. The sheer responsibilities of a one-newspaper town generally have made for a more objective newspaper.

The most priceless asset a newspaper has is its integrity and reader confidence. This far outweighs monumental plants, high-speed presses, distribution systems. So, not because of idealism or dedication necessarily, but just common sense, the publisher accepts the responsibility of single ownership and seeks to give more in service, not less, more effort toward objective news, not less. He is not going to jeopardize his position before the most important body of opinion of all——the reader and the community. After all, that's what counts.

Another trend I shall mention. Originally, I had expected to make it the central theme of my talk today. That is the proposed investigation or study under the auspices of a newspaper-based organization, Sigma Delta Chi, the research to be financed from some tax-free foundation, of irresponsible charges by self-serving politicians of a "one-party press." Just a year ago from this same forum, Norman Isaacs of the Louisville *Courier-Journal*——an editor whose opinion I respect and a newspaper I certainly regard as having the highest standards——launched the proposal for such a study covering the 1956 presidential campaign. I accord Mr. Isaacs full credit for sincerity of conviction that such a study would have been a service to American newspaperdom. The advocates of such a move are just as much entitled to their opinions as those to the contrary. Happily, and I use the word advisedly, for I feel strongly on the subject, the whole question has been disposed of. After a comprehensive poll of publishers, large and small, the verdict was adverse. The entire project has been completely dropped. There is no useful purpose served in kicking around or keeping alive the corpse of a dead issue.

I felt such a proposal was a disservice to American newspapers and expected to say so emphatically. My thinking was that it represented something utterly futile, would settle nothing; political demagogues would continue to make the same accusations whenever it served their purpose, as they have a perfect right to do, because this is free America. Responsibility in the premise is individual, not collective. All the resolutions and probes on earth wouldn't put integrity into a publisher and/or editor if it wasn't there basically. Just to measure the news content carried and not the editorial page or the columnists or the commentators would have made such a study without value. Yet otherwise you approach the danger line of control or an attempt to influence opinion in a probe outside the news columns. Other minor implications, such as appealing to a tax-free foundation for funds to conduct the study, didn't sit well. But prime and first responsibility must always be in the individual ownership of newspapers with the final judgment lodged with the readers. Fail in your obligation to them, it won't take you long to have something to worry about. You can't figure reporting in inches of space that each party got. The party or side that makes the most news will get the most news columns. This is inevitable. Editorial page, that's another thing. That's as it should be. This comparison was especially noticeable in 1948 when Mr. Truman with his whistle-stop campaign ran rings around the Republican nominee in making news. Even though a huge majority of newspapers were not supporting him, he got the news columns. On the editorial page, conviction and belief were the test——not newsworthiness.

The long-range aspects of free speech and of free press are not too happy. A totalitarian government moves first to circumvent the right of the people to know and the ability of the people to know by muzzling the press. The bigger government grows, the greater the threat. Social trends the world over all point to government getting bigger and bigger. So, it is well to be ever alert. Here in our own United States I have a sneaking feeling a return to hardboiled reporting will kick open more doors to governmental secrecy than all the congressional probes or all the speeches of alarm that can be made. What is happening elsewhere justifies apprehension and fears.

Here at home I return to my original premise that newspapers will be more effective in their appeal to public opinion by stressing responsibility of the press as indivisible from freedom of speech and press. Reducing it down to simple terms, it means truth in the news. Truth in the news with every broad and full implication.

Truth in the news——but truth tempered with mercy, decency and humility.

Truth in the news——truth that means not being controlled or unduly influenced either by Big Business, Big Labor or Big Government. That last is becoming the more important.

Truth in the news——which encompasses telling fairly and intelligently what the news means, the background, not just parrot-like recording.

Truth in the news——truth which does not slavishly follow either a party line or an economic line or a cult. Too often you know just what a newspaper is going to say on an issue before you pick it up. Both liberal organs and conservatives fail to deviate often enough from their cult to be interesting. Nonconformity is more exciting at times, more useful.

Truth in the news——which can encompass hatred of intolerance and oppression or pushing folks around. Tell the facts.

Truth in the news——but truth dedicated to high ideals, community service, national service, with a first obligation the readers' right to know. That's our first and eternal job and responsibility.

That's what I mean by responsibility of the press.

This I believe.

J. MONTGOMERY CURTIS

5   Responsibility for Raising Standards

■

Former President Harry S. Truman used to have a brass plate on his White House desk with the legend The Buck Stops Here. So it is with the publisher, Mr. Curtis states, the man at the top, that the initial and ultimate responsibility for raising standards rests. Elsewhere in this volume, Clifton Daniel disagrees——claiming that responsibility rests equally with the editor and reporter. But Mr. Curtis' remarks on the role of the publisher is just one of the many stimulating comments on newspapering today that together make the following article a particularly valuable survey of the ethics, morals and humanity of American journalism. Another opinion of Mr. Curtis' that is sure to provoke controversy is his statement that really good and responsible newspapers enlarge both their profits and their audiences.

Mr. Curtis' review of aspects of contemporary journalism is contained in an address he delivered on October 21, 1960, as part of the dedicatory ceremonies for Howell Hall as the new home for the school of journalism of the University of North Carolina. At the time of his address, Mr. Curtis was Director of the American Press Institute. His speech is printed here in a somewhat abridged format.

WHO IS RESPONSIBLE for insuring that each day's newspaper fulfills the highest standards of newspaper journalism? To what extent is the responsibility shared?

What is the current record of success and failure in discharging the responsibility? What are the rewards for success and the penalties for failure?

What are the prospects for improving the record?

To prepare for accurate and complete answers, may I begin with what appears at first to be an almost childishly elemental question? Just what is today's newspaper journalism? I raise the question because there are many misconceptions and extremely limited views, some of them found in the most unlikely places, including some newspaper offices. Let us consider a few of the misconceptions.

To some journalism students, a newspaper may be merely an opportunity to make a living without being bored until some distant time when literary genius flowers. It should not be news that many years ago newspapers ceased being a brief stepping-stone for the gifted or a permanent haven for the untalented.

To some intellectuals, including a sprinkling on some university campuses, the newspaper is performing a splendid public service when its news and opinions support the intellectuals' views, but the newspaper is an irresponsible menace when it disagrees.

To a few journalism professors, a newspaper is a place where you write, edit, and put type in a form.

To many politicians the newspaper is a bulwark of democracy when it endorses them but is a leech on the body politic when it endorses their opponents, regardless of how fair and conscientious the news coverage has been.

To some of the news and editorial men, survivors of an old and narrow school, the newspaper is an unprincipled business enterprise when they cannot command all the space and manpower they want. This is wrong.

To some newspapermen on the business side, from the same old and narrow school, the newspaper is a hopelessly inefficient operation headed for bankruptcy when the editor demands the performance of reader services from which there is no immediately obvious financial return. This is equally wrong.

To the reader interested in foreign affairs, some newspapers appear distressingly parochial. To the reader interested primarily in local affairs, some newspapers appear to be concerned far too much with distant parts of the world.

To the businessman, who may also be an advertiser, the news-paper seems unfriendly when it prints the hopes and arguments of labor. To the labor leader, the newspaper is also unfriendly when it prints the hopes and arguments of management.

So it goes. Each viewpoint is conditioned understandably by personal interests and, consequently, all of these concepts are inade-quate and often completely wrong.

What then is today's newspaper and what makes it so utterly different and so much more difficult than most other undertakings? The difference and the difficulty are caused by a unique combination of problems which must be solved if the newspaper is to succeed. Let us consider seven of them:

There is the primary function of not only offering the reader, but *persuading* him to read a daily, printed, preservable account of the news——all of the news from everywhere——through words and pictures. Today, this is an incredibly difficult job because of the wide range of subjects which now are news——and it is also incredibly expensive.

There is the function of newspaper leadership and public service to the community. That means an effective editorial page and public service reporting to improve the community. The need for this never ceases, and it requires the highest skills.

There is the function of the marketplace in which the newspaper links buyer and seller. That means advertising and the urgent need for more and more revenue to support the ever more costly news function. And the advertising function grows more difficult as other media intensify competition.

There is the job of operating a modern, complex factory for manufacturing the newspaper but with this difference——how can you be efficient with mass, assembly-line production methods, as other manufacturers are with a standardized product, when each day's newspaper varies in the number of pages, and the content of those pages is different each day?

There is the job of selling and delivering the product and servicing the buyer and constantly promoting sales to new buyers and reselling old buyers. That is circulation, a function requiring higher and higher talents.

There is the job of overall business management which must insure that income exceeds outgo if there is to be enough money to improve and expand the newspaper.

And throughout these six functions, each with its own group of problems, runs the necessity of earning, promoting and maintaining the highest respect of the public——a public containing many diverse elements which are going to resent the newspaper if it is independent, as it surely must be.

(Considering the rare combination of talent required for these seven functions, let alone the exceptional skills required by each one of them, is it any wonder that there are fewer newspapers today than there were just a few years ago? Publishing a successful newspaper of quality is not a simple, easy job [it never was]. The highly skilled and devoted newspapers survive. The others perish.)

What does all of this mean in the context of responsibility? Can it be expressed in a capsule? Perhaps.

As one of the four indispensable institutions of a free people, the newspaper is the only one which must be a successful private business enterprise in order to preserve its freedom and protect the validity of its service. The other institutions——representative self-government, schools, and religion——are supported by taxes or philanthropy. Only the newspaper must survive on the sale of its services and, incidentally, make enough money to pay its own taxes and philanthropies to support the other institutions.

Obviously, this peculiar kind of an institution requires the highest ethical standards for news, for editorial leadership, for advertising acceptability, for business practices, for relations with the community. But again and always, with a difference. The standards cannot be applied and enforced by law (except for laws necessary to protect the individual from abuse) because law means government and government participation in any way means loss of freedom.

Who, then, does apply and enforce the standards? There are many echelons of responsibility but all of them begin and all of them end with one source: the ownership of the individual newspaper. Upon ownership alone rests the responsibility for providing that most difficult product—a newspaper on which true quality is wedded with successful management. Ownership can and does delegate the *application* of standards to executives and staff members. Ownership delegates responsibility to those of us who serve newspapers. But, unless the owner is responsive to the highest standards and also possesses the required administrative skills, the newspaper will not be a quality product with successful management.

How successfully are newspaper owners fulfilling their responsibilities today? That question can be answered accurately but first a word of caution. Whenever you hear or read an opinion which begins "The newspapers of the United States are or are not . . .", beware. There are more than 1,700 dailies and almost 10,000 weeklies. A valid generalization would have to be based on reading each one of them for a considerable time with a knowledge of each newspaper's community——an impossible job.

Therefore, I will confine my answer to the more than 500 newspapers which come to American Press Institute seminars where newspapermen analyze, dissect, and criticize each other's newspapers and operations. From this experience extending over 14 years and involving the constant reading of many newspapers, we may draw a few conclusions.

Almost all of these newspapers *are* fulfilling their responsibilities. When any of them slip it is not intentional and the recovery is rapid. More and more newspapers each year are making a better and better record of living up to the highest standards. Of course, there are the exceptional and isolated cases, as there always will be in a land of freedom to publish, but the fact that these receive so much emphasis among newspapermen proves that the great majority of newspapers are faithful to their standards.

But you do not have to rely upon my conclusions. There is plenty of evidence. One test is public acceptability of the newspaper by the readers and, consequently, use of the newspaper by advertisers. What is the record of the last decade or so?

With scarcely any exceptions, those newspapers which have been faithful to their trust and high in professional competence have a record of steadily increasing circulation and steadily increasing total advertising lineage. It is true that in some rapidly growing areas, the increase in newspaper circulation is not keeping pace with the increase in the number of dwelling units. Who can reasonably expect otherwise in this age of mobility? It is also true that some categories of advertising revenue have declined. Who can reasonably expect otherwise in this day of intensive competition? It is also true that a considerable number of newspapers do not have a record of steadily increasing net profits in these difficult days, but all of the owners known to me are making enough profit to support the institution entrusted to them. This is but one of the rewards for fulfilling the highest standards in ethics and competence.

On the other hand and with a few exceptions, those newspapers which have not upheld high standards applied by superior professional competence have had increasingly difficult problems of survival. There have been cases where there was an insufficient economic base for the operation of two or more newspapers, but in the main it has been the best newspaper which has survived. That is one of the rewards for success.

Good publishers are the first to say that they have been helped immeasurably by the steady increase in public taste which is based upon an increasingly educated public. In most areas the public today rejects the irresponsible newspaper. As the months and years go on, I think *the public will more and more reject those newspapers which do not have a basic respect for the news* and which fill their inside columns with trivia. Many such papers have died or been absorbed. That is the final penalty for failure in fulfilling the responsibility.

Anyone who wishes to challenge these conclusions should first consider that the total circulation of newspapers has increased steadily through the years and total advertising lineage has increased—— both the results of ever-growing acceptability by a public which is more selective in its reading tastes than ever before.

Thus, the first essential is to produce an excellent newspaper every day. Of course this involves everyone in the operation——the reporter who is carefully checking the spelling of a name; the editorial writer who is searching for the most effective phrase in the best of taste; the headline writer who rejects the trick of luring the reader through distortion; the advertising manager who is rejecting revenue from a questionable source; the general manager who is adhering to the most ethical business practices; the production man who is striving for the cleanest, most legible page; the circulation man and all the other executives who are training their staffs as fine representatives with the public; the switchboard operator who handles the rough complainant with courtesy; and right through to the carrier boy who carefully places this precious product in a protected and convenient

place for that one person towards whom all this effort is aimed——
the reader.

Beyond this first essential of producing an excellent newspaper each day, what else is being done in the field of higher standards? There are so many examples that I will have to condense the report and even then omit many of them.

We begin with the fact that the solution to almost all newspaper problems is to produce an excellent newspaper. This requires better and better newspapermen with a degree of competence higher than ever before, and a sense of dedication as complete as any we have ever known. What is being done in the field of developing newspaper people?

The *Wall Street Journal* through its Newspaper Fund is now in the third year of a vast and effective program to improve the teaching of journalism in high schools and to acquire summer newspaper jobs for the most gifted high school students. The idea is to catch them young and train them correctly.

Almost everyone here can recall the days when university journalism graduates were looked upon with great skepticism in newspaper offices——and for valid reasons. Many had been poorly trained. Today, in the case of many journalism schools, that is not true. The graduates are not only welcome but in many cases the superior graduates are sought.

Going one step further, what is being done for the experienced newspapermen of all newspaper departments? The API is an example. We were founded in 1946 by newspaper owners for the purpose of improving the fidelity to standards and the professional skills which that requires. To date, there have been 2,581 newspapermen at the Institute from 591 newspapers. And the number of participating newspapers increases each year. *Newspapers have been more than willing to finance an Institute which is devoted to only one purpose——improvement of newspapers through constructive criticism exchanged by newspapermen and experts from related fields.*

There are many other organizations working to improve newspaper performance. Publishers, editors, editorial writers, managing editors, general managers, financial managers, circulation managers, advertising managers, production managers——all have their organizations on the national level and some extend to regional and state levels.

Training programs are being conducted by individual newspapers. Wire services have their organizations of managing editors. The list is even longer than this.

I would not pretend that all of these organizations do consistently effective work, but I would emphasize that none of them would exist without the support of newspaper ownership. The judgment of the effectiveness of each organization is best left to those who support them.

All of this work is actually only a continuation of something which started many years ago——the self-auditing and self-policing of their industry by the newspaper owners. They began by forming the Audit Bureau of Circulation to bring high standards into that end of the business, and they have been at it ever since in every other part of the newspaper operation.

What of the future? Again, this rests upon the quality, interests, ambitions and capacities of *newspaper* owners. The record of those present owners known to the American Press Institute should be quite clear by now. Over the coming years the problems of economic survival, intense as they are now, may well increase. There will be the recurring problems of labor, and I hope that labor will show an increasing desire to share the responsibilities for successful newspapers. There will be the age-old problems of newspaper inheritance in which we watch to see whether the son of the publisher is as effective as the father, or whether the daughter of the publisher skillfully chooses the right husband for journalistic competence as well as for love.

There will be many other problems but I can see nothing on the horizon which will prevent the newspaper institution from continuing and from improving as long as we have devoted publishers who have good people working with them——all engaged in one of the most vital, fascinating, and difficult jobs in the world——producing an excellent newspaper each day.

It has just occurred to me belatedly that I have been talking all this time about responsibility for standards, and I have not defined a single standard. Of course dedicated newspapermen know what they are. The definition I like best appears by implication over the editorial page masthead of one newspaper. It reads as follows: "The policy of our paper is very simple——merely to tell the truth." That is the policy of the St. Petersburg (Fla.) *Times,* and it speaks volumes in 12 words. And every newspaper owner should read the "Standards for Ownership of a Newspaper" written in 1947 by the *Times* Editor, Nelson Poynter. I will provide them later.

(*Editor's Note*: *Limitations of time prevented two sources of quotation from being used in Mr. Curtis' speech as delivered. The material, as recorded by Mr. Curtis, is appended here because it is of value to students, faculty members, and newspapermen.*)

Members of the university community and the newspaper community might well ponder the affinity between a good newspaper and a good educational institution. This affinity was never expressed more thoughtfully or clearly than by the Very Rev. James J. McGinley, S. J., president of Canisius College in Buffalo, New York, on the occasion of a dinner honoring Mr. Kirchhofer. Here is what President McGinley had to say about the good newspaper and the good educational institution:

Each must serve but also lead a community, voluntarily. Neither can be true to its commitment and also indulge in the quest for sheer popularity. Both must be open to frank evaluation and criticism, daily. Neither can become complacent and stay alive. Each demands concentration by all co-workers and often requires a type of discipline and self-denial which borders on the ascetic. Each must blend the new and the old, the local and the distant. Each must make responsible decisions on what to feature and in what proportions. Above all, each in its area of responsibility must be consistent, truthful and convinced.

Responsible newspaper owners have thought long and earnestly about the futures of their newspapers. One who has recorded his thoughts is Mr. Poynter. On August 6, 1947, he printed his "Standards for Ownership of a Newspaper or Radio Enterprise." For the sake of brevity, I have deleted the phrases referring to radio, but of course the standards apply equally to newspaper and radio. Here are Mr. Poynter's words:

This is a guide for my heirs, trustees, executors, courts or their advisors who have any responsibilities in disposing of any of my newspaper or broadcasting properties and equities. These standards shall be used as a yardstick in choosing the purchaser of the St. Petersburg *Times* . . .

which I own. A fair and equitable price must be realized from my properties but my executors shall be under no obligation to sell my interests to the highest bidder, but they may accept any offer from any bidder for any amount deemed by them to be fair and reasonable, and upon any terms deemed by them to be acceptable in view of the following:

(1) Ownership or participation in ownership of a publication . . . is a sacred trust, and a great privilege.

(2) Any publication . . . has unusual obligations to the community in which it operates, and any new owner must be sensitive to this.

(3) The owners of a publication . . . cannot compromise with the integrity of the news and information that is sold or given to the public.

(4) A publication . . . must be aggressive in its service to the community and not wait to be prodded into rendering that service. A publisher . . . must share the zeal and enthusiasm for what is new each day. He does not belong as an owner unless he has such enthusiasm.

(5) Adequate and modern equipment is vital for successful publishing . . . but it is secondary to staff.

(6) A "chain" owner cannot do justice to local publications. . . . His devotion and loyalty to any one area is bound to be diluted or divided if he has other ownerships and interests.

(On this point may I comment? There are "chains" and "chains." Certainly there are those which do not measure up at all in the field of responsibility to the community or public service. On the other hand, may I emphasize that there are some "chains" which have newspapers of the highest integrity, which allocate autonomy to the local editor and which have no superiors in the field of public service to the community. For example, The Charlotte *Observer* in this state is a Knight newspaper, and I could not name for you another newspaper which is more devoted to its community and its state. However, these are Mr. Poynter's words and let us continue.)

(7) I expect every member of any staff to be above average in his respective job. I expect my successor to demand standards of his staff as high or higher than mine. A concern that expects its staff to be above average must be willing to pay staffers above average.

(8) Any modern capitalistic institution must expect to provide pensions that promise honest and dignified retirement to members of the staff who have devoted their lives to the institution.

(9) Mere ownership in a paper . . . does not entitle an individual to a salary. All salaries should be commensurate with the services rendered to the institution.

(10) A publication . . . cannot best serve its community if it is

encumbered with outside interests. Its editorial policy should not be tinctured with ownership in enterprises not related to newspapering. . . .

(11) To maintain a strong editorial policy, a newspaper . . . must be in a strong financial position. Reserves must be built. Debts must be reduced and extinguished.

(12) To qualify as an owner of a newspaper . . . , a prospect should have a well-rounded appreciation of the contribution that is made by all departments in publishing . . . the technical——sales——distribution departments——and above all, the creative or editorial departments.

(13) A payment of not more than six per cent dividends on the present capitalization should be considered fair until debts are discharged, reserves built and technical equipment brought up to a position of second to none on the West Coast of Florida.

(14) Dividends beyond six per cent should be equalized with bonuses to employees on a formula which I expect to perfect in the coming several years, a formula that recognizes length of service and contribution to the enterprise.

(15) A publication is so individualistic in nature that complete control should be concentrated in an individual. Voting stock should never be permitted to scatter.

EVERETT T. RATTRAY

6   The Weekly Newspaper's Responsibility to Print the News and Raise Hell

■

"Boosterism" as the editorial policy of a small-town weekly newspaper today is an evasion of its responsibility, says Mr. Rattray, editor of The East Hampton Star (New York State), in the following essay written especially for this volume. The true and highest responsibility is for civic improvement, reform and truth-telling——no matter where the chips may fall.

In genteelly acerbic fashion, Mr. Rattray's comments range over the whole spectrum of the special world called weekly newspaper journalism. That he takes his responsibilities so sincerely and energetically augurs well for the continuance of not only his own weekly, but others with equal courage, dedication, and as clear an understanding of the special value and peculiar function of the small-town weekly.

The radio, TV, the big-city dailies put the Americans everywhere in touch with the larger world. But it is only the small-town weekly that has the responsibility to keep him directly and informatively involved with his own immediate world of sewage repairs, school bond issues, zoning laws, etc. To fulfill this responsibility with honesty and industry is no mean feat——in terms of both integrity and effort. Editors like Mr. Rattray are to be commended for their dedication and their ideals.

A NEWSPAPER'S JOB, according to the oldtimers, is to print the news and raise hell. Some editors and publishers would say that their job——printing the news and raising hell——was identical with their responsibility, and some newspapers do their job just that way. Yet it is also true that a good many more, big and little, do not.

Printing the news as it happens, accurately and thoroughly, very often amounts to hell-raising without the need for editorializing. How many papers do their job in either department? Not as many as should.

There are roughly 8,000 weekly newspapers in the United States and 1,700 dailies. At a guess, one in ten of either category fulfills its responsibility to print the news and raise hell, to report and criticize on the events, public and private, around them.

I would give the smalltown, suburban, or big-city neighborhood weeklies a slight edge over the dailies, however, when it comes to keeping the public eye trained on the affairs of local government. As few weeklies feel that they must report national or international news, it is not surprising that they should devote a higher proportion of their space to the city council or the school budget.

A good weekly will cover the city council or town board a good deal more thoroughly than the New York dailies can afford to cover the doings of the various branches of the city government. Unless the weekly is published in an unusual town, there will come a day when just reporting a certain government transaction is equivalent to raising hell.

A town board, for instance, decides after a series of rural slum fires to amend its building code and require masonry, rather than tin-pipe or composition chimneys on all dwellings. An amendment is adopted, and shortly thereafter a councilman proposes a revision ——composition vents should be allowed for gas furnace installations. He is the board's expert on gas furnaces, for he works for the local tank-gas firm. The paper points this out, and as far as the town board is concerned, hell has been raised.

A village board of trustees is considering a municipal parking lot. At a public hearing, the village attorney expresses himself forcefully about what he calls meddling on the part of the ladies village improvement society, which wants to save some trees to shade the lot. The paper reports his remarks straight, and hell is raised.

Small potatoes? Of course, but it is big news to people who are close to their small local government, and important news if it opens a public peephole into wrongdoing or poor judgment.

Such small potatoes sometimes grow. Several years ago, when Robert Moses proposed——for the nth time——to build a parkway down the narrow strip which is today the Fire Island National Seashore, several newspapermen questioned the practicality of the idea. They attempted to find out how much it had cost over the years to maintain, and repair after storms, a similar Long Island State Parkway on Jones Beach, a sand strip much like Fire Island and just west of it.

To their surprise, they found nothing in the public record to show how much this had cost. They asked the Long Island State Park Commission, which Mr. Moses had headed since Hector was a pup, for the figures and were refused. Several weeklies and a business-oriented daily went to court, and won the right to examine the Commission's books. They got the figures and printed them.

Today, Mr. Moses is no longer Chairman of the Long Island State Park Commission. He is no longer free to follow his every whim in New York State, and other newspapers and public figures are no longer afraid to criticize him. There is no roadway down Fire Island, through the Sunken Forest and over the marshes, either.

No one would claim the suit over the Jones Beach Parkway maintenance costs was solely responsible for this massive onslaught of *lèse majesté,* but it certainly did some of the damage. People who believe that government by Commission and Authority should not be questioned, and that public spending kept private ought to be allowed, may not even approve, but they ought not to be reading this. They ought not to be in the newspaper business, either.

It is my belief that any newspaper, weekly or daily, that reports accurately the doings of local government over a period of years is bound to make that government a better one, and make its area a better place in which to live. The worse the government to begin with, the more radical will be the improvement.

There is a big *if* involved, however. This reporting can only be done if the paper survives. Survival means money from advertising, unless the publisher is a multi-millionaire with a yearning for a tax loss. Can there be survival in the face of community disapproval, including the dislike of most of the advertisers?

Hazel Brannon Smith of Mississippi and other Southern editors who do not follow the mores of their white communities in regard to the Negro exist under these conditions, but it is hard to see how. In the rest of the nation, though, even the most idealistic editor will rarely find himself at odds with the majority of his readers at once. A good paper will eventually offend them all, but most likely do it a few at a time. Survival ought to be possible.

There are times when, feeling sorry for myself, I force myself to consider what it would be like to hold my job down in a Louisiana or Mississippi small town, without abandoning any convictions. The thought tends to brighten up the grass on this side of the fence.

Survival, yes; but can a weekly be started today without a sugar-daddy or a rich uncle? With luck, and with hard work, one can. A friend publishes a weekly he founded six or seven years ago. The paper was, and is, the only one published in a township——a very small one, but they all have a certain amount of required legal advertising. He has no shop and has one helper, plus a hard-working wife. His printing bill would, I guess, run about $150 a week (this is a very small paper, literally) and his gross income from advertising and his 1,000 or so circulation, plus printing orders he picks up on his rounds and farms out, is perhaps $400 in a good week.

He is not getting rich, but he is publishing a weekly newspaper and editing one. His town is a better place for the paper. He reports what goes on, and he has at least one editorial a week. He rocks the boat regularly.

Another acquaintance runs——I hesitate to say edits——a bigger weekly. The owner is easily sickened by a rocking boat, so the three or four editorials a year are confined to deploring Communism, drunken driving, or riding bicycles on the sidewalk. When the man who is called editor feels strongly about something, he writes himself a letter, which is printed, name and all.

This, I suppose, fits the big-city idea of weekly newspapering. It happens, and so does what Ben Bagdikian wrote about in *Harper's* a while back——the use of canned editorials and other puff material. Mr. Bagdikian, to judge from the howls in trade journals and at press meetings, struck very close to the bone with a lot of editors and publishers.

The mass of garbage he described is riper, and larger, than anyone outside the trade can imagine. Many within the business, protected by secretaries or mail clerks, would find it hard to credit a weekly editor's report on the unsolicited "suggested editorials" or matted features sent out by various special interest groups. Some editors can tell from the envelope what is inside and throw it away; others read it all, and find a certain amount of material which is adaptable for use in the advertising columns or as editorial inspiration; others sort out the gems and use them, often never knowing exactly which lobby they are helping out.

Several of the purveyors of this stuff actually send out catalogues periodically, with a check-what-you-want return postcard. Editors who immediately discard the catalogue are missing a good chance to build up a file of stereo mats for miscellaneous ad use, but that is neither here nor there.

The use of this political and business propaganda as news is irresponsible, but it is no more irresponsible than any other perversion of the newspaper's function as a relater of truth. The truth can be perverted by omission ("bad for the community"; "we'd rather you forgot about that"; "the boy's mother is deathly ill") and by commission.

Sins of commission include the airing of anonymous charges, outright lies, or even artful picture cropping. A year or so ago, some papers carried a wire-service photo of a race riot. It was the same shot in all. A white youth was in the foreground, and a Negro youth was leaping a hedge behind the white. In some papers, the Negro had one hand high, and in the hand was a knife. In others, the picture had been cropped so that he appeared to be giving a friendly wave as he jumped.

Another irresponsibility, duller but just as sinful, particularly evident in the weeklies, is home-town boosterism to the point of a complete loss of perspective. A paper afflicted with this ailment will spring to the defense of its town in the face of any criticism, no matter how justified, and will tend to judge news by its imagined good or bad influence on the town if reported.

A certain amount of defensiveness can mean a lively source of material for an editor. A rivalry between towns or cities may be fanned, within reason, and it can be a running story. Smaller cities and towns, though, are a good deal like big families, and too many papers react to criticism, or what they consider criticism, like a mother of a maligned child. Reason is ignored, and emotional editorials——often aimed at other newspapers, "the Northern press," for example——use the small errors almost inevitable in any reporting as evidence of sinister motives.

Sooner or later, any community large enough to support a paper, even the smallest weekly, will have a crime or accident story big enough to attract national attention. And, after the fire that kills half a dozen children from a poor family or the raid on the volunteer firemen's smoker, the folks back home, including the editor will claim that they have been misjudged. They will be self-conscious in the extreme, and they will want to strike back. They will have seen the event from an entirely different angle, they will wish it never happened, and they will be generally unhappy.

Some communities, and some papers, simply ignore the unpleasant. The uproar generally dies down with time, and they feel that the ensuing quiet has vindicated their back-turning. Others go into a flurry of explanation and correction.

The responsible ones try to find out exactly what happened, and why. Unless an event occurs close to press time, weekly editors generally have much more time to seek out the details of a major story in their bailiwick than does the daily editor who covers the same event. A lucky weekly editor will have time enough to collect all the clippings from the dailies, to compare them, to find the unanswered questions and contradictions, to sort out the loose ends, and to compile the most complete and accurate account of any——combining the unoffered but available legwork of the daily reporter with his own staff's (more likely his own) finishing touches.

If it is a big enough story to warrant all this work, it will deserve editorial comment. Who will be better fitted than our editor to comment on it? No one, probably, provided the editor can retain his perspective and his sense of humor during a community crisis.

My town, a resort which has come to expect genteel publicity on the social pages of the New York dailies, underwent such a crisis last summer. A party at a house rented for the season by a group of young men and women most easily described as beatniks was raided, and twenty-two persons were arrested, seven of them on narcotics charges. Within twenty-four hours, the news had appeared in papers as far away as South Africa.

The raid took place early Wednesday, giving us twenty-four hours to do the story and a chance to capitalize, as described above, on the work of reporters from the dailies. We had time to gather complete data on those arrested, and to check the details of the charges—— something the daily reporters had not had time to do before writing their initial stories.

The follow-up stories in the closer dailies continued for four or five days, and by the second Thursday (there was no doubt in anybody's mind about the raid warranting more than our first story; local people talked of little else for several weeks) we had a pile of clippings, several unanswered questions answered, and a more complete account than anyone else. We also had a long editorial which, we hoped, put the affair into perspective.

In the following weeks, we followed the case, and reported it when all of those jailed——some of them were held without bail by the local Justice of the Peace——eventually got out, either when bail was ordered set by a higher court or when charges were dropped. Other papers, the ones that had found the summer resort scandal so attractive for the first few days, either ignored the subsequent details or reported them partially. We plan to follow the affair until the last case is disposed of. The complete story needs to be told for its own sake, for the interest those at home have in what came of it all, and for the way all the facts sometimes have of changing the initial outlook on such an event.

Some of our readers would undoubtedly feel better if the matter were dropped. Most of them, however, seem to find that an event that only aroused resentment and a strong wish that it had happened someplace else at first has become, when reported in detail and with care through its aftermath, understandable and an occasion for reasoned concern rather than hysteria.

This sort of thing is the weekly newspaper's job, not the panting boosterism which generally amounts to telling the folks at home how good they are, since no one else, barring a few out-of-town relatives and moved-aways, reads the paper.

Of the American weeklies printing editorials regularly, and probably a minority of them do, a good many devote much of their
comment to congratulations to the oldest citizen on her birthday, the
Lions Club on their barbecue, or the Girl Scouts on their cookies.
Taking into our accounting those other weeklies regularly using
canned editorials about the sacred right to work, the American Way
of Life, and the need for more highways, it would appear that
editorials interpreting local events and commenting upon them in an
intelligent and honest fashion occupy but a small portion of each
Thursday's newsprint across the nation.

Why should this surprise anyone? The situation is no better with
the dailies. Newspapers are newspapers, and their responsibility is to
print the news and raise hell. Most of them, weekly and daily, are not
performing this function very well.

S. GEORGE LITTLE

7   The Responsibility of a Newspaper Syndicate

■

There is much in print in the current critical literature on contemporary journalism that deals severely with the influence of the Newspaper Syndicate on the quality of the Press. This body of opinion contends that today's newspaper editor relies too much on "canned" features and consequently depends less on his own taste, initiative and personal sense of social ethics and responsibility. A secondary criticism of the Newspaper Syndicate suggests that a newspaper too heavily loaded with syndicated material sacrifices information and depth to mere entertainment.

A spirited defense of the special role and responsibilities of the Newspaper Syndicate and its positive contributions to modern newspapers is given in the following essay, written especially for this volume by S. George Little, President of the General Features Corporation. With vigor, conviction and impressive sincerity he outlines the unique criteria of standards the ethical newspaper syndicate should adhere to, and suggests the vital role an imaginative and dedicated Syndicate can assume in the growth and scope of today's newspaper.

LIKE THE JET PLANE, space satellites, electronic typesetters, television, and motion pictures, newspaper syndicates are children of the twentieth century——an age when improvements and new developments in all media of communications have advanced at a tremendous rate. Although the first press service in America was established in 1848 by a group of six papers in New York——primarily to handle shipping news——it was not until after the turn of the century that newspaper syndicates began to come into their own and become an important part of the world-wide communications network.

Newspaper syndicates have multiplied and flourished to the extent that today there are more than 275 organizations in the business of distributing features to newspapers all over the world. There are almost fifty categories of features, ranging from political commentary, to the care of children, to crossword puzzles; and, while most of the syndicates have only a few features, fully eighty percent of syndicated material found in newspapers throughout the world is serviced by no more than the top dozen or so leading syndicates. Obviously it is imperative that these largest newspaper syndicates realize their tremendous responsibilities to the public; it is no less imperative that the smaller syndicates be fully aware of their responsibility too.

To the typical newspaper reader, there is one criterion alone by which he judges the content of his newspaper: *Is it worth reading?* The goal of every editor and writer deserving of his position as a member of the Fourth Estate is to provide a positive answer to that question. He does it by offering readers features that are informative and entertaining. But, more significantly, a feature must also be *important* and *interesting* before a reader will be completely satisfied that it is *worth reading.*

Here, in a nutshell, is the key to what I feel is the function of a responsible newspaper syndicate: to offer readers information and entertainment that are worth reading, that are important and interesting, and *that are available only through the medium of his local newspaper.*

Generally speaking, the obligations of a newspaper syndicate embrace four areas of responsibility: (1) to the newspaper-reading public; (2) to the newspapers themselves; (3) to the authors and artists who produce the features (and who are, of course, an inherent part of any syndicate); and (4) to itself (its officers and other employees who are directly involved in the business of feature syndication).

Before it can possibly serve the best interests of the reading public, a syndicate must first examine its own linen. It must be dead certain that its material is the best available and is without the blemish of vicious ideas, impropriety, or unprincipled and irresponsible opinion that may, however well disguised, be disseminated among an unsuspecting public.

To accomplish even this much sounds like an impossible job. But is it? Difficult, yes; but not impossible.

First of all, in its development of features, a syndicate is limited only by its own values and rules——its own integrity. Ideally, it should not be the dupe of any political or religious group, but should strive to produce features that reflect the highest ideals of whatever point of view is expressed. (In this respect, large syndicates are better able to research and present opposing ideas more freely and accurately because of their access to unlimited information in every field.)

As the syndicate involves itself with these problems of what has been called "The Narrow Range of Opinion," the question of censorship naturally arises. To what extent should a syndicate censor its material?

I think it is self-evident that if a syndicate selects features produced only by highly *responsible* writers and artists, the problem of censorship partially resolves itself. The responsible columnist will not indulge in wanton vilification or scurrilous diatribe; the responsible artist will avoid jokes that are in bad taste and will keep the cleavage of his voluptuous comicstrip heroine within acceptable bounds.

There should be a distinction made between features that are meant to entertain and those that are meant to inform. For example, the so-called "sob sister" columns which are a polyglot of the pseudoscientific and of synthetic humor patently based on real human problems should not be condoned by the ethical syndicate. Not only can such "advice" seriously confuse many readers with similar problems, but, wrapped in its veneer of indelicate quips, can also do irreparable harm.

This is not to say that entertainment and information cannot be combined successfully and in a responsible manner. It can, and it is. But humorous entertainment is best confined to comic strips and panels and those columns that are obviously humorous in intent. Advice or information, especially in the areas of mental and physical health, should be factual and carefully distinguished from any humor that might be imparted within a given column.

No less important than producing the best features possible for a newspaper-reading public is the syndicate's special obligation to the newspapers themselves.

According to the late Dean of U.S. Journalism Historians, Frank Luther Mott, there are eight concepts of news which invite the attention of readers. They are 1) news as timely report; 2) news as record; 3) news as objective fact; 4) news as interpretation; 5) news as pictures; 6) news as sensation; 7) news as human interest; and 8) news as prediction. The role of the syndicate is to satisfy each and every one of these aspects in order to complement and strengthen a newspaper's own locally produced news.

Since few newspapers can alone afford the services of the top authorities in every field of interest, it is up to the syndicate to marshal just as much of the best available talent as possible through their syndication process. In this regard, it is a syndicate's *obligation* to pioneer and create for the benefit and improvement of newspapers——not imitating what has gone before, but originating new and dynamic features to help build greater newspaper readership and responsible standards.

It is important to note at this point that a newspaper syndicate's efforts toward producing unique and significant features are necessarily limited and largely shaped by the demands of newspaper editors and, as a matter of course, their readers. The most successful syndicates realize that newspapers are controlled by subscribers, that advertising is there because of readership and circulation, and that subscribers often buy a second newspaper solely for certain features that they regularly read. The editors of the most successful newspapers realize this, too, and choose carefully in their selection of features. Many rely heavily upon readership surveys, others upon their own knowledge of and feeling for their readers' interest in their particular circulation areas.

Thus, a syndicate's "pioneering" efforts are tempered by newspapers and succeed in direct proportion to prevailing demand. Yet the responsible syndicate resists fashioning its features to the dictates of questionable opinion and goes ahead with news programs, all the while seeking to provide the best in entertainment and factual reporting. Also, these syndicates should be aware that good features make big names instead of big names making good features!

Worth mentioning here is the fact that the ethical organization does not pirate away the talent of a competing syndicate without due regard for all existing obligations. To do so often results in a kind of professional suicide to the reputations and future success of both syndicate and its acquisition. It may be true that the practice of "pirating features" is sometimes the fault of the columnists or artists as well as of the unscrupulous syndicate, but a responsible syndicate should no more go seeking a competitor's talent without leave than a man go in search of a new mate in his neighbor's backyard. Business ethics and morals are fundamental to the activity of responsible newspaper editors.

The rules which govern the activities of the responsible newspaper syndicate ultimately involve, then, a system of values and an integrity not unlike those rules which determine a man's personal conduct. The main distinction is that, because of its greater potential influence in shaping the lives of men and affairs, the syndicate has a responsibility different more in degree than in kind. To preserve its integrity, a syndicate must not be dominated by any one group and must work independently of, but in harmony with all segments of the people and the press. It should, and does, function to complement the work of every newspaper, from the smallest to the largest metropolitan daily.

Significantly, the extent to which its function is performed is a measure of the virtue of any agency. The ethical, responsible newspaper syndicate should therefore do everything possible to live up to those basic obligations mentioned above.

Insofar as a newspaper syndicate has done this much, it has performed its function; insofar as it has fulfilled its peripheral obligations to the public, to newspapers and to itself, it has done its duty.

RUSSELL KIRK

8 The Freedom, Responsibility and Power of the Student Press

■

In this era of increased student activity across the nation's college campuses, the undergraduate newspaper and periodical serves an ever more vital and more vocal role.

To whom is the student editor responsible? What are his freedoms and his responsibilities? Should his journal reflect the affairs only of the faculty and the academic life, or should it comment on the undergraduate's involvement with the larger world outside the campus?

The distinguished conservative fictionist, philosopher and polemicist Russell Kirk hurls some prickly challenges and poses some disturbing questions in his spirited critique of the excesses of today's student editor——or what he calls excesses. His more liberal opponents may rage at some of his traditional concepts, but even they will find it hard to dismiss completely the hard-core criteria of reason and taste that underlie his traditionalist's stance.

I HOLD that the student newspaper or magazine ought to enjoy a higher degree of freedom than does the public, commercial publication; that is, the editors and contributors should be secure in a greater latitude of judgment and expression than are the editors and contributors to most periodicals. For the student press should share in the privileges and immunities of academic freedom.

Academic freedom, as I have written at considerable length in one book and several articles, is a body of rights peculiar to institutions of learning, and necessary to the functioning of those institutions. The Academy exists for the conservation and the expansion of the realm of Truth. In the Academy, things may be said and written which it might be imprudent to say or write in the Marketplace. Often the opinions of the Academy will be unpopular; but often, nevertheless, they will be right.

For the sake of Truth, and for the welfare of society, the Academy is endowed with this freedom. But the Academy also, and correspondingly, is charged with high responsibilities. It is a principle of classical jurisprudence that every right is married to a duty. If a man enjoys privileges, justly he must assume certain balancing burdens. The Academy has to pay for its freedom. Scholars enjoy the right to teach and to seek the Truth, with few limitations. In return for this right, they assume the duty of being truthful in their utterances and their lives. They are guardians of civilization. They must vindicate their privileges by obedience to the norms of candor and taste and good order.

Now although academic freedom is primarily designed for the teachers and senior scholars in a university or college, it also extends in considerable degree to students. This was so in the medieval universities, and ought to be so still. Therefore it extends to the student press. The ordered liberty of the student press ought to be especially respected, indeed, because the press often claims to be the representative voice of the student body, and because it is a training-ground for responsible writing and publishing in the world beyond the Academy. Excesses of zeal, imprudence of judgment, and even intemperance of language ought often to be tolerated in the student press when similar offenses would not be tolerated in the ordinary press: for often it is better that the indiscretions of youthful judgment be endured than that the faculty of forming resolute opinions should be discouraged.

Let me suggest here, then, some of the more important rights and duties which pertain to the student press. Though I name the rights first, I emphasize that the duties are equally important.

First, the student press has the right to comment candidly and fairly upon the status of the students at the university or college in question, and upon educational problems and standards there.

Second, the student press has the right to discuss intelligently, so far as it is able, affairs beyond the bounds of the Academy.

Third, the student press has the right to publish the opinions and the original writing of such students as do work that deserves publication; and to print, so far as space allows, deserving writing from contributors outside the student body.

These are not the only rights of the student press; and these are not absolute liberties, but are subject to prudential considerations, as are all real rights; but this brief catalog may serve to suggest the nature of the privileges of the student press.

Now for the duties of the student press. If I name more duties than I name rights, it is not because I mean to burden student editors with obligations, but rather that student editors, like nearly everyone else nowadays, tend to talk much more about their rights than about their duties.

First, the student-press has the duty of accuracy. The Academy being dedicated to Truth, and academic freedom being dependent upon respect for Truth, the student publications ought to be even more reliable than the general press.

Second, the student press has the duty of decency. Because it enjoys liberty, it ought not to indulge in license. The temptation to shock and scandalize ought to be resisted; the college paper ought not to imitate the gutter press. Ethical understanding is at least one of the principal ends of the higher learning, and college and university publications ought not to give the lie to the idea of a university.

Third, the student press has the duty of loyalty toward its sponsor or proprietor, the university or college. At most institutions, the college subsidizes student publications in some degree, and assures them continuity and protection. Commonly the college would be liable in suits at law for libel. The college makes possible the existence of such publications, in most cases. Therefore the student press ought to refrain from actions which would seriously discredit the parent institution, and possibly cause serious damage.

Fourth, the student press has the duty of respect for persons. It ought not to revile or ridicule college officers or faculty. While temperate and even severe criticism of the institution's policies and staff ought to be possible, this criticism should not degenerate into abuse, and it ought not to infringe upon the equally important academic freedom of professors. The student editor needs to bear in mind that the Academy is a physical and intellectual community and to exercise charity for the sake of the common interest.

This is no exhaustive list of the duties of the student press; but it may serve to suggest the nature of such obligations.

So much for first principles. Indulge me now in a few anecdotes which may illustrate the distinction between liberty and license in the student press. There always will be some tension between the student press and its sponsors. I hold that the student press ought to be indulged, so far as possible, in errors of judgment and tone, for the sake of encouraging exercise of editorial abilities. But there are times when the student press, abusing its privileges, must be checked.

About twenty-five years ago, when I was an instructor at Michigan State College, the *State News* published an editorial denouncing in no uncertain terms an event during the summer session of the college: the "Wolverine Boys' State," a convocation sponsored by the American Legion which utilized some of the facilities of the college. This "Boys' State" brought together boys from many towns in Michigan, their expenses paid by posts of the American Legion, to hold a kind of juvenile legislature, in which they would become acquainted with Michigan government and parliamentary procedures. To establish some order in their domestic arrangements, the Legionaires in charge had the boys organize a quasi-military group, with marching to sessions of the Boys' State, saluting of the flag, and the like.

When this convocation came to an end, the student editor published a long unsigned editorial describing the affair as "Fascist," militaristic, and undemocratic. He did not spare the vitriol. The editorial was abusive, inaccurate, and unjust. At that time a Communist cell existed at Michigan State College——a "Marxist Discussion Group"——and it is possible, as some persons then alleged, that the student editor was prompted by members of this cell.

This editorial awoke no violent protest. The American Legion in Michigan, as a body, did not remonstrate. One Legionaire, living in the upper peninsula, did write a letter of complaint to the *State News,* sending a copy, I think, to the president of Michigan State College, Dr. Hannah. The college's administration acted abruptly upon this complaint. The college suspended the student newspaper for the

summer, dismissed the student editor, and appointed a faculty advisor, with much greater powers than any faculty advisor had possessed before, to act as censor. I believe that the member of the
American Legion who had complained was surprised and rather
rueful at the harshness of this action.

At the time, as now, I thought the offending editorial a bad one,
and the student editor misguided. But the editor had shown some
courage, originality, and vigor. He had done a serious thing: exposing
the college to the risk of political retaliation, and possibly of a libel
suit because of that epithet "Fascist." Yet I thought the college
administrators intolerant and imprudent in taking action so harsh and
hasty——and also timorous, dreading as they did a single letter of
criticism. One editorial mistake, even a serious blunder, any college
administration ought to be prepared to forgive——and even to
countenance, if need be. Such suppression is no satisfactory model
for freedom of the press——responsible freedom——in the world
beyond the Academy. An editor ought not to be treated as a mere
office-boy. I said as much in a formal latter of remonstrance which
was printed in the Lansing *State Journal*, and which did not endear
me to those in the seats of the mighty at MSC.

Here the educational institution was more at fault than was the
student press, I think. Let me speak briefly of a different sort of case,
however: one which involves the University of Chicago and occurred
this year.

Mr. John Ciardi, in one of his fits of splenetics in the pages of the
Saturday Review (June 27, 1959), exploded into rage against Dr.
Lawrence Kimpton, Chancellor of the University of Chicago. Mr.
Ciardi is a man of the Left. He is also a good poet, and has said
sensible things on various subjects; his politics, I think, are confused
and at variance with his inner nature. His attack on Chancellor
Kimpton, under the title "The Book Burners and Sweet Sixteen," is
an interesting example of what is called "disintegrated" or "ritual-
istic" liberalism, uniting perhaps with a Marxist detestation of things
established and of "bourgeois morality."

Dr. Kimpton's offense is that he suspended publication of the
Chicago Review, a quarterly edited by students and published by the
University of Chicago Press, on the ground that one issue, like some
others before it, contained much obscenity. Mr. Ciardi endeavors to

prove that this issue was not obscene, by arguing that certain courts in this land might possibly let it slip by, supposing the *Chicago Review* were brought before them in a prosecution for obscenity, with a verdict, substantially, of "not proved." Since certain American courts seem unwilling to admit that *anything* is pornographic, this argument of Mr. Ciardi's does not convince me.

Chancellor Kimpton's administration of the University of Chicago has been prudent and conciliatory. Unlike his predecessor in office, Dr. Kimpton has leant over backward to avoid interference with faculty and students. Dr. Kimpton certainly is no enemy to freedom of expression. Take this passage, for instance, from his convocation address in June, 1957:

The first intangible that one always feels around a great university is a sense of freedom. It is not a postured, self-conscious thing, and one rarely hears the word on a great campus. Those who shout freedom loudest are generally those who are concerned to express their own unorthodoxy and deny the privilege to others. The freedom of a great university is as natural as the air, and no amount of shouting will produce it. The scientist and the scholar pursue their research in whatever direction it leads them, with no other motive than the discovery of truth itself. But it is also a disciplined freedom, except that the discipline is imposed by the facts and by the character of the scholar. . . . Personnel officers are so careful to obtain the good organization man, the kind who fits in happily with the routines of the office, that the new and significant can hardly happen. I do not mean that we have to cherish the deviant, the odd-ball, simply because he is this way, but I come very close to recommending this.

This, I think, is a sound general policy for a university; and Dr. Kimpton has not violated it. He reluctantly suspended the *Chicago Review* only after months of protest against its character from friends of the university, and indeed from students. The *Chicago Review* commenced publication several years ago as a vigorous and promising magazine of ideas, brought out by the undergraduates. But more recently the University Press assumed the responsibility of publication; and about the same time, editorial control passed into the hands, for the most part, of an undergraduate *avant-garde* clique ———the sort of young persons who try to be emancipated but succeed only in being unbuttoned. In the number which Dr. Kimpton had to censure, several of the more nihilistic beatnik writers, of national notoriety, fulfilled Ambrose Bierce's definition of Realism, in his *Devil's Dictionary:* "Realism, *n.* The art of depicting nature as it is seen by toads."

Some of the attitudes of these writers have been sufficiently analyzed by Mr. Edmund Fuller in his *Man in Modern Fiction.* Four-letter words sprinkled the pages of this number of the *Chicago Review,* as of some earlier numbers. It was as if the contributors had reasoned, "D. H. Lawrence was a great writer. He sometimes used four-letter words. I will always use four-letter words; therefore I will be a greater writer than was D. H. Lawrence." The trouble with this syllogism is that Lawrence was a great writer despite, not because of, his Anglo-Saxon improprieties.

In the earlier years of the *Chicago Review,* most Chicago students were proud of the quarterly published in their name. Recently, intelligent Chicago students——some of them graduate students with considerable experience of the world, not easily scandalized——have spoken with dislike and contempt of the quasi-salacious latter-day *Chicago Review.*

Now the point really pertinent is whether a great university is compelled to publish and subsidize——and lend its name to——any superficial clique of undergraduates which has contrived to gain control of a student publication. Whether or not the contents of the *Chicago Review* might escape Post Office censorship or prosecution for obscenity is almost irrelevant. The girlie magazines generally manage to evade the laws against pornographic publication; but this does not mean that the University of Chicago Press has a moral obligation to publish a student-edited *Playboy* or *Escapade.* A university presumably has standards of truth and taste superior to those of unscrupulous commercial publishers. That the student editors of the *Chicago Review* took themselves seriously; that they presumably did not mean to encourage seduction, rape, and onanism, nor yet narcotic addiction——these considerations do not alter the fact that their magazine was indecent according to any received principles of morality and taste.

Undergraduates possess no inalienable right to injure a university's reputation and to outrage a university's friends, alumni, and students, at a university's expense. Most of the former editors of the *Chicago Review* are now bringing out their own magazine, *Big Table,* which is expected to find itself in trouble with the Post Office Department. They have a right to write and publish what they like, so long as it is within the law, and so long as it is at the expense of their own pockets and reputations, not charged against a university that is expected to bear the blame but to have no hand in policy.

Mr. Ciardi, Pharisee-like, concludes his denunciation of Chancellor Kimpton thus: "There can be no compromise with the book burners. There is only the duty to hold them in disgust, and the hope that they can be made to understand the scorn of freer and better men." As a genuine gentleman never calls himself a gentleman——if I may be allowed an aside——so a freer and better man never calls himself a freer and better man. I do not think that Dr. Kimpton has acted unjustly or imprudently. The liberty of the student press does not include the license to foul one's own nest.

The rights of the student press, I am saying, ought to be broad; and the responsibilities of student editors ought to be serious. I am advocating the self-discipline which Dr. Kimpton commends among professors. The less control there is within, Burke observes, the more control there must be without. The real freedom of the student press is directly proportional to the decency and discretion, quite compatible with editorial vigor and independence, by which editors ought to govern themselves.

In conclusion, permit me to say a few words about the power of the student press. It can be considerable: not in the sense of influencing national elections or reproving the conduct of American foreign policy; but in the sense of developing real literary and editorial talents among the rising generation, and of forming students' opinion on the questions which most nearly concern them.

Some few student papers are so well financed and staffed, and connected with such large universities, that they can aspire to a format, a range, and a role very like that of successful commercial newspapers. Yet even these few——and certainly the great majority of student publications——ought to be concerned primarily not with covering the news round the globe, or with sermonizing on political and moral questions which puzzle the most accomplished statesmen and philosophers. The first concern of student publications, I hold ——and the realm in which they can exercise the greatest influence for good——is the range of subjects and problems directly affecting the Academy. The improvement of academic standards; the struggle against apathy among students; the stimulating of students' discussion of philosophical, literary, scientific, and political questions; the encouragement of logical argument, lucid exposition, and spirited critical and creative writing——in such matters the student press can be superior to the popular press, and make itself worthy of the privileges of academic freedom. Mere clumsy imitation, with insufficient knowledge or experience, of commercial newspapers and magazines is unworthy of a college or university publication. Sometimes I hear it argued that a college paper ought to model itself on popular papers, and attempt coverage of scandal, politics, and professional sports, because the undergraduates can't be bothered to read an ordinary daily paper. Well, the Academy, after all, is a sanctuary; and there are advantages in being insulated, for a few years, from obsession with the giddy whirl of modern life. Modern man has been a good deal harmed by what D. H. Lawrence called "chewing the newspapers." If the student is to chew any newspaper, it ought to be a publication taking an intelligent interest in the life of the mind. A good student newspaper or magazine can do much to elevate, in the long run, what Arthur Machen called "that damnable vile business, journalism."

9   The Editor I Wish I Were

■

Perhaps there never was——or ever will be——an editor with the Faustian characteristics and qualifications Mr. Dilliard demands. But his Commandments to Greatness may still serve as a rich source of inspiration for every editor with the integrity and vision to aspire to perfection. Whether a journalism undergraduate or an editor-in-chief of a great newspaper, Mr. Dilliard's criteria are of inestimable value as a guide to maintaining a continued sense of responsibility and dedication to the editor's calling.

The Editor I Wish I Were was the eighth annual William Allen White Memorial Lecture, which Mr. Dilliard delivered on February 11, 1957. Mr. Dilliard's remarks, which he made while holding the post of Editorial Page Editor of the St. Louis Post-Dispatch, *appear here in an abridged format.*

THE EDITOR I wish I were knows his nation. He knows the cities and the countryside, the wonders and the beauties in all forty-eight states and territories. He visits the national parks on vacation trips. He has stood atop Gay Head on Martha's Vineyard and looked west to the setting sun and he has watched it rise in the east from the height above Avalon on Santa Catalina Island. He knows the greatness, the diversity and the capacity of his nation from having seen it with his own eyes and walked about it on his own feet. When predatory interests seek to invade the national domain, as at Dinosaur National

Monument, he rises up in righteous indignation against those who would trespass on ground that he himself owns.

The editor I wish I were has been around the world. He travels in distant as well as neighboring countries. He knows that he must write about faraway places and he must print news concerning them. And he knows that peoples overseas will seem less strange and their decisions and reactions to us less peculiar if he has met them in their home lands. He knows that travel helps him to understand and that understanding is fundamental to his work as an editor.

Let me say here to the students in the room that I hope none of you will look regretfully to the time you may be required to spend in military service as your contribution to the national defense. Your years with the Army or the Navy or some other branch of the service may turn out to be a broadening and educational experience that you otherwise would be denied. Many an American is a better informed citizen of the world because of military service overseas. My editor, to adapt a phrase of John Wesley, knows that "the world is his beat."

The editor I am describing reads his own paper thoroughly. That goes without saying. But he also reads other papers. He may not read all these at the same time but he rotates from a list that includes, among others, *The Washington Post, The New York Times, The New York Herald Tribune, The Christian Science Monitor* and *The Wall Street Journal.* His list also includes the *Baltimore Sun,* the *Providence Journal-Bulletin,* the *Milwaukee Journal,* the *Louisville Courier-Journal and Times,* the *Chicago Tribune,* the *Kansas City Star and Times,* the *Des Moines Register and Tribune* and the *Atlanta Constitution.* From time to time he reads papers from Denver and Detroit, Minneapolis and Sacramento, from Richmond and Raleigh and Nashville, from Little Rock and Watertown and Beaumont. He knows that editors such as William T. Evjue of the *Madison Capital Times,* the Gitts of the *York Gazette and Daily,* William B. Johnstone of *Lewiston Morning Tribune* and Charles A. Sprague of the Salem *Oregon Statesman* regularly are far ahead of many large city editors in the exercise of editorial leadership.

My editor receives from England the weekly air mail edition of the *Manchester Guardian,* for he knows that in the dispatches from Alistair Cooke in New York and Max Freedman in Washington he will read some of the keenest and most perceptive reporting to be found anywhere about life and events in the United States. He keeps in touch with the great traditions of Charles Prestwich Scott, for a half century guiding genius of the *Guardian* who once summarized his journalistic philosophy in a half dozen words: "Opinion is free; facts are sacred."

To be as fair as possible my editor reads differing views on the major issues of the day. He sees what Marquis W. Childs has to say and also David Lawrence. And he appreciates the opportunity he has in following the informed, constructive editorial columns of Walter Lippmann, developed as they are against a 40 years' view of world affairs.

The editor I am describing reads books because he knows, as William Allen White knew, that books are news, because they present ideas that newspaper readers soon will be acting on, because they explain the past and light the way of the future. He is familiar with the monumental publishing projects of his time in biography, in history, in the social sciences, regional life, in the messages and papers of the great Americans——Franklin, Adams, Jefferson, Lincoln. He knows there is value for him as an editor in a novel such as John P. Marquand's *Point of No Return;* a biography such as Catherine Drinker Bowen's *Yankee From Olympus;* in poetry such as Stephen Vincent Benet's *John Brown's Body.* He knows the editorial worth in history such as Roger Butterfield's *The American Past;* in drama such as the Koestler-Kingsley *Darkness at Noon;* and a study of a current problem such as Corliss Lamont's *Freedom Is as Freedom Does.*

My editor reads magazines. And not just *Life, The Saturday Evening Post, U.S. News & World Report, Business Week, Holiday, The New Yorker,* the weekly news magazines and *Fortune.* He keeps close track of *Harpers* and *The Atlantic,* the *Saturday Review, The New Republic* and *The Nation.* He is aware of the admirable studies of important issues that appear in *The Reporter,* and *Freedom & Union.* He recognizes among achievements of *The Progressive* its public revelation of a certain Senator in his real colors. He finds a case for the conservative side in politics in the new *National Review.* In *Frontier* he sees a mirror of the burgeoning life of the Pacific Coast and in *American Heritage,* for the first time, a publication that worthily reflects the greatness and wonder of the American story. He knows that a religious weekly such as *The Christian Century* can have the rare editorial talents of the late Paul Hutchinson. He knows that insights and points of view that he otherwise would not share are provided by *The Commonweal* and *America,* by *Together, The Churchman* and *The Christian Register.* He is familiar with the contribution to our culture of the quarterlies——*The American Scholar, Foreign Affairs, The Yale Review* and *The Virginia Quarterly Review*——and of the "little magazines," published often by university groups.

My editor turns to the publications of the scholarly professions, such as the *American Historical Review,* the *American Political Science Review, Social Research* and the journals and reviews of the law schools. He keeps his eye on the *Bulletin of the Atomic Scientists* and *Scientific American.* He does so in the knowledge that historians, economists, political scientists, sociologists and teachers of law, along with physical scientists are among his most significant news sources. For information about his own profession he reads not only *Editor & Publisher* and *The Quill,* but *Nieman Reports, Public Opinion* and *Journalism Quarterly.* Yes, he reads many magazines, and because he does he knows the history of *Collier's* back to Norman Hapgood and the editorials of Louis D. Brandeis in the crusades of a half century ago. And knowing that, he knows what is lost when, for whatever reason, a *Collier's* prints its last issue and disappears.

The editor I am talking about may have scoffed at television. For some years he may have resisted having a set in his home. He does so no longer. He deplores what is cheap and trivial and bad on the air waves. He knows there is a lot that is good and he encourages it.

A few minutes ago I said that the editor I have in mind reads newspapers. I did not make an exception of the comic pages for he reads them, too. Not every comic panel and every adventure strip but his favorites and enough of the others to know in general what is going on in the world of Dick Tracy, Li'l Abner, Moon Mullins, Buz Sawyer, David Crane and Juliet Jones. And why does he read the comics? Because in Lichty's "Grin and Bear It" is some of the richest of contemporary humor. Because the Bumsteads and the Wallets picture the American family in a way that no other presentation can do. Because mothers and fathers keep in touch with the military life of their sons in part through Beetle Bailey, Sarge, Cookie, Zero and Killer. Because "Steve Canyon," a flawlessly drawn adventure story, backs an adequate, well-supported defense as staunchly as any member of Congress. Because the little people in Schulz's "Peanuts" ——Lucy who builds up a snowman and kicks it to pieces, then builds it up again and kicks it down again, "torn between the desire to create and the desire to destroy," her brother Linus finding security in life in a towel, Schroeder devoted to Beethoven and his piano, the hapless Charlie Brown and all their colleagues, including the dog Snoopy——go far in explaining thought and action in mid-century America.

My editor knows that as Clare Brigg's "Days of Real Sport" was a later version of Tom Sawyer and Huck Finn and Kin Hubbard's "Abe Martin" successor to Josh Billings so is Walt Kelly's "Pogo" our generation's "Br'er Rabbit" and "Popeye" its combination of Paul Bunyan and Mike Fink. Although he has read about World War II in the memoirs of the generals and in the big, thick green volumes published officially in Washington, he knows that an indispensable part of the history of the war was written "Up Front" by Bill Mauldin's bearded infantrymen, Willie and Joe. Yes, my editor has a few moments for what——for want of a better name——is still called the comic page.

Now I want to note another group of characteristics of the editor I am endeavoring to describe. He makes it a rule to be courteous. The reader who telephones him or writes a letter does not know that the editor receives countless demands on his time and that if the editor yielded to even a small part of the requests and invitations he could not do his work. My editor looks on each contact with the public as an opportunity to create good will for his newspaper. He always remembers that his newspaper owes its continued existence to its readers. He does not bow to them but he treats them as the individual human beings they are.

My editor is co-operative. He joins with his associates to produce the best newspaper possible. He knows that this process has no place for wasteful jealousies and personalities. He makes his decisions on the merits of the issues regardless of their origin or support. He solicits and welcomes the suggestions of those who work with him.

He does his part in creating on his newspaper an atmosphere of free and friendly interchange.

A strong characteristic of my editor is his curiosity. He wants to know the "why" of things and in a world that is full of new developments he is always asking about the "how." In his community, he may not learn everything first but he knows more new things than anyone else. In the words of that great Washington correspondent son of K.U., Raymond Clapper: He never overestimates the information of his readers and never underestimates their intelligence.

My editor has imagination. While he takes genuine satisfaction in believing that the press of the United States is the best press in the world, he is continuously aware that our press not only ought to be but could be infinitely better than it is. As he is able to see the need for improvements, so is he able to see the opportunities close at hand through which he can make his own contributions toward improving the press in appearance, in content, in service, in leadership.

The editor I am describing is a man of conscience. He recoils from the dishonest and he abhors the untrue. He believes, as did William Allen White, who said: "The only excuse an editor has for being is that his paper shall print the news. The question that comes to every man running a newspaper is: What is news? That he must settle for himself, and having found a rule, must stick as closely to it as possible. When an editor begins monkeying with his conscience, stretching his rule to shield his friends or to punish his enemies he is lost."

The editor who has the imagination to see what he ought to do and the conscience to know how to do it falls short unless he has the courage to be the editor he knows he should be. So my editor has courage that stands up to the test. Sometimes he needs courage in dealing with large numbers of people or strong group interests. Sometimes he needs courage in private consultations with his superior editor or publisher in situations about which only the two of them will know and for which his superior in the end may be truly grateful. But whatever the situation he finds himself in, courage he has and nothing else will take its place.

My editor has judgment and this ability to judge the circumstances tells him when his criticism, to be convincing, should be moderate, when it should be carefully argumentative, when it should be strongly condemnatory. He does not roll the heavy artillery into action if a spatter of birdshot will suffice. Neither does he rely on a rabbit gun when the blast of a howitzer is required. He is forthright and for a model of forthrightness he recalls what William Allen White said in the *Gazette* in 1925 on the death of Frank A. Munsey, a newspaper publisher who had buried many newspapers and magazines. He wrote:

"Frank Munsey, the great publisher, is dead.

"Frank Munsey contributed to the journalism of his day the talent of a meat packer, the morals of a money changer and the manners of an undertaker. He and his kind have about succeeded in transforming a once-noble profession into an eight per cent security.

"May he rest in trust."

The editorial on Frank Munsey shocked so many people that William Allen White took the time to explain it to Nicholas Murray Butler, president of Columbia University. He wrote:

"Probably I was a little rough on Frank Munsey but the whole tendency of the times in newspaper consolidation and standardization, I think, works badly. I would rather have the press as it was in John Milton's time, or Benjamin Franklin's time, when a man with the proverbial shirt tail full of type could express himself, air his views and get it off his chest, rather than to have the mass production of newspapers owned by investment bankers and filled full of stupid syndicate matter and conventional opinions. It is a bad thing for the newspaper business and it is a bad thing for the people. And Munsey and his kind are getting halos for doing a bad thing. I have no quarrel with Munsey, personally, but I had to say what I said for the craft I loved."

The editor whose portrait I am attempting to draw has his convictions but he respects the opposite opinions of others. In 1940 the great question in the United States was: What if anything should this nation do about the war which Hitler had unloosed in Europe? William Allen White was chairman of an organization known as the Committee to Defend the United States by Aiding the Allies. One of the readers of the *Post-Dispatch* wrote to the editor at Emporia to express the view that this nation ought to avoid all involvement in the war situation. William Allen White wrote in answer as follows:

"There are, of course, two opinions held honestly by intelligent people in the United States. One is that to help the Allies keeps the war away from America by letting them fight the war in Europe rather than to wait until the Germans conquer Europe and turn their greedy eyes westward. The other opinion is your opinion and many fine, wise people hold it. There being two sides, perhaps the best thing each of us could do is to respect the honesty and integrity of each other's opinions and realize that there must be differences if there is progress in the world.

"All that you say I had considered before taking my position and felt that on the whole I was right, yet not without doubts as probably you have in holding yours."

I have brought the original of that letter and also gladly leave it for the historical center and collections over which Miss Jean McKnight so efficiently presides.

I am describing an editor who has informed himself on many things, one who knows that he can never know too much to do his work well. But let me make very clear that he also knows that he does not know it all and that he never will. He is continually aware of how much more he needs to learn every day from others to be accurate and fair in dealing with the ever more complex problems that arise in the news at all levels. He acts on the principle that guided the life of the late Justice Louis D. Brandeis, a principle that is particularly applicable to every newspaper man whatever the part he plays. It is this: "You opinion is no better than your information."

My editor takes his work seriously and he is aware of the in-escapable responsibility that is his when he uses the printed word—— and also when he does not use it. He also can step outside himself and see how he looks to others. When I was in high school I read that Edgar A. Guest, the writer of newspaper verse, would make a talk in St. Louis. Eager to hear any newspaper man, and certainly one from far off Detroit, I skipped an afternoon of classes. The truancy was no mistake. For I will never forget a story the poet told. A newsboy rushed up to a man who came out of a building in a large city. "Paper, paper, mister," said the newsboy. "No," replied the sour-looking, gruff man, as he brushed the boy aside. "I don't want a paper. I'm the man who makes them!" The newsboy saw in a flash what was wrong and so he called after the departing editor: "No wonder I can't sell any!"

Once I heard a colleague distinguish between two editors of the editorial page of the *Post-Dispatch*. He said that George S. Johns "loved justice" and that George Johns's successor, Clark McAdams, "hated injustice." The editor I am describing knows both emotions. He loves justice and he hates injustice.

My editor criticizes others every day. In turn he takes the criticism that is directed at him. He points out the failings and short-comings in others. When he is criticized he weighs with earnestness and humility the criticism for the truth that may be in it. And in fairness he frequently gives his critics their say in print. When he is wrong—— and even the ideal editor I am describing can make mistakes that call for correction——he prints an honest retraction to set the record straight.

I have spoken of some of this editor's characteristics. Independence is another. He is careful not to engage in activities that will embarrass or compromise his independent position. He is sparing in his friendships because he knows that friendships outside his newspaper may at any time force the hard choice between personal kindness to a friend and devotion to duty as an editor. He knows that an editor seldom loses his independence in a sudden collapse of his position. The editor loses his independence rather by small concessions which follow one after another until that precious asset is gone. And so my editor is vigilant against the seemingly harmless yieldings that may set dangerous precedents.

As my editor cherishes his own independence, he does not ask conformity in others. He recognizes the right of people to be themselves in what they think, in how they live, in their likes and dislikes.

One of the characteristics that most marks my editor I have not yet mentioned. This is his enthusiasm. He has zest for life. He communicates his enjoyment of his work to others. He finds too much to do ever to become cynical. And while his range of informational interests is wide, he makes of himself an authority recognized as such among his fellows on a subject worthy of his study and time. And he has learned the value of outside interests, whether some sport, hunting and fishing, gardening, collecting, making things with tools, engaging in music or art.

My editor's temple is his newspaper. He may be a member of a religious affiliation but he never allows church opinion to influence his judgment as an editor. He worships at the shrine of journalistic truth where no religious body holds a monopoly. He is a communicant with those who place the public good above all else.

There is one more characteristic of the editor I have been seeing in my mind's eye about which I must tell you before we bring this class hour to a close. I refer to his devotion to the improvement of the professional group to which he belongs. He has a long view of freedom of the press back to the stirring times of John Milton. He knows the stories of the colonial press heroes——Anthony Haswell, Matthew Lyon, John Peter Zenger. He measures himself against the sacrifice of Elijah Parish Lovejoy in defense of his printing press at the burning warehouse in Alton, Illinois. He remembers the price Don Mellett paid in Canton, Ohio.

And remembering what these brave men did for his free press heritage, my editor works year after year to protect it and to improve it——in the American Society of Newspaper Editors, in the American Press Institute, in the National Conference of Editorial Writers, in the American Newspaper Guild, through the professional foundations and other groups that may be open to him. He encourages better training for careers in journalism and he welcomes research in the colleges and universities that will help him make the press beneficial to our democracy.

He is always on guard against those who violate the people's right to know. He is as quick to speak up when news is arbitrarily withheld in Washington as when it is suppressed in Argentina. He condemns a dictatorial Peron who tramples a great newspaper underfoot and he protests when an Attorney General, in charge of the Department of Justice, makes it a rule not to hold press conferences.

My editor does not keep silent when his government tells him that he cannot send reporters to a country with which we are not at war, as the Eisenhower Administration has now told our press with respect to reporting the news from China. He speaks up at once in defense of his right to go after the news and to tell his readers what it is. And he can speak up on a country weekly as well as on a city daily for if the metropolitan editor's freedom is trespassed by government so is the freedom of the rural or small town editor violated. My editor applauds the stand of Gardner Cowles, publisher of *Look* magaine, in calling on the State Department for an open hearing on the move to revoke the passport of reporter Edmund Stevens who had the will to defy our Government's foolish ban on travel to China. My editor knows from the case of William Worthy of the Baltimore *Afro-American* that the United States can only harm itself in aping the restrictions that the Communists have imposed in the past.

Above all else my editor knows talk is cheap and that only performance counts. He expects to be appraised not for what he professes, but what he does. He knows that high-sounding resolutions and stirring speeches about the glories of a free press——yes, and lectures such as this one——are empty words unless they are practiced day by day, week to week, year after year in news columns and on editorial pages. My editor wakes up repeating the warning of the first Joseph Pulitzer: "Our Republic and its press will rise or fall together." He goes to bed at night asking himself what he has done this day to help his Republic and its press to rise.

That great American, Judge Learned Hand, once ventured a belief concerning a jurist about to pass on a question of constitutional law. He ought, said the wise Judge Hand, "to have at least a bowing acquaintance with Acton and Maitland, with Thucydides, Gibbon and Carlyle, with Homer, Dante, Shakespeare and Milton, with Machiavelli, Montaigne and Rabelais, with Plato, Bacon, Hume and Kant."

I am well aware that in describing "The Editor I Wish I Were" I have set standards higher than those which Judge Hand established for the bench. And this is as it should be, even though you will say that no one man is or could be the editor whose portrait I have been drawing this afternoon.

With that I will agree and then say:

Why should our standards not be as high as we can envision them?

Why should we not be like the pole vaulter who keeps raising the bar and going up to the new height and over and raising the bar again and going up still higher and higher and higher?

For freedom of the press——in William Allen White's America ——amid a world as threatened as ours——who among us can do less than try and try and then try again?

NORMAN E. ISAACS

10   Conscience and the Editor

■

Touching upon such controversial topics as The One-Party Press, the Newspaper Guild and the question of licensing newspapermen, Mr. Isaacs' comments pull no punches when it comes to facing up to the multi-faceted problem of running a responsible newspaper. An advocate of self-evaluation and criticism by and of the Press, he offers ten provocative criteria for judging just what makes a good newspaper. That a good newspaper is a public good may be best expressed in Mr. Isaacs' concluding words: ". . . democracy will rise or fall on the quality and integrity of its journalism."

Now Vice-President and Executive Editor of the Louisville (Ky.) Times, Mr. Isaacs delivered Conscience and the Editor as the sixth annual William Allen White Memorial Lecture. It appears here in a somewhat abridged format.

WE HEAR a great deal about the tremendous improvements in newspapering. And there have been great strides these last fifty years. There are new technical improvements being adopted constantly. We have improved in all of the ways in which the genius of science has opened the doors.

Our personnel has improved correspondingly on all levels of journalism. Our staff people today are better educated than those of a generation ago. For the most part, they are better behaved. And almost all of them come into our profession with high and shining ideals.

Fortunate, indeed, is the young college graduate who wins a place on a good newspaper. There he soon learns that these great technical advances are simply a modern tool to do the basic job better——that the essential quality of good newspapering remains the same as it was a generation ago: That a newspaper has a mission and a character and courage.

If we have produced a group of cynics it is those who have entered journalism only to find that the technical advances are little more than a handsome facade——that it covers up a shell: a functioning technological unit going through the mere motions.

We have heard entirely too much these past several years about newspaper economics; too much about the threat of radio and television competition, which is again purely an economic consideration; and entirely too little about our moral values, which are, after all, what newspapering is all about.

Certainly, the profit factor is a vital one. Without it, we can have no independent press. A newspaper's owner, therefore, is rightfully entitled to a *reasonable* return on his money.

Most of the journalistic troubles we have today can be traced to three groups of people within the profession:

1. Editors and publishers who have somehow lost the saving grace of humility, whose consciences have become elastic, who have permitted editorial judgments to slop over into the news columns, who use their newspapers to play favorites, who——to put it indelicately ——have too often permitted their minds to become something like concrete: all mixed up and permanently set;

2. Owners of newspapers who still seem to think that great profits are possible out of their newspapers if only certain economies can be practiced, mostly by cutting down on news space and squeezing news expenses; owners who are not newspapermen by calling, who neither understand nor accept the fact that it is immoral to inflict upon their communities newspapers which are biased, incomplete, inefficient and which keep the citizens uninformed about matters which the citizen has a right to have; and

3. Those employees of newspapers——news employees——who have become so fascinated with their Guild activities that they pay less attention to newspapering than to their union activities; and who have lost, in the process, their objectivity about life; and who have

confused newspapering with mass production of some sort or another to the extent that initiative and enterprise are all but stifled on those papers where they operate.

The economic facts of newspaper life are interesting in themselves. The trends of the last few years are such as to raise hopes that within another generation newspaper ownership may largely be concentrated in the hands of men of conscience who regard journalism as a professional calling.

For newspapering has ceased to be alluring for the financial speculator. To establish a newspaper today takes millions of dollars. Those already in newspapering can make a respectable and reasonable return. Men of good sense have long since become accustomed to the reality of the situation.

The mortality rate in newspapering has been high these past several years, which only underlines this point I am making about profits. And the indications are that if the country were to run into economic difficulties, more than a few newspapers will join the list of the departed.

In short, the trend to newspaper monopoly continues. Today, in more than 90 per cent of the cities of America, there is only one newspaper.

And this alone poses the moral question clearly for all newspaper executives. In all these instances, we have become virtually the sole fountain of information for our communities. Does not conscience demand that we give all that we have to protect these wells of information from taint and corruption?

It seems to me a duty far more vital and compelling than the preoccupation with technical progress which grips so many in our profession these days.

The new engraving process, the teletypesetter, the improvements in matrices, all these are well and good, but yet all of them have served only to place more emphasis on speed and standardization. More and more newspapers are squeezing themselves into the pattern in which the mechanical contrivances threaten to dominate the whole enterprise. We cannot and we must not tolerate a journalistic process which produces only a robot press.

We are standardized enough as it is and if we allow centralized editing, we will only be opening the door to still further——and justifiable——criticism of the American press.

Criticism of the press has been going on for years, as much from within as from outsiders. A good deal of this inside-the-craft criticism has been sound and intelligent.

Unfortunately, the reaction of a majority of editors and publishers has always been more heated and ill-informed than wise. Some of our colleagues deplore public criticism of the press by editors. This is the kind of nonsense that simply invites still more criticism. As Aldous Huxley has put it, facts do not cease to exist because they are ignored.

Let us, for a moment, consider one pertinent example of how the press behaves. Let us consider the performance of newspapers in the 1952 presidential campaign. I am not one of those who accepts the "one-party press" phrase. I consider it to be a gross overstatement and, therefore, a self-defeating one. There are enough ruggedly independent newspapers, and enough of them are powerful, to make the blanket labelling an absurdity.

The facts are clear enough. It is true that a very large proportion of the press has allied itself editorially with one of our two major parties. While I do not relish this preponderance of support for one party, it does not seem to me that the press' honor is thereby endangered. The real threat is in what I referred to earlier——the insidious contamination of news columns with editorial bias.

In the 1952 campaign, a majority of our newspapers, I believe, acted with fairness and equity and performed their news duties with honor. But there were sufficient newspapers which conducted themselves with vulgar and boorish displays of one-sidedness to make it clear that all was not well within journalism.

Some of these newspapers were guilty of the most outright form of campaigning in news space; some were guilty of news suppressions. It was obvious not only to us in the profession, but to readers who were deeply offended.

It seemed to many of us that some form of study was called for in order to ascertain with some accuracy how much of this type of distortion had occurred so that we could be at once better prepared to answer our critics, who would have the public believe that all were guilty, and in order that we ourselves could assess our collective and individual conduct.

Nevertheless, all of the proposals made were rejected by the newspaper profession. Some of the arguments made against such studies were on utterly specious reasoning. And some were presented on sincere and perfectly valid grounds.

To many of us, the best argument presented was on the admitted practical difficulties. And there were obviously many. Going back over burned ground is always hard. It is posing a great problem to re-assess a news-judgment situation a year or more old. The time and costs involved in this type of re-evaluation would be immeasurably greater than if a current study could have been made.

Since that campaign two and a half years ago, countless editorials have been written in defense of the press. Let a newspaper which supported the Eisenhower ticket make some criticism of the adminis-tration and you can almost bet on it that this will be cited as conclusive proof that those who have talked about a "one-party press" are thus revealed to be liars and charlatans. Perhaps some of them are, but this doesn't prove it.

Let's be honest with ourselves. We have another campaign coming up next year. I propose that right now we formulate plans for a nationwide, on-the-spot study of the press' performance in the 1956 presidential campaign.

How to do it? We have five major newspaper organizations——the *American Newspaper Publishers Association,* the *American Society of Newspaper Editors,* the *Associated Press Managing Editors Asso-ciation,* the *National Editorial Association* and *Sigma Delta Chi.*

Each of these organizations could make contributions, according to their means, to a committee which could be organized quickly to coordinate and direct such a study.

There need be no great debate about how to arrive at the makeup of such a committee. One way of doing it might be to choose a seven-man committee. This might be done by first taking the presidents of the four associations serving in the field of journalism education——the *Association for Education in Journalism,* the *Association of Ac-credited Schools and Departments of Journalism,* the *American Society of Journalism School Administrators* and the *American Council on Education for Journalism.* Add to this the directors of our two noted in-service training groups, the *American Press Institute* and the *Neiman Foundation.* And, if I were the one who had the choice, my selection for a seventh man, to serve as chairman of the group, would be Mr. Kent Cooper, the famed "KC" who served American newspapering for so many years as the guiding genius of The Associated Press.

I feel sure that the journalism schools and departments of the country, given proper directions by those skilled in communications research, could then do an intelligent and objective study of our total performance *as we do it* in 1956.

Let us have an end of abuse of each other on grounds of motive. Let us find out what the facts are in this situation.

Have we anything to gain from such a study? Everything!

If we are, as we claim to be, men of conscience who are issuing fair newspapers, then the facts will be so clear that we can adequately refute all the charges of bias that are made. More important, we will demonstrate to the nation that we who use our editorial columns and the power of our printing presses to criticize others are willing to be weighed on our total performance in the "goldfish bowl" which we adovcate for all others.

Let us not forget that we, too, have been on trial before the American public for a long time. Let us now start answering some of the $64 questions ourselves, instead of merely writing editorials about other men who decline to be questioned.

It is a curious thing, the twists that make men's names live. And of one thing you can be sure. It isn't the dollar that a man is ever remembered by——unless he has put the dollar to some humanitarian purpose.

Men's memories live because they have stood for something constructive, something courageous, some nobility of the spirit.

The other day, I had occasion to comment on something that had struck me as I was reading up on Mr. White's era in journalism. I mentioned something odd that I had run into connected with the name of Frank Munsey. Two of our brightest young reporters looked puzzled. I asked if they had ever heard of Munsey and they shook their heads.

I explained to them that Munsey was known as the destroyer of newspapers. In describing Munsey, I went to Oswald Garrison Villard who wrote that "the striking fact is that in his own narrative,

Munsey voiced no ideal or aim save . . . to publish something and to earn much money by doing so."

What had struck me as the curious thing was that in the journalism history books which I checked, more attention was focused on William Allen White's savagely bitter comment about Munsey than to the man's career.

And I got the odd feeling that Mr. White's editorial "Rest in Trust," is about all that will keep Mr. Munsey's name alive. What a tragic memory to leave behind!

It is equally tragic that we have in journalism today some men who worship the dollar more than they do principles.

Mr. White wrote that editorial because he was angry to the core about the elevation of the dollar sign above the spirit of journalism. Yet we can't forget that Mr. White himself was a sound and prudent businessman. Nevertheless, to him being an editor took precedence.

Making his newspaper pay its way was important, but he epitomized Thomas Carlyle's great phrase: "Everywhere in life the true question is not what we *gain,* but what we *do.*"

If this could only become one of our guiding principles!

It would bring the day of professional operation that much closer.

Many of us in newspapering have lifted our voices in behalf of such a professional attitude. Three years ago, here in his William Allen White Lecture, Mr. Edwin Canham of *The Christian Science Monitor,* spoke eloquently against the idea of licensing journalists.

I agree with him that any license, even if granted by other newspapermen, would be repressive and intolerable. Mr. Canham made the point that if the great press martyrs of the past had been forced to depend on licenses being issued by a majority of their colleagues, they would have been suppressed before they ever started.

At one time, Mr. White advocated licensing, but I am sure that had he been alive to hear Mr. Canham, he would have instantly agreed with his argument.

Licensing in itself means nothing. The Bar and Medicine, in many instances known to newspapermen, have shown themselves extraordinarily reluctant to revoke licenses even when the offenses against professional conduct have been flagrantly outrageous. Journalists could hardly be expected to operate at a higher and more rigorous standard of ethics.

The kind of professionalism we need is one of the spirit. More of our people must come to it——more and more and more——if we are ever to attain our proper stature as servants of the people.

And this goes not only for owners of newspapers and for editors, but for every staff member, too. It means not only the members of the American Newspaper Publishers Association, but the members also of the American Newspaper Guild.

A newspaper with a decent and intelligent management needs no Guild. Unfortunately, however, not all managements are decent. In these cases, where newspapers are run on backward and penurious lines, the staff's only recourse sometimes is the Guild.

And the Guild has to exist if for this reason alone. The Guild has a perfect right to try to organize newspapermen. It should continue to press for higher wage standards——and for better working conditions.

But it has long seemed to me that it could do these things without resort to the spiritual tyranny of the union shop, the shop stewards, and all the other union techniques which may be suited to making automobiles, but which serve only to destroy a part of newspaper originality.

It's time for the Guild to come of age, too.

All of us——publishers, editors, business managers, circulation directors, promotion managers, staff men of all types——have got to get back to the fundamentals of newspapering.

We've got to stop looking for a gimmick or an angle. They mean nothing. The fortunes poured into cheap promotions, into contests, into stunts of all varieties, have produced nothing but cheapness.

Recently, in *Editor & Publisher,* I read a report of a talk by an advertising executive to newspaper advertising representatives and I have not read such utter nonsense and claptrap in years.

This gentleman was deploring modern newspapering. He called it static and unchanging. It bores people, he said. He said that newspapers had become "dependent entirely on the news that somebody else makes."

And he recommended that we go out and "make" the news. On television and radio, he said, opinions are given freely. People are interested in opinions. They are controversial. And while he did not say so, I got the distinct impression that he was advocating an even greater freedom in news-writing latitude.

What he said was that newspapermen must "bite the dog" and bring back the "scoop" and the "extra" to win public interest.

This is the kind of advice we don't need. The "scoop" isn't quite as dead as the dodo-bird, but it's close. And so is the extra.

What the gentleman has forgotten is that radio revolutionized journalism. Radio is a medium of instantaneous transmission. Radio helped kill the extra. One doesn't want an extra with three paragraphs of bulletin material, already heard on every radio station in the nation. What the reader wants from his newspaper is the *complete* story. He doesn't want opinion. He wants interpretation. He has a right to his own opinions. And the public, I hardly think, wants us to go out and start making our own news. The day of Cardiff Giant is dead, too, I hope.

What we need are good newspapers. And this is the best newspaper promotion in the world. Just, plain *good* newspapers.

And what is a good newspaper?

First of all, it's an *honest* one. It prints the news without playing sides. It tells what happened as objectively as it knows how.

Second, it's an *adequate* newspaper. It is one that isn't trying to squeeze nickels on news space, while it spends dollars partying advertisers or running big promotion ads for contests. It is a newspaper that gives the reader a comprehensive picture of what is going on——as comprehensive as it can make it.

Third, it's a *just* newspaper. It's a newspaper that doesn't pretend that everything it prints is bound to be 100 per cent accurate. It's a newspaper that isn't afraid to confess that it made a mistake and one that does its best to rectify the error. It's a newspaper that gives equal prominence to the story of the man who has been cleared as it did to the story that he was accused.

Fourth, it's a *courageous* newspaper. Courage doesn't mean any constant flexing of editorial muscles. It means a newspaper that doesn't particularly go hunting fights, but which isn't afraid to get into one when it considers the fight important. It's a newspaper with some iron in its soul.

Fifth, it's a *clean* newspaper. And that doesn't mean being prudish. It means a newspaper that doesn't seek out cheap sex stories just to sell a few extra papers. It's a newspaper that has a sense of balance, a newspaper that doesn't have to apologize when it goes into the homes of its readers, a newspaper that tells what it has to tell with a sense of simple dignity.

Sixth, it's a *growing* newspaper. That doesn't mean growth in size particularly. It means growing in competence and in skill and in understanding. It's a newspaper that keeps on learning. It's a newspaper growing with its city.

Seventh, it's a *readable* newspaper. It is one that has a sense of knowing that a jumble of type makes it hard on the eyes. It's a newspaper that is trying to get away from the days of the old-fashioned disorder, the state of visual confusion. It is one that looks tidy and crisp. It takes pride in being neat.

Eighth, it's a new newspaper that *leads,* not follows. It takes the high road of public service. It doesn't act as the organ of the chamber of commerce or the merchants, or the labor unions, or the country club, or the politicians. It leads in its editorial expressions, in the interests of *all* the people.

Ninth, it's a newspaper with *manners.* It is a newspaper courteous to its readers. Its reporters act like gentlemen. Be it a child on the telephone or a tramp in the office, the newspaper gives both a hearing.

And, tenth, and most important, it's a newspaper with a *conscience.* It's a newspaper dedicated to the service of the reader, of the community, of the state and of the nation. It has principles, ethics and morals. It believes in itself and in its mission. It is conscience that makes a newspaper different from every other industrial organism in society. It is conscience that gives a newspaper its individual character. It is conscience that makes a newspaper perform above and beyond the call of duty.

Given these ten attributes——or any substantial portion of them ——and you have a good newspaper.

There are more than just a handful of such good newspapers in this land. And not all are big papers. William Allen White proved that they didn't have to be big to be good.

These good newspapers are respected ones. They produce reasonable profits for their owners. More important, they have made their owners distinguished and effective citizens.

Why aren't there more? Because newspapermen are human beings, like every other group in society. And human nature being what it is, newspapermen——like manufacturers, or doctors, or lawyers——are antagonistic to criticism.

We newspapermen seem to think we have a vested interest in the way newspapers are written, edited and printed.

We haven't. The only vested interest we have is in seeing to it that we try to do an honest job, that we try to report the truth, that our papers are fair and just. That's the vested interest: Our consciences.

What we need is what Mr. White called the "best American trait" some twenty-nine years ago. He was asked the question by *The New York Times*. He said the best American trait was "intelligent discontent."

That's what we need in this country and what we need in newspapers.

We need people in our newspapers who love newspapering with the same passion as did William Allen White.

We need people who seek no material riches. We need people who seek only the richness of usefulness to society. We need men and women who recognize the printed word to be the most powerful weapon in society and who seek to be its servants, not its masters, men and women willing to serve journalism as Schweitzer has served medicine. Men and women who realize instinctively that democracy will rise or fall on the quality and integrity of its journalism.

CLIFTON DANIEL

11 Responsibilities of the Reporter and the Editor

■

What is the practice of journalism? Is it a trade? A craft? A profession? Or is it something higher and nobler than any of these——a calling? Clifton Daniel boldly labels his work as a calling and, accordingly, delineates a lofty and inspiring set of rules to match the majesty of his chosen role in life. Committed to no party, ideology, pressure group or other vested interest, Mr. Daniel sees the responsibility of the editor and the reporter as being solely devoted to the public at large.

Mr. Daniel's comments were contained in an address he delivered on October 21, 1960, as part of the proceedings of the dedicatory ceremonies for Howell Hall as the new home for the school of journalism of the University of North Carolina at Chapel Hill. Mr. Daniel is the Managing Editor of the New York Times.

A LONG, LONG TIME AGO——maybe 35 years ago——I read one of those articles in a boys' magazine called "Choosing a Career."

It said that if you wanted to be a newspaperman, if you wanted to write, the best thing to do was to start writing. It didn't say anything about going to journalism school. It just said, "Send in something to the local paper."

So, I did.

As I remember, it was an account of a basketball game. It got printed. And I have been a newspaperman ever since.

It didn't occur to me then, and I have never since allowed it to cross my mind, that the only reason my piece was printed was because the editor had nothing else to fill the space.

Having one item published was enough to convince me that I was God's gift to journalism. I was pretty soon writing all the local news in the Zebulon *Record*. Mark Ethridge said that, as a high school boy 50 years ago, he got 50¢ a day——$3 a week, on his first newspaper job. In Zebulon, 20 years later, they paid me $5 a week. That's inflation for you! They paid me $5 a week in the summertime. I went to high school in the winter.

I had other duties as well, and the chief one was working in my father's drugstore. That was a lucky coincidence, because there was no better place in town to gather news.

The chief of police and the deputy sheriff used to hang around there all the time. We took calls for the doctors. Visiting politicians dropped in to shake hands. They still do; we had a well known one down there just last week. In fact, in my day, nearly everybody in town came down to the drugstore for one reason or another during the week.

I can still remember one night when a fellow walked in, apparently holding his head on with his hands. His throat was cut from ear to ear. I got a doctor for him and a news story for the Zebulon *Record*.

In time, I became more interested in the news than in the place where I gathered it. I deserted the drugstore for the print shop. I am not at all sure that my father, who is here tonight, thinks I made the right choice.

However, his interests and mine happily coincide on this occasion. He is one of many druggists in North Carolina who were interested in getting a new building for the Pharmacy School, and I was one of many newspapermen interested in getting better quarters for the School of Journalism.

We are both pleased at the way this game of musical chairs has turned out.

The School of Journalism . . . It sounds very grand. When I was here journalism occupied a single classroom. And there was one professor, whose name has already been fondly recalled several times today, O. J. Coffin.

It was not a school of journalism in those days. There were no textbooks, just the dictionary and the King James' Version of the Bible, as Governor Hodges said this morning. And so far as I could tell, the course was taught entirely out of Mr. Coffin's head.

Whether that was a good system of pedagogy I cannot say, but it did produce a fair number of pretty good newspapermen.

However, times have changed. The demands on newspapers and newspapermen have increased. New means of mass communications have developed alongside the newspapers, and they call for new technical skills. The institution that was dedicated here today is designed to serve those new needs, and is admirably equipped to do so——in both physical and intellectual terms.

Those of us who have been asked to address you on this day of dedication have the task of trying to enunciate a few ideals and principles to guide the School of Journalism in its further development, and to guide its graduates in their future careers.

Responsibility is our theme——the responsibility that the press and its people owe to the society that sustains them. My variation on the theme is "The Responsibility of the Reporter and Editor."

If I wanted to be brief and get everybody home early——and I hope you will get home in time to watch the TV debate [Kennedy and Nixon]. To quote Mr. Ethridge again: "My man's winning and I want you all to run home and hear him." (I'll leave you to guess which one is my man.)——If I wanted to get you home early, I could simply say that the responsibility of reporters is to get the facts straight and spell the names right. And the responsibility of editors is to fire them if they don't.

As far as it goes that is really not a bad creed for newspapermen, but there is a little more to it than that.

I began to be concerned about my responsibilities as a newspaperman here on this campus more than 25 years ago. I was a member of one of the political parties that we formed every spring to contest the student elections. I was asked to be my party's candidate for president of the student body. I declined because I already had the notion——perhaps somewhat presumptuous——that I was a newspaperman and that newspapermen should stay out of party politics.

Looking back, I see that I was taking myself a little too seriously. I don't think the integrity of the Fourth Estate would really have been compromised. But the fact is that I have never since been seriously tempted to deviate from the rule I laid down for myself on this campus at the age of 20.

It's *my* rule. I don't insist on it for everybody. There have been great editors and great reporters who were active in party politics. In North Carolina the first name that comes to mind is Josephus Daniels. But, in talking about the responsibilities of reporters and editors, I began with the basic assumption that journalism in America is a calling——not a trade, not a profession, but a calling ——that is not necessarily above politics, but should certainly be apart from politics.

This may sound very austere and self-denying, but I mean it to sound that way. The man who embraces journalism as a career should be no less dedicated than the parson or the doctor. Like them, he should have his own standards——standards that are not subject to change by the shifting winds of public taste or political expediency.

"There is no sure guide for all situations," as my colleague, Anthony Lewis of the New York *Times* said at Harvard last spring, "but I think it is clear that the reporter must not become entirely committed——an obvious special pleader. His instinct should be all the other way. If he has a concern for the public good . . . he must reconcile himself to satisfying that urge by uncommitted reporting. Justice Frankfurter has put it that the reporter is an educator, not a reformer. I accept that definition, with the proviso that the educator must be allowed to harbor within him just a little of the spirit of reform."

The reporter, Mr. Lewis says, must satisfy his concern for the public good by uncommitted reporting. To translate that into practical terms, a reporter may belong to worthy organizations, he may contribute to good causes, he may campaign for civic virtue and public betterment, but he should never commit himself irretrievably to one cause, one organization, one course of action.

In the words of the Code of Ethics of the American Society of Newspaper Editors:

Freedom from all obligations except that of fidelity to the public trust is vital.

A journalist who uses his power for any selfish or otherwise unworthy purpose is faithless to a high trust.

Promotion of any private interest contrary to the general welfare, for whatever reason, is not compatible with honest journalism.

Actually, the reporter who understands his mission has a higher destiny than mere dedication to a single private cause, however noble. His function in our society is to create and preserve an atmosphere in which all noble causes may flourish.

The press in this country has been called "the fourth branch of government." Its importance to the structure of our democracy is certified in the Constitution. In fact, there would be no democracy without a free press.

Show me a country where the police can stop the delivery of the morning paper, and I will show you a nation of slaves. Show me a country where the reporter is prevented from digging for the truth, and I will show you a nation in chains.

These facts impose a peculiar responsibility on the journalist. It is a responsibility, not to his employer, not to a particular paper, not to a particular point of view, but to the public and to his own conception of the obligations of his profession.

The publisher, the man who meets the payroll, is not alone responsible for the conscience of the profession. In this I do not quite agree with what Gordon Gray said this morning. Each reporter and each editor is the keeper of his own conscience.

"The modern journalist," as Louis M. Lyons has said, "is an employee. But his responsibility remains to serve the reader as his client. That describes the responsibility and the whole of it. He departs from it or compromises with it at the peril of his soul."

Mr. Lyons' conception of the responsibility of the journalist is based on the premise that information is essential to people who propose to govern themselves, and that those who supply the information must be above partisanship and self-interest.

In other words, the duty of the reporter and editor, in Walter Lippmann's terms, is to do "what every sovereign citizen is supposed to do, but has not the time or interest to do for himself"———that is, to gather information, pick out what is important, digest it thoroughly, and without passion or prejudice relate it to the problems of the day.

If the press is going to discharge this function fully, it must be among the bravest and the boldest. It must say what no one else dares to say, what no one else can afford to say.

It must tell the people what they *need* to know, not what they would *like* to hear. If you ask me *who* decides what the people need to know, I can only say, "the editor." If he can't do that, he has no right to the title. If he allows someone else to do it for him——the government or some special interest——he forfeits his freedom.

There was a time when newspapermen seemed to be more outspoken than they are today, more contemptuous of authority, more defiant of restraints on their freedom. Nowadays, when we are engaged in a desperate competition with world Communism, it is sometimes suggested that in the national interest the newspapers should voluntarily restrict themselves.

This issue arose not long ago when it was proposed that the press limit its coverage of President Eisenhower's trip to the Soviet Union ——(the one that was cancelled in May) and its coverage of similar visits by Soviet leaders to this country.

A number of editors were questioned by the Associated Press Managing Editors Association. *Nobody* voted in favor of the press limiting its own freedom. One editor wrote:

". . . if anybody proposes to limit the number of newsmen accredited to cover important international stories, let him do it if he dares. If such restrictions are imposed and found to be disadvantageous, let the enterprising newspaperman evade and defy them if he dares. If these opposite interests clash . . . then let the courts and the Congress draw the line, if they dare.

"But let's not circumscribe ourselves with our own pencils."

I like that fellow's spirit. It is the spirit with which I think we should meet the problem of official restrictions on news.

Somehow, I feel we newspapermen complain too much about the concealment of news by official quarters——"top secret" labels on inane documents, closed meetings of city councils, secret sessions of legislative committees, and so on. And we rely too much on the politicians to open these doors *for* us.

The classic function of the aggressive reporter and editor——a part of the responsibility they owe to the public——is to open doors——

open them with the power of the press——pry them open, blow them open.

As Arthur Krock has said, "There is nothing that loosens up a news source like a good swift kick in the pants."

A lot of fun would go out of the lives of newspapermen if we were denied that function and that pleasure. Readers would miss something, too.

Of course, the issue of responsibility arises sometimes in matters more serious than a local political fight. It sometimes involves national security.

Obviously, American newspapermen must not be irresponsible in the reporting of news that might affect the safety and security of our own country, our own homes. But the primary responsibility for safeguarding our national interests must rest always with our government. Mr. Gray spoke today of disclosures that have affected our national security. One asks, who made those disclosures in the first place? I suspect they were made by public officials, not newspapermen.

When Nikita Khrushchev arrived in this country last month, newspapers and broadcasting stations around the country received thousands of letters, telegrams and telephone calls urging them to boycott the visit, to ban Khrushchev from their news columns.

So far as the Associated Press could learn, there was not a single daily paper in the country that kept Khrushchev off its front page. However, there was one that gave him only six paragraphs on his arrival in New York. The New York *Times* printed 27 columns, more than three full pages, and a very angry woman in New York called me up and demanded to know why we published a picture of that "Russian Pig"——as she called him——on Page One. She said we should have printed pictures of President Eisenhower and the American flag instead.

While I appreciated her patriotism, I tried to explain——although she was too angry to listen——what I felt the responsibility of the press to be. Restricting news of Khrushchev's visit presupposes that it is more important for the press to show its disapproval of him than to inform the public of what he is and what he is doing.

Perhaps the Russians would not have us so much on the defensive today if we had not, journalistically speaking, turned our backs on them for a whole generation and ignored what they were achieving in education, industry, and science.

There are still people who think it is unpatriotic to call attention to the Soviet challenge or to publish news that is in conflict with the opinions and policies of our government.

What is the responsibility of the reporter and editor in that area? The answer is not simple, but it seems to me that, up until the time we are actually at war or on the verge of war, it is not only permissible but it is our duty as journalists and citizens to be constantly questioning our leaders and our policy.

Some people argue that newspapers should not print facts that might embarrass our government in its relations with other governments. But it may be that those very facts are the ones our people need to know in order to come to a clear decision about our policy.

In the Soviet Union, I discovered on a trip to Moscow last spring, there is now a "Press Group" attached to the Premier. It is composed of the editors of *Pravda* and *Izvestia,* the two leading newspapers, and other journalists who regularly travel with Mr. Khrushchev. They do not merely report on the activities of the Premier. From time to time they issue statements supporting him. That is the ultimate in subservience of the press to the state.

In our democracy, the purposes of the press and the government are not necessarily always identical.

For example, although our government does not recognize Communist China and prevents the Chinese government from being seated in the United Nations, there is no doubt in my mind that American newspapers should have correspondents on the Chinese mainland. We need to know what the Chinese Communists are doing because someday they may be doing it to us.

It is nothing less than folly to let this great power grow up in the Pacific without our having any first-hand knowledge of its aims and accomplishments and its potential. Here is the most populous country on earth, and we have not a single diplomatic or journalistic representative there to tell us what is going on.

Looking back and second-guessing, I would say that we made a mistake in not sending our correspondents to China in 1956 when we had the chance. The Chinese government offered to admit a long list of newspapermen. But we declined. We did not want to embarrass our government. We did not want to offend the sensibilities of those whose sons had died in Korea or were imprisoned in China.

I think we were wrong. I think we overlooked our primary loyalty, which is, as I have tried to suggest, to the American public——to give the public the information it needs to make intelligent decisions on our national policy with regard to China.

Our government has since changed its mind. A certain number of correspondents are now free to go to China. But Peiping has also changed. The Chinese are not prepared to admit our correspondents except on terms that Washington is unwilling to meet.

Without going into the diplomatic intricacies of this question, let me say only that any effort by journalism or government to break this impasse and to see that the American people are informed about China would be a contribution to our national security.

In an election year, there are inevitably proposals, from inside the profession and outside, that the newspapers should guarantee equal space and equal billing to the two candidates for President.

Of course, we should give them an even break. But the principle should not be carried to ridiculous extremes. Newspapers should be edited not with a tape measure, but on the basis of the best news judgment of competent, serious, responsible reporters and editors.

As one editor has said, if a newspaper prints a story about Mr. Nixon's infected knee, there is no obligation to "balance" it with a story about Mr. Kennedy's knee.

Or, to quote Louis Seltzer of the Cleveland *Press,* "It's ridiculous to suppose that the statements, speeches and activities of each candidate will be worth exactly the same space every day. The candidates will make the news, and the Cleveland *Press* will report it——in relation to its hard news value, and not in relation to any unrealistic effort to make the lines come out exactly even every day."

A good reporter knows pretty well when he is leaning toward one side or the other, and so does his editor. The only answer to that is: Don't do it.

Again and again these days we hear that factual reporting is not enough, that stark objectivity is out of date, that the news has become so complex that is must be explained, that interpretation is now necessary.

A good deal of this talk is beside the point. Of course the news should be explained. There is nothing new about that. The Protestant Reformation was no less complex than the present-day debate over the separation of church and state. The Emancipation Proclamation required no less interpretation than the Supreme Court's decision on desegregation.

The news has always required interpretation, but interpreting the news does not exclude the possibility of objectivity in reporting it. As I have said, a reporter knows pretty well when he is being objective, and so does his editor. The important thing is that they should appreciate the need for objectivity and its relationship to the role they play in our democracy and that they should constantly strive for objectivity.

So far this evening I have talked only about editors who handle the news. I have said nothing about editors who comment on the news, who write editorials, who voice the opinions of their newspapers. Frankly, I have very little to say about them, because I have more or less deliberately isolated myself from them——as I have abstained from party politics.

From one day to another I have no knowledge of what the New York *Times* is going to say on its editorial page. I have no need to know. I would rather not know. My employers would prefer that I not know. At this moment, for example, I have no idea whether the *Times* will come out for Nixon or Kennedy, although Douglas Edwards, Walter Winchell, Leonard Lyons and quite a few others seem to know.

It's not my line of work, but it is commonly said that the editorial pages in this country have very little influence on public opinion and public policy. If so, I can suggest only that they do not say very much that is pertinent to the problems of our people.

The editorial columns are all too often taken up with ill-conceived, ill-informed, ill-digested expressions of opinion on matters that are of little real consequence to the people who buy the paper.

Newspapers have to make themselves necessary to the people. Editors have to make themselves, and their leadership, essential to the community.

However, they cannot expect to be rewarded very substantially for whatever contribution they may make. As my friend Thomas Griffith of *Time* magazine has said, in a lovely sentence, "Newspapermen must warm themselves by their own fires."

It is perhaps one of the attractions of the business that it pays so badly in comparison with what it is expected to do. Becoming a newspaperman is an almost certain guarantee of martyrdom——you will make everybody mad sooner or later——and martyrdom is a very exalted state.

Still, as Mr. Griffith says, "A good journalist is a rewarding sight. . . . He must have a zest for events. . . . He must have a dedication to facts and a scent of humbug. . . . He must cultivate skepticism while avoiding cynicism. . . . He must learn to cover . . . causes for which he can have sympathy but must not display loyalty. . . . He must be incorruptible. . . . He must go where he is not wanted, and be resistant to those who are too welcoming. And for all of this, his hours will be long, his pay inadequate, and his standing in the community not particularly high."

But, he serves a great ideal, and, if he serves it well, he need not take off his hat to any man.

So, in a few sentences, let me at last recapitulate.

What is the responsibility of the reporter and editor in our democracy? Stripped to essentials, it is this:

To serve the public——not the profession of journalism, not a particular newspaper, not a political party, not the government, but the public.

To put information in the hands of people who must be their own rulers.

To make that the supreme obligation of their lives.

To bring intelligence, skill and devotion to the task and, I hope, perform it with some grace and wit.

It is to this last point that I address my concluding remarks. We all came here today to dedicate a beautifully refurbished building, designed to become one of the nation's leading centers for education in the techniques and ideals of modern journalism.

We dedicate not only the institution. Those of us who are journalists, teachers of journalism, or students of journalism must, to paraphrase Governor Hodges, dedicate ourselves as well. We should bring to the practice of journalism the heartiest possible sense of responsibility and all the intelligence, skill, devotion, grace, and wit that we can muster.

JENKINS LLOYD JONES

12   The Inexact Science of Truthtelling

"When should an editor not tell the truth?" Mr. Jones, editor and publisher of the Tulsa Tribune, asks.

That there are such occasions when it is not ethically right to tell all of the truth may come as a shock to the neophyte journalist or journalism student schooled in remote absolutes and not mundane realities.

In matters of bad taste; in situations that lay the newspaper open to libel actions; in matters of questionable justice——these are some of the instances when it is more human of the editor to err by omission than sin by commission.

Using some real and some apocryphal illustrations for his controversial thesis, Mr. Jones makes a witty and tartly pungent case for selective truthtelling.

The Inexact Science of Truthtelling was delivered by Mr. Jones as the ninth annual William Allen White Memorial Lecture on February 10, 1958, at the University of Kansas, Lawrence, Kansas. It appears here in a slightly abridged format.

WITHOUT inspiration and idealism the profession of journalism is merely a sorry form of diary-keeping, an endless succession of statements of fact, like the log of a dull captain on a very dull voyage.

But I propose not to inspire you, but to perplex you. For I wish to ask this question: When should an editor not tell the truth?

I believe that honest perplexity is just as much a part of the pro-

[157

fession of journalism and education for journalism as honest conviction is. The strong, immature mind is a mind of many convictions. It
is a mind that loves and hates, worships and abhors, admires and
detests many things. It is youth that has recently discovered that his
father doesn't know everything, and is now certain that his father
doesn't know anything. It is youth whose political opinions and social
observations are stretched or amputated to fit the Procrustean bed of
his self-image. And that self-image is his conception of himself as a
fearless liberal who will drive away the shibboleths of an evil past, or
as a staunch and clear-sighted conservative who will defend to the
death the eternal verities.

I have no quarrel with such minds, although it is sometimes
wearisome arguing with them. It is, indeed, the youth that has no
strong convictions at all who is hopeless. But when a strong young
mind begins to grow into a condition of maturity and balanced
reasoning it suffers a series of distressing shocks, namely, the discovery that the copy-book maxims are not always correct.

Love doesn't always laugh at locksmiths. Ask any convict.

There have been cases where the course of true love ran smooth as
hell.

Murder does not always out.

Truth crushed to earth sometimes stays down for the count.

And, saddest of all, there seem to be times when honesty, if that
means blurting out the unvarnished facts, is not always the best
policy.

It is this latter circumstance which I wish to relate to the problem
of journalism.

We will not consider venal editors who lie for profit, or cowardly
editors who are constantly trying to rationalize sins of omission
because they fear a fight. I want to talk about the perplexities that
assail the vast majority of our editors today, men of decency and
devotion, men who are not afraid of a righteous brawl, men who are
trying to do a good job for their readers and their communities.

The editor who claims that his newspaper prints all the news all the
time is either a liar or a fool. We often tell our readers only half-
truths. We are constantly sweeping facts under the rugs.

The New York *Times* has a slogan—"All the News That's Fit To
Print."

I believe nearly every editor will subscribe to that slogan. The argument starts when you get down to the last three words. What is "fit to print"?

Well, the old-time tabloids and the latter-day scandal magazines proceeded on the theory that anything was fit to print that didn't bring on a successful libel suit or an enthusiastic horsewhipping. The peddlers of scum and slime and smut even invented an elaborate system of innocent-sounding synonyms, which were adjudged libel-proof, but which didn't fool——and weren't supposed to fool—— their evil-minded readers.

Happily, there has been a public revulsion against this garbage. At least in the field of daily newspapers those papers that had the lowest standards have, in general, had the greatest recent circulation difficulties, and those that have tried to do a good job with significant news have, in general, prospered most.

So my gorge rises every time I see a movie or a television program in which people are harassed as blackmailers who threaten to "spill it all to the papers." The fact is that the average newspaper in America today is not remotely interested in most of the stuff that makes for blackmail. Nor should it be.

No there is a great deal about our communities that we do not tell. And we do not tell it because for a variety of reasons we consider it nobody's business, not even ours. Still, when editors get together in shop talk you will find a wide range of disagreement as to just where the line should be drawn.

We are, for example, often guilty of double standards. Here is a case. Think with me for a moment and tell me what you would do.

As in all cities, we, in Tulsa, have several celebrated bums. Our most eminent bum is a panhandler who makes whisky money by selling yellow-jacket pills to other bums. These pills have often been seized and often analyzed, and always they have turned out to contain nothing but bicarbonate of soda. This is a brilliant and godly idea, for not only is bicarbonate of soda no transgressor of the law, but it soothes the lacerated stomach linings of the unsuspecting customers.

Anyway, our particular bum has only one glory in this life and that is his complete bumness. So, when we occasionally run a little story to the effect that he has crossed the 1,000 mark or the 1,200 mark in his arrests for drunkenness and vagrancy, he is consumed with pleasure and gratitude and offers to buy our police reporter a beer.

Now take the case of another drunk, this time a professional man of wide and favorable reputation, a pillar in his church and community, with a fine wife and intelligent children. On one evil night he took aboard one Martini too many and crashed his car into a tree. Our boys saw him when they got him to the station. He was without doubt pie-eyed. Stricken with remorse, he was admitting it to everyone.

Of course, his friends hurried down and got the charge reduced to reckless driving, and he later paid a fine——all of which our newspaper recorded. But did we tell the real truth? We did not. No one was hurt. Damages were paid for the wounded tree. We never told on this man although his family knew it and so did his intimate circle. But his reputation as far as the general public is concerned remains unblemished. And he has never taken another drink.

Here is a double standard. The dereliction of the bum is published. The dereliction of the solid citizen is not. The first had no reputation to lose. The second could have been vastly injured. Were we wrong to give the gentleman one more chance?

But here is another double standard:

When a local woman suffers a miscarriage the home town newspaper never mentions it. We consider it a private tragedy that will be known, anyway, to the family friends and that is of no particular concern to anyone else.

Yet when the same misfortune occurs to a movie actress like Marilyn Monroe or Elizabeth Taylor it goes on page one. How can we justify this? Has the actress forfeited her right of privacy? Many of our readers find escape from their dull and humdrum lives by peering into the personal affairs of celebrities. How far should we pander to this reader interest?

I don't know. We used both the Monroe and the Taylor stories.

There is a sound axiom in journalism that when a man runs for public office his past becomes public property. The people have a right to know what type of men are seeking to do the people's business. Each election year we examine with great care the records of the candidates, and particularly of the candidates of the party to which we don't belong.

Yet for many years an ex-convict has been holding public office in my community. He doesn't belong to my party, but we never point to his penitentiary term. Why? Well, he does a good job. He has been re-elected time after time and has grown gray in public service. There has never been a suspicion of graft or malfeasance. So, although a few old-timers may know about his record, neither the newspapers nor, more strangely still, his political opponents ever mention it. Are we wrong?

One of our perpetual puzzles is whether to recall the criminal record of a dead citizen. Consider the vast difference in reader interest between these two apocryphal stories:

"Mr. Gerald Cantonwine, 68, house painter, of 2273 E. 38th St., died yesterday in a Tulsa hospital after a long illness. He was born in Danville, Ill. and came to Oklahoma in 1920. He is survived by his widow, Mrs. Mamie Cantonwine, prominent southside church worker."

Or:

"Death, which he had eluded in a dozen blazing gun battles, finally came yesterday to Jerry (The Gimp) Cantonwine, prominent early day bank robber. The once-celebrated thief and gunman succumbed in a Tulsa hospital after a long illness. In 1922 Cantonwine, originally from Danville, Ill., was convicted of four bank robberies and a gold shipment theft. He served 15 years in McAlester penitentiary. On his release he married "Flaming Mamie" McGuire, his former look-out girl, and took up housepainting. The Cantonwines lived at 2273 E. 38th St. His widow is now the only survivor of a gang that once included Gaspipe Flynn, Brassknucks O'Toole and Nitro Burke. She is a member of the Altar Guild at All Saints Church."

Of the two, which story would you run? Personally, the story I would run would be much closer to the second than the first, although it needn't be so cruel. But a prominent criminal record is a legitimate part of an obituary notice. A completed penitentiary sentence may, as we say, discharge a man's debt to society, but he cannot expect society to erase from its memory the crime that put him there.

Still, this is a very rubber standard on our newspaper. If a man's criminal record was long ago and not too remarkable, and if we can assume that the vast majority of his acquaintances are unaware of it we usually skip it on what, after all, is his final story.

This perplexity applies not only to obituaries. It can be a problem of marriages, too. For example:

A short time ago our boys heard that a girl figure in a prominent criminal case, who had done time in prison and subsequently been released, had quietly married a local man. As good reporters should they ran it down and confirmed it.

But the girl's mother appeared breathless at the office and begged me to kill it. I argued that there was nothing disgraceful about getting married. The distraught mother was not to be put off with any such sophistry.

"You are anxious for the story," she said, "only because my daughter had committed a crime. You want to interest readers and you know that readers love to gossip. My girl, as you know, has been under the care of a psychiatrist. He recommended the marriage. He said that if she can have a few months of happy quiet homelife right now it may change her whole life for the better. I don't have to tell you what the consequences may be if you choose this moment to start the tongues clacking and the neighbors gawking."

Well, she had me there. We certainly weren't after that wedding as a society item. Besides, I knew she spoke the truth when she mentioned the precarious emotional condition of the girl. So I killed the story.

Several days later our opposition woke up and did a big piece on the marriage. Everybody thought we had been scooped. Our managing editor and city editor have been looking at me with gentle scorn ever since. It's obvious they consider me less of a newspaperman than a patsy. I'm quite sure they're right. But I sleep wonderfully these nights.

Still, there is another side to this coin. Our obligation to protect the apparently repentant criminal is nothing compared to our obligation to protect the innocent public. Yet there are plenty of sentimentalists who think that what a large part of the criminal element does is none of the public's business.

Consider the New York State youth court act which, if it isn't repealed, is scheduled to go into effect next April. The act would consider all offenders under the age of 21 as children. They would not be arrested——only apprehended. A man of 20 could have completed his military service. He could have had a long record of robberies, thefts and assaults. But his record could be buried in the super-secrecy of the youth courts. A suspicious prospective father-in-law couldn't find the truth. An unsuspecting employer is denied the right to protect himself.

Oxie Reichler, the editor of the Yonkers *Herald-Statesman,* is conducting a vigorous and so far unsuccessful battle to end this odd-ball notion that people of 20 are still children and that if juvenile crime is wrapt up like a mummy it will somehow evaporate. How long must a human being remain a juvenile?

At the age of 12 English boys used to go to sea as midshipmen. At 16 Napoleon was a lieutenant in artillery and David Porter was commanding his first ship. At 17 Mohammed was proving an able camel trader and Mozart had completed his second opera. Juvenile delinquency is never much of a problem where children are allowed ——even required——to assume responsibilities as soon as nature makes them ready for responsibilities.

But consider New York State, where the period of legal irresponsibility is already up to 18 and where the most elaborate legal blocks are thrown in the way of letting the press or the public know just who among youth is committing crimes. Does it work? We have the statement by New York City Police Commissioner Stephen Kennedy to the effect that in the five boroughs crime among persons between 16 and 20 is going up at the rate of 12 percent a year, and crime among children under 16 is increasing 32 percent a year.

Here is where dishonesty, based upon the same pseudo-psychology that has reduced progressive education to an absurdity, is apparently a long way from being the best policy.

The effort to twist laws to prevent the press from informing the people is well advanced in many areas of government. Bureaucrats are human, and human beings like to conceal their mistakes if possible. Who among us does not? So all kinds of flubs and bloopers are hidden in sealed files marked confidential and secret. And in departments in Washington where there is not the slightest question of leaking information of value to a potential enemy many records are withheld from reporters under broad provisions of the so-called "housekeeping" directives. These directives require employees to do what is necessary for the welfare of their departments. Good Lord, there's a wooden horse, bigger than Troy, itself.

But here, again, perhaps I must perplex you. Many of my colleagues in the newspaper business have leaped to the conclusion that all public affairs, not directly connected with national defense, must be conducted in the open. Once again we hear the ghost of Woodrow Wilson pleading for "open covenants openly arrived at!"

I disagree. I think that much of the important business in a republican form of government will be carried on behind closed doors. I see few dangers in that. I see many advantages. For it is only behind closed doors, as William R. Matthews of the Arizona *Star* has pointed out, that most politicians——yea, even statesmen—— honestly express their views and try to get at the meat of the question. As soon as the doors are open, or as soon as these gentlemen arise in a congress or a legislature, they start speaking for the gallery. Our slang word "bunk" arose from the days when a backwoods North Carolina legislator kept making bombastic speeches which he hoped would be published back in Buncombe County.

I don't mean to imply that legislative voting should not be in the open, nor that the public should be denied the right to appear before all committees, nor that any legislator should be excused from explaining why he voted as he did. But I do mean that in every city hall, every courthouse, every state capitol and in the National Capitol, the White House, and the various Washington departments no sound policy is decided upon without frank exchange of views. And a frank exchange of views is rarely reached with the public and the press looking over the shoulders of the policy makers.

The government of ancient Athens was an absolute and complete democracy, with all deliberations carried on in the goldfish bowl of open desire. But Athens became smothered with oratory, paralyzed with demagoguery, and finally wound up with such an unstable mobocracy that nearly every able Athenian was banished from the land.

Our struggle in America is to maintain a republican form of government that can do three things: remain responsive to the wishes of the people, provide a large measure of administrative stability, and stay flexible enough to meet the immensely complex problems of our age. If, in the pursuit of these aims, the boys want to retire now and then for a private conference, I'm not going to hurl myself against the door.

As you can see from these apparent contradictions I don't consider the business of truth-telling a simple one.

I have tried to point out to you that a newspaper that sought to publish all the facts all the time would:

(1) lay itself open to ruinous libel suits, since many things that are true and provable are not privileged,

(2) be an accessory to blackmail and stand guilty of bad taste, since much that is privileged is also merely degrading,

(3) be responsible for many injustices since some truths which are privileged and neither profane nor pornographic are cruel and unnecessary, and

(4) paralyze our popular government by insisting on a level of reporting so free that it would destroy deliberation.

On the other hand, I have pointed out that it is not only a right but a duty of the press to hammer down those barriers to truth-telling that are based upon zany theories of social justice, or that are raised to protect inept bureaucrats from the consequences of their own stupidities, or that for any reason are designed to shroud those things which can be included in, as Harold Cross has put it, "The People's Right To Know."

This latter is a bitter, serious battle. At the moment we are not even winning it. But America is lucky that men like Russ Wiggins of the Washington *Post,* Jim Pope of the Louisville *Courier-Journal,* Herbert Brucker of the Hartford *Courant,* and Congressman John Moss are waging an incessant fight for more light in dark places. Without the right to learn the truth the press is powerless to fulfill its obligations to the community. But, alas, it's time for another paradox:

The newspaper's obligation to the welfare of its community is so fundamental that there are even times when a newspaper must print a lie.

A few weeks ago Springfield, Missouri, was shocked when a robber stabbed two store proprietors to death and then escaped. After several days of searching the police discovered the murder knife hidden in a pipe a block from the scene. By agreement between police and reporters this discovery was concealed.

Instead, the Springfield *News and Leader* gave page-one play to a phony story to the effect that the next day the police intended to make an inch-by-inch examination of the area in an effort to find the weapon. Shortly after midnight that night a furtive figure stole up to the pipe and began searching it anxiously. The police leaped from the ambush and had their man.

Is there anyone who can say that this fake news story was not fit to print? Happily that's a rare, rare case.

The inexact science of truth-telling involves essentially the difficult business of selecting facts. The proper selection of facts gives a reasonably accurate picture. The improper selection can give a false one.

I once had a personal lesson in this matter. Some years ago we had a police chief of whom I was very suspicious. We rode him editorially at all times. We reported with glee those occasions when the police department looked silly or when the chief put his foot in his mouth.

One day he stopped me. "Why are you giving me the business?" he asked.

I assumed an air of righteous innocence.

"Is there anything that we have said that isn't true?" I demanded.

He looked at me hard for a moment and then walked on.

A month or so later I was preparing to leave for one of those South American police states that require a certificate of good conduct before they will grant a visa. So I asked our police reporter to get me the usual form letter from the police department.

An hour later a motorcycle officer delivered a "To-Whom-It-May-Concern" letter over the chief's signature that read:

"An examination of our files fails to reveal any instance in which Mr. Jones has been convicted of a felony. However our files are very incomplete."

And appended to it was a note in the chief's handwriting. "All this is true, too," it said.

How shall an editor select his facts? Is the primary purpose of a newspaper to uplift, to inform or to entertain its readers? We all like to think that we succeed in doing all three things, but we are constantly putting our thumbs on the scales.

One of the best-edited newspapers in America is *The Christian Science Monitor*. Its influence goes far beyond the boundaries of its church. In its early youth it tried to print nothing but good news, but it rose to greatness after it began printing quite a bit of bad news, but doing it in a constructive and hopeful manner.

The *Monitor*'s test for the news that's fit to print seems to be this: Is it the kind of news a truth-seeking reader needs to know about or is it merely a distressing accident of no social significance?

So, two weeks ago, when the Nebraska gunman, Charles Stark-weather, was busy murdering 11 people the *Monitor* looked the other way. Not a line did it print about a story that had the entire world looking on with gruesome fascination.

But the *Monitor* did print an item about a group of Chinese students who had tried to kill Chou En-lai with a penknife. This leaves me confused. I'll take 11 home-grown murders any day over a botched assassination 9,000 miles away.

And, ladies and gentlemen, I'm sure that you, too, are confused enough by now.

If you want to live by inflexible rules, stay out of the newspaper business.

If you like inexorable and unquestioned truths, go into engineering or accounting or chemistry. The laws of stress and compression are unchangeable. If properly done, the debits will always balance the credits. A given catalyst in a given compound will react tomorrow as it did today.

But not so the newspaper business. It is a business as variable as human beings. The editor is torn between that which is popular and that which is instructive. He must understand that uncompromising honesty carries cruelty in its saddlebags, and that too much gentleness will help evil thrive.

He is constantly wondering how to play the unaccountably brilliant speech of the candidate he isn't supporting and the unaccountably dull speech of the candidate he is. He perspires over profound editorials, knowing all the time that it is the picture of the fireman getting the cat out of the tree that will draw 100 percent reader interest.

He hates to be maudlin and inconsequential, yet he is losing his grip if he doesn't realize that the tear-stained face of the baby abandoned in the bus station may carry a more powerful social lesson than reams of statistics on parental delinquency.

He tries to be consistent. He lays down rules for reporters and desk men. And then there's a midnight call from a frantic mother and the rules go blooey. And the next morning he detests himself. He snarls into breakfast and doesn't throw bacon to the dog.

The science of truth-telling remains inexact.

All day long the editor flies by the seat of his pants in a thick cloud layer, with the compass swinging and the artificial horizon turning circles. But somehow the paper gets out. Somehow the right guesses seem to balance off the boners.

And then a truly great truth dawns on him. How sterile are the routine professions. How dull the easy businesses! The thing that makes journalism one of the most challenging callings on earth is its very perplexity——its wide areas of error——the utter impossibility of doing it as well as it ought to be done.

The editor wouldn't have it any other way. He goes home to the supper table whistling.

And he feeds the dog.

NICK B. WILLIAMS

13 America's Third Force: The Watchdog Press

■

Journalism has been called, among the more publishable names, "the fourth estate" and "the fourth branch of government." In the following concerned and reflective article by Nick B. Williams, editor of the Los Angeles Times, it receives still another pertinent, timely and memorable title: "America's Third Force."

Reasoning that the highest responsibility of the Press is to create an informed climate of free-wheeling, intelligently conceived opinion in America, Mr. Williams charges journalism with the trust of being the interpreter and guardian of our two-party system of government.

In this era of increasing distress over the tinder-box issue of "managed news," Mr. Williams stirring defense of the Press' right and duty to seek the truth wherever it may lie contains a heartening measure of courage and encouragement to newsmen everywhere.

America's Third Force: The Watchdog Press was given, without the title accorded it here, as an address before the World Affairs Institute on December 9, 1964, by Mr. Williams in Pasadena, California.

FOR SOME TIME, I have been debating with myself as to just what the role of the mass media is in our twentieth-century world. And I think I have the answer. It is our role simply to be there when those who

think they are losing a political contest or an argument feel the urge
to find a whipping boy.

I cannot tell you when all this began, for my active interest in
politics started with the first election of Franklin D. Roosevelt, who
did not really need to lambaste the media, but who on occasion did it
anyway, probably just for the practice.

But Harry Truman was a devotee of whacking the press, and after
him Adlai Stevenson gave us equal space with Eisenhower as a target
of his criticism. Then Richard Nixon temporarily almost lost his
sense of proportion in blaming the media on two occasions. And all
this reached its climax in 1964 when Barry Goldwater and his more
enthusiastic followers made the media, and "certain columnists and
commentators," a major issue of the campaign.

But I am happy to report to you that Barry Goldwater, perhaps
believing that if you can't lick 'em, join 'em, himself will become once
again a columnist and a commentator for the Los Angeles *Times* and
other newspapers, and we hope his opinions are at least as vigorous
as those of his critics.

But the point of all this is that the mass media have been thrust
into a role which they did not consciously seek, and which I believe,
judging from their reactions, they did not fully anticipate.

For this kind of criticism, this kind of direct and vigorous attack
(and from the leaders in turn of both the political parties) almost, in
effect, seems to me to be setting up the mass media as a sort of third
party: a third party, or third force, that always will be, and must be, a
party of opposition; a party without the responsibility of directing or
participating in government, but with the responsibility of criticizing
and commending and independently investigating both the party that
is in power and the party that is out of power.

And this role in our domestic affairs may indeed be greatly
intensified by the current state of weakness of the formal party of
opposition, the Republicans.

Already there are indications that the media, both printed and
electronic, are moving rapidly in the direction of this greater role as
an independent critic of the party in power.

This has always tended to be true, for newspapermen traditionally
have felt a compulsion to act as the independent watchdogs of the
public: to search out scoundrels in government, those who cheat and

steal, but also those who abuse their powers in pursuit of their own ideologies, or what they believe are the ideologies of those who elected him.

This compulsion must have gained strength with the frank contention by Arthur Sylvester of the Defense Department that government had the right, and on occasion the duty, to manage the news.

Sylvester's statement, which did no more than openly confirm the intentions of all administrations, past and present, nonetheless has since been taken somehow to mean that the media accepted the principle of managed news or that they were powerless to do anything about it even if they wished.

Nothing could be much further from the truth.

I think it is conservative to say that the mass of the media reporters do not think of themselves as a non-selective, non-discriminating, non-critical, non-investigative transmission belt between the government——any goverment——and the public.

On the other hand, I think it is equally safe to say that the mass of media reporters and editors have no intention of letting themselves become a dogmatic organ of the opposition, condemning without investigation any act of the government, or the governing party, whether or not it makes sense.

Yet there is no question that reporters and editors of the mass media do believe that they have the obligation to report even the most dogmatic instances of opposition, even the most blatant examples of managed news——not necessarily as the truth but as the allegations of contending factions.

And once these attempts to manage the news, or these dogmatic instances of opposition have been faithfully and accurately reported, then the real work, the significant work, of the media begins——or should begin——their own attempts to discover all the qualifying facts, the contradictory facts, that may well not have been stated in the expositions of the contending factions.

With this kind of role, and I think most of the media representatives practice it, it seems inevitable to me that the media will be attacked constantly, and in turn, both by government and the opposition.

This, I think, creates the greatest opportunity for fair, for diligent, and for intelligent reporting, and for fair and intelligent editorial evaluation, that the media could possibly seek. For it distinctly casts the media in the role that they always have contended to be their own——that of militant representatives of the general, unorganized and unaligned public. Which means, in effect, a permanent and unaligned party or force of opposition, truthfully, a fourth estate.

Such a role has its obligations, but even more importantly, it has its perils.

For if the media are to succeed, and even to endure, as an extra-political force with responsibility only to the general public——and without direct and accountable responsibility to all the many kinds of minorities (economic, racial and geographic) that go to make up either of the two political parties, with all their blind loyalties and half-blind enthusiasms——if the media are to succeed as an extra-political force of criticism, then also they must become an even greater force for expanding the general public's comprehension of the issues of our time.

If the media are to base their position on reason——and they can successfully base it on nothing else——they must have supplied to the public the data essential for reaching a reasoned conclusion. And the public must have absorbed enough of this information to agree, at least to the extent of giving some validity in power to what the media are contending.

This is an awesome prospect.

It is enough, I'm sure, to make most of us lament the good old days, when our responsibility might be no heavier than the selection of the best comic strips, the better gossip columns, and the best of nickel-catching headlines. But for the metropolitan press, and for the metropolitan or nationwide electronic media, that time is forever past.

Whether by our own underestimation, or simply by the thrust of the "with-us-or-against-us" attitude of the two political parties, the mass media now find themselves more and more cast in the role of representing the general public, of conducting a nonpartisan forum in current events, and of educating their public, the base of their support, in such areas as economics, science, diplomacy and foreign affairs.

As we now must conceive of ourselves as a third political force, so too we must now conceive of ourselves as a group of agencies for independent research, independent of political and governmental agencies, but also independent of each other.

More and more, we must conduct our own research in the foreign nations of the world, to determine for ourselves, and for the general public, the thinking of foreign peoples and their leaders, rather than to rely upon interpretations of these by our own governmental agencies.

More and more, we find ourselves committed not only to tell the general public what our government thinks for instance about West Germany, and what our opposition party thinks about West Germany, but also what the governments of France and the United Kingdom, or Soviet Russia and Hungary think about West Germany.

And we must probe even deeper. We must try to tell our public what the public of West Germany thinks about its domestic and foreign issues, and what the public thinks in France and the United Kingdom, Soviet Russia and Hungary.

In doing all this, it may indeed develop that the opinions in each case are parallel, or close to it, but it also may develop that they are in conflict.

Let me give you an example, based on the previous example of West Germany. An American reporter, knowing the goals of our present national administration, and believing, as he well might, that they made sense, would find in West Germany a considerable enthusiasm for the proposed multi-lateral force, particularly if he spoke only to the faction of the Christian Democratic Party that is in power in Bonn. If that was the sole report he sent back, Americans might well believe that the multi-lateral force ought to begin at once.

Yet if this American reporter talks also to other West German politicians, particularly those who built the Paris-Bonn axis, he will find less enthusiasm.

If he talks to British politicians and military people, he will find wariness that amounts almost to opposition.

If he talks to the French, he will find violent opposition.

If he talks to those in the Communist nations of East Europe, he will find opinion that ranges from dogmatic opposition all the way over to absolute terror.

It is the duty of the media reporter, then, to report *all* these degrees of opinion on a subject of such importance and to report them with equal weighting, equal diligence. For our responsibility, as I see it, is *not only* to support the purposes and the conclusions of the current administration or its domestic opponents. Our responsibility is to distribute a full range of information, upon which the electorate, and possibly even the national political parties, will be able to take action.

A great danger, it seems to me, would arise if the media began these sorts of investigations with preconceived notions. It would arise most certainly were we to feel that our mission was to substantiate the conclusions of our own government or, conversely, were we to feel that our mission was to prove that the conclusions of our own government were cockeyed.

And perhaps the greatest danger of all, both to the media and the general public, would arise if we or the public were to believe the media infallible.

Our mission, then, as a third force, as a permanent, if sometimes shapeless, structure of opposition, must be not only to seek an independent point of view, based on our independent research and reporting, but to submit it to our readers only——I repeat that, *only*——as a contribution to public debate.

All this discussion of a third force might presuppose a degree of conformity among the media that does not actually exist. For not only are there differences in the way the Washington *Post* reports the news and the way the Chicago *Tribune* reports it, but there are indeed differences in the way the Los Angeles *Times* reports the news in 1964 and the way the Los Angeles *Times* reported it in 1954.

Even the concept of reporting has changed. In the latter part of the twentieth century it is no longer simply a matter of recording automatically with pencil and pad, or even with a camera. Most of the media now believe that their staffs are intelligent enough to understand more than what they are told, or what is obvious. There is of course danger in this method, but there were dangers, equally great, in what we call "objective reporting." And even this has become a political issue——with conservatives condemning "interpretive reporting," condemning it on the theory that editors, and particularly publishers, lose control when a reporter "interprets." This, I think, is nonsense, for the selection of facts can be just as interpretive and just as opinionated. But that is a technical or professional argument.

The important thing to remember is that the newspapers, or the television networks, grow both in the quantity of their individual work and the quality of their work as they develop better personnel. The mass media, not being infallible to begin with——any more than the political parties are infallible——and being by nature fiercely independent, increase their skills at varying rates. And certainly I do not consider their role as a third force to be an unmixed blessing, either for the media or the nation.

There are indeed these differences in skills and attitudes, yet competing newspapers, and competing networks, demonstrate in their daily play of the news a remarkable similarity. They have developed a mutual understanding of what their public considers to be news, a feeling for the public mind that is the first essential of any opinion-molding force. They react to this understanding much more rapidly than do the political parties, much more rapidly than government; and they know, much better than the political parties or government, just how far they can go in departing from what the public is ready to accept or absorb. Their barometers are attuned to their circulation figures and they get a new and accurate reading every day.

I think that all I have been saying here today about the mass media and their role as a third force, a critical force, further implies that the media, however much their components may vary in quality and attitude, nonetheless do provide as a whole an element of continuity in our political and economic life that not even the political parties give us. Consider, for instance, the durability as an institution of a Lippmann, a Sevareid, an Alsop, a Marquis Childs, a Walter Cronkite, a Gallup or a David Lawrence.

For the careers, the really great and impressive careers, of Walter Lippmann and David Lawrence run consecutively and consistently beginning in the era of Woodrow Wilson more than half a century ago. No political personalities of prominence in either party have endured so long. And during this half century, the actual characters of both the parties, the goals for which each now contends, have changed far more than have the characters or thinking of Lippmann and Lawrence.

These two enduring newspapermen, and others who have been

active for lesser but still long periods of time, point up not only the continuity of the third force of journalism, but also its broad range of attitude. And it is this broad range, from left to right (two descriptions I find more and more distasteful), that gives the third force its greatest impetus. It is the kind of spectrum of opinion that most of the media now practice. For the concept of the broad range, the concept of presenting opinion and information as a basis for debate, has become generally adopted in all the media.

I suppose this could be called the confession by the media of their own doubts about their infallibility. And in the formative stages of national policy, I am inclined to think that the more doubts we have——both the media and the general public——the better our policy will become. For doubts mean debate, and debate means examination, and examination means research and study——and the media welcome the challenge to supply information for it.

I want to repeat again that this sort of prospect does concern the responsible executives of all the media. For they feel thrust upon them and their organizations a role that, as I said in beginning this discussion, they did not fully anticipate. Not since the Civil War period have newspapers felt so strongly the pressures (on the one hand) from what they believe to be their true course as suppliers of information and divergent opinion as the basis of debate, and (on the other hand) from political enthusiasts of both the parties, centered on the theme of "you're either with us or you're against us."

Television's history is not so long, yet the pressures there are at the greatest in that medium's history.

But so long as the media, both printed and electronic, keep foremost in their minds that they are responsible only to the vast and often inarticulate general public, they will be able to maintain their position of criticism, of information, and of broad-ranging opinion as the basis for debate. If they can do that, and do it effectively, they will indeed have become the third force in our policy-making process.

RICK FRIEDMAN

41   A Negro Leader Looks at the Press

Reporting the racial ferment in America today is one of the most difficult and challenging responsibilities journalism must face. How good
a job is the press doing on this vital issue in our national life? Whitney M. Young, Jr., executive director of the National Urban League
presents his candid opinions in the following article by Rick Friedman, feature writer for Editor & Publisher. Mr. Young's comments
appeared in the July 18, 1964, issue of that publication.

*Whitney Young, Jr., 45-year-old executive director of the National
Urban League, has been in the news almost daily during these tense
days and nights of civil rights conflict. As one of the* Big Five *Negro
leaders, his words as well as his face have been appearing in countless
news stories, columns and editorials all over the country.*

*Mr. Young heads a 56-year-old organization of Negroes and whites
which has undergone dynamic growth since he became its executive
director three years ago.*

*The National Urban League is a nationwide professional community
service agency dealing with improvements of Negro life. It works in
the areas of education, job retraining and equal opportunities, "the
meat and potato problems of the average Negro," according to Mr.
Young.*

*The League was founded in 1910 to secure equal opportunities for
Negroes. It is non-profit and non-partisan and is interracial in its*

leadership and staff. The League has 500 full-time employes and 6,000 volunteers; offices are in 66 cities and 30 states.

In civil rights, the League stresses persuasion instead of picketing, education and self-improvement rather than pressure. Mr. Young's weekly column, "To Be Equal," is syndicated (E&P, May 9, page 58) to 30 newspapers. The Urban League's "Human Relations Beat" appears in 50 Chicago area weeklies.

SITTING in his mid-Manhattan National Urban League office, Whitney M. Young, Jr., appearing relaxed, smoking a cigarette and taking advantage of a short break in a tight schedule, summed up civil rights news reporting this way:

"Newspapers, despite superb spot coverage, have been guilty of emphasizing the conflicts between the whites and Negroes and minimizing, if not completely ignoring, areas of cooperation between the two groups. The in-depth series too often is the exception to this rule. We need more of them."

GETTING ALONG

Leaning forward to crush out the cigarette, he elaborated. "Floyd Patterson moves out of Scarsdale because of racial problems and this makes news. But for 12 to 15 years, there have been situations in the suburbs where Negro kids are the most popular ones in the neighborhood.

"Yet, to the general public, conflict is the norm. Negroes and whites getting along in the same neighborhood are considered oddballs. The public thinks that any white person who cooperates is offbeat.

"Big Business in this country, the principals of major corporations, the top people in government——it's easier for us to enter into discussion with them today than it was in the past. Before, they watched civil rights like it was a spectator sport.

"Now, they realize that business is being hurt, that it doesn't do them any good to have the Klan represent America overseas, to have free enterprise shown as not working for the American non-white. These people realize now that the real test of free enterprise is when it helps those who may be different.

"Now, we walk into the offices of presidents of the largest corporations at THEIR request. They want to know what they can do. Now, we speak before groups of city managers, mayors, industrial boards, builders, real estate federations who never had a Negro on their programs before.

"But these positive, new positions taken by American industry are not always played up in our press. Newspapers are not informing readers of what the role-models of the country are doing to advance civil rights."

But aren't many of these corporations that invite you to private breakfasts and luncheons, reluctant to let the press know about them?

"Sure," Mr. Young admitted. "But the press has to convince these men it's to their own interest for such stories about them to be publicized; that if the public thinks these corporations aren't discriminating, such stories could improve their images. The Urban League has been glad to cooperate with the press in breaking down resistance to getting the real stories from corporations doing their part in advancing civil rights."

Violence in Harlem

Mr. Young moved to what he considered a second error in civil rights coverage! "Too many newspapers give the impression that violence, vandalism, crime, murder are new things in Harlem——and give them a racial overtone. The truth is that violence has been a way of life in Harlem for years, just as it has been in white, poverty-struck communities.

"The big difference today is that, in addition to Negroes getting killed, some white persons are also getting killed. Now, the white community finally cares. Now, many newspapers are trying to identify a problem that was always there before white people were getting killed."

He paused to light another cigarette. "My own wife isn't safe in Harlem. The single fact of color is no guarantee of her safety. I don't want Harlem safe just for white people. I want Harlem safe for ALL human beings.

"Contrast this poor coverage with the superb stories the press has done on the war on poverty——almost totally free of racial overtones. The *New York Times* and the *Washington Post* are two examples."

IRRESPONSIBLE LEADERS

The third area of bad reporting, according to Mr. Young, was when some newspapers promote and project irresponsible Negro civil rights leaders. Often it is the press itself that makes these men leaders, Mr. Young contended.

"Somebody gets up and says he's going to start an all-Negro political party and the next day there are headlines, front page stories, editorials. But does any one pick up the phone to find out that this man has no backing, no members, no money and no power?

"The World's Fair stall-ins were the same type of bad reporting. Responsible leaders in Philadelphia, Cincinnati or Boston could have told any reporter who asked that they were not going to send in cars to have them impounded on the Long Island Expressway. Anyone who checked could have found out that the stall-in people had poor organization, no money. All the national Negro organizations were opposed to it.

"Something happens in civil rights and the newspapers call up outstanding personalities like James Baldwin or Louis Lomax or Willie Mays and ask what they think. Baldwin and Lomax are excellent writers but they are responsible to nobody but themselves. They are responsible to no organization so they can make statements that get front page space.

"I don't question the integrity of their statements. But do newspapers call Frank Sinatra to comment on foreign policy? Or John O'Hara to comment on wheat to Russia? The racial situation is complex and it takes organization, know-how to comment on it. Lomax can say what he wants. I have to speak for the Urban League, its thousands of members and its 56-year-tradition.

"The press gives somebody such as Malcolm X a chance to air his views. Then when he does, they rush in panicky and report them."

Are you suggesting that the press ignore someone such as Malcolmn X?

"No. But I expect the press to report him objectively. When Malcolm X draws a crowd in Harlem, not 10 in 1,000 would follow him to a separate state or to Africa. Let the press find out who in the crowd would follow him. Let the press report Malcolm X in a more subjective way instead of just saying he's out to start rifle clubs. Let the press find out how many would follow him, where he gets his money, whether he's a con man or not, who is behind him.

"Let the press put him in proper context and cover him just as they do James Hoffa."

Mr. Young named the United Council on Civil Rights as an example of responsible Negro leadership. It is made up of heads of seven leading Negro civil rights organizations—Wilkins (NAACP), King (SCLC), Foreman (SNCC), Farmer (CORE), Mr. Young, Mrs. Dorothy Height, National Council on Negro Women, and Jack Greenberg, head of the NAACP Legal Defense Fund. These leaders meet regularly to decide what collective action they will take on civil rights.

But hasn't the press covered these meetings?

"They know about the meetings and when we hold them. We've been written up. But they don't seek us out when something like the Christmas boycott idea pops up. Baldwin, Lomax, Rep. Adam Clayton Powell pushed it. Our United Council rejected it because a boycott would hurt a lot of small retailers who employ Negroes. As with the stall-ins, we felt the Christmas boycott would be almost useless——any demonstration is useless when it's not focused, not specific.

"This was another failure on the part of the press to project responsible Negro leadership, the kind of leadership which produced the March on Washington last year. After that march, we suggested that Negroes keep marching to libraries, adult education centers, retaining centers, PTA meetings, if they wanted to put meaning into the March on Washington. It was almost a year before a wire service picked up this plea."

But adult education, job retraining, they don't present as dramatic a story to reporters as Malcolm X or the stall-in, do they?

"To a good reporter, job retraining is dramatic. Otherwise, he's lazy, has no creativity, no imagination," Mr. Young countered.

"When the Urban League takes 40 girls about to become domestic workers and retrains them so that 30 of the 40 are now working with major corporations, that's *dramatic,* isn't it? The *New York Herald-Tribune* showed how a beautiful piece could be done on this subject.

"The press should be informing the public of this positive aspect of civil rights."

AMERICAN TRADITION

Mr. Young lit another cigarette. "The press has failed to tell its readers that what the Negro is doing is nothing more than what Americans have been doing since Susan B. Anthony and the Woman Suffragists right up through the labor movement.

"But let a Jesse Gray show up overnight and create a rent strike and it gets top play."

Doesn't it deserve top press play?

"All I'm asking is for a little more balance in newspapers. For somebody to pick up a phone and talk to more responsible sources. In these critical times, the press cannot afford to give incorrect information. Reporters have to look beneath the headlines, to the person who can deliver the correct story."

What about the positive side of civil rights press coverage? Do you think there is one?

"Sure," Mr. Young said. "Many newspapers have helped gain public acceptance on civil rights laws in not only school desegregation but in other areas such as fair housing and employment. Depth reporting in this area has been outstanding.

"These laws got good local support from newspapers. Newspapers made segregation something undesirable. In many areas, it became unfashionable to discriminate openly. Last Summer, the *Chicago Daily News* did a series on civil rights that ran an entire month. It was a top job.

"Because of newspapers, many people no longer feel free to articulate primitive prejudices. So some of these same people form a new rationale, a more polite one and the word 'nigger' no longer is the thing to say unless these same people get delayed on the Triborough Bridge by a civil rights demonstration.

"I think the challenge to newspapers now is to make sure people don't accomplish their old segregationist objectives with new, more subtle schemes, ones that involve property, standards of education, a new vocabulary such as *neighborhood school concept.*

"This is the real challenge to newspapers, to all media——make it as much a status symbol to have diversity as it once was to have sameness. Make the norm inclusiveness instead of exclusiveness. Make people see that their own self-interests will be served by integration. Assure the insecure, frightened, unsophisticated who surround themselves with sameness that diversity won't put them in danger.

"The real challenge to the press is to create the kind of climate where people will have to apologize for anything that is all-white, except their own families, as a sign of insecurity."

ROBERT J. MANNING

15   Journalism and Foreign Affairs

■

Must the Press always be an adversary of the government?

Does the public have a right not to know?

Would journalists be more responsible in their reporting if they served some time as government employees?

These are just a few of the many challenging questions Mr. Manning submits for consideration in the following article on the special responsibilities inherent in reporting the government's foreign policy decisions to the American people.

A keen critic of journalistic ethics and a propounder of some unorthodox (and sometimes unpopular) concepts on the nature of these ethics, Mr. Manning's remarks were voiced before the National Editorial Association at Washington, D.C. on March 13, 1964.

At the time of his comments, Mr. Manning was Assistant Secretary for Public Affairs. Currently he is Editor of The Atlantic.

ONE IN MY LINE of government work, when he faces an audience of journalists, has the difficult choice of talking directly about his own work or dabbling more generally in foreign affairs.

The second alternative is probably easier, and certainly less risky. But I would prefer to talk tonight mostly about our business—— journalism and foreign affairs. I think there is much we can discuss; so I'll take the risk that before the night is out, I'll have proved myself akin to the Mark Twainian Daniel whom God, as the story goes "ordered forth into the lion's den, but he slipped and came in tenth."

Information gaps are probably inevitable in the best informed societies, and ours is no exception, however clearly defined the issues of foreign policy may be. What I have been struck by in the past few years are the special reasons for such a gap today——and the special peril it holds.

The reasons lie, of course, in the nature of our world. We live at the floodtide of change in all the continents. We are confronted with a totalitarian ideology that seeks our destruction. And we are riding the crest of a revolution in science and technology.

Each of the challenges we face would tax the wisdom, the ingenuity, and the patience of any generation of Americans. Together they pose a test greater than any our nation has confronted. Most acutely, they pose a test of public understanding.

This is a test made difficult by our history. We Americans are the product of a century of precious isolation. We developed our nation behind the protective shield of great oceans. In the mid-19th century Alexis de Tocqueville wrote that the American system of government was the best ever invented by man. He predicted it would be adequate to meet the needs of our society for many generations, unless the United States became actively involved in foreign affairs. The perceptive Frenchman did not try to predict what would happen in that eventuality because he considered it unlikely. Needless to say, it has happened, and with a vengeance.

Since World War II we have catapulted to a position of world leadership and full world responsibility. Yet our training as a nation for such leadership and responsibility has been minimal. The great and complex problems of this age are difficult enough for our policymakers to comprehend. How then are they to be adequately explained to and contributed to by the general public?

This Republic is in great peril when the public is inadequately informed. We see in many parts of our country today the results of public confusion on questions of foreign policy——a growing sense of frustration, among some groups, that has given rise to extremism; a quest for easy, quick "answers"; a search for scapegoats; a demand for such contradictory "solutions" as smaller budgets and "total victory," higher tariffs and freer trade, cheap security and reckless venturesomeness.

Without question, the subject matter of foreign policy is growing more complex. A great deal is happening all the time in foreign affairs all around our planet and, with the advent of rockets, in outer space as well.

We have our own national interest, our own set of foreign policies and foreign crises. These are diverse and complicated to a degree that frequently agonizes the most knowledgeable experts. But ours is a world of 120 other countries, of 120 other foreign policies, of 120 other sets of national goals or national appetites. Keeping track of what is going on, and translating it into terms understandable by large numbers of citizens, is a task that challenges both the press and the government departments concerned with foreign policy, primarily, of course, the Department of State and the White House.

The relationship of you, the press, and us in government in our open society is not a simple thing. It is at least as variegated as human nature and vulnerable to human frailty. The traditional stance of the press confronting government is the adversary relationship; its heraldic sign is crossed swords with bar sinister on a field of spilled ink. In domestic political matters excessive coziness between any element of the press and a reigning political group quickly and properly draws criticism.

In foreign affairs, however, I question whether the old-fashioned adversary relationship is sufficient to the delicate task our nation faces these days on the world scene. When you print the news, to an important extent you make the larger facts. What the press chooses to emphasize frequently becomes the postulates of public opinion (though I have some reservations on this point) and as such can become an important ingredient of policy. In such a situation is the public interest best served when the press and government stand on separate pedestals and snipe at each other across a mythical abyss? I think you will agree that the answer is no——and that journalism as well as government is aware of the need for something more. I suggest that accurate reporting perhaps requires a closer relationship than may have been traditional, perhaps a closer one than some here tonight would consider wise or possible.

On the basis of long experience in journalism and two years' experience in government, I suggest a direct cross-fertilization between American journalism and American government. Let me be as precise as possible, so as to avoid misunderstanding: The separation of journalism and government is as basic and as advisable as separation of church and state. Government intrusion into the functioning of journalism——whether by censorship, by regulatory controls, by economic penetration, or political manipulation——would represent serious jeopardy to our political system.

That accepted, there is more to be said about the subject. Countless times in these last two years I have wished that officials in government knew more about journalism, its needs, its practices, its uses, and its shortcomings. Even more convinced am I that journalists——most of them——need to know more, much more, about government, how it works, why it works and, sometimes, does not work; how decisions are made and how they are not made; what are the facts as against the myths and misconceptions.

There is one direct way to accomplish this. Journalism should encourage some of its top established hands, and some of its more promising new hands, to take leave for intervals of a year or two in government service. The government would profit from the infusion of versatility, energy, and enterprise that makes a good newspaperman. The newspaperman would become a wiser and more valuable craftsman. On his return, the newspaper reader would be better served and better informed.

The opportunities for newspapermen in government are not by any means confined to information work (which in many ways is the least demanding and least rewarding of the many activities for which a competent newsman is fitted). The governmental careers of men like Carl Rowan, William Attwood, and John Bartlow Martin, to name a few, suggest the high quality of service and imagination that a journalistic background can produce.

I suppose there are still some editors and publishers who, while sipping at the 19th hole with leaders of industry, banking, and commerce, will shake their heads and maintain that a newspaperman who enters into public service somehow taints himself for further journalism. It seems unfortunate that such thinking should survive the kerosene lamp and the automobile crank. I can think literally of no activity that has been more educational to me as a journalist than these past two years in government. In a time when, as H. G. Wells says, "human history becomes more and more a race between education and catastrophe," I heartily recommend a few semesters in Washington or at an embassy overseas.

Whatever steps might be taken to alter or improve the old adversary relationship, one point must be emphasized from the outset: It should neither suggest nor require any abdication of the critical faculties of the reporter and editor. Quite the contrary, the more thorough knowledge which skilled reporters today accumulate about what is happening in foreign affairs serves to invigorate, not weaken, the function of responsible criticism. On a subject like South Viet Nam——unquestionably one of the most difficult and sensitive issues confronting us——the access to information within the government that has been available to the press has provided the basis for the considerable number of well-informed and critical editorials that have appeared in recent weeks.

Irresponsible criticism is, of course, a different matter, but there is a very high correlation between misinformation, or lack of information, and the kind of wild criticism that graces the "hate sheets" of the right and reveals itself in the latent paranoia of a few newspapers and correspondents around the country. The reckless charges that pass for comment in these forums cannot survive exposure to information. It is no coincidence that with rare exceptions the writers (I hesitate to dignify them, and besmirch the craft, by calling them reporters) who regularly produce the most startling accusations about the State Department do not call my office or any other section of the Department to ask questions or check conclusions. Apparently they feel their concoctions will clang more loudly if not muted by the facts.

Leaving aside this category——in which, by the way, I place none of the regular State Department correspondents——it does seem to me that on the whole the job of communicating information about foreign policy is one that the press and the government have in common, not one in which our interests are opposed. The basic elements of my present job are remarkably similar to that of a reporter: to get out the news——fast, accurate, and as complete as possible. Nearly always my associates——several of whom are also former newsmen——and I are in the position of working with, not against, the reporters who cover foreign news and call us daily, if not hourly.

Information flows from the State Department in many ways. In testimony last year before Congressman [John E.] Moss's subcommittee on government information, James Reston of the New York *Times* described the Department as a "gabby outfit." Ours is a house with many windows, and its daily information output is enormous. Anyone who, as I have, has served as a correspondent in a foreign capital will vouch for the truth of the statement that nowhere in the world are reporters given such complete and unfettered access to the makers and shapers of foreign policy. As a practical matter, every State Department reporter has a government telephone directory which tells him what every officer in the Department does and who's in charge of what desk, area, or section. A reporter is not confined to a few known sources. Whatever the subject that arises, he can quickly pinpoint the individuals with responsibility and can call them directly, by direct dial, without having to filter through a central switchboard. Even home telephone numbers are provided——and are regularly used by reporters with late-breaking deadlines. The newsmen assigned to the State Department make wide use of this access-by-telephone every day. It is a source of information at least as important as the regular press briefings by the Department spokesman and the Secretary of State. Naturally, as in any area, he has to build his own network of sources who are able and willing to serve him. But the sources are there to be cultivated.

In addition, considerable use is made of background briefings. This is the device, treasured by reporters everywhere, whereby a high official will discuss subjects but not for direct quotation and not for attribution. The stories that result are generally authoritative and accurate, and they contribute greatly to the supply of information publicly available about United States foreign relations. They provide important guidance on the government's thinking on a given topic.

I have listened to a lot of nonsense about the so-called iniquity of the background briefing, but most of it comes from distant critics who make me agree with Josh Billings that "it is better to know nothing than to know what ain't so." Anybody with experience in reporting knows two things. One is that a reporter is only as good as his ability to separate fact from fancy, bogus from real. Another is that there is no such thing as goldfish-bowl diplomacy. Show me a businessman who conducts his business in a high-pitched voice at noon on Main Street, and I'll show you a diplomat who does his work by talking out loud on the front page of the Washington *Post*.

Heisenberg's principle of uncertainty in nuclear physics has a close analogy in foreign relations: It is usually not possible to describe a diplomatic situation publicly, however accurately, without changing it and making it different. The public comment itself becomes part of the situation. An on-the-record statement by the Secretary of State, be it a prepared speech or a response to a question, is instantly filmed, recorded, printed, and otherwise communicated, with all the speed of modern telecommunications, to a mixed audience of friends, partners, skeptics, and enemies all around the globe. Many are ready to seize on a single ill-considered word and blow it up for propaganda purposes. As a consequence, important comments issued formally on the record by high officials often must be planned as carefully as a surgical operation so that no listeners anywhere can have reason to misunderstand or abuse what is said.

That is why most newsmen highly value the background device, which permits a policy officer to speak freely and informally to let reporters in on his thinking without giving our cold-war adversaries the same access. At the briefing conferences conducted twice a year at the Department for the press and other media a mixture of on-record and background discussions have been used. After the most recent conference, we asked the participants to comment on this point; the 800 replies we received favored background briefings by four to one.

In a sense the background rule makes it possible for the government to take a reporter into its confidence. This calls for good faith on both sides, and it is nearly always present. The exceptions are happily infrequent, though no less irritating when they occur. It is a procedure that can be abused. It is an abuse, for example, for the government to use this method to float trial balloons, as a way to sample public opinion without choosing sides in advance, or in any way to mislead or misinform. It can be abused by reporters who fail to maintain the distinction between it and on-the-record briefings. But despite these pitfalls, its overall utility is great. The fact that a knife can be used to kill is no reason to eat with our fingers. The best safeguard against misuse of backgrounders lies in the skill and integrity of the reporters themselves. What is said on background or not for quotation is subject to the same acid tests of accuracy and relevancy as any other government pronouncement, and rightly so.

Let me examine another aspect of the government-press relationship. It is frequently argued that it is the government's responsibility to keep secrets, the responsibility of the press to get them and print them. "The press lives by disclosure," opined the *Times* of London in 1851. If a foreign agent came into the State Department and managed to procure secret information, he would be liable to prosecution and a heavy sentence. When a reporter does the same thing, he wins praise from his editor and gets nominated for prizes. The story is printed, and either way our enemies can read it.

In the year 1964 I think that this simplified, traditional view of the role of the government and the role of the press is out of date. I prefer to think that the responsibility both for informing the public and for maintaining certain areas of nondisclosure is one which is shared by the press and the government. To be sure, the press's responsibility is heavily weighted toward full disclosure: I would not wish it otherwise. But I believe, and I think I speak for the majority of reporters, that we would lose an important ingredient of the relationship of trust that is basic to how the press gets along with government if the press did not recognize its responsibility in circumstances of great national importance to help us keep some secrets.

I feel that I am on solid ground when I say this because I know from my experience in the past year that with rare exceptions the reporters who regularly cover the Department of State do recognize this responsibility. I know one reporter, for example, who is still sitting on a dramatic first-person story of his involvement in a recent great international crisis. Many others have happened upon or otherwise uncovered information which if immediately divulged would have caused us serious difficulties. They did not immediately rush it into print, recognizing that to do so would not serve their own interests as responsible journalists seeking to report the news accurately and fully, and might seriously prejudice American foreign policy objectives or national security.

THIRST FOR FOREIGN POLICY INFORMATION RISING

The responsibility for getting the news out is also one that we share. A great many things happen each day, only a few of which come to public attention——not because they are kept secret but because they are not considered news. The press itself is highly selective. Only a fraction of the information that pours into a typical city room survives the cutting and paring process called editing and makes its way into print. Douglass Cater has written that the power of the press,

> . . . stems from its ability to select——to define what is news and what isn't. In Washington on an average day, a good many hundreds of thousands of words are spoken, tens of dozens of "events" occur. The press decides which of those words and events shall receive the prompt attention of millions and which, like timber falling in a deep and uninhabited forest, shall crash silently to the ground.

Several independent studies show that an average of 3 to 8 percent of general news space in American newspapers is devoted to foreign affairs items. The average daily newspaper content of foreign news is four to eight columns. Foreign news actually sent by the Associated Press on its main ticker averages 22,000 words per day, or 27 columns. If nonduplicating items from other wire services plus special reports are included, it can be calculated that the average American daily newspaper provides its readers with well under 20 percent of the foreign news actually reported each day. I simply do not think that is enough.

The problem of making manageable the vast outpouring of news on foreign policy that becomes available each day challenges journalism in many ways. The press often still practices methods of makeup, construction, and play that were in use half a century ago. As a result, editors often seem to be overwhelmed by the torrent of events and their readers have served up to them a daily collection of fragments. That approach to foreign affairs may have made sense when the United States was involved in only one crisis at a time. It no longer suffices today, when we are participants or ringside spectators to 15 to 20 crises at a time. The frequent result is that each day's news on each topic is apt to be so brief, so fragmentary, as to be more misleading than no news at all. Too often, each day's fragment remains a fragment. As a result, in the words of the late Joe Liebling:

> Our present news situation, in the United States, is breaking down to something like the system of water distribution in the Casbah, where peddlers wander about with goatskins of water on small donkeys, and the inhabitants send down an oil tin and a couple of pennies when they feel thirst.

Ironically this comes at a time when the national thirst for foreign policy information is rising. The American people want to know what is happening, how it affects them, what we are doing about it. By any indication, including public opinion polls, more people are concerned about foreign policy than at any time in our history. Still one hears editors insisting that "the people" don't want to read a lot of foreign affairs guff. I do not believe it.

The inability of the daily media to keep abreast of this rising level of interest is reflected in the success of other enterprises, particularly magazines, which give at least the impression of providing a fuller, connected account of foreign news. Volume of information is not the problem; what is needed rather is a more reflective approach to foreign news which relates the snippets to one another, which locates an event in history as well as geography, and which takes more profound account of the fact that other people's domestic politics often influence their foreign policies.

SOME WORDS OF CRITICISM

I do not want to abuse your hospitality, and I therefore hope that some words of criticism will not be taken amiss; they come from a deep sense of involvement in the profession of journalism and a desire to see improvements. I do not presume to tell you how to behave——for I recognize that there is no mightier potentate than the proprietor of an independent newspaper. Many of you, I know, are editors or publishers of weekly newspapers, and I understand there is solid backing to the claim that weeklies are more extensively and carefully read than many dailies. I understand also that in many cases the weekly is the only newspaper its readers read. On both these counts, therefore, it is depressing to know that so many editors of weeklies disdain to provide their readers with much coverage of national and foreign affairs. I realize there are staffing and money problems, but in this age of communications wizardry, joint efforts, and speedy travel, the weekly community could easily and cheaply build up a service providing solid, well-written, and well-thought-out material on the big world issues.

Another more general characteristic of journalism today should cause more concern than it seems to be causing. The press today suffers from a bad case of complacency and self-righteousness and is noteworthy among all fraternities that perform public services for its lack of self-criticism.

Our press today is keenly, sometimes even stridently, assertive of its rights and prerogatives, but it has a bad case of laryngitis when it is time to talk about its responsibilities. If Congressman Moss will excuse me, I would like to say that the intellectual quality of a great deal of the testimony delivered to his subcommittee after the Cuban crisis was so low as to remind some of us of the old description of the Platte River in midsummer——two inches deep and a mile wide at the mouth.

When it comes to actual performance, I think the press in this country can be described as not only the freest and most imaginative but also the most responsible and best in the world. (One could make some reservations; for example, I would say that the very best in British journalism surpasses most of the best in ours.) But we cannot afford to stop where we are and be satisfied. There is still too much tendency among editors to operate on the old-fashioned presumption that the reader has the IQ of a 12-year-old child. There is still that ancient reflex that is mindful of the old Chicago city editor who once in anger called his staff together and said, "What this newspaper needs is some new cliches." There is great truth in the indictment that the press is generally too greatly preoccupied by entertainment, by what it takes to reach the easier side of reader interest.

I have the impression that journalism is not doing enough to recruit and properly train top-level people. I have been struck in years since the war to find that newspapers and magazines, even some very good ones, have to go out and cajole people into journalism. The tendency to call it a profession and pay as if it weren't is still strong, once you get away from the metropolitan areas.

As for the long vaunted "power of the press," where does that stand today? I confess that I am in a somewhat ambiguous state of mind; there are moments when I believe too many in government attach too much power or influence to the press; then there are mornings when I question that this is so. I think we have to concede that the power is indeed very great but that in general the press today is powerful more as an exciter than a provoker, and for the most part a channeler of other people's ideas and arguments. There has been a vast increase in analytical and interpretive reporting since the war, but still not a great deal of political, intellectual, theological, or philosophical inspiration comes with the average newspaper in America.

So the power of the press directly to influence is in great part a negative power, as it is exerted today; it stems in large part from others' ideas. This is also related to the power of omission that comes from the fact that each day the writers and the editors have to choose which large segments of a very large news budget they are *not* going to pass on to the public. I don't mean to suggest that there is not still in our press the power to do great good (and bad)——great power to make or break careers or ideas——but it is clearly limited, and the chief limit is set by the ability and the willingness of the possessors of this power to use it.

HANDLING OF FOREIGN POLICY NEWS

Coming back to my home ground, the handling of foreign policy news, I would like to comment, if I may, on two other tendencies that seem to me to create problems for all three elements——the newspapers, the readers, and the government.

One is the newspapers' feverish preoccupation not with what has happened but what is going to happen tomorrow. I know State Department correspondents who spend literally hours trying to learn the names of new ambassadorial or other appointees before candidates have even been selected. One prestigious newspaper over a period of several months had two separate "exclusive" stories reporting that a certain official had been picked as ambassador to two different capitals. The diplomat did not go to any one of those posts, and when he was actually appointed to his present post the newspaper neglected to report it. This overpreoccupation with getting ahead of events, to be the first to report what is *going* to happen, results in a lot of wasted motion, a lot of incorrect or highly premature stories, and any number of woes for government officials. More than that, however, it takes journalism's eye off the big part of the game——what *has* happened, what does it mean——to the detriment of us all.

Even the best writers and reporters——and I believe that the corps that covers the Department of State and foreign affairs in Washington

is by and large the most diligent and most talented group in journalism——are not always able to rise above the mixture of bugaboo
and custom that dictates the structure and the play of stories. They
are seriously handicapped by their editors' assumption that it is still
possible to report the world's major convolutions as if they are
innings in a ball game. This frequently leads to the scorecard wrap-up
of a number of otherwise unrelated episodes in foreign affairs, a
device that few reporters like but one that many editors cannot resist.
Usually the attempt is made to summarize a series of events around
the world as "victories" or "defeats" for U.S. policy.

Nothing is easier, and few things are more misleading, than to
chart the tides of foreign relations with a limited set of phrases taken
from the vocabulary of the sports page. The relations of nations in
the world arena are not like a ball game; victory and defeat are not
determined by the number of times a ball goes out of the park.
Evaluating progress in the cold war——forward, backward, sideways,
up or down——is a subtle process, one which the most penetrating
analysts usually avoid. They see all too clearly the folly of trying to
pick out who's ahead from day to day or week to week.

In a world where ideology confronts ideology, and both face the
quickening tides of nationalism; where foreign policy pronouncements by the leader of a nonaligned state may be motivated by his
domestic politics, and may in fact conflict with firm private assur-
ances to the contrary——and are understood as such by all concerned; where around the globe nations and peoples above all are
seeking their own form of development, their own definitions of
progress; where Communist states swap insults and plot their own,
nationally oriented paths in foreign and domestic policy; where our
own alliances experience the natural retrenchments that must occur
in a changing world——in such a world "victory" and "defeat" are
usually no more than words to be played with.

One of the occupational hazards of trying to keep score in foreign
affairs is that it sometimes makes the practitioner look silly. Not even
on the AP's weekly top-ten listings do teams plunge from victory to
defeat and back again with the erratic swiftness ascribed to U.S.
policy.

About three months ago a prominent weekly publication put together a scorecard roundup which opened with the sentence: "Russia,

the facts are showing, has lost the cold war." Two months later it printed a similar wrap-up which began: "Troubles of the world look somewhat less alarming than at any time in many years." A third installment, four weeks later, was summed up with this opening sentence: "America is going from defeat to defeat in almost every corner of the world." It even carried a map pinpointing the "defeats." Surely this must have strained the credulity of some of the magazine's readers. I venture to suggest that the world has not changed that much in three months, and to deal with the matter in such a sophomoric manner verges on insult. The cold war goes on, neither won nor lost, but invariably changing in its manifestation. America is not "going from defeat to defeat" (nor does a globe have corners).

A reporter must always guard against reporting the plausible as the actual, and this is certainly true in foreign affairs. What is likely or logical does not always happen in foreign policy; reporting likelihoods as facts before they come true is not far removed, it seems to me, from other kinds of misreporting.

There is an important difference, it seems to me, between the right of a reporter to pursue information about foreign policy, or any other subject, and the responsibility of his newspaper to print all the data thus uncovered. The right of the reporter to try to find out what is happening is limited only by his enterprise. I do not think any check beyond present security restrictions should be placed on a reporter's right to cover the news, which should be limited solely by his enterprise. But the obligation to disclose by publication is not so absolute.

The press discloses in the name of the public's right to know. But the public also has a right to have its interests defended and advanced in the field of foreign policy and national security. These two rights may come in conflict, and when they do, the public may well prefer success to disclosure. There have been many episodes in the past two years——of which the Cuban missile crisis was the most dramatic ——where the success of American policy depended very directly on the preservation of a period of privacy during which the policy could be formulated and carried out, where disclosure would have spelled defeat.

Where in these cases does the public interest lie? The public, I submit, has a right *not* to know when knowledge can gravely compromise our security or damage our foreign policy. Many reporters, among them the most able, respect both these rights. But their responsibility is less great than that of their editors, who are the ones who finally select what is printed——and is thus disseminated to the world at large, as well as the American people. It is not an easy responsibility to live with; it raises questions to which no single answer is right.

It is not for a government official to presume the right or the wisdom to settle this problem; it is journalism's to contemplate, and I am sure that many of you have pondered it.

PARTNERSHIP BETWEEN JOURNALISM AND GOVERNMENT

I have devoted much time to criticism because I have assumed that you share with me a belief that healthy criticism is always needed among those who labor in the world of ideas. I have not taken pains to reiterate the obvious—that the American press today is indeed the "fourth branch of government," in some ways the branch that is least captive of custom and least fearful to tread where the timid fear to enter.

A revelation of government service has been the discovery that this great partnership between responsible journalism and responsible government——wary, sometimes abrasive, sometimes argumentative ——works, and it works for the country.

A great nation devoid of intelligence, wrote Horace Mann, is "an obscene giant," destined despite its power and capacities, to "rush with the speed of a whirlwind to an ignominious end." We are together in striving to assure that this does not become our epitaph.

The perils we live with today are perhaps more subtle than those of World War II or the early days of the cold war. But they are no less real and probably more pernicious. Undeclared warfare backed by the challenge of thermonuclear weapons is a greater danger than we ever faced in the past. These are problems for all of us in press and government. To a very real extent we are partners in adversity.

PAUL MILLER

16   The Press and the World Scene

■

Reporting the world scene is becoming one of the most technologically advanced and vitally important areas of today's journalism. Basing his comments on the activities of the Associated Press, Mr. Miller envisions a day when transmitting news and photos by satellite will be a routine occurrence. Because the wire service is international, its bureaus are so many embassies throughout the world. And Mr. Miller urges that these bureaus report the news fairly and accurately as part of the wire service's implicit responsibility towards the amelioration of hostilities among foreign countries and the creation of a climate of international understanding.

Mr. Miller's ideas are set forth in the following article, an address he delivered on October 30, 1964, on the occasion of the two-hundredth anniversary of the Hartford Courant. Mr. Miller's speech is presented here in a slightly abridged format. One of America's most distinguished reporters and publishers, Mr. Miller is president of the Associated Press and The Gannett Company.

ADVANCES in the handling of international news remind us of journalistic progress since October 29, 1764. These run from newsgathering techniques through the production of the newspaper in its final form.

There have been wholesale changes in content, format and the philosophy of newspaper publishing. Instead of pastepot and shears, today's editor has a vast array of tools, electronic and otherwise, for collecting and processing news from all parts of the world.

[199

Not only has the reporting profession grown up. The circulation and advertising arts have been fostered and cultivated to a point where they have made possible financial independence for the press ——an independence which has placed the guidance of American newspapers largely in the hands of professionals.

Through their skills, marvels of ingenuity and invention have transformed newspapering into a much more effective means of mass communication. And with these changes——and because of them ——have come today's miracles of international news reporting.

If you examine the first issue of The Courant, you will find that nearly 80 per cent of its content was "foreign" news. Much of this was pastepot-and-scissors stuff. But the historic fact of The Courant's survival and growth attests that this newspaper was then as now meeting a need.

Yet "reporting" then was indeed different!

Consider an item from the first issue of The Courant. It is date-lined Madrid, July 10, 1764. This indicates it was some three months reaching Hartford. It begins:

"From the frequent arrival of couriers and the profound silence observed in relation to their dispatches, it is judged that there are some serious affairs on the carpet; and the more so, as the court is augmenting its forces by sea and land, and ships of war are building in all the yards of the kingdom with more ardour than ever."

Well, high-speed teletype circuits have replaced couriers, carrying news dispatches around the world. Attribution is almost mandatory. The time lapse between a news event and publication has been reduced from months to minutes. Many newspapers, including The Courant, no longer include the date in a dateline.

The Associated Press already has transmitted both news and photos via satellite. Within a comparatively short time, this will be routine.

In reviewing The Courant's two centuries, there is a temptation to belittle similarities and to dwell on change. But The Hartford Cour-ant became a force for good long before the age of science; indeed, long before the United States came of age as a nation. What made The Courant prosper is what keeps it prospering——the conscientious effort to serve its readers.

What I am about to say on the gathering, editing and transmission of foreign news is merely a progress report——not a last word. Among other things, in the foreseeable future it will be no more unthinkable for a reporter to go into outer space than it was for reporters to land in Normandy with Eisenhower.

In fact, the general manager of Tass, Soviet News Agency, told me that he had a commitment that he would have a Tass correspondent aboard when Russia undertakes its first manned voyage to the moon.

On hearing this, an associate of mine in Rochester wrote me a note: "How about us? Should someone, like The Associated Press, be making moves in this direction?"

Apparently as an afterthought, my associate wrote:

"P.S.——Please don't interpret this as a suggestion that The AP president go to the moon!"

The world has been shrinking, yet at the same time it has grown much larger. It takes only a few hours to cross the oceans. Yet there are many more individual countries to visit than there were even 25 years ago. The United Nations started with 50 members. Now there are 112; and it is growing so rapidly that the total figure may change even before this report is printed.

Some of these countries may not amount to much to the average American, but all are potential makers of news. And from time to time each has an interesting situation (to say the least) that needs to be reported. Today's press has the responsibility of telling their stories amid many overwhelming domestic and foreign issues, cold wars and hot wars.

The day is past when most of the news of Africa, for instance, could be gathered from the colonial offices in London and Paris. Even if African news were available there, our concept of unbiased news would make such an arrangement unthinkable.

Well how, then, is foreign news collected?

It is gathered painstakingly and at great expense by specialized organizations. The Associated Press invested $6,805,003 in foreign coverage last year. It and other news-gathering organizations exemplify for the most part the highest principles to be found in the individual newspapers they serve. Sensationalism largely is passé. Intelligent searching for trends, causes, ideas and cross-currents is the rule. For such work, the agencies of international news collection seek correspondents of integrity, political independence, enterprise and broad education. They come mostly from the ranks of outstandingly successful domestic newsmen.

The United Nations seems to have a better chance of success than had the League of Nations. If so, much of the credit must go to those persons who have worked tirelessly for the broadening of international channels of news communication.

I like to think that The Associated Press is a leader in this continuing effort at global enlightenment. It is the agency I know most about, but it is by no means alone. There are United Press International and Reuters, France Presse and the Japanese agency; National Broadcasting Company and the Columbia Broadcasting System and American Broadcasting Company. Then there are the foreign staffs of individual newspapers here and abroad; not to mention the controlled news agencies of Iron Curtain countries, led by Tass.

Thus the accuracy of world news reports is tested daily by the sharpest competition.

During more than half of the lifetime of The Hartford Courant, there has been an Associated Press. The cooperative principle of The AP was born when New York City publishers got together in 1848 to economize on telegraph tolls. Instead of each bringing in a news story, they arranged to bring it in once, then distribute it locally among all.

Later, the principle was expanded of course. The Associated Press grew stronger and more useful with the increase in the number of newspaper members, each obligated to supply the important news of its area to all other interested member newspapers.

For AP purposes, the world is divided into strategic zones, large and small, with a bureau responsible for news and picture coverage of each. The AP now serves 8,000 newspapers, radio stations and television stations in more than 100 countries. The full-time AP staff around the world numbers more than 3,000 of whom more than 800 are employed abroad.

In Germany there are a hundred AP staffers——newsmen, translators, photographers, photo editors, teletype operators, and so on. More than 350 newspapers and radio stations in Germany receive AP news. The U.S. editor thus benefits from coverage in depth to an extent which never was possible in earlier days.

Moreover, the sharing of AP news with the other nations of the world, while serving the cause of global understanding, is thrifty, too. And there's this added benefit from the marriage of news collection and distribution:——

Newspaper readers abroad are getting a more accurate picture of America. Before World War II, tens of millions of peoples had only a fragmentary and often distorted picture of America and Americans. Though slowly, it seems, that condition is being corrected in a doubly fortunate way.

For, since the War, the AP and UPI have emerged as by far the largest of the global news agencies. Both are operated in the pattern of American journalistic independence, initiative and integrity. And besides furnishing foreigners with more and better news about life in these United States, they also are providing our friends abroad with improved ideas of unbiased news gathering and news writing.

AP news is delivered in many languages. It strives for an objectivity and factuality that will make it read and believed in every nation.

Worldwide AP expansion has proceeded apace in recent years.

Take Africa.

Before World War II all of Africa was covered by one AP bureau at Cairo, plus scattered part-time correspondents. Today there are six AP bueaus in Africa——at Cairo, Tunis, Lagos, Leopoldville, Nairobi and Johannesburg. These are backed up by roving correspondents and photographers who criss-cross the continent.

Or take Latin America.

Twenty-five years ago the AP had four bureaus there. Today there are a dozen in key spots.

And here again, roving correspondents are going into areas where staff men aren't regularly stationed.

These correspondents are seasoned newsmen. They are abroad to work——to cover an area or a capital or even a nation as tirelessly as once they covered City Hall back home. Only on the late-late show's old-time movie will you see the foreign correspondent portrayed as a lone operator who peruses the local papers while sipping an apertif at a sidewalk cafe before strolling to the cozy little cable office to file his one story for the day.

The great flow of international news into the United States has accompanied a significant change in even the smallest daily news-paper in this country. Where 25 years ago little news of foreign origin could be found, even in some of our larger newspapers, today the volume is high. There are economic and physical limitations, of course, on how much foreign news can be published in an individual newspaper. There is an occasional complaint from abroad that American newspapers are interested only in news of revolutions or disasters. This is far from true.

Foreign news must compete, and properly so, with national, state and local news. All of these today also are being reported in greater depth. And the use of foreign news is determined by the news judgment of individual editors.

It may seem to some that a government crisis gets onto front pages with big headlines while a story about a new agrarian reform measure in Peru, say, is barely mentioned far back in the paper. Still, real progress is being made in the handling of interpretive stories——stories which may have a sweeping effect on some country's life over the next century.

More and more editors recognize a double responsibility; not only (1) to see that worthwhile stories get into print, but (2) to see also that the news is presented so as to capture the interest of the reader in any part of the paper.

In the writing, transmitting and publishing of foreign news, the newsman assumes the role as educator, as Dr. Kingman Brewster suggested last night. Although editors might be the last to admit that their work is educating, they must have the skill of an educator to use pictures and charts and history to give the news maximum meaning.

Yet no newspaper could, even if it wished, force all of its readers to take an interest in any single topic or category of topics.

At most, it can present the news clearly and as meaningfully as possible.

We can all take pride in the job being done by many small and medium-size newspapers to make world news meaningful.

There was a most unusual piece of enterprise last April 4 by the Huntington (West Virginia) Advertiser. A six-column headline read, "World Picture Suddenly Seems Brighter for West." With this, in boldface type, two columns wide, was a summary of news from world centers that led into a spread of bylined articles from Moscow, Budapest, New York, Rio de Janeiro and Washington.

Here journalism and education indeed joined.

Among large newspapers, the same might be said about the uses of Pages 2 and 3 in the Philadelphia Inquirer for foreign analyses; the Page 3 showcase of foreign features in the Baltimore Evening Sun; the Miami Herald's printing of some copy in Spanish. There are many, many more.

Interest in international news is increasing as individual horizons broaden. Foreign travel by individual Americans helps build an appetite for foreign news. So does service in the U.S. military forces abroad, or in the Peace Corps; likewise, membership in student exchange groups.

As any newsman knows, everyone with a special interest thinks any report of it belongs on Page 1. Repeating: My point here is that there is no simple formula for global news presentation. At least three variables are involved——

(1) the news-gathering agency or newspaper and its personnel;

(2) the individual newspaper and its editorial patterns and practices; and

(3) the reading appetites of the rank and file of newspaper readers, for the foundation of the pyramid is the public's interest.

Those who would advance the cause of world peace and understanding would do well to understand all three. They should grasp also the importance of having international news supplied by nongovernmental agencies.

Dictatorial governments may be able to suppress international news in their homelands for a time. But The AP international report flows freely between nations. And where The AP report can be freely published, the fairness of its news presentation helps lay the groundwork for international understanding.

Therein lies one hope for continued improvement in the coverage of foreign news. Another hope may be found in the now well developed tendency on the part of discriminating readers and listeners ——a tendency to ask, "Who says so? Who is reporting it?" The public there is exerting a very real——and very proper——pressure on all to tell the whole story accurately as well as interestingly.

Reflecting on the topic assigned to me, "the foreign coverage available to newspapers . . . and what they have been doing with it," I wish I could report that the world has experienced a breakthrough in its search for brotherhood and understanding; that new patterns of news gathering have made neighbors of us all; that new editorial techniques of presentation have made what we think readers ought to have as appetizing as what we think readers would like to have.

While we can't do this, we need not be disheartened. There is wider recognition that integrity and ingenuity of high order are required of those who operate and represent our news-gathering organizations. This same integrity and ingenuity, it also is recognized, mark the newspaper editors who most effectively evaluate and present the news.

There will always be someone to rise and declaim that "American newspapers aren't printing enough foreign news." As I said at the outset, there are similarities as well as dissimilarities between newspapering now and when The Courant was born. One of the similarities, I'd wager, is that on or about October 29, 1764, The Courant's ink-and-paste-bespattered editor had critics even then who complained not about the quality of foreign news, or even about its tardiness, but simply that there wasn't enough of it.

JOHN HOHENBERG

17 Tomorrow's Foreign Correspondents

■

Are foreign correspondents more than journalists? Are they not quasi-diplomats who make——and sometimes break——their nation's foreign policy, in addition to reporting it? What is the future of the specialized art of foreign correspondence? Where will the internationally oriented reporters of tomorrow come from? What will their problems be?

In the following article, a selection from the final chapter of John Hohenberg's Foreign Correspondence: The Great Reporters and Their Times, the pressures and responsibilities of the foreign correspondent are discussed in informed and comprehensive terms.

A veteran journalist, John Hohenberg is a Professor of Journalism at Columbia University Graduate School of Journalism and Secretary of the Advisory Board on Pulitzer Prizes.

THE JET PLANES that have annihilated distance now bring swarms of correspondents to any major break on the world's news fronts within a matter of hours, and the new electronic communications marvels insure quick transmission, although at relatively high cost. But a piece of wire, a beam of electrons, and some machinery, no matter how ingenious, have never yet covered a story. Before anything can be sent, some correspondent with the understanding of a Crotius and the physique of a long-distance runner must thread his way through the crowd, get at the news, understand it, write it, and hand it to the operator.

It is not difficult to understand, therefore, why the public believes that so much of our foreign reporting today resembles an unrehearsed mob scene in a Grade B movie. This impression is not confined to the United States by any means. The unfavorable image of the mass correspondent exists, too, in Britain and Western Europe, in Japan and India, and doubtlessly in a number of other places. The Communist press, having no bothersome tradition of press freedom, merely looks on and registers sardonic comment from time to time, reaping a certain amount of propaganda benefit.

The public's notion is, of course, grievously unfair to the serious professional correspondents of all nations who provide the world outside the Iron Curtain with the bulk of its international news. But it is not based on fancy. Let there be a summit meeting, a Cape Kennedy space shot, or a grand tour by president, pope, or queen, an emergency session of the United Nations, or a sally by a Soviet potentate into the unfriendly West, and the correspondents pour in by the hundreds.

No correspondent who has ever labored in such a strained situation can forget his angry first impression that most of the newcomers were phonies, that their credentials were wangled from careless or conniving news organizations, that they didn't file every five minutes and should therefore be barred.

But on closer examination, in such instances, the so-called phonies turned out to be perfectly respectable and professional foreigners representing the major papers and other services of smaller countries, the correspondents of prestige weeklies or monthlies, and the indefatigable radio correspondents. Whether they were alone in a country, or part of a small global team, it would have been difficult to bar any of them.

The nature of the problem may be illustrated graphically by examining the foreign correspondent force registered at the United Nations. To obtain accreditation, it is necessary not only to have a letter from the managing editor of a responsible newsgathering organization, but also to be scrutinized by the wise and experienced professionals who run the UN's press section. In normal periods when there is no crisis atmosphere at the green glass house on New York's East River, a total correspondent force of anywhere from forty to fifty does the global news work. But when there is an emergency, some 500 or more correspondents, at least half of them non-U.S. correspondents, show up with their valid accreditations and demand entry to the limited press space. The United Nations, accordingly, sets up a system of priorities, with wire services and major dailies, TV and radio, taking precedence, and the smaller papers last. At its greatest emergencies during the Suez crisis and the Khrushchev visit, the United Nations had to screen out correspondents in accordance with the circulation of their newspapers, the lowest receiving least attention.

At fixed spots, such as presidential news conferences in the United States and appearances of other national leaders in places where the news media can be controlled, similar procedures are routine when attendance must be limited for any reason. But where no control is possible, the very size of the correspondents' corps and the fast movement of the principals in the news make for complete chaos.

This situation was not created overnight. It is true that there were some like Herbert Brucker who during his term as president of the American Society of Newspaper Editors blamed much of the over-coverage on the growth of the electronic media. Certainly, the development of both radio and TV created complications. But long before the birth of world broadcasting, diplomats at Versailles bitterly attacked the work of the press. And in the 1920s, in the United States, foreign commentators were accustomed to reflect ungraciously on the unique ability of the American press to fall all over itself while covering such celebrated trials as the Hall-Mills and Snyder-Grey cases. In 1935, before TV, there were international complaints against the press for the circuslike nature of the trial of Bruno Richard Hauptmann in Flemington, N.J., for the kidnap-murder of the Lindbergh baby.

The issue was muted during World War II. There was more than enough work to keep thousands of correspondents busy, and the public wanted all the news it could get. But shortly thereafter, the press's foreign legion once more stirred up angry debate. At every international conference of moment after V-J Day, the spectacle of mass coverage sorely troubled diplomats, editors, and thoughtful correspondents alike. Then, in 1959, during Soviet Premier Khrushchev's tour of the United States, the so-called Battle of Coon Rapids brought the issue to a head. That was at the Roswell Garst farm in

Iowa, which the Soviet leader visited at the head of a mob of correspondents, photographers, and technicians.

In the aftermath of that garish exhibition, James Reston of the New York *Times* wrote, "We didn't cover the Khrushchev story, we smothered it. We created the atmosphere of hysteria. We were not the observers of history, we were the creators of history."

The AP sounded out its members at that time on whether some limitation should be imposed on correspondents, but the returns were inconclusive. The debate flared again after President Eisenhower's 22,000-mile good-will tour of Asia. Robert W. Richards of the Copley Press commented sourly: "Our part of the trip was herd journalism at its worst. . . . It's stupid, ridiculous and isn't worth it. The job should be left to the wire services."

At the Kennedy-Khrushchev meeting in Vienna in 1961, the confusion became pandemonium. "Perhaps," the AP reported, "the meeting was designed to ease the nerves of a jittery world. It did little for the nerves of jittery newsmen. The joint news conference was a study in babel: Too many questions, not enough answers. Picture 1,500 newsmen all trying to ask questions in a score of languages, simultaneous translation, a la United Nations. . . . The confusion was terrific." However, no method was developed for a limitation on correspondents.

Then came the assassination of President Kennedy in Dallas on November 22, 1963. The correspondents were the eyes and ears of the world that tragic day. What they did and what they wrote, in a magnificent display of journalism under pressure, helped piece together the murder of John F. Kennedy for a stricken nation and showed the rest of the world that it was closing ranks behind Lyndon B. Johnson, his successor. The period during which the news agencies and newspapers, the news magazines, the TV and radio stations poured out the story in the United States sent a thrill of sorrow and compassion around the world. It brought a Pulitzer Prize to Merriman Smith of UPI. The kings and the dictators and the democratic leaders all heard the news first from him and his fellow correspondents in Dallas, as did the humblest citizens. Halfway around the world, outside Madras, an unlettered Indian sweeper woman asked her employer in wonderment, "Is it true that the King of America has been killed?"

Yet, there was criticism of the role of the press as well as praise.

When Lee Oswald was led manacled before the TV cameras as the alleged slayer and himself was shot and killed before 40,000,000 witnesses by Jack Ruby, the proprietor of a strip-tease emporium, the New York *Times* wrote: "The Dallas authorities, abetted and encouraged by the newspaper, TV and radio press, trampled on every principle of justice in their handling of Lee H. Oswald." To which the Dallas *Times Herald* added that the police made the second murder possible by accommodating the press in announcing the hour for Oswald's transfer. Nevertheless, on March 14, 1964, when Ruby was convicted and sentenced to death in Dallas, the proceedings were on TV.

"It will be a long time," Brucker wrote, "before the full story of what happened in Dallas is told. But there seems little doubt that TV and the press must bear a share of the blame."

Again, Brucker raised the cry for pool coverage on a limited scale but, for all his eloquence, he did not rally many from the profession itself to his side. This was not so much because of any presumed invasion of the rights of a free press; rather, as it was put by Wes Gallagher, general manager of the AP, a pool could very well result "in hundreds of newspapers depending on the reportorial skills of Joe Glotz of the *Toonerville Blatt*. This is not the type of service the members of the AP should receive."

Granting the "priceless values" of unrestricted news coverage, Brucker pleaded nevertheless, "But why should that mean also that we must allow regiments of reporters, photographers, broadcasters and their camp followers to multiply without limit or purpose? They all see the same thing. And all they do is get in each others' way, if indeed they do not distort or besmirch the event whose independent course they are supposed to chronicle.

"Publishing an infinite variety of news and views is one thing. A thousand eyes on a single event is another. Just how many lads *does* it take to watch one rat hole?"

If there had been a great revulsion against herd journalism, it would have come early in 1964 when Pope Paul VI was trapped in a screeching mob in the Old City of Jerusalem, partly because the Jordanian authorities failed to provide security, partly because there were too many journalists, real and fancied. But the Pontiff made no protest at the time, nor did any move to limit correspondents gain many supporters.

As Milton Bracker wrote in the New York *Times* just a short time before his death: "The symbolism of where the Pope was, and what he did, as recorded by TV, radio, tape recorder, color camera and typewriter was more important than the degree of serene piety he was able to attain while doing it. . . . It is now unmistakably apparent to millions of people around the world, including many to whom the Pope was a vague figure . . . that he is actually one of the most important human beings on earth."

There is bound to be a further increase in the numbers of correspondents. That means there will be more incidents, more protests, more pressures for self-regulation by the press under threat of some more arbitrary intrusion. It is possible, of course, that some more responsible system may be worked out on a trial-and-error basis. In the United States, at such a major event as the presidential election night of 1964, the New York *Times* and other newspapers contracted with CBS News to obtain fast voting totals and the AP contracted with NBC News for a similar service, enabling TV to concentrate on the immediate news and the press to put its major effort on detail and analysis. Some such division of labor and responsibility, arrived at through sheer necessity, will be required if the problem of the multitude is to be resolved. Herd journalism has reached such a hopeless state of confusion abroad that it is nothing more nor less than an international disgrace. Some form of regulation, voluntary or not, is bound to come by public insistence if for no other reason.

The foreign news editor of the New York *Times,* Emanuel R. Freedman, once asked a dozen journalism graduate students where they would want to be assigned if they worked for him. With one exception, the youngsters chose London or Paris. The nonconformist, a trenchcoat type, bravely chose a supposedly wild and uncivilized area, Hong Kong.

Freedman, having piloted his staff into a Pulitzer Prize in international reporting, wasted no time explaining the missing factor in the calculations of the would-be correspondents. He needed no correspondents in London, Paris, or Hong Kong. "Where we do need young corespondents of good health, energy, and ability," he went on, "is in Africa, particularly sub-Sahara Africa and East Africa. That is where a great deal of news will be made from now on, and we want good people, trained people, to cover it. Also, we need more young and active correspondents in Southeast Asia. We want good people, too, who are trained to appreciate the growth of India and Pakistan, and we look just as hard for specialists in Latin America. But they must be trained journalists first."

He was asked about the linguistic qualifications of correspondents of the future and set back his auditors once again. "It is all very well to cultivate an expert knowledge of Spanish, French, and German," he replied, "but to some Russian will be more useful. And to young people who want to get on as foreign correspondents, I'd say that it was important to learn such languages as Chinese, Japanese, Hindi, Urdu, and Swahili. We can't cover the world from Washington, London, Paris, and Hong Kong, and our correspondents can't go on not knowing languages that are spoken by far more people than there are in any country in Europe except Russia."

Slowly the global news network is being extended to cover the missing factor in international correspondence. It may take years to right the imbalance, costs being what they are and journalistic budgetary efficiency being in short supply. While all newsgathering organizations jealously guard their profit-and-loss sheets, it is scarcely a secret that some American managers pay as high as $50,000 a year to maintain a correspondent abroad while others do a more modest job for $18,000. These figures do not include transmission costs of messages and articles.

Some foreign newsgathering organizations claim to be able to cover the United States at $15,000 a year per correspondent, with transmission costs extra, but some kind of subsidy is probably involved. The figure given by a first-rate Indian newspaper manager, who said he had to spend $25,000 a year to maintain an American correspondent before even a single message was sent, is undoubtedly more realistic. The wire services, being able to concentrate their staffs and arrange for less movement per correspondent, have the lowest individual costs.

If there is any single factor that encourages the transmission of news from the world's underdeveloped areas, it is the British penny-a-word rate, formerly known as the "Empire Rate," which is available to any bona fide correspondent transmitting press messages from one part of the Commonwealth to another. On October 1, 1941, on the initiative of Brendan Bracken, then Minister of Information, the rate was set to stimulate maximum news exchanges between Commonwealth nations during World War II. Cable & Wireless Ltd., by 1945, was handling 2,000,000 words a week of press material. Six years later, the file was down to 500,000 words a week, but even this was 136 percent more than the prewar total. The extent to which foreign reporting between Commonwealth countries has increased since is shown in the 1,320,000 words a week of press material that were handled at Commonwealth Rates in the twelve months ending in April, 1963. The totals were issued by the British Post Office Overseas Telegraph Services at Electra House, London, now the operative agency.

Few seriously believe that the Commonwealth Rate is economically feasible, particularly with the coming of the trans-Atlantic and trans-Pacific telephone cables, and the expanded microwave system for overland transmission. These new links, with their manifold channels for the transmission of messages and pictures and teletypesetter tapes at rates of up to 1,000 words a minute, have greatly reduced disruption of service. While the radio communications satellites eventually may be a challenge, the cables operated by multinational agencies have come to stay. And although they are efficient, they are also expensive.

Thus, it may fairly be said that all the wire services benefit from the Commonwealth Rate. Reuters may be aided more than the others because much of its traffic is between Commonwealth countries. But Agence France-Presse routes its Far Eastern service from India and Singapore through London, then back to Paris, in order to take advantage of the penny-a-word rate where it does not have radio teletype service which is paid for on a time basis. The American agencies and newspapers do much the same thing where it is to their advantage.

Press Wireless, Inc., an American cooperative that is privately operated, also reduces the transmission costs to its members, which include the most powerful organizations engaged in the dissemination of international news. And the International Telecommunications Union, a specialized agency of the United Nations, exists for the purpose of trying to equalize transmission rates, press and others, a process that has made comparatively little headway in recent years.

If correspondence in the world's underdeveloped areas is to be substantially increased, some international arrangements similar to the Commonwealth Rate will be necessary. Those who are familiar with the operation of the British arrangement have speculated, for example, on whether there could be a NATO Rate, binding together the nations of the Atlantic alliance, or a SEATO Rate for Asia. It would take something like this to make correspondence between African nations and Asian nations more practical for more newspapers. As the matter now stands, such agencies as Reuters are handling the bulk of the traffic between African nations south of the Sahara, and all four global agencies are fighting for a share of the business in Asia and Latin America as well.

The distribution of correspondents for American news media on a global basis in 1963 illustrates the problem in general, since they are the most prosperous and therefore able to maintain the largest group outside their own borders. A recent census taken in eighty-four countries by John Wilhelm, director of McGraw-Hill World News, gave these totals:

OVERSEAS CORRESPONDENTS FOR U.S. MEDIA 1963

Area	U.S. Citizens	Local or other nationals	Total
Asia and Australia	109	146	255
Europe	285	341	626
Middle East	17	47	64
Africa	20	39	59
Latin America	84	145	229
World Totals	515	718	1,233*

* Of this total, 310 are listed as stringers. Since there are literally thousands of stringers, these presumably are the ones who were considered by the checkers to be more or less permanently employed and file at regular intervals. J. H.

Wilhelm's total appeared to be more realistic than some of the previous efforts at such a census, although he couldn't please everybody. Admittedly, he failed to list some correspondents. He was also too charitable in extending his definition of a foreign correspondent to some part-timers, stringers, and free-lancers. And he was ungenerous to the wire services and the New York *Times,* which in 1964 still maintained the best foreign service in the world.

Without underwriting every figure in his survey, an independent check indicated that he had at least outlined the main trends in the growth of the work of American news media abroad. London was still the leading news center overseas, with a listing of 183 correspondents, 73 of them Americans. Paris, Rome, West Germany, and Brussels all were reasonably well covered in Europe. In Moscow, there were 16 correspondents for American news media. By contrast in the Far East, only Tokyo and Hong Kong rivaled the European news centers. India, Pakistan, and Indonesia all were underrepresented, as was much of the rest of the world.

The dictates of national pride, plus the undoubtedly more economical operation, were the chief factors in the very large engagement of non-American citizens by the American news media, particularly the wire services. At the home office of Reuters in London, seventeen nationalities were represented in the editorial department in 1964, and there were almost as many in the home office of the French news agency. By and large, the trend toward the internationalization of the global news agencies, in personnel as well as in service, had been long overdue. It was brought about by sheer necessity.

As far as American newspapers were concerned, American correspondents still predominated in the mid-60s.

The main reason for the gain in American foreign coverage was the establishment of new foreign services and combinations of older ones. Among the newcomers was the combined Washington *Post*-Los Angeles *Times* service and the Copley Press service. The older New York *Herald Tribune* and Chicago *Daily News* services also effected a working combination.

There was growth, too, in the staffs of the three national TV-radio chains, NBC, CBS, and ABC, and spot foreign coverage by Westinghouse radio. The news weeklies all broadened their foreign staffs, with *Time-Life* as the leader by far. The specialized staffs, including those of the *Wall Street Journal,* McGraw-Hill, and Fairchild, also gained. Smaller syndicates were in operation, such as North American Newspaper Alliance, while the *Patriot-Ledger* of Quincy, Mass., was running a foreign background service for small papers known as "the poor man's New York *Times* foreign service." Among the papers that maintained foreign specialists in the home office, ready for service where needed, were the Miami *Herald* and Miami *News* in

Florida, the St. Louis *Post-Dispatch,* and others. It was one way to beat the cost of a permanent foreign service.

Such pressures resulted in gains in Latin American coverage in the mid-60s. Fourteen new bureaus were established by U.S. media alone in Latin America, notably in Mexico City, Rio de Janiero, and Buenos Aires. Reuters joined the other three global agencies in opening a special service to Latin America. The Latin American journalists themselves began moving at a faster rate to cover their own continent.

Yet, there and elsewhere, the bare spots——the missing factors ——continued to trouble every thoughtful and discerning editor. They were doing what they could with available resources, but they knew it wasn't enough. Great stretches of Africa and Asia, in particular, were still without representation in the world's news network. And in a country as important to the United States as the Republic of Korea, where 55,000 American troops still remained after an uneasy ten-year truce, not a single U.S. national was permanently assigned. While the Korean correspondents in the area were first-rate, the great concern about non-American correspondents there and elsewhere remained the possibility that they could be put under pressure by their governments in time of crisis. The answer from the agencies was what it always has been, "We can get men in there in two hours, if necessary."

Impressive though the gains were, they did not cancel out the reality that the great bulk of foreign news was still brought into the United States by the wire services, principally UPI and AP with Reuters maintaining a foothold. After that came the newspapers—— the New York *Times,* New York *Herald Tribune*-Chicago *Daily News,* Washington *Post*-Los Angeles *Times, Christian Science Monitor,* Chicago *Tribune,* Baltimore *Sun, Wall Street Journal,* Washington *Star,* Copley Service, and a scattering of others; the news weeklies, *Times-Life, Newsweek,* and *U.S. News and World Report;* McGraw-Hill and Fairchild, of the specialized services, and TV-radio chains, NBC, CBS, and ABC, with Westinghouse showing new foreign interest for radio alone.

The old Paris *Herald,* as the New York *Herald Tribune's* Paris edition was still known to newsmen, carried on despite the challenge of the New York *Times International Edition.* Although the *Herald* was not a great money maker, it was in better shape than its rival in early 1964. At that period, the *Times* had suspended publication of its West Coast edition, and it also had to change its original concept of the international edition as a mere duplicate of the New York edition. The *Times*'s troubles with its satellite publications did not, of course, affect its overall position which remained affluent.

While no one can guarantee a completely accurate count of all the permanent foreign correspondents outside the Iron Curtain, most knowledgeable editors believe the American force represents from one-quarter to one-third of the total. This is predicated mainly on the roughly 625 foreign correspondents in the United States in 1964, with slightly more based in London and Paris. The smaller European newspapers, particularly the Swiss under the leadership of the *Neue Zürcher Zeitung*, cover Europe more intensively than do the Americans. The British put considerably more manpower into the Commonwealth countries. As for the French, Agence France-Presse is putting up a stubborn and determined campaign to get back into major competition in Asia, Africa, and Latin America, as well as in Europe. The fact that various French government agencies paid a substantial sum in annual subscriptions to Agence France-Presse, as reported in *L'Echo de la Presse et de la Publicité,* indicates the interest of the nation in this effort. There is one other difference with American practice: most great newspapers in England, Europe, and Japan want more direct news from Moscow and Peking than does the bulk of the American press.

It should not be imagined, however, that American newspapers are the most prosperous in the world or that American news coverage dominates the world media outside the Iron Curtain, despite numerical superiority. The British, the West Germans, the Japanese, and the French are all serious competitors. While the *Times* of London may have lost part of its intellectual leadership to the *Economist* and some of the Sunday newspapers, the old Thunderer still maintains a small staff of foreign correspondents and sets the pattern on many a major foreign story. There is substantial influence, too, among the smaller foreign staffs of the London *Daily Telegraph,* the *Guardian,* the *Observer,* and the *Sunday Times,* while the *Daily Mail* and *Express,* the mass circulation leaders, can always kick up a row.

The influence of the United States is even less apparent in the columns of the French press where *Le Monde, Figaro,* and *France-Soir* usually set the tone of a thoughtful and well-ordered foreign coverage. If the critical content of French foreign correspondence has increased in recent years on most news bearing on American foreign policy, it is readily understandable. The French have elected to go their own way, within Gaullist reason; it is reflected, therefore, in their press. The 100 percent American, in fact, will search in vain for a foreign newspaper of standing anywhere in the world that is a mere echo of Washington. From West Germany to Japan, from Italy to Korea, from Scandinavia to India and Pakistan and the Philippines, it is a hard but scarcely unpalatable truth that foreign correspondents writing on American affairs reflect their national interests to a very large extent. The same thing is true when such correspondents venture to explore those areas of the world that constitute the missing factor in international coverage.

In view of the sophisticated methods of the newer censors over three-quarters of the earth's surface, such diversified reporting is likely in the long run to be a help rather than a hindrance to international understanding. Thus, there is essentially little difference between the lack of direct censorship in most Communist bloc countries and Red China, and the very heavy, virtually punitive censorship that exists in a number of the newer nations of Africa and the Middle East. The end result is the same.

As the AP put it in its annual report for 1963: "The traditional censor is not the only foe of a free flow of information. Just as effective is censorship at the source——a reluctance by responsible officials to talk to newsmen or even make themselves available to answer questions.

"Still another formidable weapon is 'responsibility censorship.' This entails reprimands to newsmen for articles after they appear in print. Sometimes there is expulsion or threat of expulsion from a country."

The comment of Earl J. Johnson, editor of UPI, is pertinent in this connection: "Experience in global reporting teaches us that almost no government anywhere would scruple to take advantage of a supine press. . . . There is no doubt that official restrictions tend to dampen news initiative. In countries which have had censorship over the years, editors begin to accept it as a way of life."

Just before the 1963 revolt in South Viet Nam, Joseph Alsop, Marguerite Higgins, and *Time* magazine bitterly accused a few resident American correspondents in Saigon of being unfair to the regime of Ngo Dinh Diem. The defendants replied in kind.

It was the most violent argument over journalistic practice since the McCarthy era. Yet, despite the charges of the Alsop-Higgins-*Time* alliance, most of the foreign correspondents familiar with Saigon tended to support the chief defendants——Malcolm Browne of the AP, Neil Sheehan of UPI, and David Halberstam of the New York *Times*. In fact, Charles Mohr, chief *Time* correspondent in Southeast Asia, resigned in protest over his magazine's highly unusual role in the affair and joined the New York *Times*. Sheehan went to the *Times* a year later for more conventional reasons.

Nobody accused the correspondents of lying except, of course, the embattled Diem government. Alsop conceded that what they had written was "true or part true." What he objected to was what he termed a "high-minded crusade" against President Diem. Miss Higgins, on her part, took offense at the repeated stories out of Saigon that the United States and the Diem forces were losing the war against the Viet Cong, the Communist guerrillas.

"Reporters here," she wrote angrily, "would like to see us lose the war to prove they're right."

As for *Time,* no model of disinterested journalism, it complained piously of distorted and exaggerated reporting: "The reporters have tended to reach unanimous agreement on almost everything they have seen. But such agreement is suspect because it is so obviously inbred. The newsmen have themselves become a part of South Viet Nam's confusion; they have covered a complex situation from only one angle, as if their own conclusions offered all the necessary illumination."

To which Halberstam replied with no less vigor and forthrightness: "What's been exaggerated? The intrigues, the hostility? It's all been proven. We've been accused of being a bunch of liberals but even that's not true."

As a matter of fairness, the critics of the resident correspondents of

1963 should have looked at the record a year earlier. Had they done so, they would have found the redoubtable Homer Bigart writing of his experiences as a New York *Times* correspondent as follows:

"Saigon is a nice place to spend a few days in. The food and wine are good, the city is attractive, most hotels and restaurants are air-conditioned. But to work here is peculiarly depressing.

"Too often correspondents seem to be regarded by the American mission as tools of our foreign policy. Those who balk are apt to find it a bit lonely, for they are likely to be distrusted and shunned by American and Vietnamese officials."

Just how far the Vietnamese government and the infamous *Times* of Viet Nam might have gone in their war on the correspondents will never be known. For at 4:14 A.M. on November 1, 1963, the first bulletin on the military revolt in Saigon banged into the New York office of the AP. It came, not from the correspondents in Viet Nam whose output was tightly controlled, but from Bangkok. Tony Escoda, an energetic and talented Philippine citizen who had taken no part in the argument, scored a 42-minute beat for the AP over his American opposition. It was some time before the regulars in Saigon could get their stories out through censorship. But when they did, the fact that the Diem regime was overthrown and its two leaders killed bore out the worst forebodings of the resident correspondents.

Browne, Sheehan, and Halberstam were credited with having helped change the policies of the U.S. government in Viet Nam by their accurate reporting that the war was being lost at a time when all officials on the spot were claiming victory. "We maintained an independent position," Halberstam said. "While we were sympathetic to the aims of the U.S. government, we had to be critical of the representatives of our government who created a policy of optimism about the war that simply was not justified. There was no choice for us. We had our duty to our newspapers, the public that reads them, and that was to tell the truth." Browne and Halberstam won a Pulitzer Prize for their work in Viet Nam. Sheehan, despite his excellent work, was unfortunate enough to have missed the reporting of the revolt, having been recalled to Tokyo for two weeks at the time.

Even though the revolt did not produce a strong government, and in early 1964 was succeeded by still another coup, the argument against the resident correspondents was dropped. Alsop and *Time* went on to other things. So did Miss Higgins from a new base, *Newsday,* at Garden City, N.Y.

The Viet Nam affair demonstrated anew that foreign correspondents, like all other journalists of consequence, are able to exercise an entirely independent ability to shape the news in an open society. It is a unique function that not only approaches diplomacy but, at times, actually becomes a part of the diplomatic forces that bear on the conduct of international relations. As such, it can serve as a stimulant in changing the course, and sometimes even the character, of the flow of international news for public consumption.

There is nothing particularly new about this. George Wilkins Kendall was no mere fact-gatherer when he was under fire with the American armies in Mexico in 1846 and 1847 while he was the war correspondent of the New Orleans *Picayune.* He was the glorifier of the spirit of manifest destiny and he pretended to be nothing else. Nor did William Howard Russell topple the Aberdeen cabinet and save Britain's beleaguered forces in the Crimea a few years later with pat-a-cake journalism in the *Times* of London. Well-nigh a century later, no reader of Ernie Pyle's World War II pieces for the Scripps-Howard newspapers could fail to be moved by his personal involvement with GI Joe, a powerful factor in creating a toughened national morale.

Until the advent of an era when a whole civilization could be destroyed by a careless or accidental act, putting in flight an unstoppable missile carrying a hydrogen bomb, there was no serious thought of curbing the power of the journalist in the Western world. His news-generating function, even when used to excess, was viewed as a desirable part of the Western liberal tradition. Indeed, the Constitutional guarantee of freedom of the press was upheld, even when it was irresponsibly abused, on the ground that the right to untrammeled publication was worth the cost of the excesses. Yet, in the sixteen years that followed the birth of the atomic age, three Presidents spoke out in one way or another against what they considered to be security violations of the American press. To keep the record straight, such alleged violations were consistently denied and not one was ever proved.

In any event, President Truman issued Executive Order #10290, setting what he called "minimum standards" for government procedures in 1951 and thereafter for handling security information. While President Eisenhower modified the order, he struck out in another direction by commanding Defense Department officials to measure any proposed news release by determining whether it would make "a constructive contribution to the primary mission" of the military. Finally, in the sodden aftermath of the Cuban invasion disaster in 1961, President Kennedy challenged American publishers as follows: "Every newspaper now asks itself, with respect to every story, 'Is it news?' All I suggest is that you add the question, 'Is it in the national interest?' "

Viewed in this context, the events in Saigon preceding the violent end of the Diem regime take on a deeper meaning. If the American authorities there did consistently mislead reporters and investigate their news sources, as David Halberstam has charged, then certainly the press was entitled to ask whether such actions were in the national interest. It took all the tact and diplomacy of Henry Cabot Lodge, in the role of American ambassador after the Saigon uprising, to smooth over the difficulties between the American mission and the correspondents and prepare the way for his successor, General Maxwell Taylor.

What Lodge could not do was to lay down, with finality, a position between the press's insistence on the public's "right to know" and the government's effort to substitute for it, in sensitive cases, the public's "need to know." Many have attempted to provide a workable policy that would satisfy both these conditions, but none have succeeded. The reason is quite clear. It was stated as follows by Clifton Daniel, one of the most distinguished of the New York *Time*'s foreign correspondents:

"If you ask me who decides what the people need to know, I can only say, 'the editor.' If he can't do that, he has no right to the title. If he allows someone else to do it for him——the government or some special interest——he forfeits his freedom."

It would be both an indignity and an injustice to the professional foreign correspondents of well-nigh two centuries to consider their efforts as a mere prelude to some thunderous development in the international reporting of tomorrow. Furthermore, it would not be true. Changes, on the whole, come slowly in journalism.

With all the troubles that lie ahead of tomorrow's foreign correspondents, they will do very well, indeed, if they are able to maintain the right to present an independent point of view in international affairs to a sufficiently large and appreciative audience. If they can manage to attract a greater audience, or extend their services to places where independent voices are not now heard, then a free society will be deeply in their debt.

Unless circumstances change drastically, however, the odds may often be against them in their quest for news. The spread of censorship and of authoritarian press methods is not likely to be halted and rolled back very soon. Nor is the deadly contest between the independent nations and the regimented society of the Communist states on the way to a quick settlement, regardless of the thaw in Eastern Europe and the Sino-Soviet conflict. In such a situation, the independent correspondent is likely to encounter increasing difficulty.

MARK F. ETHRIDGE

18 The Newspaper That Will Endure— A Summing Up

■

Despite the onslaught of such scourges as television, higher over-head and the situation of there being no newspaper competition in ninety-six percent of American cities, Mr. Ethridge believes the news-paper will endure——in one form or another. The reason——and it is a two-fold one——is that together with a rising standard of intelli-gence among readers there is a corresponding rising standard of re-sponsibility among newspapers. The two factors interacting upon one another give strength to each other. Moreover, there is also the fact that there is nothing——but nothing——like a well-edited, objec-tive, vigorous newspaper to give people an in-depth insight into the important issues that concern them.

Mr. Ethridge's lively comments are contained in the following article, an address he delivered on October 30, 1964, on the occasion of the two-hundredth anniversary of the Hartford Courant. Mr. Ethridge is editor and vice-president of the Long Island Newsday.

MOST of what has been said today about communications, particu-larly newspapers, should be put against the background of a socio-logical revolution which the United States is undergoing.

When he was inaugurated as president of Yale University, Kingman Brewster, the speaker of last night, said, among other things, "The next decade of our trusteeship must cope with three revolutions: the explosion of knowledge, the burgeoning population and the uncanny development of automated machines and mechanized intelligence." Dr. Brewster would now undoubtedly like to add as the fourth revolution which we are witnessing and in which we are living, the fight for civil rights.

I don't know of any industry that has been more affected by the sociological revolution that has taken place since World War II than the newspaper business. It manifests itself in many ways as far as we are concerned:

In the decline of the number of newspapers. In the past ten years, 202 dailies have died, or reverted to weeklies. In the same time 171 have been started, most of them suburban. No new newspapers have been started in cities of more than 100,000 in the past 15 years, except in Portland, Oregon; Phoenix, Arizona; Jackson, Mississippi, Atlanta and Oklahoma City. The first three have died. Since I entered newspaper work 35 percent of the dailies have disappeared.

In the trend toward monopoly, merger, printing corporations and 24-hour newspapers. Ninety-six percent of the cities in the United States have no daily newspaper competition. Chains, or groups, as some of them prefer to be called, control 50 percent of the circulations of daily newspapers. There are 23 states with cities that have no daily newspaper competition, several more with only one competing newspaper situation. The trend toward monopoly, merger and 24-hour operations will continue, I venture.

This sociological revolution manifests itself in the fact that 20 percent of the American population moves each year, chiefly to the cities and the suburbs. Dr. Gallup said today that whereas 80 percent of the American people were farmers a century ago, only a tenth of that number, 8 percent, are on the farms now.

The mass migration has created a host of problems: the decay of the core of the cities, the creation of slums, the disruption of tax structures, the extreme employment sensitivity to the shifting of defense industries, the demands of the urban and suburban counties for greater and fairer representation in their state legislatures and in the lower House of the national Congress, shifting the balance of power from the rural to urban and suburban areas of the country and in the demand for a greater measure of civil rights, sometimes leading to riots.

It has affected newspapers, too. There has been a decline in the number of metropolitan newspapers and a great increase in suburban papers. Department stores and shopping centers in metropolitan areas have followed their customers to the suburbs and have created new shopping habits. The young marrieds of whom Dr. Gallup spoke shop together in large part. Where they don't the woman can wear shorts to the stores, get free parking and put her baby in a shopping cart. These changing habits have been a boon to suburban newspapers. Since I know it best, I shall use Newsday as an example.

When Harry Guggenheim and Alicia Patterson founded Newsday in a garage in Hempstead, L.I., the population of the two counties in which we circulate, Nassau and Suffolk, was 604,000. Today, that population is 2,400,000. The circulation of Newsday has just passed 400,000 and it is the eighth largest evening paper in the country—— the 17th largest of all dailies. Obviously, since it carries a bigger weekday advertising linage than any New York paper, it has drained off enormous revenues from the New York newspapers. It is the biggest, but only one of the 106 newspapers in the two counties. Our situation is not unique. In the two counties which Los Angeles claims as the metropolitan area there are 26 daily newspapers, one of them with more than 150,000 circulation. What is indicated is that there will be further rationalization of metropolitan newspaper situations. In ten metropolitan areas which he studied, Dr. Ken Byerly of the University of North Carolina found that suburban newspapers had more circulation than their metropolitan counterparts.

This sociological revolution has also manifested itself in the phenomenal growth of television as an advertising medium and as a medium of news accepted by the people and as an instrument of public communication and public service. Television's effect upon newspapers can be demonstrated by two or three figures. In the past five years there has been a decline of more than 16 percent in national advertising in newspapers, almost all of it going to television. Since 1956, the peak year of newspapers, the decline has been more than 25 percent. Last year, for instance, the top 100 national advertisers spent 56 percent of their money on television, 20 percent in general magazines, 17 percent in newspapers and the other 7 percent in radio and other media. Television combined with suburbanization has made it more difficult to keep up the circulation of afternoon papers. A man used to get two papers; now he gets a morning paper and usually his community paper which gives him the news of schools, sewers, tax rates, etc.——the things by which he lives.

There is one other factor in the sociological revolution which has been mentioned by speakers here today as affecting all branches of communications. That is the measurable rise in the intellectual level of our people, a rise which Dr. Gallup stressed. It exists; it was stimulated undoubtedly by the GI bill and sputnik. But it is a factor with which all media of communication must reckon. Speaking at Marquette three years ago, Wally Carroll told of Willie Stevens, the so-called "idiot boy" of the Hall-Mills murder case. Wally said that pasted on the typewriter of a foreign correspondent was a picture of Willie. Asked why, the correspondent answered, "I have to remind myself that this is my average reader."

"Today," said Wally, "the world of Willie Stevens is behind us. Whatever the newspaper reading public of that time may have been, it is no longer so today. . . . It is to these readers of new tastes and interests and their new sense of responsibility that we in the news-papers must give more serious attention."

I grew up in a newspaper generation that, if it did not regard Willie Stevens as the average reader, was certainly taught that we must write for the twelve-year-old mind. What I am afraid of today is that the mirror is being turned back toward us and that too many of our readers regard newspapermen as the twelve-year-olds; that too many of us have been mired in the old-fashioned concepts of the functions of newspapers while the intelligence level of the American people has risen. I frequently think that too many of us regard our methods as unalterable as the laws of the Medes and the Persians. Then I wonder where the hell the Medes are.

If in what I have said you are listening to a Jeremiah, let me disclaim pessimism. Hamilton Basso in "The View From Pompey's Head" had one of his characters say that he was "still a little blinded by the dust of wonder that had got into my eyes." That happened to me more than 50 years ago when I first discovered newspapering. As a realist I have tried to diagnose the disease; as one who believes strongly that newspapers will endure, let me suggest a few ways in which that may be assured.

What I believed when I became a publisher 30 years ago, I still hold to: not only the best, but the cheapest box office attraction a newspaper has is its editorial and news content. Give me a newspaper that prints the news fully, fairly and fearlessly, interprets it intelligently and comments upon it vigorously and I will take my chances on survival.

I believe strongly that newspapers are indispensable to the full enlightenment of the American people and that in altered form they will survive through any period in which we may be interested. Television is capable of excellent documentaries and spot coverage of major stories, but inherent in its structure is the necessity for a great measure of entertainment. But neither television, which must paint with a broad brush, nor radio, no matter how local, can give extended coverage or satisfy the hunger of people to know about their schools, sewers, free-ways, local tax rates, juvenile delinquency and other problems closer to them than Baghdad or Moscow. Nor can they compete with metropolitan newspapers in depth coverage of significant stories, national, international or local.

If we of newspapers are to endure——and we will——we must recapture our editorial pages from the columnists and write in the vigorous tradition of Greeley, Cobb of the World, Watterson, Grady and other giants of the editorial pages.

We must recognize that there has been a lift in the intellectual level and a change in the habits and tastes of our readers——a more serious concern for things that affect their survival. There has been, in my time, a change for the better in the newspapers' concept of their responsibility to the public. There is less cheapness, less tawdriness, less pandering to the baser emotions and fewer newspapers that do it than when I came along. There is more sober and generally more independent discussion of issues; less blatant partisanship.

There is better reporting; more background information, more reporting in depth, more interpretation of the news, more graphic aids for the reader, a keener awareness that eternal vigilance is indeed the price of good government, as Monty Curtis said. I have never known an administration, national, local or state, that did not try to manage the news when the news was unfavorable and I don't suppose there will ever be one. The newspaper is still the best weapon against concealment of civic wrongs of all sorts.

When I think of public service, I think of young fellows with whom I have worked or who have worked for me: of Mike Johnson, who won a Pulitzer prize for exposing the dock racket in New York; of Dick Berger, who voluntarily went to jail in Kentucky and helped reform the prison system; of Buford Boone, who defied the mob at Tuscaloosa; of Bob Caro of Newsday, who broke up the mail order land schemes that were fleecing older people who wanted to retire and those dozens of others of whom Monty Curtis knows. There can be no underemphasis on the newspaper that wants to endure of its obligation to its role of public protector.

We must, I think, look to our manpower and its constant improvement. We must develop specialists: science writers, business writers, competent critics and specialists in public affairs. We must hire men who know as much or more than the people to whom they are writing, or know how to find out. Journalism schools can contribute mightily to that. Since Neil Luxon of North Carolina sent his cry into the wilderness——a cry for fewer and better schools of journalism ——the first faint echo has been transformed into an insistent demand for better education, not in the techniques, but in the content of journalism, in the problems with which newspaper men have to deal.

We must keep up with production techniques, with automation. Newspapers are at least a generation behind in the sort of research that would make production more efficient. I am glad to say that the ANPA has in recent years greatly stepped up its own research. Many small newspapers are going to offset printing; many larger ones are embracing all sorts of labor-saving electronic devices, including about 10 which have computers. "Automate or die!" has become almost a slogan among newspaper managers. Needless to say, in a great many places, notably New York, automation is meeting with the bitterest resistance on the part of the unions and more trouble can be anticipated. But automation must come if more newspapers are not to die, and with it perhaps facsimile transmission of whole news pages as has now been instituted in Japan.

But when all the things I have mentioned have been done, the newspaper that will endure must stay with the fundamentals. A cub reporter's techniques are no substitute for informed counsel of able and fearless editors willing to combat bigotry and fanaticism wherever they occur. Our stake in the world is too high for us to be playing from ignorance and prejudice. Every newspaper which hopes to survive in a contracting field, every editor who is worth his salt, must deal with the problems of his region, his country and the world.

For the newspaper that endures, a fitting masthead might be Pulitzer's injunction, "Never be satisfied with merely printing news; always be drastically independent, never be afraid to attack wrong by predatory plutocracy, or predatory poverty."

And above all, in the spirit of what Monty Curtis has said, but in the words of Harry Ashmore, we must remember that "The free press was conceived not only for the protection of the verities, but as the cutting edge of change."

ROLAND F. WOLSELEY

19   Understanding Magazines:
Social Responsibilities and Effects

■

Is the American magazine a force for the devaluation or enhancement
of the quality of our national life? Does the lure of advertising reve-
nue debase and corrupt the social contribution of the magazine? And,
last but certainly not least, just what is——if it exists at all——the
social responsibility of American magazines?

Leavening his academic approach with dry wit and no little sophisti-
cation, Professor Wolseley damns with faint praise and often praises
with almost inaudible damns the complex involvement of the maga-
zine as the innovator and reflector of American social life.

The essay, appearing here in a somewhat abridged format, com-
prises Chapter Twenty-Two of Professor Wolseley's latest book Un-
derstanding Magazines, published in 1965 by the Iowa State Uni-
versity Press.

Professor Wolseley is the distinguished Head of the Magazine De-
partment, School of Journalism, Syracuse (N.Y.) University.

A MAGAZINE PUBLISHING COMPANY decided to reject advertising for
a product thought to be harmful to its users. Such a decision is a
demonstration of social responsibility.

A magazine editor and his staff adopt a policy of making certain,
when writing about any subject, that what they print gives all the

legally publishable facts and points of view necessary to meet the reader's needs. This practice, also, is exercising social responsibility.

Magazines of any kind are social institutions and have social responsibility as well as social effect. And the larger the circulation and the more readers the greater the potential influence and hence the degree of responsibility.

So far in this book we have seen how magazine companies are organized and how they operate, what some of their many thousands of publications are like, how they are organized, and what their staff members do. In this chapter we need to consider the obligations to society of such an institution as the magazine business and its effect upon our society.

MAGAZINES AND SOCIETY

What are the social responsibilities of magazines?

They share with all journalism, whether printed or electronic, the obligation in a democracy to provide the people with a fair presentation of the facts, with honestly held opinions, and with truthful advertising.

Louis M. Lyons, curator of the Nieman Foundation for Journalism at Harvard, addressing a magazine editorial conference of the Magazine Publishers Association, indicated a difference in the responsibility, however, of the newspaper and the magazine. He said:

I believe the role of the magazine is quite different from that of the newspaper. I want something quite separate. I think the substance of the magazine should be a quite different fabric. The magazine should give the reader something to chew on, to mull over, something to stir his imagination, to reflect about, not only to broaden his awareness of current issues, but to lead him to consider matters that are not now and may never be current issues, but should engage the attention of the questing mind.[1]

That no medium, and certainly not magazines either as a whole industry or by types, has achieved perfection in fulfilling these and other obligations is evident to anyone who can read. Periodicals, being the result of human work, have numerous shortcomings. Magazines as a whole may come closer to being perfect than the more

---

[1] "Reader's Choice," an address by Louis M. Lyons, March 27, 1963, Washington, D.C., MPA Release, p. 2.

hurriedly produced media because there is more time in which to eradicate faults or achieve virtue, but this is not yet proved.

No one yet has invented a machine that rings a bell when magazine reading matter or advertising copy is unfair or in some other way unethical. Value judgments must be left to the changing human mind. Intelligent editors made decisions and offer interpretations and opinions based upon facts; and facts themselves, when joined with new facts have new meanings. Readers, being possessed of more or fewer facts than the magazinists themselves, as the case may be with different individuals, arrive at their own interpretations, often entirely different although based on the same facts.

THE MEANING OF SOCIAL EFFECT

All publications, as do all institutions and persons, have some social effect. Nothing, in our interdependent world, functions without bearing directly or indirectly upon society or some segment of it. A magazine publishing company may not intend to be a social institution, that is, one with a social purpose, but it cannot escape having a social responsibility. Whether a magazine firm should have a social purpose at all or whether such a purpose should be the main reason for being is a constantly debated matter, settled more by the nature of the economic order than the desires of owners.

A social institution may be defined as one devoted to the whole good of the whole people. Theoretically, that is the purpose of all properly run organizations. It is the guiding principle of the school, the church, the professions. This definition is admittedly unsatisfactory because it is vague about what the phrase, "the whole good," means. If, to achieve "the whole good of the whole people," it is thought necessary to destroy some of the people is such action to be condoned? Obviously not. Yet, for general purposes, magazinists must use some such definition as a working principle and must seek to approximate the ideal.

The magazine world, as we have seen in earlier chapters, is almost wholly within the world of business. At its best, business benefits all of the people. But if a magazine publishing company is part of an economic order which makes it dependent upon public support through purchase of magazines and of advertising space, the magazine can be socially beneficial only to the extent that such dependence permits.

William L. Chenery, for many years editor of *Collier's,* observed while speaking at the University of Virginia that "The national magazine of mass circulation can treat only those national problems about which millions of people . . . are willing to read. . . . [The magazine] is not an endowed educational institution. It is a business operation primarily for profit. If it does not interest its readers, it cannot endure."[2]

Therefore if the public will not read certain types of content, it will not be exposed to ideas and facts in that content. As a result such content is withheld by editors. Here is one of the several points of contact between magazine and public that relate to the publication's social responsibility and effect.

THE ATTEMPT AT FAIRNESS

Frederick Lewis Allen, while editor of *Harper's,* once described a common editorial experience on that and other magazines: "We at *Harper's* are called, from time to time, communists, fascists, New Dealers, reactionaries; brutally savage toward the nation's enemies, pacifistically tender toward the nation's enemies; anti-Russian, anti-British; victims of conspiratorial propaganda of the Russians, of the British; anti-business, anti-farmer, or the tools of each."[3]

The lengths to which readers go in their attacks upon publications that displease them or satisfy them can be illustrated by the experience of *Parade,* magazine supplement to newspapers which distributes eleven million copies a week and therefore has possibilities of receiving numerous letters. On an article that appeared in the early 1960's it received twelve thousand letters. About another topic one reader wrote:

"Your entire reason leads me to believe that you are a lackey of

[2] William Ludlow Chenery, "The Magazine and Public Opinion," address delivered at the University of Virginia, July 13, 1936. *Vital Speeches of the Day,* Aug. 15, 1936, p. 718. See also "Causes and Effects," *Collier's,* Dec. 15, 1950, p. 70.

[3] Frederick Lewis Allen, "The Function of a Magazine in America," address prepared for delivery at the 36th annual Journalism Week, University of Missouri. *University of Missouri Bulletin,* Aug. 10, 1945.

the Russian embassy. Take your suggestion and go to hell! Now, when I open my Sunday paper, my first act will be to completely destroy *Parade* Magazine." And, sure enough, the next Sunday Jess Gorkin, the editor who relates this incident, received the latest issue, torn up and the pieces stapled together.[4]

Editors who receive such reactions may think they have been unfair until they read equally vigorous mail on the other side. Then they come to conclude that perhaps they have been impartial, after all, or perhaps not entirely clear. In any case, they are having a social effect; they are reaching people's minds. And since they have such an effect they have social responsibility.

The owner, publisher, editor, or writer for a magazine does not work in a vacuum, nor can he for long content himself only with making or losing money. His presence in journalism, in fact, is likely to mean that he has other motives: to express himself, to influence others, to gain power, to assume responsibility. He wants to have some kind of influence upon the society around him and to be of value at this time in history, i.e., to have a social effect.

Attempts at Influence

That magazines have not saved the world needs no proving as we look around at it; that many have made an admirable effort is easily demonstrated. Over the years since their existence, general as well as specialized magazines alike have championed numerous socially desirable causes, conducting crusades year after year. Some have given analysis and advice, others have raised money, supported political parties, undertaken exploration, or under dangerous conditions sponsored investigations of crime or political corruption. A segment has explored unpopular social ideas, often surviving to see them widely accepted.

The effects, good or bad, have been accomplished largely, however, through magazine content rather than organized action. Three departments have been influential: advertising, editorial, promotion.

The advertising department has offered word, camera, and brush

---

[4] Jess Gorkin, "Challenges Faced by Mass Media," in John E. Drewry (ed.), *Better Journalism for a Better Tomorrow* (Athens, Ga.: University of Georgia Press, 1963), pp. 127–28.

pictures of new products and services, has conveyed general information and ideas. Through its literature, the promotion department has supported the advertising. Both have stimulated desires for products and services, influencing the progress of business and industry. Living standards of readers have been affected in consequence.

The editorial department has influenced the language of readers, has been a creator or molder of cultural standards and interests, and has purveyed facts and ideas that readers might not otherwise have been exposed to. Editorial content has affected people's dress, eating habits, and use of their spare time.

What might be considered the official concept of the influence of the general magazine has come from the Magazine Advertising Bureau. Placed first among general effects is the shaping of public opinion. "The national magazine does not have the spot news function of either the newspaper or the radio. But being edited with deliberation, it is read with equal deliberation, and therefore has the unique ability to form a *mature* public opinion, nationally." It also is a reflector of American life. Said the MAB: "Life is not the daily headlines of the newspaper, nor is it the artificial dramatics thrown out daily, hourly by radio. The solid values of the lives of millions of American families are reported by the national magazine, unsensationally but vividly and accurately, in articles and fiction, in pictures and illustrations."[5] The contrast with television might be added.

Wood, in his study of American magazines, declares that the magazine is one of "three major forces affecting and controlling national public opinion." With newspaper and radio it "first created the public opinion they affect." He reminds us that the magazine is read more persistently than any other medium, is less perishable, and is read attentively. It provokes results, receives reactions. Much magazine material later goes into books and motion pictures; reprints are made.

"The character of a given magazine limits its audience," he says, "thus, to some extent, the spread of its influence, its educational force, its persuasion to belief, and possibly to individual or social action."[6]

---

[5] Undated bulletin of the Magazine Advertising Bureau. No. 2, p. 2.

[6] James Playsted Wood, *Magazines in the United States* (New York: Ronald Press Company, 1956), p. 305.

EFFECTS BY TYPES

Wood properly qualifies his generalization by using the word *given.* The effects of the comics are unlike those of literary magazines, and within the specialized magazine world the effects of one technical journal only in a superficial way resemble those of another.

Led by *The Reader's Digest,* condensed material and pocket-size magazines have stimulated popularized reading by the middle-class public, have spread certain social positions and attitudes, and have increased demand for short, quickly read publications. The digests made the portable magazine among the most popular of those published, one of them being of world influence.

With magazines of seven or eight million circulation setting the pace, the women's group, with which may be associated the service and shelter books, has been principally responsible for influence wielded by advertising departments on homes and families of the middle class. They have to some extent standardized housekeeping tools, widened the variety of cookery, introduced or popularized certain habits (such as more frequent bathing and shaving, use of deodorants, and hair coloring), and called attention to books, motion pictures, and art works, considerably broadening their effect. Not a minor result has been the introduction of fictional stereotypes; most heroes and heroines of fiction in women's magazines seldom are like realities.

The confession magazine, more and more an imitator of the slick in content, has had a changing influence. In its early days it played a psychological role: it offered spiritual release for uneducated or immature readers (whether adults or adolescents), enabling them to experience adventures of the more daring and unorthodox without personal risk. Now, except for a surviving group offering stories of sex adventures and crime detection, it is achieving on its own economic level a standardization in reader habits and practices similar to the women's slicks.

The circulation and advertising leaders among men's magazines have turned away from tales of wartime bravery to tales of bedroom exploits, holding as admirable man's sexual domination of women and gratification of his dreams of wealth, power, and comfort. They encourage their readers to a hedonistic philosophy of life and to be patrons of entertainment.

The religious magazines, less given than they once were to regularizing moral concepts, now are influencing their readers to apply their religious principles to social concerns as well as to personal conduct. Some have helped bring social movements into existence, such as the civil rights groups, and mustered support for social legislation.

Literary magazines have started movements, erected critical standards and founded schools of criticism, introduced new writers, maintained the following of older ones, and provided an outlet for work not marketable to the public through general or consumer magazines. Henry Mills Alden listed the following famous writers as owing their first publication to magazines: Scott, Johnson, Coleridge, DeQuincey, Lamb, Hazlitt, Shelley, Keats, Wordsworth, Hunt, Eliot, Landor, Trollope, Thackeray, Poe, Twain, and Longfellow.[7] In our own day *The New Yorker* alone has nurtured dozens of new writers, as have the little magazines.

Magazines for juveniles have had definite effects, since their readers are in formative years. A youngster's heroes once were provided almost solely by books and magazines; today radio, television, motion picture, and recordings also have strong influence, perhaps stronger. The religious juveniles have built concepts of right and wrong in human conduct and of individual responsibility at home and in the church. They have aroused loyalties. The secular juveniles in more recent times have been simplified versions of magazines for grown-ups——witness the departments in *Ingénue* and *Seventeen,* for example. Their effect has been at once to create little adults and to encourage youthful independence and also standardization of mores among adolescents. The comics have appealed to childish imaginations so effectively, and with so much questionable content, that they have been treated as social phenomena to be studied as seriously as are educational practices and policies.

The effects of specialized magazines are vertical, rather than horizontal. A clothing publication or a food magazine affects the profession, industry, business, or other group it serves by conveying

---

[7] Henry Mills Alden, *Magazine Writing and the New Literature* (New York: Harper & Brothers, 1908), pp. 42–52.

news created by the group, evaluating trends within, providing an outlet for ideas, and stimulating business through advertising. The company magazine has established itself as a bulwark or dam against ideas that its publishers deem undesirable or has helped to stimulate business.

EVALUATING THE EFFECTS

This discussion of the social responsibilities and effects of magazines has to this point attempted little evaluation. Not much attention has been given by scholars or critics of the magazine to these effects or to their merits. Journalism in general, or specifically the newspaper, radio, or television, has been subject to evaluation, but not much space has been accorded to judging the magazine's performance. For many years there has been an open season for passing upon the effects of journalism as a whole and newspapers in particular. Almost all the judges have been adversely critical of papers, and many have lumped magazines with them, for the term *the press* always has been ambiguous.

Insubstantial as criticism of magaizes has been, what is its point? A few commonly held views are these.

The adverse critics say: (1) they are too much inclined to give the public what it wants; (2) they deprive the public of the fullest knowledge of facts and ideas; (3) through advertising content they stimulate desires for possessions that cannot be gratified by the average reader's income; (4) they present only conventional or ultra-conservative viewpoints; (5) they evade their duty to provide leadership in solving social problems; (6) they are time-wasting, distracting the reader from more valuable uses of his leisure; (7) they have failed, as employers, to give minority racial groups responsible positions on their staffs; (8) they knuckle in to advertisers; and (9) they deal unfairly with their employes by discontinuing publications on short notice.

The favorable critics counter that: (1) magazines have helped produce the high standard of living in this country through their advertising copy; (2) they have helped stimulate mass consumption of goods and, thereby, mass production; (3) they have therefore contributed toward the lowering of the cost of living; (4) through their popular education materials they have created a better informed public; (5) they have "merchandised," as one proponent put it, new ideas; and (6) they have played an important role in every national crisis, be it war, depression, flood, or recovery from such disasters.

As with so many arguments, this is not a clear case for either pro or con. To begin with, most critics of either side are talking exclusively about the consumer magazine and, as usual, overlooking all the rest, which as we know are fifty times as numerous, and in some instances just as influential. Accepting the consumer scope, some parts of each set of criticisms may be accepted as true. The charge that the magazines are but mirrors of the public mind cannot be disputed; as Godkin of *The Nation* put it long ago in a letter to President Charles Eliot Norton of Harvard: ". . . the press would not be what it is without a public demand for it as it is."

Because magazines depend upon public support, they must gratify public demand to assure support. It follows that unpopular ideas will get short shrift in the mass periodical, such ideas as the consumer cooperative movement, diplomatic recognition of Communist China by the United Statess, and mental telepathy, for example, either are ignored or presented unsympathetically. The subject of racial and religious intolerance likewise was ignored, except by certain specialized magazines, until progress was begun in the United States toward decreasing such intolerance, and the press ran less risk, as a result, in discussing it. With progress came open discussion in countless magazine articles and even fictional treatment in the women's magazines.

Magazine advertising sometimes does make readers dissatisfied with their present washing machines, cameras, mixers, or vacuum cleaners; the less self-controlled consumers do implicate themselves in endless installment buying. To balance these detriments, however, are the greater sanitation and efficiency made possible in part by the lower prices and greater availability of tools resulting from better merchandising. Magazines are time-wasting to time-wasters; other readers should not be deprived of occasional trivial reading to protect them from themselves.

The charge of knuckling in to advertisers is one of the most often made and of great importance in considering whether magazines are interested in their own welfare rather than that of the commonweal.

Certainly a hat-in-hand attitude toward advertisers was obvious in the policy of the Curtis Publishing Company's management, before the change in control of the firm early in this decade. When a new format for the *Saturday Evening Post* was agreed upon by the staff (that is, by those who did not resign in protest), specimens of it were shown to potential advertisers in a much promoted preview. The question arises, since this is common also when new commercial magazines are launched: are magazines intended primarily for readers or for advertisers?

H. W. Kastor & Sons, an advertising agency, has declared that some magazines dropped advertising for Bantron, a smoking deterrent, after tobacco companies had exerted pressure on them. *Advertising Age* looked into the matter and published several statements by unnamed publishers in confirmation. One large periodical said it never carried Bantron advertising "because we decided against it." Taking such copy "would be bad business," for the magazine had much cigaret linage. Size of copy is an important factor here; small purchases of space were accepted.[9]

A vigorous general statement has been made on this general problem by Dean Theodore Peterson of the University of Illinois College of Journalism and Communications:

One response of magazines to television, I think, has been to treat advertisers with all of the deference accorded a pregnant queen when the crown needs a male heir. Now, magazines must have advertising, I know, and the publishers have been bowing respectfully to advertisers at least since 1896, when Edward Bok of the *Ladies' Home Journal* broke with traditional format by jumping fiction into his advertising pages to increase their readership. But in recent years, their bowing has become lower and lower, and more and more respectful. Let me mention just three manifestations.

First, many publishers have designed their magazines more for advertising exposure than for reader convenience. At their mildest, they simply permit odd-shaped advertisements to chew up their editorial pages. At their most extreme, they dare the reader to find the editorial features. As Louis Lyons has remarked, a reader cannot miss the advertisements in a magazine even though he may have a hard time finding and completing an article he wants to read. Mr. Lyons could have cited the large-circulation magazine that made readers detour around 6¾ pages of advertising to finish the last half of a sentence.

---

[9] "Magazines Confirm 'Cigaret Censorship,' " *Advertising Age,* April 6, 1959, p. 1.

For another thing, many publishers have blurred the distinction between editorial matter and advertising matter by carrying advertisements deliberately designed to trick the reader into thinking they are editorial features.[10]

Examples of editorial independence exist, also, in the consumer magazine world. *The New Yorker*'s thumbing of its nose at advertisers is widely known; in the days of Ross it prohibited its own advertising salesmen from appearing on the floor housing the editors' offices. *Good Housekeeping, Redbook,* and *Saturday Review* in recent years also have demonstrated independence of advertising pressures in specific instances reported in the trade press.

The pressures put upon magazine publishing companies are strong. Typical of what happens occurred when *Life* carried a picture story on the pharmaceutical industry. That business considered it unfair, for it said that consumers are overcharged for drugs. Several important firms then dropped *Life* from their advertising schedules, including Abbott Laboratories and Parke, Davis & Co.[11]

An unnamed magazine publisher, commenting in the Bantron situation described earlier, said: "When the copy runs in small space, there isn't any argument. When it appears in full pages, somebody asks one of your salesmen casually why you run 'junky' ads like Bantron, and points out that they don't 'do anything' for the book. And pretty soon you start losing tobacco business. No threats, no intimidation."

During 1963, the Washington State Pharmaceutical Association told its drugstore members: "Check your magazines . . . eliminate those which have articles detrimental to your business." Its special target was *The Woman,* since discontinued, which had published an article encouraging patronage of discount houses.

The Reader's Digest has several times been dropped from advertising schedules for its articles that offended certain businesses. The American Tobacco Company, in 1957, removed $1,250,000 in advertising from it because of a cigaret article; in 1961 the American Dairy Association cancelled its schedule because of two articles it

[10] "Where's the Editorial?" from an address before the Periodical Publishers Association of Canada, *Advertising Age,* Oct. 7, 1963.

[11] "Parke, Davis Also Drops 'Life' Ads Because of Article," *Advertising Age,* Dec. 5, 1960.

considered detrimental to the dairy field. Four pages were dropped and the magazine accused of "lack of courage" because the association was not notified in advance of the articles' publication. But the ADA's general manager of that time said that the Association had "no desire to dictate the editorial policies of any publication."[12]

Such pressures come, also, from other sources than business: local governments, self-appointed guardians of public morals, and patriotic societies. Typical was the banning of *Time, Life,* and *Look* in 1956 from the nine high school libraries of Bossier City and Parish in Louisiana.

Extremely wealthy publishing companies can ignore pressures, but few firms are extraordinarily strong in their resources. Because the majority of publications are issued by small firms there has been sufficient feeling of insecurity in the journalistic world in recent times to produce even more caution than usual. What may be worse is a mind set, resulting from the dependence of magazines upon advertisers, that the advertisers and not the public comes first. Advertisers, after all, bring far more money into the treasury than does the public. On that excuse omission of troublesome facts and ideas is being justified.

Charges about advertiser influence are heard mainly about consumer magazines. But they also are made, if less loudly and possibly with greater validity because so many more could be involved, about the specialized magazines. Because most are small and more vulnerable, the chance of pressures succeeding is greater.

Peter Bart, advertising news writer for the New York *Times,* reported that the Society of Business Magazine Editors had surveyed 103 of its members "soliciting their candid opinions about advertiser influence on editorial operations." About 22 percent of the editors acknowledged that it was accepted policy on their magazines "to give preference to advertisers when gathering information for articles." About 55 percent said that advertising salesmen exerted "some influence" in selecting and researching articles. One-third said they made a "special effort" to publish illustrations sent in by advertisers.[13]

Protests came at once, charging slanting by the *Times.* These were

---

12 "Dairy Men Drop 'Digest' Schedule," *Advertising Age,* April 3, 1961, p. 7.
13 Peter Bart, "Advertising: Loss of Editorial Independence," New York *Times,* Feb. 12, 1964.

from business magazine associations as well as from a few heads of companies known, however, for the high ethical quality of their operations.

The assertion that the public is better informed because of magazines can be accepted if "better informed" is taken relatively. "Better informed about what?" is a legitimate question. The American people as a whole may be better informed about current affairs than the inhabitants of many other nations but are they well informed enough to make democracy work to the limit and to the full advantage of the people? The revelations of pollsters about what the people do not know raise doubts.

Yet the magazine does not exist in isolation; it is only one medium of mass communication. It should not have to carry full blame for failures shared by all other media. It is blameworthy to the extent that it makes no attempt to provide facts, to the degree in which editors and publishers lack interest or courage in dealing with controversial subjects, unorthodox ideas, and topics of limited appeal although important.

A single, all-inclusive statement about the social effect of the magazine in the United States is difficult to frame. No comprehensive studies have been undertaken. But it appears that the consumer magazine has lost the dynamics that made it powerful in the days when it was a personal organ or a tool for social pioneers. As it has become the product of a business it has had to follow business methods and standards lest it not survive. The business periodicals, numerically by far the largest group, naturally are subordinate to the business motive. Any magazine is likely, under such conditions, to invoke blessings upon the existing social order and warn readers away from social experiments that threaten to change the fundamental economy upon which the magazines are dependent.

THE MAGAZINE'S SOCIAL ROLE

If the magazine shares its social role with other media, those who produce and use it must have some idea what that social role might be.

A business society prevents the magazine from fulfilling the role of the institution wholly devoted to the welfare of society as are, for example, church, school, and the professions of medicine and nursing. It is left to play a part short of full devotion to the commonweal. If magazines indiscriminately use the fear motive in advertising, they are not bettering society; if they ignore significant social ideas for fear of adverse reader reaction, they are doing less than their best to help mankind. But where shall they position themselves? How far ahead of the public may they safely be?

Paul F. Lazarsfeld and Robert K. Merton tackle this problem in a general manner and point out a procedure for the magazine, among other media of mass communication. They examine the argument that the level of esthetic taste has deteriorated in "the measure that the size of these audiences has increased." They say there is a fear "that the mass media deliberately cater to these vulgarized tastes, thus contributing to further deterioration." They declare that they have been able to find little knowledge about the social role of mass media and their effect upon the community.

Many critics of mass media make them "targets for hostile criticism because they feel themselves duped by the turn of events." Reformers have helped make available more leisure but people use it in radio listening, movie going, and, the authors might have added later, television gazing. Such media seem somehow to have "cheated reformers of the roots of their victories." Instead of spending time reading Shakespeare or listening to Beethoven's music the public turns to sex novels, television Westerns, or pop singers.

Messrs. Lazarsfeld and Merton ask how best to use mass media "for moving toward designated types of social objectives." They answer by suggesting that propaganda, whether for good or bad social motives, must satisfy one or more of three conditions if it is to be effective: (1) monopolization; (2) canalization rather than change of basic values; and (3) supplementary face-to-face contact. Monopolization they illustrate by wartime censorship in a democracy, the taking over or use of channels of communication for war propaganda. Creation of popular idols by mass media is another example. Canalization perpetuates existing behavior patterns or attitudes. Magazine fiction offers an example. In most short stories the heroine is beautiful and desirable; the hero, handsome and virile. Supplementation is a follow-up on the presentation of a point of view through mass media, achieved through local centers of organized face-to-face contact, such as reading rooms and clubs. It "serves to reinforce the prevailing culture patterns."[14]

Dr. Lazarsfeld went a step further, in an address before the Institute of Communications Research at the University of Illinois, when he said:

Do we "give the people what they want" or do we believe that there are experts who know the best balance for the total supply which the mass media provide? It is not too difficult to suggest an answer. Obviously we do not want magazines and radio programs in this country to drive audiences away. But almost no one would propose that the media be based on the lowest common denominator; publishers and broadcasters have a cultural responsibility. Their business is affected by public interest. Thus the best solution would be to have mass media aim just slightly above what would be the simplest level at any time. In this way, we shall have a general acceptance of media content, as well as a slow, systematic intellectual progress to which the media, themselves, will contribute.[15]

He admits that the recommendation is more easily made than carried out. Consciously or unconsciously, however, Dr. Lazarsfeld's philosophy seems to be followed by certain editors. The increasing quantity of material dealing with such social problems as divorce, birth control, crime, sickness and disease, and denial of civil rights to minorities has increased the popularity of women's magazines among women who desire more than fiction and advice on everyday household life.

The progress made in introducing new ideas through magazines can be judged by the difference in the climate of public opinion during an earlier period of magazine history.

The social effect of some of the policies of Edward Bok was tempestuous. This editor of the *Ladies' Home Journal* related in his autobiography the medical opposition, in the 1880's, to a department of questions and answers for prospective mothers. He describes, also, the results of a policy of refusing patent medicine advertising advocated by John Adams Thayer, advertising manager, and supported by Cyrus H. K. Curtis, the publisher. Curtis returned a check for the

---

[14] Lyman Bryson (ed.), *The Communication of Ideas* (New York: Harper & Brothers and the Institute for Religious and Social Studies, 1948), pp. 113–14.

[15] Paul Lazarsfeld, "Role of Criticism in Management of Mass Communications," in Wilbur Schramm, ed., *Communications in Modern Society* (Urbana, Ill.: University of Illinois Press, 1948), p. 195.

equivalent of five pages of advertising because it came from a patent medicine manufacturer, although the money would have met the magazine's payroll for three weeks. When Bok launched a campaign to improve small-house architecture he found architects unalterably opposed. Finally obtaining the assistance of one, he offered readers full building specifications and plans to scale.

"A storm of criticism now arose from architects and builders all over the country, the architects claiming that Bok was taking 'the bread out of their mouths' by the sale of plans, and local builders vigorously questioned the accuracy of the estimates. But Bok knew he was right and persevered. Slowly but surely he won the approval of the leading architects."[16]

Bok, who wrote an autobiography in the third person, conducted campaigns that would be considered tame today. Far more controversial problems are dealt with now, yet public opinion has so changed that the effect, so far as readers are concerned, is not very damaging.

---

[16] Edward W. Bok, *The Americanization of Edward Bok* (New York: Charles Scribner's Sons, 1922), p. 241.

HY STEIRMAN

20   The Publisher's Responsibility: A Matter of Public Trust or Private Conscience?

■

A usually unquestioned premise inherent in most of the pieces in this anthology has been that the responsibility of the Press has been, first and foremost, to the public. In the following essay, written especially for this volume, Mr. Hy Steirman, the publisher of Coronet Magazine *and* Paperback Library, *challenges the premise in a lively and unorthodox fashion.*

Putting his own sense of ethics and conscience before the will of the public, Mr. Steirman believes, is the only honest way the public can be served with truth and with taste. Basic to his contention is his view of the editor and/or publisher as the synthesis of his collective readership; ergo, to please himself is to please his audience.

Mr. Steirman's view of publishing, based on nearly twenty years' experience as editor and publisher, however controversial in its ramifications, clears a common ground upon which members of the Press of all shades of opinion and levels of integrity can stand: for indisputable indeed is his central thesis, that without the integral honesty of the editor/publisher there can be no honest Press and, as a corollary, no honestly informed public.

Still in his early forties, Mr. Steirman has had a full generation of experience as an editor, writer and, since 1958, magazine publisher. Since 1961 he has been publisher of Paperback Library. *In whatever spare time Mr. Steirman finds, he lectures and teaches on writing and publishing.*

> Question: As the publisher of *Coronet Magazine* and Paperback
> Library, what do you see as your responsibility to
> the people who buy your publications?
> Answer: I feel I owe no responsibility to the people who pur-
> chase my publications.

This statement is not intended to be high-handed or arrogant, just truthful. The only responsibility I have is to myself, and if to mine own self I am true, then my readers will have been served well.

Publishing, like baseball and medicine is a business——big business. Baseball may be a game to youngsters and a sport to adults, nevertheless it's big business when you realize that a Willie Mays, a Mickey Mantle and a Sandy Koufax each earn about $100,000 every year for playing games. A doctor may be saving lives and working for the greater good of mankind, but it's also the way he earns his livelihood. A publisher who manufacturers the Bible is also publishing for the greater good——but it's also the way he earns his living.

I believe that next to show business, the most electrifying profession is publishing. The public realizes that from this hallowed profession emerged such writers and editors as Benjamin Franklin, Horace Greeley, William Randolph Hearst and Winston Churchill. A publisher is protected by the Constitution's guarantee of Freedom of Speech, one of the Four Freedoms powerfully restated by Franklin D. Roosevelt during World War II.

There is an unusual psychology about the printed page. Words in print, to the average reader, contain the truth. Here is a power that can be used or abused. Most publishers understand the trust placed in them and scrupulously uphold that trust. But not all publishers are scrupulous. Thus the public's conditioned reaction to things in print is sometimes taken advantage of; instead of being objective, the truth is sometimes colored, slanted, purposely misleading or inflammatory.

Perhaps this is best exemplified by the Dreyfus case. Forged evidence helped convict Captain Alfred Dreyfus of treason. Misleading information turned over to the newspapers by the military cadre of France helped keep the people inflamed against the Captain.

Col. Picquart who had proof of his innocence was transferred out of the country and later imprisoned. Though Dreyfus was sent to Devil's Island, many brilliant minds were at work trying to prove his innocence. When the real culprit, Major Esterhazy, was uncovered, a rigged court martial was arranged where he was acquitted. The military refused to admit it was wrong. Yet few newspapers published the readily available facts.

Two days after the Esterhazy acquittal, a new newspaper, *L'Aurore* published "J'accuse," written by the famous novelist Emile Zola. It denounced those who tried to suppress the truth. Though it landed Zola in jail, it was the turning point in the fight to prove Dreyfus innocent.

All this indicates the power of the printed word——a power which can be used for good or evil. The responsible publisher publishes responsibly; the irresponsible publisher publishes irresponsibly.

Besides his responsibilities to himself as a publisher, a publisher usually finds himself in the position of slanting material based on his own principles, his attitudes and his experience. A Catholic magazine publishes the Catholic viewpoint, a Jewish magazine publishes the Jewish viewpoint, the trade union magazine publishes its particular pro-labor slant. All these are well intentioned, but nevertheless slanted. For magazines published in a democracy, one slant counter-balances another. The *Nation* is an extremely liberal magazine, while the *National Review* is extremely conservative. *Reader's Digest* has one viewpoint, we at *Coronet* have another. Just as water reaches its own level, each magazine, because of its slant, finds its own audience.

Every publisher plays his role in this design. *Pravda,* the official voice of the Kremlin has a responsibility——it must publish the views of the Kremlin. Thus it is an external house organ of propaganda. That is its purpose and function. But the New York *Times,* the St. Louis *Post Dispatch, Life Magazine* and *Newsweek* publish what the publishers and editors please, and present it in a format that tries to appeal to the reader. In a democracy you pay your money and make your choice of reading material.

Besides being a business in a democracy, publishing is also a gamble. The man who decides ultimately what will or will not be presented in his book, magazine or newspaper, is taking a chance that the people he is trying to reach will buy what he prints.

That is why newspapers try to get as broad a base of appeal as possible: the lures are comics for kids, sports for sports buffs, racing tips for the horse players, stock market news for the tycoons, menus, ads and fashions for the ladies, a teen-page for teeners and news for them what wants it. Newspaper publishing being a gamble, the idea is to reduce the odds by making the gamble minimal.

Getting back to my own two fields, magazine and paperback books: both cater to different areas of interest. A general magazine like *Coronet* must base its appeal on a certain amount of immediacy to newsworthy topics in such diverse areas as politics, medicine, self-help, science, etc. Also, most people like short humor as well as profiles about interesting people. Then, too, we mustn't neglect controversial articles where we take careful aim and fire a volley of critical opinion at a particular target. In *Coronet* we have lashed out at bad nursing homes, the shortages of ambulances, the fight between eye doctors and optometrists, etc. People have come to expect it. I feel that I publish these controversial articles to please myself; to bring out into the open things that I feel strongly about. And deep down inside I hope there are as many people as I think there are who would like to read about the same thing. I often refer to this as "stomach-thinking." A magazine, therefore, is a multi-interest publication which tries for appeal in many areas.

A book, on the other hand, is mostly one of singular interest, and may be categorized into science fiction books, Westerns, love, sex, biology, autobiography, historical romance, philosophy, gothic, general interest, current events, commentary, general fiction and others too numerous to mention.

Sitting out across the country are some 120 million readers with diverse interests, different reading abilities and intelligence levels and varying psychological needs. They are the judge and the jury of what I and every other publisher offer for sale. If what I put out does not appeal to them or please them, they don't buy my books or magazines. You see, just as my responsibility is to myself first, the reader's primary responsibility is to himself. The public owes me no responsibility to purchase what I produce. On the other hand, if a publisher can please this audience (not all of it, just a small segment of it) then he will be successful.

In other words, if a publisher is a responsible person, he does not have to be responsible to anyone but himself. It is he who must live with himself and his own brand of honesty, integrity and morality. The publisher who is less responsible may have fewer or no scruples; he may publish hard-core pornography in order to make money. While he caters to a certain segment of the public eager to pay for his wares, his irresponsibility goes beyond the area of good taste. Like any other extreme, his product comes under the careful scrutiny of society.

Responsibility means being answerable to or held accountable for one's actions. A publisher must publish within the confines of the community in which he operates. Even this varies. There is an expression that says "One man's meat is another man's poison"——so too, with publishing. It was D. H. Lawrence who said, "What is obscene to one man may be the breath of genius to another." His literary masterpiece *Lady Chatterley's Lover,* was banned in the United States for decades. But thirty years later it became a bestseller when Grove Press decided to battle the censors——and win. Thus a publisher, if he has ideas, fortitude and money, has a responsibility not to his reader, but to his society, which has rules and regulations called laws.

If a publisher does have a responsibility, and even as I feel not to his reader but to himself, this responsiblity is strictly a moral one. Every man sets up his own standards of morality.

I would like to invent an axiom right this minute for all books and periodicals. The greater the audience, the greater the moral responsibility of the publication. It's a premise that should stand up because it sounds so academic but it doesn't.

Let's take the subject of the relationship between smoking and cancer. *The Saturday Evening Post* (circulation 6,600,000) has never mentioned the subject. *McCall's* has had only one non-scientific article on it (circulation 8,500,000).

To their credit, *Life* (circulation 7,500,000), *Time* (circulation 3,500,000) and *Newsweek* (circulation 2,000,000) have published definitive stories on the subject.

Perhaps the magazine most active in anti-smoking campaigns has been *The Reader's Digest* (26,000,000 circulation, world-wide). However, *The Reader's Digest* falls prey to other shortcomings.

In the interest of starting a controversy right now, are the nudes in *Playboy* obscene or are they to be considered art? *Playboy* has been getting a wider acceptance, along with an increasing circulation. Publisher Hugh Heffner says there is nothing wrong with displaying the female form. Most great artists delighted in painting nude women, from Rembrandt to Rubens, including Michelangelo who painted them on the Sistine Chapel.

The question is, was Michelangelo right and Heffner wrong? Is an old nude more socially acceptable than a new nude? If nothing else, Heffner has proven that twentieth-century males like their females to be less bulky than were the sixteenth-century ladies.

If we all returned to the Garden of Eden, I'm certain that no Dior or Balenciaga gowns would be clothing the girls in the Garden. They'd be nude unless Eden was in the U.S.A. Critics, thinkers and philosophers have said for years that Americans are timid about nudity and sex. Yet these are the best-selling items in newspapers, magazines, books, movies, art and advertising. One commentator who viewed the nudes, semi-nudes and girdled girls in the ads in the New York *Times* Magazine Section, called the paper "The Pious Pornographer." I, personally, don't know if these ads sell more copies of the New York *Times,* but I'll bet they don't hurt the sale of the paper.

Now let us move to a question of publishing taste and judgment——the publisher who distributes a so-called "dirty book." A religious or highly moral person might say, "Arrest and jail the pornographer." However, a more liberal-minded thinker might say, "This is a free country. We cherish freedom of speech and every man has his right to be heard. I believe this is a work of art and not pornography."

We now have a paradox where one segment of the population finds a book acceptable and another finds it unacceptable. Is it possible to be responsible to only one segment of the reading public?

Take another publisher who thinks everyone in the country should know more about rabbits and their contribution to America. He wants to educate the public. His rabbit book is published and he sells none despite wonderful reviews in the New York *Times* and *Life.* Here the publisher's idea has the approval of the critics. He has honestly discharged his "responsibility" to the reading public. But the public isn't interested. With this artistic triumph behind him, the publisher goes back to work, probably as an employee of the publisher who feels he has no responsibility to the public.

All of which poses an interesting question of ethics: How could a publisher have a responsibility to the reading public if the reading public has no responsibility to him?

Just what are my responsibilities to myself? I'm a publisher and members of my staff have often heard me say, "Okay, let's publish this and get in a few points for our side." This usually refers to honesty, integrity and often publishing at a loss. And it means articles like exposing pious rackets in lifetime dance lessons and reducing aids; exposing a Nazi who entered the U.S.A. under an assumed name, with the help of powerful friends, but who later turned out to be the commander of a concentration camp during World War II.

The latter example is an interesting case. I had what I believed was sufficient proof to expose this man, despite the fact that my attorney advised me I would be sued and that just to defend myself in court would take more money than I had. But I have to live with myself. I had spent five years in the service fighting enemies like this man and I decided to put everything I had——and more——on the line to back up the principles I had fought for. The story was published. True, I discharged a "responsibility" to the public; but, in essence, I was doing it for myself. The public also benefited when I discharged my responsibilities to myself.

The above cost me only money, and I lost nothing more. I never regretted I had but one small bank account to give to my country.

Magazines with specific interests are specialty or trade publications. A magazine dedicated to supermarkets has a responsibility to feature, inform, educate and even advise its special-interest readers of what is taking place in the industry, what is done at conventions and what laws in Congress may affect their lives.

A law journal does three things: it informs, educates and records. Any professional magazine has these responsibilities.

A general interest magazine must first know its audience, then attempt to appeal to it. Bless the publisher whose own ideas and personal interests appear in his magazine, and who joyfully discovers that this is also what the readers want.

Factors that affect a general magazine are many. The life and death of a publication is based on its ability to entertain (in the broad sense) and keep the reader coming back for more. That is why it is the most difficult and most risky of all publishing, for it depends on the allegiance of a notoriously fickle public prone to changing its tastes in reading.

Millions of people may enjoy the magazine, but if it is too heavily dependent upon advertising and has incorporated the economics of this income into its budget, this can spell disaster. Why? Because it must meet its budget. Next to lack of editorial savvy, over-dependence on advertising can kill a publication. Witness the deaths of *Collier's* and *American Magazine* and take into account the tremendous losses of the *Saturday Evening Post* today despite the fact that nearly seven million people buy this magazine regularly.

There are publishing concerns that are publicly owned and have a responsibility to the stockholder. The motto is, "Make a profit or else." If it doesn't, management changes. If it does, it continues.

No matter how lofty his or her position, the person who reads does so for a variety of reasons. To relax, to be amused, to be entertained or thrilled, to be informed or to be educated.

If every person who buys a magazine or book published by my firms is pleased, I have fulfilled my responsibility to myself as a publisher. The contents of the publications fulfilled the promise on the cover; the reader was told in a direct manner exactly what was for sale; after purchasing same, the customer found it to be so. Thus the contract between the publisher and the reader is complete and valid.

As editors and publishers of a general magazine and a line of mass-market paperbacks, we know we are Mr. Average Person and that our tastes are in concert with our readers. We are the common denominator of taste and ideas and appeal. Our particular publishing project has found its target. We have communicated. With a wide range of publications, everyone finds his own brand of reading.

A publisher's credo might be called for to crystalize just what a publisher must do in order to understand his responsibilities to himself. These nine commandments of responsibility sum up how I feel publishers should conduct their businesses:

1) Be a responsible person.
2) Be true to himself.
3) Have a viewpoint and stick to it.
4) Try not to be dull.

5) Don't publish toothless tigers. (Promise her Arpege then give her sewage. Don't promise her something on the cover the publication does not deliver inside.)

6) Publish at a profit.

7) Utilize good taste at all times.

8) Don't preach hatred.

9) Check, then recheck facts.

ROLAND F. WOLSELEY

21   Responsibilities of the Religious Press

■

Professor Wolseley outlines seven special responsibilities incumbent on the religious press. Implicit in his list is an eighth responsibility ——to always live up to the other seven. Because the religious press is not dependent on advertising or competition for circulation, they are free, he suggests, to attain the highest possible standards of journalism. But Professor Wolseley by no means condemns the secular press, per se; indeed, one of the most challenging points in his provocative article urges a "secularization" of the religious press, meaning more involvement with the larger world and the development of religious journalism that is far more than just a "house organ" for God.

Professor Wolseley's article is based on a paper presented at a 1963 meeting of Catholic, Protestant and Jewish editors under the auspices of the National Conference of Christians and Jews. It appeared in the November, 1964 issue of The Catholic Journalist.

I SHOULD FIRST OF ALL like to make clear that whatever I say about the responsibilities of the religious press applies only to that press as it exists in the United States. The situation in this country is sufficiently complex without complicating it by adding the problems that beset the religious press in certain other lands.

I want to discuss the responsibilities of the religious press in a pluralistic society like ours rather obliquely. I shall do so by ap-

proaching my assigned subject from two side angles before facing it
directly.

One is the angle of the monistic society. We might consider for a
few seconds this question: are the responsibilities of the religious
press in a pluralistic society any different from those in a monistic
society?

I think that they are, and rather obviously so. A society that has no
independent units, as does ours, would give the religious press an
easy time of it in many ways. In a monistic society there is only one
religion, and while the conflicts and stresses within that one layer
would be enough to keep an editor alert, they are less of a problem
than those occurring in the many-layered society that we live in on
this continent.

In such a society there might be not only one religion but also a
single language and one set of moral standards.

Another angle of approach to my subject is from the viewpoint of
the secular press. Are the responsibilities of the secular press greater
than those of the religious press in our pluralistic society?

In theory they are as great but in practice they are not, simply
because the secular press does not accept all of its responsibilities. It
is exempted, by tradition or mores, from certain responsibilities that
are taken seriously by the religious press.

For instance, the secular press, or at least the major part of the
daily press, is given to frequent use of news stories that emphasize
conflict without much thought to the social consequences. As a result
labor is always opposed to management or vice versa. If, for example, a meeting is addressed by a speaker who in an isolated answer
to a question notes a conflict he is likely as not to find that all the
moderate and conciliatory assertions he made are subordinated to
that one item of conflict. Now and then the religious press also over-
emphasizes conflict, but it is uncommon there and common in the
secular press. Note these words from the headlines over the news
stories in the first two pages of a conventional U.S. general daily:
slash, pull, bans, threaten, invoking, fight.

SECULAR PRESS RESPONSIBILITIES

The responsibilities of the secular press are generally thought to be
these four:

1. To inform the people, so that they can make decisions in a democracy based on full knowledge of events.

2. To provide opinions and other means of influencing the people, so as to guide them through a world of complex facts.

3. To entertain, in the broader sense rather than merely to amuse them.

4. To assist the economic system by printing advertising.

Only two of these——to inform and to influence——seem to me to be necessary and appropriate for the religious press to assume as its function as well, in any sort of society. If the religious press does not inform and influence it is betraying its sponsors, who established it to carry on their own objectives, the most important of which is to influence, that is, to propagate the faith.

I suppose there is no harm in the religious press fulfilling the entertainment function, but it should be distinctly subordinate to the other two, certainly. As for the advertising function, I see it only as a necessity for survival and not at all meaning that any religious body should be committed to support of an economic order that rests so heavily on advertising as does ours. I can see a service function in the press of religion carrying advertising, but the line between service and dependence must be drawn sharply.

Clearly, then, the responsibilities of the religious press in a pluralistic society are as great and also as complex as those of the secular press. As I see them they are greater. For they include at least these seven:

1. *To serve God.* I hesitate to use that expression, "to serve God" not only because it is such a well-frayed cliché but also because it is so obvious and also so sweeping and perhaps meaningless unless it is spelled out. Let us accept it as the charter and agree that to take up the responsibilities that come after it is the way this paramount responsibility is implemented.

2. *To inform.* This means that is has the obligation to provide facts to each part of the society as well as to the whole. This means, also, that ecumenical publications are needed as much as publications that serve single divisions. It means, furthermore, that all publications must induce the layman to become informed about his own group's views as well as about the events occurring in the larger world of

religion. It leads to all sorts of problems of format, content, editing, financing, and distribution of publications.

3. *To educate.* This responsibility is not the same as that of informing and certainly not the same as that of influencing, although education does influence, as a side-effect. An informed person is not necessarily an educated one. He may have only isolated facts. He may be well informed in some areas, but not including religion or whatever his version of religion may be. Education implies systematic accumulation and retention of knowledge, development of thinking power, adjustment to any situation in life, and the ability to use the resources of information. The religious press to some extent performs this function through its educational publications, to be sure, and with varying degrees of success. This responsibility, like influencing, has its external implications.

4. *To interpret.* In fulfilling this responsiblity, the press explains the meaning of religious events and shows the significance of secular events from the viewpoint of religion (question: which religion?). The massive failure, in my opinion, of the grass roots church or temple to shed religious light on world events may come in part from the shortcomings of editors who do not or cannot take this responsibility seriously, thereby failing to help pastor, priest, and rabbi. It also means to explain the policies of the church to its members, a responsibility more successfully carried out.

5. *To persuade.* This is the opinion-making function. It is the evangelical function. It is not commonly shared by editors of all religious papers and magazines because not all religions support the view that they should make converts or seek to mold opinion through journalism. But the majority do believe in taking this responsibility. It is one of the best lived up to responsibilities in the list.

6. *To reconcile.* For most of the history of religious journalism, this has hardly been accepted as the press's function. On the contrary. If you scan the back issues you see many religious publications that have done much condemning of other religions——even of denominations——than their own. Not that this has ceased. But there is less of it, partly because religion has a common enemy in certain anti-religious political theories and partly because more editors have come to realize that direct attacks on other faiths harm all faiths in the long run, especially in a pluralistic society.

7. *To develop loyalty*. One of the most common responsibilities and one of the most eagerly discharged by the religious press, this one hardly needs explaining. Religious journalists, if anything, have in my view been too zealous in this endeavor, for they pursue this aim so enthusiastically that you all have seen them reach the point of printing articles about the all-Methodist football teams and the all-Catholic basketball teams and making prideful comparisons of the number of persons of each faith in the national Congress. But making these distinctions in the religious affiliations, if not devotion, of our Representatives and Senators seems to say that it is more important to have 19 members of a certain denomination in our government than it is to know that some of these churchmen are among the worst obstructionists to social progress. Yet that latter observation seems never to be made.

DISAGREEMENT AMONG EDITORS

I realize that among editors like you there will be disagreement about the best way to carry out these seven responsibilities. Especially is this true when it comes to that responsibility I have called influencing. One needs merely to read widely in the religious press to see its diversity. This variety is a healthy situation in a democratic society, where differences of opinion are encouraged and are essential to intellectual and spiritual growth. The fact that *The Pilot* of Boston and *The Tablet* of Brooklyn do not always agree, anymore than *Motive* agrees with *Together* or *American Judaism* with *Orthodox Jewish Life*, does not invalidate my basic insistence that the religious press as a whole and in its separate units has certain responsibilities in our society.

How well these responsibilities are being accepted it was not my assignment to determine. But they are not being carried out either sufficiently or sufficiently well, in my opinion. And they never will be if the religious press in America remains more or less as it is now, in its understanding of its responsibilities. It is not that the editors alone can change the situation. The change must come from the proprietors of the press: the religious bodies behind it.

Why? Because the religious press is so much a servant only of religion and too little a servant of all society, that is, of God, as religion at its best should be.

QUESTION THE "HOUSE ORGAN"

The religious press in a pluralistic society has a far greater obligation to serve God through serving all society than it does in a monistic society. For God's work is more difficult in the many-layered society.

In reflecting upon their responsibilities, then, the owners and managers of the religious press alike must, in my opinion, question whether the house organ type of religious publication is sufficient for the task. They must decide whether it is not time again for the churches, as agencies of religion, to put religion to work more firmly through journalism by entering the world of secular publishing, doing so fully possessed by motives of religion instead of those of commerce.

FRANK K. KELLY

22   Who Owns the Air?

■

The title of the following article sums up one of the most enduring controversies in the American mass communications industry. Are the broadcasting and television systems a national natural resource owned by the people and only leased to private capital? Or do the owners of the communications systems own and have absolute control of the air?

The vital topic receives a thorough, soundly reasoned discussion by Mr. Frank K. Kelly within the framework of testimony he offered before the Federal Communications Commission on January 12, 1960, in the course of its extended hearings on broadcasting practices. His remarks, suggesting as they do, that the FCC serve as a more active "watchdog" on broadcasting stations and their programming, serves as an effective counter-argument to the laissez-faire positions taken by Dr. Stanton and Mr. Sarnoff elsewhere in this volume.

Mr. Kelly's point of view grows out of studies undertaken by the Fund for the Republic and its Center for the Study of Democratic Institutions. Mr. Kelly is a vice president of the Fund and Staff Administrator of the Study of Mass Media. His testimony is published here in a somewhat abridged format.

I wish to make it clear that the views I am presenting are reflections and ideas based upon the studies undertaken over the past two years by the Fund for the Republic and its Center for the Study of

Democratic Institutions. But my views do not necessarily reflect those of the directors or other officers of the Fund, or of the Consultants to the Center. It might be noted, as a matter of interest, that the studies launched by the Fund and the Center were begun long before the so-called TV scandals created the present atmosphere of excitement and concern.

As an educational foundation, engaged in studying the impact of modern democratic institutions upon freedom and justice in our society, the Fund does not make recommendations concerning legislation. The Fund, through its consultants and researchers, attempts to explore the basic issues confronting Americans today, with the hope that its explorations will show what the issues really are. The impact of the great new electronic medium of communication is obviously a matter of primary concern in any consideration of contemporary society.

The many complex matters before this body relate to one of these issues with which the FCC must deal under its mandate from Congress: How can a federal agency regulate a communications medium without engaging in censorship? There are no easy answers to this question——including the frequent admonition from the broadcasting industry that the problem is so delicate it should not even be considered by FCC.

To get at the root of the question, we tried to obtain a comprehensive picture of how the FCC has operated. We asked several former members and one present member of the Commission to tell us exactly what kinds of jobs they had to do, what authorizations and restrictions they felt they had, what problems they repeatedly encountered. We asked broadcasters, advertising agents, program executives, news editors, writers, and television critics to tell us what they expected from the FCC and what they received. Some of this material has been published, and some of it is in the form of working papers. We will be glad to make all of our reports available to the Commission if members wish to see them.

To judge from the statements of all these people, it might be concluded that the FCC has an impossible task. It was not functioning effectively for a variety of reasons. The more we studied the complexities of the problems in broadcasting, the more we realized the difficulties facing the agency. The FCC was expected to administer the Federal Communications Act for the "public interest, convenience, and necessity"——but it was virtually impossible to get agreement on what those words meant.

Was it in the public interest to use most broadcasting time for entertainment and advertising? The broadcasters and the sponsors evidently felt that it was. The general public, by its response, seemed to agree.

Was it in the public interest to give so little attention to the development of educational television? Many educators seemed inert or confused on this question, the Commission was harassed and confused about it, and the general public didn't seem to care much one way or the other.

Was it in the public interest for most broadcasters to avoid discussions of controversial issues——to "play it safe"? Most broadcasters, naturally determined to conserve their financial investments, considered it a duty to avoid risks. The FCC, reluctant to interfere with programming, did not know what to do. The public, again, seemed largely indifferent.

Interpretation of the "public interest" clause in the Communications Act is one of the most difficult assignments the Commission has. Beyond providing for essential broadcasting facilities in all communities needing such facilities, the Commission has moved slowly and hesitantly and has encountered great counter-pressures from the vested interests of broadcasting. A point constantly emphasized in our studies was that the FCC, as now constituted, was subjected to so many pressures, for so many reasons, from so many groups in our society, including the Congress which created the agency, that a new set of legal safeguards for FCC members, giving them positions comparable to those of federal judges, might well be in order.

In my own view, the responsibility for seeing to it that broadcasters supply a higher level of programming rests not only on the FCC but on the leaders of every community where broadcasting stations are located. Community leaders should let the FCC know when they believe their local broadcasters are falling down, and protests should be followed up by demands for remedial action. As things now stand, the FCC too often hears only from those who have a direct financial stake in its decisions.

Perhaps the most significant change which could be made in the present atmosphere of broadcasting would be positive recognition of the fact that broadcasters do not own the channels they use. The American people have only the vaguest conception of this fact.

In my view, the FCC could and should issue a policy directive to all stations, requiring them to emphasize in their dealings with the public that they are using a public facility under a renewable license granted by the United States government. Stations should be required to make public announcements of the dates when their licenses expire and should be required to publicize the summaries of program schedules submitted to the FCC with applications for renewals. Audiences should be informed that printed copies of these program schedules would be made available to any listener without charge.

It is essential that the public recognize the role of the broadcasters as that of trustees, not as owners of the broadcasting air. Such understanding would, I believe, do much to strengthen FCC's hand in dealing with the powerful forces that seek proprietary control of the airwaves.

If the broadcasting spectrum happened to be a relatively unlimited natural resource, the dominant American tradition would place it in the area of almost complete private development with a minimum of government intervention.

But the spectrum is not unlimited. It has definite boundaries. As a limited natural resource, belonging to all the people, and capable of earning a fair return for those who are licensed to use it, it comes under the American tradition of government regulation for the benefit of the public. Congress and the FCC have shown some confusion on this question over the years since the passage of the Radio Communications Act in 1927. But generally the broadcasters have been encouraged to behave as though the licensed channels were their private properties.

The attitude of the broadcasters has been made evident in many instances. A recent speech by Robert W. Sarnoff, chairman of the Board of NBC, contained this revealing sentence (emphasis mine): *"We* should consider the most effective methods of *using our own facilities* to create wider understanding of *our medium* and how it functions in everyone's interest." The sense of proprietorship came through in every line.

It is perhaps natural that the broadcasters regard the air as their private medium. But it is not natural, or healthy, for the FCC to regard itself as simply a service agency for the broadcasters. In this context, the public is regarded simply as a collection of spectators ——people who have no rights except that their dominating tastes must be satisfied in order to keep the broadcasters in business.

The broadcasters insist that there is no conflict between commercial broadcasting and the public interest——and therefore there is neither need nor justification for regulation beyond the allocations of channels. Here is Mr. Sarnoff on this subject, in what I believe to be a fair summary of the position of the industry as a whole:

(1) "Broadcasting, as a mass medium, best serves the public interest through programming which meets the desires and interests of the majority of the people.

(2) "Broadcasting assumes a secondary function of programming for minority tastes and interests and, by doing so, offers the majority continuing opportunity to absorb new interest.

(3) "Broadcasting's responsibility to the public is harmonious with its responsibility to advertisers, for the more effectively it serves the public, the greater value it offers advertisers.

(4) "Broadcasting depends on public acceptance of its programs in competition with all other forms of entertainment and information and can best serve the public through the free play of competition, and with a minimum of government regulation.

(5) "Broadcasting, as the nation's greatest unifying communications force in peace or war, is entitled to the standing and privileges of other free communication media."

In attempting to reach these five goals, broadcasters rely on audience-rating systems to discover "the desires and interests of the majority of the people." Our study shows that whole categories of programs tend to vanish from the air when the ratings are low. Other types flourish in great numbers when the ratings are high. Room for shows with less than the widest audience-appeal can be found only in marginal time periods.

Industry spokesmen contend that broadcasting's responsibility to the public is harmonious with its responsibility to the advertisers. The assumption in such a statement is that the broadcasters are adequately serving the public by renting out their channels at prime viewing hours to those who have enough money to buy time. This assumption underlies all of the industry's pronouncements. Under this policy, the largest possible audience has to be assembled for every program upon which the broadcaster relies for revenue—— because advertising rates are based on costs per thousand viewers. In practice the "secondary function" of programming for minority tastes loses priority and often all but disappears.

In terms of freedom of expression, broadcasting is certainly entitled to equal standing with the other media. But there is a notable difference between broadcasting and the press: in the print-media, advertisers do not as a matter of settled policy hold control of the placing and presentation of non-advertising matter. The press, with all its faults, inherently has far more independence of commercial forces and a more direct responsibility to the mass of paying customers who are its audience. This fundamental economic difference between the media puts broadcasting in a significantly different category from that of the printed press.

Life and *Look* are mass media appealing to national audiences comparable to those claimed by network television. But the operating premise of the proprietors of these periodicals is that they are in business to sell magazines, not goods. The assumption is that if they sell enough magazines, advertisers will buy space to reach the audience attracted by the editorial policies controlled by the proprietors; a column rule separates the space in which an advertiser makes his pitch and that in which the magazines' editors set forth their own picture of the world; if the column rules are not always inviolate they are still there, and nothing comparable exists in television.

In a controlling, economic sense broadcasters are totally and finally accountable to advertisers. There is no offset in circulation revenue, and no provable measurement of audience of the sort by which the printed media guarantee circulation on the reasonable assumption that those who pay for a copy of a publication are almost certainly going to read it. No proprietor of a newspaper or magazine will admit that his advertisers dominate his editorial policy and dictate the non-advertising content of his publication——even when there is a reasonable suspicion that this is true. On the other hand, no broadcaster will deny——except in the special instance of news and commentary—— that advertisers can, and frequently do, dictate program content.

In both radio and television the practice of turning over the entire production of major programs to advertising agencies has been common. The present talk among some broadcasters of adopting the "magazine concept" of programming is an admission that such a concept does not now exist. A reading of the broadcasting trade journals will demonstrate that this notion has already been flatly rejected by the advertisers——and I know of no one who seriously believes that of its own volition the industry is capable of denying the advertisers the last word on a program content.

It was proposed by a participant in one of our discussions that the FCC require all stations to carry educational and informational programs several hours each week in "prime evening time"——the hours between 7 and 10:30 P.M. This is closely related to a suggestion made by John Fischer, editor of *Harper's*, who urged that broadcasters, in return for the financial rewards of commercial broadcasting, underwrite such public service programs.

Edward R. Murrow, one of television's best-known commentators, urged the largest advertisers to buy time for programs which would tell "what is really going on in America." In their reaction to the TV scandals some of the networks are doing something like this voluntarily——and this has been hailed, primarily by apologists for the industry, as a heartening sign of a new trend in broadcasting. Even so, such notable prime time contributions as the excellent CBS and NBC documentaries on President Eisenhower's recent foreign tour still account for only a fraction of the pay-off hours and stand out in naked contrast to the standardized entertainment fare that surrounds them.

These departures from the norm are patently public relations devices and cannot be taken as reflecting permanent policy decisions. One does not need to be a cynic, only a student of the record to assume that programs of this calibre will inexorably find their way back to the Sunday afternoon "intellectual ghetto" once the public relations experts conclude that the public reaction to the quiz scandals has subsided to a safe level and that there is no clear and present danger of fall-out in terms of FCC regulation or Congressional action.

Another proposal made at one of our conferences called for a sizable expansion in the FCC's staff to make possible closer checking on the services rendered by the broadcasters; another participant recommended that Congress should give the FCC the funds to resume open hearings in communities across the country, with the people being invited to give their opinions of the mass media in their area. These proposals were designed to give the FCC the means to determine whether stations were actually living up to the public service plans described in their application for license.

It has been proposed also that licenses for broadcasters should come up for renewal every year or every six months, rather than every three years. Under this plan, probationary licenses would be issued to stations with poor records——the stations to be required to improve their community services before gaining full reinstatement.

Another proposal offered at one of our conferences was that the FCC should be transformed into a Federal Communications Court, thus separating the judicial functions of the FCC from the purely administrative functions.

Dean Louis Mayo of George Washington University Law School made two suggestions: (1) community audits of the services performed by the mass media, the audits to be supervised by the FCC and reported to the FCC; and (2) continuous analysis and evaluation of the mass media by an independent, privately-financed group of leading citizens.

There were also several more sweeping proposals discussed at some of our meetings——proposals which would change the fundamental structure of broadcasting.

What we now have is a privately owned broadcasting system, theoretically controlled by a few proprietors and managers but dominated by a few advertisers, and nominally regulated by a federal agency.

In theory, there are two drastic alternatives to this system: to turn everything over to private enterprise, freed of any form of governmental regulation; or to establish a broadcasting network financed and operated by the government.

Advocates of the first idea feel that the remedy for the problems in the present system might be found in taking all governmental regulatory powers out of the picture. With the total withdrawal of regulation, there might be a "healthy scramble." All commercial broadcasting would be moved to the Ultra-High-Frequency band, and free competition would determine what kind of service would be supplied to the public. This apparently is technically possible, but the burden of our findings is in accord with those of the "Bowles Report" to the Senate Interstate and Foreign Commerce Committee——mixed in detail but generally pessimistic.

The general feeling seems to be that the re-establishment of unrestricted competition in TV broadcasting has become practically impossible. Broadcasting now is largely confined to the limited VHF band——and the public has a multi-billion-dollar investment in VHF receivers that freezes it there.

The other drastic alternative considered in theory was the establishment of a governmental broadcasting system. The BBC and the Canadian systems have been suggested as models which the people of the United States might consider. The basic objective would be to develop a broadcasting system of high quality with adequate arrangements to satisfy the intellectual and cultural needs of minorities. An independent governmental broadcasting system, operated by a public authority after the fashion of TVA, has been suggested by Walter Lippmann and others as a yardstick by which to measure commercial programming as well as a source of information and education.

Questions were raised at our meetings on whether the establishment of such a network would be regarded as a violation of the First Amendment. Precedents were cited for governmental operation of broadcasting facilities, and the consensus was that such a network could be organized on a constitutional basis.

However, most of the participants in our discussions were strongly opposed to governmental intervention of this type. Many expressed the belief that the function of the government should be limited to protecting the individual's freedom of speech without entering directly into the operation of the mass media. The usual fears of the danger of converting a public system into an official propaganda medium were also voiced.

No one contends that the FCC does not have the power of regulation——although the broadcasters, as their vested interest in the medium has increased, have come to add always the modifying "minimum." It seems to me to be quite clear that the public's definition of "minimum" regulation does not coincide with that of the industry. For example, Mr. Sarnoff's statement of policy, which I have quoted, stresses the fact that broadcasting "assumes a secondary function of programming for minority tastes and interest." The testimony you have heard so far makes it abundantly clear that that function is not being adequately fulfilled. It follows, then, that broadcasting does not always "serve the public through the free play of competition"——for the very good reason that by its nature there is no full and free competition in broadcasting. Millions of Americans have access to only one TV station; those who have access to more than one channel usually find a slavish imitation of program content among the three networks during the prime viewing time——and a preponderant diet of old films during most of the rest. Finally, Mr. Sarnoff's claim that broadcasting is inherently entitled to the "standing and privilege of other free communications media" simply flies in the face of the facts. Each broadcasting station is licensed by this agency. That license gives the station a monopoly over a valuable part of the radio spectrum; the limitations of the spectrum make it certain in most instances that mere possession of a license will guarantee a substantial profit even when there are competing stations. By these elementary tests, then, broadcasting has many of the characteristics of a public utility.

Certainly I am not suggesting any form of censorship or of direct control over program content by this or any other public agency. I recognize that at some point regulation could come into collision with the First Amendment, whose guarantees of free speech and a free press certainly apply to broadcasting as well as to the printed media. At that point I would stand for freedom.

But I submit that the proposals discussed here stop well short of that critical point. They do *not* call upon FCC to assume jurisdiction over program content. They do call upon FCC to set certain standards of performance as a measurement by which it may determine whether a broadcaster is entitled to a valuable public grant in return for a contractual guarantee to serve the public interest. Moreover, it should be noted that the most important of these proposals point away from excessive federal regulation and in the direction of greater diversity of broadcasting and genuine competition for the attention and the dollars of the public——our historic device for protecting the public good with a minimum of official interference.

It is the FCC that has divided the radio spectrum, granted the licenses, and placed the broadcasting in the hands of its present proprietors. If there is to be a change in the present pattern——which by public test has proven inadequate in important respects——only this agency on its own motion, or by Congressional direction, can bring it about. Given greater diversity and real competition, I believe many of the present ills would disappear, and others could be left to private ministration.

To that end I would call your attention to the recommendation of Senator Benton and others for the creation of an independent citizen's commission to carry on a continuous review and appraisal of the mass media. Whether this be done by presidential appointment or other official act, as Mr. Benton has proposed, or be created and supported by purely private means, it should be made up of interested, informed, and concerned citizens completely independent of the industry. Having no regulatory or coercive powers, such a commission would encounter no conflict with the First Amendment. It could perform a critical function in regard to program content properly denied to this agency but clearly needed by a developing industry which has demonstrated that it cannot sustain its own declared standards of responsibility and taste in the face of commercial pressures which dominate it.

Such a commission might cause pain to some of those who now control broadcasting. But if it succeeded in mobilizing public opinion it would also free the medium of the tyranny which forces it to base most programming on the advertiser's estimate of the common denominator. With its great financial resources, and its still exciting if largely unrealized potential, television commands the greatest pool of creative talent our country has ever known. Yet this talent has no effective command over the medium, with the result that the creative urge is frustrated and often perverted. At the least this is a tragic waste of a great natural resource; it may also be a positive threat to the national interest in a time when there is general agreement that we need a new spiritual awakening. I do not believe that anyone in the television industry could seriously challenge the statement that television, which was hailed at its advent as a means toward new intellectual stimulation, has instead become an opiate. Indeed, by implication, this is conceded by the leaders of the industry who have appeared before you and defended their performance on the ground that they are giving most of the people what they want.

The performance of the broadcasters is a proper matter of public concern, as is the performance of the proprietors of the printed media. The role of the government in determining what that performance shall be is, of necessity, essentially negative; the government may define certain outer limits of free speech on grounds of obscenity and libel, and it may set general standards that must be met in return for governmental bounty in the form of monopoly broadcast licenses or mail subsidies.

We are all of us properly concerned that there be no trespass beyond these limits that would inhibit freedom of expression. But we need to be equally concerned that the safeguards we erect do not in fact serve to reduce the diversity of what we hear and see and read to the point where we have access only to minor variations on a single monotonous theme.

The government has an obligation to see to it that there is a fair field for broadcasting. Private citizens——educators, philanthropists, and ordinary viewers and listeners——have an obligation to see to it that the field is occupied by the bold as well as the bland. At the end of the first decade of TV it is obvious that neither obligation has been met.

ROBERT W. SARNOFF

23   Television Journalism:
The Shackled Giant

■

Mr. Sarnoff's recommendations for achieving a higher standard of television journalism are based on the premise that the medium can only be truly responsible if it is entirely free from governmental restrictions. Eloquently and fervently, he pleads for the removal of the "equal time" provision of the Federal Communications Commission statutes; and goes on to urge the use of television in areas of public life where it is currently restricted: the federal courts, Congress and the Senate. Mr. Sarnoff's laissez-faire position is in general agreement with Dr. Frank Stanton's concepts of the relationship between television and government and is in opposition to Mr. Frank Kelly's suggestions for continued governmental monitoring. Together these three views offer a comprehensive and authoritative look at one of the most important and lively controversies in American mass communications today.

Mr. Sarnoff, who is President of the Radio Corporation of America, delivered Television: The Shackled Giant as an address before the Economic Club of Detroit, Michigan, on December 7, 1964, when he was Board Chairman of the National Broadcasting Company. It is presented here in a slightly abridged format.

IT WAS NOT LONG AGO that some tried to discount the influence of television simply by refusing to own a set, or, owning one, by ignoring it. One can no more do that today than one can deny the social and economic impact of the automobile by declining to use it. For, like the automobile, television has run a rapid course from its origin as a private novelty to its emergence as a public necessity.

At its beginning the primary mission of television, as of radio before it, was entertainment, and although it has developed far greater dimensions in the intervening years, its spectacular growth has been based on the quest of a nationwide audience for laughter and fiction and fantasy.

In 1949, there were 700,000 television homes. Today there are more than 52 million. Over the same period, advertising expenditures in the medium have risen from less than $58 million to more than $2 billion. And now color has won a firm and growing beachhead, while America's appetite for television continues to increase. Currently, the average family watches television more than five-and-a-half hours a day, in response to the program schedules that have been shaped by an aggregate of considerations. Foremost among these have been public popularity, the need for a broad base of commercial support and the continuous striving of broadcasters for innovation and diversity.

And as an effective instrument for demonstration and sales, reaching millions of consumers in their homes every minute, television has revolutionized the speed and efficiency of our marketing and distribution system——the core of an expanding economy rich in production capacity.

The warm embrace of its audience and its advertisers has not altogether shielded television from the cold blasts of criticism. One need go no further than the television columns——and sometimes the editorial columns——of his daily newspaper to find a constant questioning of television's entertainment schedules and a cataloguing of its flaws and failings, some real and some imagined. This must be expected by a medium that undertakes to meet so many varied—— and often conflicting——tastes within our multiple society. It is often constructive criticism and it underscores the importance television has achieved in the lives of millions of Americans.

Valid criticism can serve television, and, more important, its audience. It would be a great misfortune for both, however, if a debate that turns on the variables of taste in entertainment should obscure a most salient fact about television: that it has become the foremost medium of news and information for a public that must be informed if it is to survive as a free society.

The massive influence of television journalism is demonstrated by survey results showing that more than half the nation gets most of its news from television.

A single news program on NBC, for example——"The Huntley-Brinkley Report"——reaches more than 36 million people a week.

In the Cuban nuclear confrontation two years ago, when the moves and countermoves of the United States and the Soviet Union followed each other with stunning swiftness, television's immediacy and constant availability in reporting these critical events placed them in prompt and comprehensible order.

Its live, on-the-spot coverage of great public events——addresses by national leaders, the national political conventions, the orbiting of a man in space——gives our people a means of direct participation in the life of the nation no other medium can provide.

And in four shattering days in November 1963, television demonstrated with great distinction its unmatched power to envelop an entire population in the details of national crisis and grief and, as a further dimension of its singular capacity, to unite the public in spirit and in purpose.

Television is now a basic part of the American press. With its reach, immediacy and directness it has unique capabilities for informing the public and engaging them in the affairs of their society. As a consequence, it, too, has taken on the classic responsibility of the press to serve as the public's watchdog in relation to the activities of politics and government.

The principle of a free press was established as the cornerstone of our democratic society by a generation of men who still bore the scars of a tyrant's lash. Its purpose was to protect the public's right to unfettered dissemination of views and information so the public itself could forever determine the direction of that society.

Our founding fathers insisted that their institutions be fully visible, and this visibility so struck the visiting French aristocrat Alexis de Tocqueville that he wrote in his historic treatise *Democracy in America:* "The American learns to know the laws by participating in the act of legislation; and he takes a lesson in the forms of government from governing. The great work of society is going on before his eyes, and, as it were, under his hands."

The American society has grown considerably more intricate since de Tocqueville wrote those words. Few Americans can know their candidates for public office personally, and the town meeting has bowed to the voting machine. The operation and scope of federal government have removed much of the workings of his nation from the individual. The intimate relationship between our people and their institutions has been altered by the inexorable force of technological, social and political change.

The pace of change has had a profound effect, too. Events succeed events with overwhelming speed, and time for decision, action and reaction has been compressed into history's microseconds.

In the fanciful world of mythology, the more difficult problems were solved by gods and giants. In our own time we have been aided by the fortuitous arrival of a communications giant——television—— that cannot solve our problems for us but can assist an entire population in understanding them.

For all these reasons, the public's stake in freedom of the press applies with particular forcefulness to television journalism. Yet it is in television's most essential area of information service that its capacities are seriously restricted——in political coverage, in dealing with controversy, in reporting on the public business.

Paradoxically, these shackles——which do not apply to any other medium——have been forged by government itself in the name of the public interest. Two arguments are generally offered to justify them, and both are invalid.

One is based on fear of television's power and unique capabilities. A medium so influential, it is argued, should be regulated to assure its responsibility.

This is precisely the theory used to argue for repression of the printed press when its force was first felt. We have come to recognize, however, that danger does not lie in a free news medium, but in a regulated one. A regulated press is vulnerable to official pressures, to timidity, to accommodation. A free medium of journalism is independent of these forces which can threaten its integrity. In an open society, the greater the freedom of the press, the less the danger. And in such a society, television's power as a communicator is a public asset to be developed, not a public danger to be restrained by laws and regulations.

The other argument for restriction rests on the circumstance that television uses a public resource, the frequency spectrum; that it therefore has been licensed by the government to operate in the public interest; and that consequently the government should represent the people by judging what is in their interest.

The fallacy here lies in the assumption that in the field of journalism the government can better judge what is in the public interest than the press or public itself——and assumption directly contrary to the Constitutional guarantee that "Congress shall make no law . . . abridging the freedom of the press."

The Supreme Court has ruled that broadcasting is included in the press whose freedom is guaranteed, and the Federal Communications Commission has explicitly acknowledged this. Additionally, the Communications Act expressly forbids the Commission from censoring radio and television broadcasts.

Restrictions on television's news function cannot be justified by invoking the precept that "the airwaves belong to the people." On the contrary, that precept demands that the people's resource be used in their service to provide a free flow of information and ideas unfettered by government restraint. The government's licensing authority over television, designed to promote efficient use of broadcast frequencies in the public interest, is not a license to the government to control or influence the function of a free press.

Although the arguments for regulation do not stand the test of principle or logic, there are in the law, in the stated policy of the Federal Communications Commission and in the practices of legislative and judiciary bodies the elements of an effective control over television's journalistic expression.

Perhaps the best known is the so-called equal-time requirement, imposed on political coverage by Section 315 of the Communications Act. With stated exceptions, it requires that a broadcaster who makes his facilities available to a candidate for political office must provide the same opportunity to all candidates for the same office ——a requirement that would shock public conscience if it were applied to the printed press.

Its effect has been to restrain broadcasters from presenting serious and major candidates who command the public interest, by requiring the same amount of air time to be devoted to candidates of splinter and frivolous parties in whom the public has little or no interest; and the by-product of this mechanistic rule has been less, rather than more, exposure of candidates and discussion of issues.

The shackles were eased, on an experimental basis, during the 1960 Presidential campaign when the equal-time rule was suspended for appearances by the Presidential and Vice Presidential candidates. The result was the historic television encounters between John F. Kennedy and Richard M. Nixon. Equally important was the great variety of special programs in which the major candidates were enabled to appear. These, together with the debates, were generally credited with making an unprecedented contribution to the definition of the issues and a stimulation of interest in the campaign and the elections.

Despite broadcasting's acknowledged record of responsibility and fairness in covering the 1960 campaign, Congress this year declined to suspend the equal-time provision. As a consequence, a significant measure of control over journalistic presentation of the campaign was removed from the hands of the broadcast journalist; and a seven-member government agency, the Federal Communications Commission, was placed in the unhappy position of having to interpret and apply a statutory control over campaign coverage.

The maintenance of the equal-time restriction had a variety of curious results, none serving the public interest.

Early in the campaign the Commission interpreted the statue to mean that the President's traditional nationwide television appeal in behalf of the United Community Fund would oblige broadcasters to grant equal-time claims by all other candidates for the Presidency.

Soon after, the Commission ruled that under Section 315, the broadcasting of Presidential news conferences would entitle all Presidential candidates to claim and receive equal time.

Later, in a more widely publicized incident, the Commission decided that a television address by the President on the removal of Premier Khrushchev, the explosion of a nuclear bomb by the Red Chinese, and the significance of the British elections did not entitle the Republican candidate to equal time. If, as a matter of news judgment, the networks had decided to grant Senator Goldwater an opportunity to comment on these international developments, they would have opened a round of claims for equal time by at least ten minor candidates for the Presidency.

Beyond these rather visible results, the most drastic, but less obvious, effect of the equal-time restriction was to inhibit the appearance of major candidates in many special programs that had been designed to give wide exposure to the principal contenders for office, their backgrounds and their views. We may speculate on the extent to which this restriction of television's capacity to present the candidates speaking directly to the public contributed to a widely noted characteristic of the 1964 campaign——its failure to develop a clear focus on the issues.

Surely, as these examples demonstrate, a law that requires a government agency to direct the manner in which the public may be informed in an election campaign is inconsistent with the aims of democracy.

On another, related front, the Commission, through interpretation and policy rulings, has undertaken to review fairness in the broadcast coverage of all matters in controversy——a function it identifies with the appealing title of "The Fairness Doctrine."

No one can argue against the desirability of fairness in reporting controversial public issues; but one can properly argue against the advisability of having the members of a government agency and its staff review the judgments of professional newsmen, editors and news executives on what is fair news coverage.

Such a process compels the regulatory agency, in the first instance, to define what is controversial and what is not, on matters ranging from major international events to local community problems. It places on appointed officials of government the obligation to judge, often without firsthand knowledge or expertise, whether the issues have been fully and fairly explored in news treatment.

Further, it invites individual and special interests to use the Commission's processes for contesting news programs they do not favor. For example, over the last two and a half years, the Commission has asked NBC to respond to fairness complaints lodged by organizations or individuals against news documentaries on social welfare practices in the City of Newburgh, New York; fallout shelters; the economic situation on the Caribbean Island of Nevis; Red China; medical care for the aged; frauds in highway construction; the New York City newspaper strike; race relations and the civil rights march on Washington, and poverty in the Lower Rio Grande Valley.

That is only a partial list, and in these and other similar cases, the Commission, after investigation, has presumably been satisfied with the fairness of the broadcasts questioned.

But that is not the issue. For even though the Commission has sought to encourage journalistic enterprise and the coverage of controversy by broadcasters, its undertaking to review their performance in this field weakens the very effort it seeks to encourage. The danger here lies in having an arm of the government that holds the licensing power in a position to second-guess the broadcaster's journalistic judgment in reporting on events and issues that at times involve the government itself.

The third main area of restriction is the official exclusion of television from places where the public's business is conducted. These include the floor of the House of Representatives and its Committee rooms; the floor of the Senate; the Supreme Court; all federal courts, and the legislative chambers and the courts of most states and localities.

Thus in our open society we have an officially sanctioned denial of its principles, and in this area the public's foremost medium of information is confronted with a closed door.

Originally it was contended, not without reason, that bulky broadcasting and lighting equipment would be an awkward intrusion upon serious proceedings. Technology can solve that problem. Now——as has been demonstrated by the experience in equipping the United Nations for broadcast coverage——it is possible for television to report proceedings in legislative chambers, hearing rooms and court rooms with cameras that are not only unobtrusive but out of sight.

So the argument has shifted to the expressed concern that some legislators or lawyers might take to performing for the cameras, rather than for their constituents and clients. If that should happen, however, their behavior would be displayed and exposed by television itself as the reporter of actuality——a course that should contribute to decorum and responsibility rather than detract from it. But even if a few should be stimulated to unseemly behavior, that is certainly insufficient reason for denying the rights of the many to attend, through television, those occasions where the public's business is conducted.

The result of all these restrictions upon television coverage of candidates, controversy and huge areas of the public business has been to by-pass the historic right of the public to free and full access to information on all matters that affect it.

To safeguard that fundamental right, certain specific steps can and should be taken. Insofar as they call for Congressional action, the time to act is in the coming year, away from the heat and contention of a political campaign, when the public policy issues involved can be considered with calm reflection.

First, the Congress should revise Section 315 of the Communications Act to eliminate the equal-time requirement completely and permanently. This provision of the law has in fact served a purpose contrary to the one anticipated and it discriminates against the medium of information best equipped to inform the public on candidates and issues.

Second, the Congress should make it clear that the Federal Communications Commission is not mandated to pass on how broadcasters cover public issues in controversy. Review by a federal agency of journalistic judgment and expression is contrary to the principle of a free press.

It is possible that a few irresponsible broadcasters might abuse the freedom such actions would give them. I do not believe, however, that this possibility warrrants throttling a whole communications medium——any more than it would warrant imposing similar restrictions on the whole newspaper field because of a few irresponsible newspapers.

Third, the doors to public proceedings should be opened to television whenever they are open to other elements of the press, so that television can use its special capacities to enable the people to witness the conduct of the people's business. This calls for abandonment of existing discriminatory rules barring television from federal, state and local legislative chambers and the hearing rooms of legislative committees.

What is needed is the establishment of an affirmative public policy declaring that the institutions of government should be fully open to television coverage, limited only by defined requirements of security and due process. In this field, official attitudes and policy development have not kept pace with television's emergence as a major communications force. In considering television and other media, the goal should always be to expand to the maximum the information that can properly be made public, not reduce it to the minimum.

There is, however, one area of the public business——in arrest, pretrial and trial proceedings——where conflicts may arise between the public's right to information and the right of the accused to a fair trial. The Report of the Warren Commission, for example, has recently expressed concern that the unrestrained coverage of pre-trial activities impedes or corrupts the judicial process. In terms both of principle and practicality, the solution to such a problem does not lie in placing restraints on newsmen in reporting available information, but in establishing standards to guide officers of the court——law enforcement officials and counsel——in divulging information that does not prejudice judicial process. Similarly, affirmative standards can be established to enable television coverage of trials, with such safeguards as may be necessary to protect the rights of the accused.

In considering these standards and safeguards, it should always be remembered that the absence of full public information about such proceedings can itself lead to infringement of an individual's rights. For access of the information media to judicial proceedings creates a two-way street: the accused, if he should suffer abuse, can reach the public; and the public can be informed as to the nature of the proceedings involving the accused.

In this special area, I am confident that if representatives of the judiciary, the bar and journalism joined in a constructive examination of the issue, they could develop a meeting ground where both public and private rights would be protected and advanced. There is an immediate need to define how television access to judicial proceedings can be enlarged to the full extent consistent with due process. This approach, I believe, holds far greater promise than codes designed to formalize restrictions on the gathering of news.

Restrictions on any part of the press threaten the principle underlying the vitality of all parts of the press. The public's stake in that principle should be supported and protected by all news media, not only to safeguard their own rights to freedom of speech and the press, but more importantly to protect the public's right to learn and to know. Print journalism and broadcast journalism have common interests and responsibilities which transcend their competitive endeavors.

Finally, it must be emphasized that the arguments and proposals I have advanced are not designed for the benefit of television. They relate directly to television's ability to discharge its responsibility to the public. The public in turn, has a responsibility to take an active role to protect its own interest in television's freedom to perform its journalistic function.

Individuals and organizations must accept and pursue this obligation by insisting that their elected representatives take whatever steps are necessary to allow the free flow of ideas, information and fact to reach their natural level of service.

Only then will television be fully able to carry out its mission of informing the people to the ultimate limits of its vast potential, as an auditor of government for the people, and a great force for fuller understanding of ourselves and institutions. Only then will we be true to the precepts of Thomas Jefferson who displayed an insight that was to prove applicable over the ages when he wrote:

"I know of no safe repository of the ultimate powers of society but the people themselves, and if we think them not enlightened enough to exercise their control with a wholesome discretion, the remedy is not to take it from them but to inform their discretion by education."

DR. FRANK STANTON

24   The Responsibility of the Press

■

Dr. Frank Stanton, President of the Columbia Broadcasting System, Inc., is regarded throughout America as one of the communication industry's most articulate and respected voices. And as president of one of the nation's leading broadcasting companies, his views are newsworthy and influential.

In the following chapter, Dr. Stanton discusses several of television's most consequential issues. His comments on TV's responsibility in reporting the war in Viet Nam; his proposal for abolition of "the equal time" clause of the FCC and his urgings to permit TV cameras in the courts and the legislatures are contained, eloquent and soundly reasoned pleas for giving TV greater scope in American life without the supervisory restrictions of the government as a possible deterrent to the fulfillment of this scope.

Mr. Frank Kelly of the Fund for the Republic presents the opposing point of view (elsewhere in this volume) in his remarks before the FCC.

There are no easy answers to the proper dimensions of governmental activity in the communication industry, but the opinions of Dr. Stanton, Mr. Sarnoff (of NBC) and Mr. Kelly together combine to offer a balanced and informed picture of TV grappling with its responsibility to the public.

Dr. Stanton's comments were first made in speeches and in testimony before the FCC as noted appropriately in the following chapter. "The Face of War" appears here in a slightly abridged format.

THE FACE OF WAR

Waldorf-Astoria Hotel, New York, N.Y.
January 28, 1966

THE PAST FOUR DECADES have seen broadcast journalism grow in competence and thoroughness until today the majority of Americans look first to radio and television for their information. Those same four decades have seen the nation's bleakest depression, the world's most devastating war, and mankind's most dramatic scientific progress.

All these put a tough challenge, first to radio and then to television, to report and interpret them accurately, vividly, and in such a way that the American people were significantly aided in carrying out effectively their decision-making duties as citizens.

But the responsibility of broadcasting in gathering and reporting the news has never been more pressing and more difficult than it is now. The overriding fact of our national life today is the war in Vietnam. It is our duty in broadcasting to bring the face of this war——the human face on the battlefield and the issues behind it—— to all the people so that they can witness it and understand it. This is turning out to be a rough job, full of perplexing and persistent problems. The forthright reporting of unpleasant facts has inspired adverse reactions both from the public and from Washington. Unjust and senseless charges of unpatriotic conduct have been made against correspondents for doing their jobs under the most difficult conditions imaginable.

I am not talking here about censorship or matters involving military security. I am not talking even about "managed news." I am talking about facts and issues that our people have to know in order to carry out their decision-making responsibilities as citizens.

There has been debate and protest at home and abroad——some of it irresponsible and thoughtless, some of it conscionable and informed. Motives and objectives have been difficult to define and susceptible of distortion. It is a war which we are fighting in double-harness, in which we alone cannot call the turns, and where our status is only that of supporters of one of the two principals. And it is an

open-ended war, unpredictable, and sometimes seeming to be inter-
minable in its consumption of lives and effort without any apparent
movement forward——a war about which it is easy to lose heart and
easy to lose perspective.

Besides its baffling intrinsic nature, the Vietnam war has also been
a baffling one for our newsmen, our reporters, and our camermen.
Operating on their own in a war of no fixed positions, they have had
to use ingenuity, persistence, and sheer guts to bring the harsh reality
of this agonizing war home to us here in the United States. They have
to provide for themselves and work in isolation from their colleagues.
For their pains——and I use the word literally——they have been
attacked more often than they have been praised.

There is an ancient proverb about the low regard in which the bearer
of ill-tidings is held. "None love the messenger who brings bad
news," wrote Sophocles. Unhappily, much of the news in any war is
bad news, and this one is far from an exception. As a result, the men
who risk their lives to get the sounds and sights of the embattled, and
the men who stay up all night to get the material ready for the air, are
treated in many cases as if they invented the events and conditions they
are reporting.

There are those, too, including some in our government, who
would like only the good news reported. Threats of reprisal, of
making a difficult job all but impossible, have not been unknown. But
failures and mistakes are an essential part of the story. If they are to
be avoided or corrected, it will not be by hiding them but only by
bringing them fully out into the open where the people have a chance
to examine them and then to make their opinion felt. For as Sophocles also wrote, "Truth is always the strongest argument."

On the other hand, in the absence of formal censorship, we
scrupulously follow the three general principles put to the news media
by the Pentagon for voluntary adoption: we will report casualty
statistics on a daily basis only in general terms, we will report troop
movements only when the enemy already know them, and we will
refrain from giving the names and numbers of specific units engaged
in individual battles. We also do everything we can to avoid revealing
the identities of individual casualties before next of kin have been
notified. All these are sensible restrictions with the sole purpose of
limiting information reaching the enemy. But in other respects——in

common with all conscientious journalists——we are not subscribing to any theory of news by hand-out, telling the American people only what somebody arbitrarily decides that they should know and concealing the rest.

This policy does not make for unanimous popularity, although we are convinced that in the long run it is the only sound one. And not all our letters are fan letters. We receive some very vigorous letters protesting that we are bringing the horrors of war too vividly into American homes, that we are reporting facts too unpleasant for the public to know, that we are showing too much of the fighting, that we are not showing enough of the fighting and too much of the draft-card burning, that we are propagandists for the war, and that we are propagandists against it.

Much of this, I suppose, is understandable. The human face of war is never pleasant to look upon, and its stark reality is far more jolting in the quiet living room on Elm Street than it is on the battleground. But the fact of the matter is that Elm Street is no less involved in this conflict because of its distance from the combat area and because fighting is delegated to a comparative few of the young. Decisions made in Washington and culminating on a steaming, tortured peninsula ten thousand miles away begin in the living room and end there. To ignore this is to deny our birthright and our responsibility as a free people.

The forces of history have put to the American people in the past troubled decade some very tough and unpalatable choices, and there are going to be some tougher ones ahead. None is tougher than the decisions we must make about the extent to which we press this war and the conditions under which we resolve it. It is as fundamental an element of common sense as it is of the democratic proposition that we had better know, as close to first hand as we can get, the realities, the facts, even the atmosphere and climate of the events both giving rise to and springing from those decisions.

It seems to me highly fortunate that this, the most difficult of all wars to report and understand, is the first war also which we have been able to report with the immediacy, the speed, and the thoroughness of modern-day electronic journalism. The reality of the Civil War was brought home forcefully to the people by the searching and ubiquitous eye of Brady's camera, but his pictures were not seen by most people for months and even years after the events pictured. The choppy films of World War I were mute and fragmented and seen only in brief unrelated sequences in the nickelodeons of the time. Even the intrepid microphone and the dogged motion picture camera of World War II for the most part kept sound and sight apart. To the family on Elm Street the war was reconstructed solely by the words of reporters, written or oral, with an occasional glimpse of what it looked like in a still picture or in a movie clip sandwiched into the news reels of movie houses.

The desperation of Vietnam, on the other hand, is witnessed every day by the vast majority of Americans in their own homes. Very possibly before it is over, it will be brought directly by satellite. War has ceased to be a far-off thing of cold casualty statistics, unpronounceable geographical names, and unread speeches by unknown statesmen. The misery of war, the pain, the death, the fear, the drudgery, the intensely felt convictions, the troubled dissents, the shrill protests, the deep determination——all these are brought full-scale to the people with whom the final responsibility for national commitments in a democratic society rests.

There is a loneliness about the burden that this nation has assumed in Vietnam, and at times a sense of despair, that could so weaken our sense of purpose as to endanger our cause. To overcome this, we need to keep before us both the issues involved and the realities that make them more than issues. This is not to suggest that the function of electronic or any other journalism is to serve as spokesmen of national policy. It is to assert that the function of all journalism is to furnish the people ultimately responsible for that policy with the facts——the shocking as well as the placid, the ominous as well as the reassuring, the dissenting as well as the agreeing. That this policy, the only sound one for a free press, is also the only right one for a free people seems to me clearly established by the attitude of the people themselves. Recent national surveys reveal that the majority of Americans understand why we are in Vietnam and generally support our using armed forces to bring about a satisfactory resolution.

The matrix of that understanding and of that support is the day-to-day events of the most enigmatic of all wars——both the tired face of combat and the heated confrontation of issues. It seems to me that there is no more important responsibility of broadcasting today than to report those events fully, accurately, and forthrightly, and to analyze their meaning candidly and decisively.

BEFORE THE SUBCOMMITTEE ON COMMUNICATIONS AND POWER
HOUSE INTERSTATE AND FOREIGN COMMERCE COMMITTEE

March 4, 1963

The position of CBS on Section 315 has so often been set forth, both before Committees of the Senate and the House and in speeches and articles, that I am sure I need not take up your time in spelling it out in detail here today: CBS is for outright, permanent and total repeal of Section 315.

The premises of Section 315 were simple: during political campaigns, the broadcasters could not be trusted to be fair and impartial in the treatment of political candidates and their parties over the airwaves. A statutory device was contrived to impose upon broadcasters a civic responsibility. The device backfired. Far from assuring the execution of that responsibility, it created over the years a chronic situation which has exactly the opposite effect; it deprived the broadcasters, by the unworkable, mathematically implausible and substantively self-defeating equal time requirement, of an opportunity to carry out their responsibility. By forcing them, in defiance of all the dictates of relevance and significance, to give equal time to the most trivial and irresponsible candidates of the most bizarre parties, it forced them also to deny time to the busy and distinguished men and women seriously aspiring to serve their nation, their states and their communities.

The crippling effect of this was recognized by the Congress in 1959, when Section 315 was so amended as to exclude from the reach of its equal time restrictions newscasts, news interviews, news documentaries and on-the-spot coverage of news events. But the amendments went only part of the way in clearing up the difficulty. In 1960, through the aroused interest of both major parties, of far-sighted officers of the government, of journalists of all the media and particularly through the efforts of this Committee and your colleagues of the House and of the Senate, at the eleventh hour of the 86th Congress, the provisions of Section 315 were suspended with regard to the Presidential and Vice Presidential offices for the 1960 election.

The suspension proved two things. Contrary to the old implications of Section 315, there was proof on a national scale that broadcasters in this country had far too much sense of responsibility, far too much maturity, far too much sheer will to survive, to abuse the freedom granted by the suspension through unfair, partial or partisan treatment of the candidates. Secondly, it proved that, released from a discredited unworkable restriction, the broadcast media could spark interest in a campaign, stimulate new interest on the part of other media and significantly advance voter participation in the election.

The statistics in terms of coverage given the Presidential and Vice Presidential candidates are persuasive evidence of the increased usefulness to the American people that an unfettered radio and television can be. In 1960 the CBS Radio and Television Networks devoted a total of 16¼ hours to personal appearances of the Democratic and Republican Presidential and Vice Presidential candidates, at no charge to them. This, compared to 36 minutes in 1956. In 1960, another 16 hours were given supporters of the major candidates. Time costs of these 1960 broadcasts exceeded $2 million, and additional time worth another $700,000 was offered to the candidates but not accepted.

There seems to me no question as to the proof offered by the 1960 experiment that Section 315 is an unnecessary and crippling straightjacket into which broadcasters, singled out among all the media, are forced. Nobody benefits from it. Nobody is protected by it. We are all better off without it. The very fact that we are today considering a move once again to suspend it for the next Presidential election is in itself evidence that we ought not to be saddled with it.

The only question is (and to me it's less a question than an unsupportable contradiction) why what has proved so conclusively a great good for a Presidential campaign——the unfettering of radio and television to cover a campaign as events and not as prohibitive statutes dictate——is not equally good for contests for the United States Senate and House of Representatives, for the governors of our states and the mayors of our cities.

We in this country live under the most demonstrably workable system of self-government the mind of man has ever devised. Not only do we have, inherent in our constitutional processes, a division of powers in our national government but we also have a division of powers with regard to the scope of national, state and local authority. Nor have these been merely legalistic or academic. They are responsible for the very survival of a democratic experiment that asked of a heterogeneous people living over a vast area, encompassing different geographic, economic and social conditions, the achievement of a free and constructive way of life that far more monolithic societies had failed to accomplish.

Any legislation that seeks to differentiate between either the national elective executive and legislative officers on the one hand or, on the other, between the elective officers of the federal government and those of state and local governments, seeks, in my judgment, to diminish the essential distinctions that have made our country the oldest, most successful constitutional democracy on the face of the earth.

What are we doing when we say that it is all right for broadcasters to have freedom, always subject to our general responsibility to be fair, to present the candidates and issues in Presidential campaigns but not those in Congressional campaigns? Aren't we saying that it is not as important, that we can be content with a mandatory restriction that we no longer consider healthful to the choice of our executive leadership?

Yet the fundamental fact of our national life is that the Congress still represents the people. The members of this House of Representatives are still more directly and more frequently answerable to the people than any officers in our national government. They are still more directly in tune with the people, not only of every state but of every region within those states. They are still charged with originating the raising of revenues, without which all other arms of the government would be powerless. They are still charged with supervisory surveillance over more intricate and extensive governmental machinery than the free world has ever seen. They are still charged with functioning on two levels, representing both the communities which send them here and the nation to whose interests they are bound by oath.

Similarly, the members of the United States Senate have distinguishing responsibilities that ought to be respected in any legislation that, intentionally or otherwise, evaluates the sources of our national authority. They represent all the people of their states. They must serve a longer term than any other officers of the federal government. They must directly confirm or reject Presidential appointments of critical importance and responsibility. They must act with the President in the field of foreign affairs. They must act with the House in the allocation of public monies and in the enactment of the laws that govern our lives.

Is there any logic at all in saying that it is not just as important to have free and full broadcasting coverage of election contests for these offices as for the Presidency? Is there any logic at all in saying there should be more restrictive ground rules for one than for the other? Is there any logic at all in saying that the division of powers is our most priceless constitutional heritage and then by legislative act putting one branch in a separate category from the other?

I am unwilling to concede that we live in an era solely of Presidential government——that if we have freedom with regard to candidates for the Presidency we do not have to worry about the Congress.

I am no more willing to concede that if our national leadership is chosen after the freest and fullest dissemination of its views on all our media, we do not need to worry about our state and local leadership. Any such notion flies right straight in the face of our whole experience as a self-governing people.

The governors and mayors, the legislatures and councils, of our states and municipalities are responsible for spending more than half again what our national government spends in non-military expenses ——well over $50 billion every year. They are responsible for the health, the education and the public safety of over 180 million people. They are the guardians of the rights and privileges and responsibilities specifically reserved to their constituencies by the Constitution. We wander on dangerous ground indeed when we distinguish between the freedom of the process by which their actions, their intentions and their policies are reported to their electorates in campaign time and those by which the President's and Vice President's are.

CBS has a basic uneasiness also about the freedom of broadcasters being conditioned by election-year to election-year *ad hoc* decisions about what the ground rules are. Principle is involved here. The principle is simply——not what is in the best interest of the candidate and not what is in the best interest of the broadcaster——but what is in the best interest of the people. The 1960 suspension proved what is in their interest. I cannot see how this can vary from year to year. I cannot see how it is even susceptible of constant reappraisal. If it was good in 1960 for the people to have the advantage of unlimited, unrestricted, unprescribed exposure of the candidates in the Presidential campaign, it can be no less good, from their point of view, in 1964 or 1968 or 1972——or all the years to come.

Up until 1960 broadcasters repeatedly asked the Congress to accept only their word that they could be trusted to be responsible, to act fairly, without Section 315. But with the 1960 suspension they proved that they were responsible and acted fairly. The Congress had the right to a test. We met the test. And now House Joint Resolution 247 proposes that we take the test all over again, though it no longer has the experimental point that the Resolution had in 1960.

I am grateful for this opportunity to restate the CBS position. I am grateful that this Subcommittee is concerning itself, now, well in advance of the next elections, with this crucial matter. I am deeply appreciative of this Subcommittee's efforts to get something specific done about it. I hope that you can see your way clear, however, to urging the Congress to face the fundamental problem and to provide the fundamental solution——and that we can be done with temporizing on a matter that, in principle and in practice, deserves and requires a clean and final resolution.

THE ANNENBERG SCHOOL LECTURE

University of Pennsylvania, Philadelphia
March 26, 1964

As events of this turbulent century pick up more and more speed every year, communications are obviously going to increase in importance. To meet the demands put upon them, they are going to have to be swift, immediate, vivid. To achieve their fundamental purposes ——which, in my judgment, are no less than the preservation and the advancement of our whole civilization——they are going to have to reach not just the relatively few who used to be in the drivers' seats, but the scores of millions whose informed participation in the democratic process alone can assure its survival in an age of persistent perils.

If we are to succeed in this, there are certain assumptions that none of us in communications can ever make. One is that we have already arrived at the highest level of social and technical efficiency that communications can reach. We have not. Another is that we have long since hit upon the final answer of how freedom of communications accords with other basic freedoms no less necessary to the good and productive life. We have not. We must recognize this unfinished business. We must always be dissatisfied with our current performance, uneasy about the weak spots, restless about the neglected areas.

It will be my premise here today that we have something very fundamental in the relation of communications to freedom and to self-government to be dissatisfied about——uneasy about——restless about. That is the lack of a public policy in this country with regard to the role of electronic communications in reporting to the people happenings within the government answerable to them. For nearly two decades now——since the end of World War II and the rise of electronic communications——this lack has persisted. It has persisted despite the pressure of events, despite social and technological advances, despite the disturbingly obvious needs and the promisingly obvious opportunities.

The Age of Electronic Communications

We are living in the Age of Electronic Communications. This does not mean the end or even the diminishing of other forms of communications——each of which will always have distinct and unique functions to carry out. But it was discovered recently, for the first time, that the burden of being the primary source of news to the most people in this country has shifted from the newspapers to television. In november 1963, the "Roper Survey of Public Attitudes Towards Television" revealed that 55 percent of the American people said that they got most of their news from television, while 52 percent named newspapers as compared to 52 percent for television and 57 percent for newspapers two years earlier. (In both cases, some respondents named both, thus accounting for the percentile overlap.)

In spite of this reliance by a majority of Americans on television for their news, the halls of the Congress of the United States are still closed to the television camera and microphone. Public hearings of the House of Representatives and, at the pleasure of the individual Committees, of the Senate, are still closed to the camera and the microphone. In the vast majority of cases, the state legislatures are still closed to the microphone and camera. The Supreme Court of the United States is still closed to the camera and the microphone. State, county and municipal courts——except in a few jurisdictions where it is up to the judge——are still closed to the camera and microphone.

The United Nations and Television

As students of communications, you are as familiar as I with the broad reasons often given for this: that the temptation to play to the galleries——to ham it up——put to the participants in these proceedings is too irresistible, that camera and microphone coverage does not comport with the dignity of these bodies, and that the distraction to the legislators is too overwhelming.

To test the soundness of these predictions, we have only to look at the United Nations, to whom we have been host country since its inception and which has always accepted electronic communications on wholly equal terms with all the other media. There television and radio are regarded as full-fledged, indispensable adjuncts of reporting, while we in our own governmental processes regard it as an intrusion and a distraction.

Every open session of every United Nations body——the General Assembly, the Security Council, the Commissions, the Committees ——is available for coverage by television cameras and radio microphones. Every chamber of any size has built-in camera accommodations, adequate lighting and permanent microphones. In times of the tensest crisis, over and over again, by simply flicking a switch, United Nations proceedings have gone out over the air live. As a matter of routine, television is used to record deliberations on tape for later broadcast.

The Responsibility of Television

The dignity of the United Nations has not suffered because of it. Delegates——despite the fact that tapes are made available to them to send home——have not played to the television audience. The debaters have not been distracted. And the force of these broadcasts in educating the people not only as to the issues but as to the United Nations itself has been incalculable.

If——in spite of the wide diversity of language and of national temperament and tradition, and in spite of the highly charged atmosphere of potential world conflict——the United Nations has no problem with television, why do our legislative institutions?

Much of the responsibility lies in television itself. The clutter and trappings of hastily assembled equipment, the harassment of unnecessarily glaring lights, the clamor of inadequately coordinated crews, the thoughtlessness of overzealous or inconsiderate personnel, the lack of special gear adequate to meet special requirements——all of these have too often characterized the live coverage of legislative events.

These deficiencies have been grist to the mills of those who would be opposed to television coverage in any case. They have been a source of discouragement to legislators favoring television coverage. In the case of judicial proceedings and their preliminaries, however, they have carried a very real danger to the administration of justice. But many of these failings of television are directly due to the lack of a realistic constructive public policy, to which I invited your attention earlier, and of suitable, inconspicuously installed facilities.

This lack is no less regrettable in the case of the higher courts than it is in that of the Congress and the state legislatures.

Up until our time and the development of electronic communications, access to the courts has necessarily been limited. Courtrooms are small, and the distances to them, for the vast majority of people, prohibitively great. And so the public rarely witnesses proceedings of the courts and depends upon the reports in the press, which has meant largely the newspapers. The quality of this coverage has been as varied as the quality of the newspapers and their reporters. Those given to sensationalism were on the prowl only for sensationalism; those with a more thoughtful sense of their mission concentrated on really significant cases. But all of them have been second-hand accounts——for the reader in no way comparable to witnessing the proceedings for himself.

The Responsibility of the Citizen

Is this of any significance? I think that it is. Ultimately, the citizen is as responsible for the quality of the courts as he is for all other government institutions. And cases before the higher courts are heavy with issues of broad social, political and economic significance that can touch upon the lives of all of us as individuals and as a people. The courts have become the forums before which contending views on the most basic philosophic and moral propositions are presented and resolved.

No less important than substantive matters before the courts are the procedures of the courts; they are, in fact, of the most fundamental importance to the democratic way of life. Ignorance of any aspect of public affairs in any society is a great evil. Ignorance of any aspect so basic as the judicial function of the government could be——as it has been in other societies——disastrous.

We do not have to correct in one swoop this anachronism of the courts being open to the public only in the context of a communications system existing before this century began. There has been, I think, too much all-or-nothing talk about this. The important thing is to break down a hard and fast categorical barring of any medium from any proceeding which both is open to the public in fact and ought to be in order to accord with rudimentary principles of freedom and self-government. Certainly, any disruption of old practices and restraints can be minimized by an approach on judicial levels that do not involve the presence of defendants or witnesses.

A Camera in the Supreme Court

The first level would be to permit television coverage of the proceedings of the Supreme Court of the United States, including significant arguments and decisions. This is just as essential as covering, by every means available, the President and the Congress. Many of the issues before the Court strike deeply into the whole moral, social and intellectual nature of our society, shape the course of our future history and define our objectives and values as a people. Such coverage involves no question of affecting the conduct of defendants and witnesses. It involves no question of sensationalism. It involves no question of compromising the dignity of the Court——any more than the dignity of the Ecumenical Council at The Vatican, of a Presidential inaugural or a state funeral has been endangered by television.

The second level would be similarly to permit television coverage of appellate courts in the federal districts and throughout the state judicial systems. Here again there are none of the problems that have been advanced as sufficient reason to close the courtroom door on camera and microphone.

The Rights of Individuals

Trial courts and adversary hearings admittedly present wholly different problems, some of which strike at the very basis of justice in a free society——the assumption of innocence and the protection of the rights of the individual. These are not just theoretic problems. They are substantive and real. The defendants and witnesses are under the protection of the courts during trials, and this is a duty and purpose of the courts that none of us would want obstructed or compromised. The problem is even more acute before the suspected or the accused is under the court's control. That there have been serious abuses by the news media of their access to the police station in such cases cannot be doubted——or that they have had the most damaging effect upon the lives and liberty of those not proved guilty of any crime.

These problems so deeply involving a conflict between the rights of individuals and the interest of society in crime are not new; they are as old as the printed news media and——for that matter——as old as the village gossip. And we are not going to solve them by more categorical bans or by closing the doors of the police station to cameras and microphones as the doors to the courtroom have been.

No thoughtful person can advocate abridgement of the right of access to the police station and to coverage of those detained prior to their arraignment. Humanity has far too often been afflicted by police brutality and unwarranted detention for anyone to look with favor on that kind of cure of abuses. Administrative and investigative arrests have for too long dogged the footsteps of men insistent upon the exercise of their freedoms. We have seen in our own time the regimentation of far too many societies in which the first crushing step to totalitarianism has been the swift, unexplained and unrevealed arrest. And our memories are too much haunted by accused who were shut off abruptly and completely from any accessibility to the outside world.

The Interests of Society

There is no question, then, of abridging the right of access of all media to coverage of police activities, including arrests, detentions and the nature of charges. At the same time, there are problems involved in such coverage that have been deeply disturbing to conscionable men and women equally anxious to safeguard the rights of individuals and those of society. In my judgment, the crux of the matter lies not in the existence of the media's access to police activities, which is essential to our basic freedoms, but in the use of that access. And this involves a re-examination not only of all the media, including television, but also of the activities of the police, of prosecutors and of defense counsel.

If photographers, reporters, interviewers, newsfilm or television cameramen are, by their methods, their lack of discernment or their zeal, doing violence to the cause of justice, the situation should be corrected.

If the police are pre-empting the function of declaring the guilt of defendants, if they are publicizing confessions, often wrongly extracted from prisoners, and by their actions compromising the rights of the accused, the situation should be corrected.

If there are prosecutors who do violence to the due process principles that we all prize, or defense counsel who seek to try their cases outside the courtroom, the situation should be corrected.

A Statement of Standards and Principles

To bring about these corrections, to bring about a wiser use of the access by news media to those accused or detained for questioning and to consider more effective and less disturbing coverage of trials, it seems to me obvious that a voluntary, inter-media statement of standards and principles for fair practices must be evolved.

In making this suggestion, I am fully aware that as much harm can be done by wild rumors that inevitably spring up in the absence of adequate news as by a flow of news that prejudices the conditions under which an investigation is made or a trial is held. The statement should not, therefore, be merely a negative series of "thou shalt nots." There are affirmative duties of the news media here, too. Unless they are carried out, there could be an assault on the rights of an accused and of a society in the dark far more devastating than the public airing of charges.

The statement of standards and principles should not lead to a conspiracy of silence on the part of the media. And since all rights are granted ultimately for the benefit and safety of the people, the public should know exactly what is in the statement——its substance, its ground rules and its rationale——for it can be made effective only by the force of public opinion. Any coercive measure would defeat its purpose and could obstruct the duties of the news media. The problem is essentially not to reduce the freedom of the media but to prevent that freedom from becoming anarchy——a tendency which was dramatized, although I do not think typified, by the case of Lee Oswald in Dallas.

A Proposal

Such a statement ought to be acceptable to all media, for the problem is not peculiar to any one medium. Nor should it be treated, I think, solely as a media problem. It is also a legal and a social problem with implications that touch sensitively upon fundamental principles of political life.

As a first step towards the construction and articulation of such a statement of standards and principles, CBS has proposed* to the Brookings Institution, an independent research and education organization in the social sciences, that it undertake to bring together a distinguished task force to make a study and report on a public policy for the television coverage of both legislative and judicial proceedings, including the pre-trial apprehension and detention of the accused. Such a task force would be composed of learned, experienced

---

* See Appendix for the text of the proposal.

and respected citizens representing the bar, the bench, the various branches of journalism, experts in government and public administration and the public. We have suggested that a gifted American widely experienced in both the law and communications be made chairman of the group. Such a name as Newton N. Minow, a member of the bar and former chairman of the Federal Communications Commission, comes immediately to mind.

We have also suggested to the Brookings Institution that it consider inviting to join it in this vital survey such organizations as the American Bar Association, the American Society of Newspaper Editors, the Magazine Editors Association, the Radio and Television News Directors Association, and Sigma Delta Chi, the professional journalism society that includes representatives of all the media. These suggestions are, of course, not inclusive; other organizations and other individuals should also be tapped for this important assignment.

To administer and conduct the inquiry and report its findings, CBS will make the necessary grant, with no strings attached, to the Brookings Institution, if the project is acceptable to it. I am happy to report that our proposals have been greeted by the Institution with interest, and the President of the Institution, Robert D. Calkins, has authorized me to say that they will be taken under immediate study.

A Definition of the Issues, Conflicts

I do not see this group providing a panacean code. But I do see it clearly and realistically defining the problems, the issues and the conflicts, and pointing the way for the orderly framing of a sensible, workable statement of standards and principles now so urgently needed.

The purpose of CBS in initiating and financing this project is to get this vital matter out of an arena of contention that only drives us further away from a solution and into an atmosphere of affirmative discussion and common purpose. From it we hope there will come a standard to which the honest and the just can repair in this difficult area. Reforms will not come overnight, but there will be a beginning, based on a consensus of informed and concerned individuals representing a variety of all points of view.

I do not know that this will solve all the problems. I do know that the problems will not solve themselves——nor will counsels of extremes be helpful. And I would hope most earnestly that all of us can soon say of communications in this advanced day that it is equal both to its opportunities and to its challenges.

Appendix

Proposal to the Brookings Institution

Background. A necessary premise of democratic government is an informed citizenry, free to find out what it needs to know in order to exercise its franchise adequately and free to question, to comment and to criticize. For this reason, Western political institutions have for centuries provided for a free press——the only means practical for a numerous and diffused people to acquire such knowledge and conduct such discussion. This principle was written into the First Amendment of the Constitution of the United States as a primary element in the national Bill of Rights. It has been fought for and recognized in the courts. It has been respected even in the midst of war and grave national emergencies. In the American democracy, it has involved access by the press to the Executive, whether the President or the Governors of the several states, to the Legislature, whether the Congress or the various state legislatures, and to the Courts, whether the Supreme Court or the district and local jurisdictions. Such free access has been held to be the basic condition of the political life of a free people.

The Current Situation. Today an integral and important part of the press in the United States is television, upon which, according to recent polls, some 55 percent of the American people state that they depend to get most of their news. This increased role of television has tended to create some new problems in the relationship of a free press to a democratic government and to illumine old dilemmas by focusing new attention upon them. Chief among the former is the closing of legislative chambers and hearing rooms to the tools of the broadcast media——the television camera and the microphone, and chief among the latter is the sensitive relationship between the administration of justice and the public reporting of police activities and adversary proceedings.

At present, television cameras and microphones are not permitted in the chambers of the Senate and the House of Representatives of the United States, or of the vast majority of state legislatures—— though their sessions are open to the public and reporters. Nor are they permitted at public hearings of the House of Representatives and——except at the pleasure of the individual committees——at those of the Senate. They are not permitted at open sessions of the federal courts or, with rare exceptions, at those of local jurisdictions. This categorical discrimination against the broadcast media, whose technical advances now make it possible for its equipment to be inconspicuous and unobtrusive (all open meetings of the United Nations General Assembly, Security Council, Commissions and Committees have been open to cameras and microphones from the beginning), deprives the American people of the fullest use of their leading news medium.

Television cameras and microphones are permitted, however, in police stations and often on the fringes of court chambers, where old problems of the rights of the individual accused or defendant have often been compromised or endangered by the nature of the coverage of all media. But there has been an essential conflict between the insistence of society on knowing and seeing what goes on in the police station and its uneasiness at the possibility of compromising the assumption of innocence on the part of those held to answer for offenses.

The fear of administrative and investigative arrests has, in our time, been strengthened by events in authoritarian societies where the police state is the chief adjunct to dictatorial power. On the other hand, many conscionable Americans have been shocked by the events of recent months in Dallas into a realization that, if it is to serve its high purpose, freedom of the press to cover police activities and trial court proceedings must itself be constantly aware of the implications of its own actions. In the past, there have been several instances where higher courts have felt it necessary to remand cases for retrial as the result of press coverage held to be prejudicial to the interests of defendants. Often police officials, prosecuting lawyers and defense counsel have dealt imprudently with the press in terms of allegations and denials. Often the working press from all the media have been overzealous, lacking in discernment or callous in the handling of themselves and their reporting functions in police and court cases.

As a result, a twofold danger faces the American society: one is a threat to the freedom of the press springing from its grave if occasional abuses; the other is a threat to the dispassionate, equitable administration of justice.

An Approach to a Solution. Abridging, restricting or repudiating access to the legislatures, the courts or the police stations is repugnant to our values as a free people and dangerous to the status of our free institutions. The only alternative is, with regard to the broadcast media, the construction of a public policy upon the need and right of television and radio to cover legislative and judicial proceedings and, with regard to all media, the adoption of a voluntary statement of standards and principles for the coverage of police activities and adversary proceedings.

In the first case, such a policy should accord with the facts of life in the age of electronic communications, the means by which the American people choose to inform themselves and the traditional responsibilities of governmental entities to make their procedures and activities known to the people to whom they are ultimately answerable.

In the second case, a thorough study needs to be undertaken by qualified representatives of the bench, the bar, the news media, and the public to define the problem, the issues involved, and the conflicts evoked, and to point the way to the orderly framing of a workable statement of principles to which all the media can subscribe.

The Proposal. The Columbia Broadcasting System proposes to make an unconditional grant to the Brookings Institution to enable it to bring together and sponsor a distinguished task force to make a study and report on a public policy for the television and radio coverage of both legislative and judicial proceedings, including the pre-trial apprehension and detention of the accused, and on the elements of fair practice for all the media in covering the latter. Such a task force should be composed of learned, experienced and respected citizens representing the bar, the bench, the various branches of journalism, experts in government and public administration and the public.

It is suggested that the Brookings Institution consider inviting to join it in this vital survey such organizations as The American Bar Association, The American Society of Newspaper Editors, The Magazine Editors Association, The Radio and Television News Directors Association, Sigma Delta Chi, the professional journalism society that includes representatives of all the media and such other organizations or individuals as may seem helpful in the planning and execution of this vital inquiry.

It is further suggested that, when they are available, the Brookings Institution make its findings fully known to the public, upon whom rests the final responsibility for the press as well as for the government.

FRED W. FRIENDLY

25   The Responsibility of TV Journalism

■

TV journalism is an increasingly important media in imparting news to the American people. Its immediacy is ultra-dramatic and thus implicitly its influence is often more powerful and far-reaching than the strongest editorials in the leading newspapers. Many millions of Americans rely almost exclusively for their information about the nation and the world on what comes across on the video screen. Men like Huntley, Brinkley, Reasoner and Cronkite are even better known today as the Murrows, Kaltenborns, Fulton Lewis, Jrs. and Heatters were in the heyday of radio news broadcasting.

How much time should TV give to acknowledgedly important news events? Since the McCarthy-Army Hearings, America has come to expect a front-seat view of the great domestic debates. The Kefauver Crime Hearings and the Kennedy-Nixon debate have further established this "tradition."

Now the country is involved in a war in Viet Nam that has not won total approval from all sections of the citizenry. Many men of good will disapprove of the Administration's foreign policy; others vociferously support it. How much does America care about the national dialogue on Viet Nam? Does TV have a responsibility to present the issues even if the potential audience is small?

Fred W. Friendly in his capacity as president of CBS News thought America did care, and should care. Accordingly he scheduled TV coverage of the hearings on the war before the Senate Foreign Relations Committee on the afternoon of February 10th. The hearings were never televised. Indignant and disillusioned, Mr. Friendly resigned his post, one of the most important in American mass communications. What follows is the text of Mr. Friendly's letter of resignation from his post as President of the Columbia Broadcasting System News Division, sent on February 15, 1966, to William S. Paley, chairman of the Columbia Broadcasting System, and Dr. Frank Stanton, president.

His resignation made the front page of the New York Times for February 16, 1966 and has provoked anew the recurring controversy over TV's responsibility to televise as a public service the great events of our country. His departure from CBS is also of unusual interest in that Dr. Frank Stanton, President of the Columbia Broadcasting System, has urged for years TV's acceptance into the courts, the Senate and the Congress. Mr. Friendly's leavetaking will be interpreted by some as self-serving martyrdom, but there will be many others who will see his action as serving the highest standards of television's responsibility to its public.

DEAR BILL AND FRANK:

This is the third time since last Thursday that I have asked you to accept my resignation as president of C.B.S. News, and this time you have an obligation to accept it.

It is important that you and my colleagues in the News Division know that I am not motivated by pique or change of status in a table of organization, or lack of respect for Jack Schneider. He is, as you have both recalled, someone I had asked to join the News Division in an administrative role more than a year ago, when he was station manager of WCAU-TV.

I am resigning because C.B.S. News did not carry the Senate Foreign Relations Committee hearings last Thursday, when former Ambassador George Kennan testified on Vietnam. It was the considered news judgment of every executive in C.N.D. [Columbia News Division] that we carry these Vietnam hearings as we had those of the other witnesses. I am convinced that the decision not to carry them was a business, not a news, judgment.

I am resigning because the decision not to carry the hearings makes a mockery of the Paley-Stanton C.N.D. crusade of many years that demands broadest access to Congressional debate. Only last year in a most eloquent letter, you petitioned the Chief Justice for the right to televise live sessions of the Supreme Court. We cannot, in our public utterances, demand such access and then, in one of the crucial debates of our time, abdicate that responsibility. What happens to that sense of fairness and balance so close to both of you, when one day's hearings, and perhaps the most comprehensive, are omitted? How can we return on Thursday and Friday of this week without denying Schneider's argument that "the housewife isn't interested"? Why were N.B.C.'s housewives interested? What would have happened to those housewives if the Supreme Court had said "Yes" to your plea for live coverage? Where would broadcast journalism have been last Thursday if N.B.C. had elected not to carry the U.S. Senate hearings on the war?

When last Thursday morning at 10 o'clock I looked at the monitors in my office and saw the hearings on Channel 4 (pool production by the way, via C.B.S. News crews) and saw a fifth rerun of "Lucy," then followed by an eighth rerun of "The Real McCoys," I wanted to order up an announcement that said: "Due to circumstances beyond our control the broadcast originally intended for this time will not be seen." It was not within C.N.D.'s control because the journalistic judgment had been by a sudden organizational act transferred to a single executive. Mr. Schneider, because of his absolute power, would have more authority than William Paley or Frank Stanton have exercised in the past two years. This, in spite of the fact that Mr. Schneider's news credentials were limited in the past to local station operations, with little experience in national or international affairs.

The concept of an autonomous news organization responsible only to the chairman and the president was not a creation of mine. It is a concept almost as old as C.B.S. News, and is a tradition nurtured by the Ed Klaubers, the Ed Murrows, the Paul Whites, and rigidly enforced by both of you. The dramatic change in that concept is, to my mind and that of my colleagues, a form of emasculation.

Actually, it is the second step of the emasculation that began when C.B.S. News was shorn of its responsibility in the news operation at WCBS-TV here in New York. Had I been in my current position at the time of this change, I should have resisted it as I do the current weakening. It denied C.B.S. News a highly professional outlet in New York, a competitive position with the other networks, and the training apparatus for the Sevareids, the Cronkites, the Reasoners of the future.

My departure is a matter of conscience. At the end of the day it is the viewer and the listener who have the biggest stake in all this. Perhaps my action will be understood by them. I know it will be understood by my colleagues in news and I know Ed Murrow would have understood. A speech he delivered to the Radio Television News Directors Association in 1958 spelled it all out:

"One of the basic troubles with radio and television news is that both instruments have grown up as an incompatible combination of show business, advertising, and news. Each of the three is a rather bizarre and demanding profession. And when you get all three under one roof, the dust never settles. The top management of the networks, with a few notable exceptions, has been trained in advertising, research, sales, or show business. But, by the nature of the corporate structure, they also make the final and crucial decisions having to do with news and public affairs.

"Frequently they have neither the time nor the competence to do this. It is not easy for the same small group of men to decide whether to buy a new station for millions of dollars, build a new building, alter the rate card, buy a new Western, sell a soap opera, decide what defensive line to take in connection with the latest Congressional inquiry, how much money to spend on promoting a new program, what additions or deletions should be made in the existing covey or clutch of vice presidents and, at the same time——frequently on the same long day——to give mature, thoughtful consideration to the manifold problems that confront those who are charged with the responsibility for news and public affairs. . . ."

Such a day was last Thursday when a non-news judgment was made on the Kennan broadcast.

Murrow went on to say:

"Upon occasion, economics and editorial judgment are in conflict. And there is no law which says that dollars will be defeated by duty. Not so long ago the President of the United States delivered a television address to the nation. He was discoursing on the possibility or probability of war between this nation and the Soviet Union and

Communist China——a reasonably compelling subject. Two networks
——C.B.S. and N.B.C.——delayed that broadcast for an hour and
15 minutes. If this decision was dictated by anything other than financial reasons, the networks didn't design to explain those reasons. That
hour-and-15-minute delay, by the way, is about twice the time
required for an I.C.B.M. to travel from the Soviet Union to major
targets in the United States. It is difficult to believe that this decision
was made by men who love, respect and understand news."

In that speech Ed also said:

"There is no suggestion here that networks or individual stations
should operate as philanthropies. I can find nothing in the Bill of
Rights or the Communications Act which says that they must increase their net profits each year, lest the republic collapse."

I now leave C.B.S. News convinced, ironically, that my leaving will
help insure the integrity and independence of the news operation. I
believe that the Senate hearings next Thursday and Friday will be
televised live because of circumstances within the control of the man
you choose to succeed me. For the kind of news executive who would
warrant the trust of the two recipients of this letter would insist upon
such a mandate. Senator George Norris, quoted in John Kennedy's
Profiles in Courage, says, "Whatever use I have been has been
accomplished in the things I *failed* to do rather than in the things I
actually did do."

I now leave C.B.S. News after 16 years, believing that the finest
broadcast journalists anywhere will yet have the kind of leadership
they deserve. I know that I take with me their respect and affection
as, indeed, I hope I do yours.

Faithfully,
Fred.

ROBERT CUMMING

26   New Hope for Television: Educational TV

■

*Must television always be damned as a "wasteland"? Are all TV
watchers "videots"? Obviously not, and to prove it there is a growing
world of television that is a fertile field for the imagination, a delight
for students, savants and just the intellectually inclined. It is called
National Educational Television (NET) and it is fulfilling many of
the responsibilities that commercial television often avoids or only
partially responds to.*

*The following article gives a brief but remarkably detailed account
of the spread of ETV (educational television). It appeared as the
lead editorial in The Music Journal for November, 1964 (without the
title given it here), and is written by the managing editor of that publication, Robert Cumming.*

EDUCATIONAL TELEVISION (ETV) is the answer. But there are questions to be aired and problems to consider. This issue, saluting ETV's
inspiring "network"——the National Educational Television and
Radio Center (NET)——evolved to encourage music educators and
supervisors to promote widespread *active* interest in ETV. We all
know that America's cultural standards have room for improvement.
Walt Whitman said: "To have great poets there must be great audiences, too." Our task is to get a response from the great audience of
today, and to build a greater audience for tomorrow.

314]

The mass media are a cultural wasteland, critics have said. This is not entirely the case. The same critics of commercial TV's cultural offerings should focus upon the present virtues of ETV; their criticisms would then hold constructive water. But they are not making every effort to review the new films being released by NET——films that seek to enrich as well as entertain. Many are still unaware of the vast potential of "quality" programming on TV, or of its possible role in teacher education and retraining. The recent Seminar on Music Education, held at Yale, decried: "Training in music should be given to teachers who are not musicians, training in teaching to musicians who are not teachers, and retraining in music to teachers now teaching music." The report admitted that "Television, like film, is handicapped by poor sound reproduction, but under expert control this medium can be of great assistance to the teacher, both in his own training and in the classroom." It was suggested that a national research institute be founded for the development of audiovisual aids for music education.

Based on criticisms aired at the Yale Seminar last year, Juilliard recently attacked the "appalling quality" of music in the schools, proposed a pilot project of curriculum renewal for six cities, and received a $308,000 grant from the U.S. Office of Education. Paul Van Bodegråven (President of M.E.N.C.) responded, representing the public school professionals, by writing to Francis Keppel (U.S. Commissioner of Education) and to Juilliard President Peter Mennin. To Keppel, Van Bodegraven attacked the "sweeping castigation of the teaching profession" on the "narrow evidence cited in the announcement," and the by-passing of dedicated school music specialists in favor of a single conservatory which has not been active in the field. To Mennin, the new President of the Naumburg Foundation, Van Bodegraven cited the destructive effect of the one-sided and distorted charges, while expressing amazement that the distinguished school "would feel the need to use such extreme and hostile ground for requesting a grant of $308,000 of *public tax funds*."

We can best come to terms with musical change through television. Theorists, teachers and practitioners should get together with the object to bring subject matter and method of teaching in line with contemporary knowledge and culture. It is happily reported that the Music Educators National Conference, in cooperation with the U.S. Office of Eucation, will hold a conference on the uses of educational media in the teaching of music in Washington from Dec. 7–11, 1964. Latest equipment, such as portable TV tape recorders, will be demonstrated. Conferees will be briefed on developments in teaching machines (programmed learning), films, radio and TV, recording devices and players, electronic instruments (stroboscope and tachistoscope), etc. Dr. Edward Maltzman is directing this nine-month project.

Is the mass media affecting our culture? Or does our culture influence our mass media? Yes, in both cases. The commercial programs are directed to the largest audience, naturally, and these become habit-forming and self-perpetuating mediocrities. But there are outstanding instances——such as the *Bell Telephone Hour,* the *NBC Opera, Sunrise Semester* or, more specifically, recent performances of Shakespeare's *Hamlet,* Stravinsky's *Noah and the Flood,* Menotti's *Labyrinth,* Bernstein's New York Philharmonic concerts, the opening of Manhattan's Lincoln Center for the Performing Arts ——which clearly indicate that culture influences the mass media. The airwaves can be used as a motivational force for good or bad. It's up to the integrity of the individuals in control. Fortunately, for the arts at least, cultural activity of variety and depth has become a common heritage and quest of the people.

To wit: When commercial TV offered the Bernstein concerts, the orchestra witnessed a totally new kind of reception on tour. Audiences would offer standing ovations with cheers before the orchestra had played a note! Maestro Bernstein stated that there was "an explanation other than musicianship to explain the extraordinary enthusiasm" of the audience. "You can't imagine," he said, "how we have been gathered in by audiences that obviously knew about us through television." In Las Vegas, scarcely a center of musical culture, and where no major symphony had performed before, a hall holding 7,000 was jammed. These cheering people were well acquainted with the New York Philharmonic. The orchestra's record album sales soon passed a million.

The chairman of the American Library Association's broadcasting committee has said: "Dramatization of classics on TV inspires people to read or re-read the classics. And public affairs documentaries have been sending people back to history books. . . . We look upon television as a tremendous motivational force. And we haven't even scratched the surface." A survey by the N.Y. Board of Education of 73 library systems across the land revealed that "TV encourages more reading . . . any story which appears on TV creates a demand for the book."

Commercial TV has shown that it *can* be educational, but not often enough. It still earns the reputation it has in many quarters———that of an *idiot box*———famous for cowboys and crime. And its best entertainment programs are incessantly interrupted by often inane commercials (though some are clever and creative) which do *anything but* double your pleasure or sell that product which so insensitively breaks the illusion. So, before the standards of commercial TV can be raised, along with the size of the audience for educational TV, we are confronted with the problem of understanding the variety and intensity of the motives of the audience. Are they brainwashed creatures of habit? Are they irrevocably attached to surface interests? Are they ready for something new? If so, when? Under what circumstances? Will we only cater to the cognoscenti? Can TV influence the *taste* of its viewers?

NET has accomplished wonders in only ten years. This issue will bear witness. Its 83 affiliate stations have a potential audience of over 75,000,000. Only one out of ten ETV stations, however, calls itself *educational*. Closed-circuit TV are wired setups, located in schools or on a campus; this is the present answer for more than 300 systems. Pay-TV is successful in several quarters. An airplane is ETV's most unique solution: it circles Montpelier, Indiana, broadcasting prerecorded lessons, reaching TV sets in 15,000 schools in Illinois, Indiana, Kentucky, Ohio, Michigan and Wisconsin! (2,000 schools use the airplane's programs put together by Purdue University and Chicago's WTTW.) A higher level of learning is promised.

ETV is soaring to great heights. From its birth in 1953, when Houston's KUHT went on the air, it has proved its ability to grow. *Changing Times,* the Kiplinger Magazine, made note of those who "visualized the time, 10 or 15 years hence, when technological change will make room for hundreds more ETV operations and when ETV stations will outnumber their commercial cousins." With steady help from the Ford Foundation, this may soon be a reality. There are over six million of America's thirty-three million elementary school students receiving ETV. We can all help to increase its great audience and gain the public recognition ETV has deserved but missed. It is hoped that NET will play an important role in the realization of a fulfilling future so creatively and resourcefully being earned at present by those (and many others) herein featured.

EDWARD BENNETT WILLIAMS

27 The High Cost of Television's Courtroom

■

Much has been said about television's enormous responsibility to the viewing public. The generalization "responsibility" is so huge and so impersonal, however, that we often lose sight of the fact that it is made up of countless specific and very human bases of application in our daily life.

One of these applications is television's portrayal of the law and lawyers in action. How true-to-life are the legal maneuvers of Perry Mason? Could any pair of attorneys practice in the style of the father-and-son team in The Defenders? What effect does TV's distortions and hyperdramatizations of the legal process have on the average American's concepts of lawyers, judges and the whole judicial function?

The distinguished attorney Edward Bennett Williams puts the TV picture sharply in focus from a dedicated jurist's point of view in the following essay, which appeared originally in the Fall, 1964, issue of Television Quarterly.

TELEVISION'S DRAMATISTS have joined their predecessors in theater and motion pictures in feeding the public appetite for courtroom conflict. The popularity of such programming with writers and producers is understandable. The advocacy system of Western law, with the direct confrontation between defense and prosecution, has possibilities of high drama and climactic resolution. And the small physical area of the action makes for relatively simple staging and low costs.

Some practicing attorneys were unhappy over the dramatic license with which writers for the legitimate stage approached criminal law. But there were few plays in a season and the total audiences were relatively small. Even when motion pictures were most popular there might be only a dozen "law" films a year, and the audience could be counted in the low millions. But a single television program may reach 40 million viewers and the programs continue 52 weeks a year. It is thus time to evaluate the effects of the dramatic image of the trial lawyer.

My misgivings about television trial justice are not based at all on the economically produced daytime programs such as *The Verdict Is Yours, Divorce Court* and *Day in Court.* My work schedule does not permit seeing these.

I have no quarrel with the technical advice given to televison's dramatists by appointed committees of the Bar Association. Much of TV'S legal drama takes place at the pretrial hearing where rules of procedure are less strict than in the actual trial. The distinction, however, is lost on most viewers.

As an attorney in criminal practice, I appreciate the stand taken by *The Defenders* in favor of the Durham Rule, a new rule in the District of Columbia on the law of insanity. I admire Lawrence Preston's persistent campaign against capital punishment and I approve Perry Mason's weekly insistence that prosecuting attorney Hamilton Burger dot every "i" and cross every "t" in observing the procedural safeguards for the accused.

Producers of programs like *Perry Mason, Arrest and Trial* and *Sam Benedict* are undeniably men of good will. They are eager to observe technical niceties of a magnificent legal system. But its magnificence is misleadingly mirrored. Perry Mason has lost only one case in the past eight years. One might expect that his services would be in great demand, that his waiting room would be overflowing with clients and that, in preparing his cases, he would be working some long days. Yet he is free——day or night——to speed to the scene of a crime and beat the police to the discovery of a murder. He practices law, as far as any viewer can determine, with one secretary, one investigator and one legal assistant.

The creator of *Perry Mason* has said the popularity of his character comes from everyman's longing for a "knight on a white horse." It is not surprising, therefore, that Mason is always forced to be a courtroom magician——an attorney who wins consistently by springing an overlooked piece of evidence or by forcing a seemingly innocent witness to confess on the witness stand that he committed the crime.

The Defenders team of Lawrence and Kenneth Preston sometimes loses, but rarely. Their losses usually occur when the playwrights are attacking legislation or a decision that can be overruled only by courts higher than the ones in which the Prestons practice. But, at least, *The Defenders* deals with real issues. It is unusual among "law" programs, and TV programs in general, in its effort to introduce substance on a weekly basis.

The unending triumphs in television's courtroom tend to confirm a notion that few who are brought to trial are found guilty. Senator Goldwater, as a presidential candidate, decried the "softness" of our Federal Courts. No one argued with this description. "Softness" in Federal Court trials? In fiscal 1963 there were 34,845 criminal cases in the Federal District Courts. 29,803 resulted in conviction. 5,042 were "terminated without convictions." Thus there were convictions in 85.5 percent of the cases. It is true, of course, that many convictions come from pleas of "guilty." But in 2,637 jury trials in 1963 there were 1,874 convictions. The defense counsel lost 71.1 times in every 100 cases.

The odds are no better in state courts. The most recent figures from California (fiscal 1962) show that jury trials ended in a finding of "guilty" 79 percent of the time. But "Perry Mason" practices in California and wins weekly. In New York, home base of *The Defenders* and *Arrest and Trial,* District Attorney Frank Hogan's office lost only three cases during one term of court.

Television has also taught the public through endless repetition that trial lawyers are a scheming, tricky lot. This has actually produced repercussions in real life. The least significant witness now comes to court expecting to be tricked, ridiculed and harassed by inquisitorial gimmicks. The number of argumentative witnesses has increased. As a result, trials slow down with unnecessary evasions.

Double and triple meanings are heard when a lawyer, in the most prosaic style, is trying simply to establish a sequence of events that can be corroborated by a second witness.

In general, TV law programs, hampered by the dramatic demands of television's chronomatic precision, too often reach for the quick and easy denouement. An actual trial is often a dull, plodding affair to watch. It has to be. The rules of evidence generally reduce showmanship to farce. But television's courtroom is pyrotechnic and there is never time to show the actuality of carefully developed facts.

To illustrate——one of the most exciting cases I ever tried would have made dull drama indeed. The case involved the Reconstruction Finance Corporation in the Truman administration. A lawyer in Washington was charged with having committed perjury in front of the grand jury investigating the RFC, by denying that he had ever given anything of value to anyone employed at the RFC. It was subsequently developed that he had given a television set to one of the employees a few years before at Christmas.

His defense was that he had forgotten about it at the time the question was asked, and that he had later returned to the grand jury to give this fact (when his mind was refreshed) but that the grand jury by that time had gone out of session.

At the trial, one of the lawyers who had worked on the case as an investigator was on the stand. In cross-examination I asked him an almost irrelevant question. It was so irrelevant that my opposing lawyer, who was a very able man, did not object because he did not figure it could possibly hurt him. I asked the man on the stand: "Now who were the other lawyers from the Department of Justice who worked with you on this investigation for the grand jury?" He said, "Mr. Smith. Mr. Brown. Mr. Black. Mr. Blue. And Mr. Johnson."

"Now you worked on this investigation for a whole year and those are the only lawyers who worked with you?"

"That's all. Those are the ones. There were six of us."

So later in the defense, I called Mr. Smith and under the guise of simply testing the accuracy of the transcription of some testimony, I asked a couple of questions that appeared meaningless and boring. Then I asked him one that appeared even more meaningless and boring: "Who were the other lawyers who worked with you on this?"

And Mr. Smith said, "Well, there was Mr. Brown. Mr. Black. Mr.

Blue. Mr. Jones"———then he named the man who had testified earlier
———"and Mr. Murphy."

So then I called the next one and I asked him the same question,
burying it in a lot of dull and meaningless other questions. Pretty
soon it turned out that Mr. Blue left out Mr. Brown. And Mr. Brown
left out Mr. Black. And Mr. Black left out Mr. Murphy. Everyone of
the prosecutors had omitted a name or added a name to those who
worked with him.

And nobody———of course this was a long trial and these questions
were buried in a melange of hundreds of pages of testimony———but
nobody in that courtroom had any concept of the significance of what
had happened. And I did not tell them! I just put it away in the
icebox.

But at the end of the trial, in the summing up, I took it out and I
said, "Now here we have the Department of Justice asking that you
return a verdict of guilty beyond a reasonable doubt against this man
whose reputation to this point has been unsullied. They are unwilling
to accord him the benefit of a mistake in recollection, and yet the
very lawyers who got the indictment all have mistaken recollections
about the very same grand jury that indicted him. All six of them
have mistaken recollection.

"I am not asking that they be indicted, because I would be laughed
down the courthouse steps if I made the ludicrous request that these
six men be indicted because each of their recollections failed them
about a transaction of *one* year ago. Yet they are asking you to
convict this man whose recollection failed about a matter *three* years
ago."

We won the case. But the making of the point resulted from
tedious, seemingly pointless questions piled up among the other
business of the trial———hardly the stuff of television drama. The vast
majority of courtroom successes are of this sort———built with plodding care and exploited with common sense reasoning. Very, very
few actual cases are won with dramatic appeals to a jury, sudden disclosures of proof or sly little tricks. A trial attorney's effectiveness is
circumscribed by the materials of his case. He learns early that he
will often do his finest, most thorough and most effective work in a
case that he must lose in court.

Another fact unrecognized by TV is that the lawyer is not the absolute factor in winning or losing a case. Take a sample of 100 cases, 50 of which should be won and 50 lost. If these cases were defended by an attorney who embodied the best qualities of Clarence Darrow, Max Steuer and Martin Littleton, this miracle man would win about 60 of the cases and lose about 40. Turn the hypothesis the other way; let those same 100 cases be handled by the least experienced and least gifted member of the Bar and the results wouldn't change much. He would probably win 40 of the cases and lose the other 60.

I have used this illustration during ten years of lecturing at the Georgetown University Law School. More recently I have repeated it in lectures at more than 30 law schools during the past three years. Increasingly, I sense the disbelief of the students; for I am addressing a generation that has matured with the examples set by television lawyers over hundreds of programs. The students seem to have accepted a point that television's dramatists have not consciously tried to make. But almost subliminally, students have come to understand that criminal cases are decided by rhetoric; that the outcome depends on malevolent tricks; that the lawyer is always the key factor in winning or losing. The student has a definite impression that deception may be more important than the difficult and grubby disciplines. They would like to avoid the digging that makes the law student a competent attorney.

Television's dramatists, while observing technical details, leave an impression that the scholarship of law is a bore——unnecessary to successful practice. But the good legal defense, like a well-constructed house, is built brick by brick, block by block. A lot of sweat and discomfort goes into both. There are no cheap shortcuts in sound construction. The architect and the construction engineer expect their buildings to endure hurricanes. The competent attorney knows that a prosecutor's case is never going to disappear before a puff of oratory.

The long and continuing popularity of television's courtroom wizards indicates that they are not likely to be dropped from the prime-time schedules. But one might hope for portrayals closer to the truth and scripts that abide with the realities of the legal profession in the United States.

FRANCIS BROWN

28 The Responsibilities of the Book Review Editor

■

For many years the common cry among critics of the Press was that critical journalism, book reviewing in particular, was in a slovenly, irresponsible and ineffectually undistinguished state. Recently, however, the success of The New York Review of Books and the revamping and revitalization of the New York Herald Tribune's Book Week have raised book reviewing in America to the level of a vibrant and responsible section of contemporary journalism.

Throughout the declining years of book reviewing, however, the New York Times Book Review maintained a consistently high standard of distinction. With a circulation of 1,400,000 readers per week, it is the most widely circulated book review in the United States. In the following essay, first given as a talk before the New York Library Association in 1964, Francis Brown, the long-time editor of the New York Times Book Review, discusses with affectingly honest self-searching the subtle aspects of the art of putting together a reasonably intelligent, highly readable book review. How to assign the right book to the right reviewer? What books to choose and what ones to ignore? To keep the scope of the Review wide or narrow it? These are just a few of the eternal problems Mr. Brown tackles as he sets about

*establishing the social, literary and esthetic criteria that determine
the character of his influential organ of news and opinion.*

MY BUSINESS is concerned with book reviews. Not book reports,
which everyone of us who's been to school has written for class
assignments, and often hated, but book reviews——and there's a
world of difference. A book report, which among other things is
teacher's way of checking on whether you've actually read a book, is
at best not much more than a dreary recital, with maybe a few
flourishes, of plot, of storyline. A book review, on the other hand, can
be an adventure for both its writer and its reader.

Well, what is a book review anyway? What is its reason for being?
Book reviews are, in a sense, only good, informed talk (written, that
is) about books. Usually this written talk is of new or current books.
It could just as well be about old ones, only then what is really a
review calls itself a literary essay.

Now there are, there have been, and there will be tomorrow all
kinds of book reviews, which is another way of stating that there is no
set formula, that there are no set rules. In the early 19th century Lord
Macaulay (he was plain Thomas Babington Macaulay then) made
himself famous in the *Edinburgh Review* by writing what began as a
book review and became an essay on the subject presented by the
book, the book itself meanwhile being lost and forgotten in the rolling
periods of Macaulay's prose. Lesser Macaulays are still writing that
sort of essay, and it can be excellent reading for what it says and as a
literary exercise, but it is not very satisfactory for anyone concerned
with the book that started it all.

At the opposite pole, or at least far removed, is the routine review
that has nothing to recommend it. The time is long gone, if it ever
was, when a book review reported only a book's title, authorship, and
content——much like those school reports of blessed memory. But
even now too many reviews are being written that are first cousins of
such a bare-bones performance. The reviewer, perhaps taught in
school that this is the way to do it, tells what a book is about, makes
a point or two of minor criticism, concludes with a general endorsement that is meaningless, and then picks up his marbles and goes
home. Such reviews are not to be taken seriously.

What do matter are those first-rate, often brilliant reviews that are the products of a first-rate, often brilliant mind that has got inside the book under review, and in telling what has been found frequently sets in motion ideas and thoughts that are stimulating in themselves, over and above what the author has done. The result may be also a well-turned piece of literary criticism. In England a generation ago, Virginia Woolf's book reviews were an instance. And while there are not many Virginia Woolfs (and as a critic she has less to say to us now than to her own time), her kind of book review has set a pattern that many have followed to the reader's great profit and delight. These are the reviews that make bright a literary editor's day.

A first-rate reviewer, whether a Virginia Woolf or not, has to have something to say and be willing to say it; and it would be well if he did not follow the precept attributed to the English wit, Sidney Smith, who is quoted as having said: "I never read a book before reviewing it; it prejudices a man so." Sometimes, to be sure, it does seem that reviewers have the precept in mind——I've seen some exhibits—— but, to repeat, I don't recommend it. However unconventional a reviewer's approach to his material, somewhere in the review he is writing, and this would seem to be fundamental, he must reveal what the book is about and what is its nature. He has to do more——and he does.

Because the purposes of the best book review are to furnish perspective, to further appreciation, and sometimes to challenge the accepted, the reviewer must ask himself a lot of questions. He must, for example, ask what does the book's author bring to it as a writer and a thinker? What is he trying to do? How has he gone about realizing his aim? Where has he failed——and why? Where has he been successful? What contribution to knowledge, to comprehension, of man and his world has he made? Where does this fit into his own previous work as an author, and into that of others who have been gleaning the same field?

Such questions are easier to ask than to answer, for their answering, and the nature of the answers, calls not only upon a reviewer's own knowledge and philosophy, but upon his appreciation of the task of literary creation. Moreover, questions that are pertinent to one book and author may be quite out of turn with others. Obviously one does not judge William Golding and Ian Fleming by the same standards.

The best critics not only have something to say, they know how to say it and want to say it. In the saying, however, there are many accents and intonations.

Americans by tradition, or so we are assured, are a kindly people; and while this quality has not prevented assault upon a man's politics or his ancestry, it has often protected him in the practice of authorship. The frequent result has been a hesitancy, almost a congenital unwillingness, to disagree with the thesis of a book and its development, or to speak out and pronounce the verdict: bad, bad, bad. There has been dislike——perhaps it is fear——of controversy; and to some extent this reflects the protective blandness that coats American life.

By contrast, there are critics who are not afraid to hear their own voices, to speak their own minds. The number, thankfully, seems to be increasing——and why not? A well-informed reviewer should not be afraid to praise when praise is due or to attack, maybe demolish, when the nature of a book so determines. It is the vigorous independence, the candor, with which a man sets forth his position that gives strength and ultimate conviction to his criticism. When he hedges, he is unfair to himself, to the reader, and eventually to the author——for from criticism the knowing author can learn much.

The ideal is always easier to describe than to attain. The root of the problem, from beginning to end, lies obviously in the critic, the reviewer, and there have never been enough good ones to go around.

To preserve the independence that should be a *sine qua non* of the profession, criticism must be as free from log-rolling and knifing as it is from the control of clique or claque. Yet one of the hardest things about assigning books for review, as every literary editor has learned (and I had to learn it too), is to keep friends from friends, enemies from foes. Perhaps there are times when exceptions can or should be made, but only when one can be certain that friendship will not count and enmity will be temporarily suspended. To repeat, the best reviewing is that which is farthest from deliberate log-rolling or premeditated knifing. In the long history of book reviewing, both knifing and log-rolling have been all too common. In early 19th-century Britain it frequently seemed that a reviewer's chief joy came not only from thrusting in the knife but in giving it a couple of twists.

A good, well-rounded book review can be a wonderfully exciting thing for it offers the excitement of discovery. The reviewer is setting forth what he has found in a book, and if the book is a good one, and sometimes even if it is a poor one, he has found a lot, whether it is new understanding of the human animal or fresh interpretation of his origins or new insight into what made John Keats tick. He shares his discoveries with the reader, just as he may take the reader on philosophical excursions or artistic digressions that the book at hand suggests. Readers may be outraged (and often are) by what the reviewer has said and the manner of his saying it, but is that bad? Dissent in itself can be exciting, can bring light into gray corners. As our culture becomes more and more unified, diversity is a quality to be cherished and cultivated. How dull it would be, how stultifying, to find ourselves in total agreement on politics, aesthetics, or what you will——and most of all on books which, by their very being, testify to man's diversity and the importance thereof.

These general observations constitute the ideal, and the ideal, alas, is too seldom realized. An editor and his staff may have the best of intentions, may have the ability, the knowledge, even the intelligence to bring off this ideal, and yet find themselves confronted by what Grover Cleveland in a quite different context described as a situation not a theory.

How is the ideal to be attained, for instance, when a book review like *The New York Times,* is faced with 8,000, 9,000 books or more a year, and can at best review only 2,600 or 2,700 of them? Obviously some good books are passed over, some poor ones are reviewed unnecessarily, some books are assigned to the wrong reviewers.

What is an editor to do about reviewers who stubbornly refuse to meet deadlines, disregard the length assigned for their reviews, kick like steers if their copy is altered (however much alteration may be in order)——who in short act like prima donnas?

How does an editor resist (and he *must* resist) the pressure of authors, not to mention their friends, and of publishers and *their* friends?

How does he settle the question of judgment and taste raised not only by readers but by the members of his own staff?

I sometimes marvel that we do as well as we do, and actually, if you press me, I'll tell you that, with occasional lapses, I think our job is well done.

But the issues that I have raised are somewhat common to all reviewing media. At *The Times,* and I suppose this must be true to some extent of other newspapers with book review sections, we are constantly aware that we are part of a newspaper, and a newspaper that boasts of its broad coverage. What exactly does this mean?

It means that first of all we are reporting, analyzing, putting in perspective the news in books, whatever their nature. It means also that we are more concerned than would be a strictly literary magazine with books dealing with current affairs, whether politics in the narrow sense or in the large. Moreover, because of *The Times'* principle of broad coverage, we feel obliged to cover (and we believe that this is right, *very* right) the many varieties of books that come from American presses. Not all the books: some are too specialized, some are unworthy. But we are speaking to an audience that is presumably as varied in its tastes and interests as the books we are reviewing. This is not a limited audience of special interests. The Sunday *Times* has a circulation of something like 1,400,000. We have to speak to that audience in many ways; we seek to guide it to the best and most significant, and we like to think that often we have planted some important ideas in the minds of our readers.

THOMAS C. WALLACE

29 Responsibilities of a Trade Book Editor

■

The American book publishing industry has undergone revolutionary changes recently: many firms have gone "public," with the result that Wall Street has dictated the publishing policy, subtly or not so subtly, of these houses; more and more firms are merging with each other and with the great electronic media, with a possible loss of the exercise of individual taste and character of the particular house; and, finally, there has been a great emancipating movement towards complete freedom of sexual expression in fiction.

With all of these larger-than-life factors affecting his role, how does the trade book editor define and meet his daily responsibilities? Thomas C. Wallace, an editor for the important firm of Holt, Rinehart & Winston, Inc., answers the question in a candid and direct essay, written especially for this volume.

His personal criteria: the exercise of taste, excellence, information and entertainment which he employs in choosing and editing the books in his charge would seem to guarantee the perpetuation of the high standards of responsibility that have always been met by American book trade editors since the development of the industry during the second half of the nineteenth century. Though an employee, Mr. Wallace has been given the responsibilities——or many of them—— of the publisher, and he fulfills them by being true to his own in-

tegrity, to his employer and that of his demanding and socially invaluable profession.

THERE ARE two types of trade (a trade, or general, book is any book which is not a textbook or a juvenile) publishers: privately-owned houses, which tend to be small or medium-sized and live off their trade list; and large, publicly-owned corporations which publish textbooks, magazines and reference works as well as general books. I have worked as a general books editor in both types of publishing enterprises.

Much has been said about the fact that an editor works for a publisher, that publishers are in the business to make money, that certain publishers prefer certain types of books (mail order specialities, erotica, cook books, what have you) and that someone under salary cannot bite the hand that feeds him.

In my experience, these are the flimsiest sort of rationalizations. A serious editor has one overriding concern: to publish, and to publish well, the best possible books, be they fiction or non-fiction, serious literature or entertainment. Not only would both publishers for whom I have worked heartily subscribe to this statement, but they have both given me support, encouragement *and* a salary in my efforts to implement my beliefs.

A careful examination of the records of such leading American trade publishing houses as Knopf, Little, Brown, Houghton Mifflin and Viking would show that "good" books sell, in the long run, better than "bad" books. By good books I mean books that contribute something——an insight into contemporary human affairs (*The Making of the President, The Lonely Crowd*); a portrait of an important statesman, composer, writer or general; a knowledge of faraway places and times (*The King Must Die, The Leopard*) or sheer entertainment (the novels of Kenneth Roberts, the mysteries of Agatha Christie).

This is not to say that silly books, vulgar books, books which are an insult to any intelligent adult, are not published every year. They are, but not because editors are forced to participate in such questionable trade. They are published because editors want to publish them, either because their own taste and inclinations are such or because they are cynically trying to cash in on a quick buck. Here I have in mind such books as ghosted celebrity confessions.

Thus it is, on one level, a truism that an editor has a responsibility to make money for his publishing house, but he has, in a far more serious sense, an obligation to publish only books which he considers to be worthwhile and of merit——even to the point of idiosyncrasy and personal preference. For, though in a relative sense trade book publishing may be a small business when compared to the manufacture of both guns and butter, still there are certainly enough publishing houses and editors in our country to ensure that a valid book will eventually find a fair hearing and a publishing home. (Nabakov's *Lolita* and Travers' *Anatomy of a Murder* were both turned down by more than twenty publishers, then became big best sellers.) And there is no need, nor should there be, for any one editor to become involved with a book which he feels does not meet his individual standards or taste. Thus the editor-in-chief of one major publishing house when asked to define the policy of his department, answered, "we have a list which reflects the personal idiosyncrasies of my editors."

So much for the selection of the books to be published, a crucial but by no means the sole obligation of a publisher's editor. For as I started out by saying, an editor should publish the best possible books and publish them well. In the area of non-fiction (and I personally have been involved with many more works of non-fiction than fiction) this means that a manuscript must be scrupulously edited both from the point of style and contents. This does not mean that an editor should tamper with or alter the substance of what a writer has to say (because if he disagrees with him he probably should not be publishing his book in the first place*). He should, merely, see to it that what the writer has written is presented in the clearest, most graceful and most responsible manner possible. Of course, in ninety-nine cases out of a hundred the author of a biography, a work of

---

* *I certainly have no wish to imply that an editor should only consent to publish books that entirely echo his own sentiments. For at this turn of the conversation someone inevitably points out the service which Houghton Mifflin performed in publishing* Mein Kampf——*a service which, by the way, was almost uniformly ignored at the time. Still, if an editor doubts the validity of an author's contentions, it is far fairer to both his own house and the author for him to pass the book by.*

criticism or a piece of popular science will know infinitely more about his subject than his editor. But the editor, as a generally intelligent and objective reader, has a duty to query and check any data which strikes him as questionable or not entirely accurate. In the case of highly technical or specialized books it is often advisable to get a reading from another expert in the field.

In this advisory capacity, the editor is serving the author and the eventual reader. He must also consider both in approving the book's format, design and typography. As these are technical matters (and as every publishing company has a production department) I will not go into them at length here, beyond saying that a book's design is certainly of great importance. All too many editors are ignorant of the rudiments of production and leave decisions of considerable significance to others who are not nearly as close to the whole problem of book-making.

It would be nice to think that in our free-market economy the most important, the most timely, the best-written books would automatically be recognized as such and would automatically be bought by the people one could reasonably expect to be interested in them. However, without being overly cynical about such matters and without even suggesting that Gresham's Law works more actively in the book publishing business than it does elsewhere in our society, it is fair to assume that when a book's sales exceed a certain "mean" (in a non-economic sense this may be equated with the remainder tables at "bargain" bookstores) level, overlooking the "star" psychology which is as prevalent in the book business as it is in Hollywood, it is due to the fact that the publisher's publicity, advertising and sales staff have successfully brought the book's special values to the attention of the book-seller and then the reading public. Coordinating and supervising this campaign is the editor, much the way a quarterback directs the other three backs on a football team.

For an editor's tasks do not end with the selection and the editing of a manuscript. His is the guiding, overall responsibility to see to it that the salesmen have a "handle" for the book, that the publicity department arranges for the proper newspaper, radio and television publicity, that the book finds its way into the hands of the right reviewers and that an effective and appropriate advertising campaign is conducted.

What I am suggesting is that an editor is a publisher in microcosm, though as he does not actually sign the checks there are certain limitations to his authority.* It is his decision what manuscripts will in fact be published. And once having made his decision, it is up to him to follow the manuscript through every phase of copy-editing, design, production, sales and promotion to ensure the most successful possible outcome to this venture of publishing, which is a most subtle combination of art and business, know-how and luck.

I have omitted two rather significant considerations in this informal discussion of the trade book editor's role in a free society such as ours——the "commissioning" of books; and the decision to publish or not to publish books which, for lack of a less loaded phrase, I shall call excessively and determinedly oriented towards sex. The first interests me a great deal, the second not at all.

In the past the writer was, more often than not, independently wealthy (for instance Virginia Woolf's proclaimed *sine qua non* of a yearly income of £100 and a room in Bloomsbury or Aldous Huxley's statement that he could afford to write because he had an ancestor who sailed with Drake). Today, however, such is rarely the case and more and more frequently a writer will approach a publisher with an idea and a request to be subsidized while researching and writing the book. Given the competitiveness of our society it is hardly surprising that even more recently publishers have completed the cycle, unleashing bright young editors with ideas and in search of the right author. Certainly the "key" word here is *right,* for unless the idea and the author are perfectly mated, the end product, as is often the case, can turn out to be disastrous. Yet the subject for no less a contemporary classic than *The Guns of August* was initially suggested to the author by her editor.

Here again it is the taste, knowledgeability and dedication of the editor (not to mention the writer) which is all important. Rather than talking about "commissioned" or "non-commissioned" books we

---

* *Unfortunately the story of one editor who turned down a manuscript after a prolonged argument with his publisher is not apocryphal. When, a number of publishing seasons later, the book came out under another imprint and to the accompaniment of rave reviews, the initial publisher asked his editor why they were not publishing books like that one. On hearing that the manuscript had indeed been in the house and ultimately declined by himself, he muttered, "If it's that good you should have fought harder."*

should think in terms of good and bad books. Similarly our current preoccupation with whether or not a book is "obscene" seems to me to be entirely misplaced. I personally see no reason to publish or not to publish a book just because it is full of naughty words and vivid sexual play, though I know it has become fashionable (as well as profitable) to bring out the worst rubbish and hide behind the rubrics of "freedom of the press" and "freedom from censorship."

Here again the prime consideration should be is it a good book, is it a significant contribution, does it really entertain? For the role of books in bringing all of us wisdom, knowledge and entertainment has reached unparalled heights. In some parts of the world the decision as to what should be published is made by the state, with all the limitations which this implies. In the United States, and throughout the Western world, book publishers and their editors decide, although aided, abetted and sometimes distracted by book clubs, best seller lists and popular magazines.

In a very exact sense they are arbiters of culture and taste, and theirs is a crucial, creative and exhilarating responsibility.

GEOFFREY SHURLOCK

30   The Film Industry and Self-Regulation

■

Over thirty years ago the motion picture industry found itself the target of self-style censorship groups. Rather than risk review (and potentially increasing control) by the federal government, the industry organized its own self-regulating agency, The Motion Picture Production Code Administration. Since that time, over sixty nations have imposed national censorship statutes on their own motion picture industries (statutes based, in large part, on the industry's self-devised Code), but America——along with Germany, Japan and Britain—— still leaves control of the motion picture's contents to the producers themselves.

The details of that Code will be found elsewhere in this volume, but in the following article, Geoffrey Shurlock, Director of the Code, outlines its history, rationale and working methods. His comments are sure to clarify the premises of the Code and eliminate the popular misconception that there are some things you just can't do (or show) on film. Mr. Shurlock makes it clear that you can do just about anything if it is done with taste and integrity.

The Film Industry and Self-Regulation was an address given by Mr. Shurlock at the Seventh Annual Freedom of Information Conference at the School of Journalism at the University of Missouri, November 16–17, 1964.

IN THIS QUARRELSOME WORLD there are not too many areas of agreement, in spite of the efforts of ecumenical councils and the

United Nations. Opinions differ, generally violently, and arguments can be had ranging from the nature of God to whether traffic should drive on the left or on the right. It is only in the last thirty years or so that we have approached agreement on outlawing such international curses as white slavery and the dope traffic. We are still trying to ban the bomb. And it may be some years before the world agrees on how to handle either the population explosion, or on the lighter side, the spread of those other world-wide inundations, American jazz and Coca-Cola.

With the movies, however, it has been easier for the world to make up its collective mind. The early flickers started out to be nothing more than the cause of innocent merriment to people who had only a nickel to spend on entertainment; and it now seems difficult to imagine how anyone could be corrupted for a nickel——even back in 1907, when the first censor board was established in the U.S. Nevertheless from their inception, there was widespread demand for somebody (generally the government) to do something about them by way of censorship; with the result that today every country in the world has imposed some form of nationwide control.

It is difficult to realize the torrent of abuse that greeted the first crude one-reelers. Not many people here today perhaps know that the movies were being damned as far back as 1896——and that was during the presidency of Grover Cleveland, which to the present generation sounds like the later middle ages of American history. In that year a contributor to the *Chap Book,* a family periodical of that era, took off as follows:

Now I want to smash the Vitascope. The name of the thing is in itself a horror, but that may pass. Its manifestations are worse. The Vitascope, be it known, is a sort of magic lantern which reproduces movement. Whole scenes come and go, and the thing is mechanically ingenious, and a pretty toy for that great child, the public. Its managers are not satisfied with this, however, and they bravely set out to eclipse in vulgarity all previous theatrical attempts.

In a recent play called "The Widow Jones" you may remember a famous kiss which Miss May Irwin bestowed on a certain John C. Rice and vice versa. Neither participant is physically attractive, and the spectacle of their prolonged pasturing on each other's lips was hard to bear. When only life-size, it was pronounced beastly. But that was nothing to the present sight. Magnified to gargantuan proportions and repeated

three times over, it is absolutely disgusting. . . . The Irwin Kiss is no
more than a lyric of the stock yards. Such things call for police interference.

That hollering for the police has not died down 68 years later.

Today there are at least 60 countries which impose official prior
censorship on the exhibition of films. (There are probably a few more
actually, with the emergence of the new African republics.) These
boards are empowered to reject films, to require cuts, and finally to
forbid them for young audiences generally below 14, 16, or 18 years
of age. Theaters violating the censor's rulings can be fined, or lose
their license. (Two years ago de Gaulle raised the age limit in France
to 18 for some films, and estabished a fine of $400 for any in-
fraction.)

On the other hand, there are four countries which do not have
government operated censor boards: Great Britain, Germany, Japan,
and the U.S. It is interesting to note that two of these are our ex-
totalitarian ex-enemies. They evidently had enough of governmental
meddling in their recent past to swing them away from statutory
censorship and into our camp.

In these four countries the regulation of films is in the hands of the
organized motion picture industry. In three of them there is some sort
of shadowy official sanction in the background which makes it either
difficult or dangerous for a producer or a theater owner to attempt to
get around submitting their films in the established manner.

In the U.S., however, there is generally speaking nothing short of
public opinion or the obscenity laws to ride herd on theater operations. Exceptions to this are four states (New York, Maryland, Virginia, and Kansas) and some twenty-five or so municipalities which
still operate censor boards and prior submission and licensing. In the
rest of the country, the theater operator is free to show any film he
sees fit.

Movie censorship in the U.S. burgeoned in the years between
1907 and 1922. The first decade and a half of this century evidently
was a great time for reform and regulation. Until the great war
blasted us awake, optimism and the conviction of human perfecti-
bility were rampant. With the advance of science and the spread of
education, man had it made; all we had to do was to make up our

minds, pass legislation, and our ills would surely disappear. In 1899 and again in 1907 the Czar of Russia (of all people) convoked at The Hague the first Peace Congresses for the outlawing of war. The first international convention for the control of dope traffic was held there in 1912. And about this time, the reformers began to eye the movies.

There was during this period in the halls of Congress, a "lobbyist of the Lord," as he styled himself, who devoted himself to warring on opium, alcohol, sex, and celluloid. Maybe because the latter was a comparative new-comer (after all, sex and alcohol had been around for several thousand years and were by then pretty well entrenched), celluloid actually came first on this country's regulatory schedule.

The first movie censor board in the U.S. was set up in Chicago as early as 1907. New York came second, in 1909, followed by Pennsylvania in 1911 and Kansas in 1913.

Second spot on the regulatory totem-pole went to sex; the Mann White Slavery Act was passed in 1910. In 1914 came the Harrison Act controlling narcotics. Alcohol had to wait until 1920 and the 18th Amendment.

Censorship was established in Great Britain in 1912. It was in that year that the British Board of Film Censors began clipping and classifying films to make them acceptable, whenever possible, to the British family. The British have always detested violence on the screen; and it is quite conceivable that their distaste was confirmed in those early days by the horrific assaults on law and order, as well as on human dignity, by such early Mack Sennet worthies as the Keystone Kops and their pie-throwing tormentors. The BBFC hasn't changed its opinion much in fifty years; just last month it made three cuts in Walt Disney's latest dog epic to make it safe for British moppets to view unchaperoned.

Not that the movies are the only sufferers from the zeal of the regulators. They are only the latest, the most widespread, and therefore the most vulnerable. It is no news to this audience that the performing arts have always been on the receiving end of brickbats from the authorities. There may well have been periods when the theater was really asking to be chastised. But the thinness of the ice upon which playwrights and actors have always skated can be most vividly judged by taking two great outbursts of theatrical glory two thousand years apart——the Greek drama of Plato's time and the Elizabethan age of Shakespeare.

Plato was a great philosopher, but at times he could sound like a bit of a prig. By the time he came to write his *Republic* he had developed a first-class blind spot for some of his fellow craftsmen. In that blue print for his idealized state, he has this to say about poets and playwrights:

Shall we carelessly allow children to hear any casual tales which may be devised by casual persons, and to receive into their minds ideas for the most part the very opposite of those which we would wish them to have when they grow up?

His answer is a pious "No." He goes on to comment:

The first thing will be to establish a censorship of the writers of fiction, and let the censors receive any tale of fiction that is good, and reject the bad. And we will desire mothers and nurses to tell their children the authorized ones only. . . . Most of those which are now in use must be discarded.

This astounding suggestion is a direct crack at those marvelous legends on which the great dramatists based their masterpieces, as well as a solid right to the jaw of Homer, whom Plato denounces by name, along with Aeschylus.

So we see, the first recorded demand for dramatic censorship is better than 2,300 years old.

Did the Athenians take Plato's recommendation? They did not. And very lucky for succeeding civilizations. What would our own culture be like without the Greek legends and their progeny, the great tragedies? Suppose the Iliad and the Odyssey had been tossed into the ash can by this board of censors.

The outcome was of course that the "censors" to whom Plato referred turned out to be the informed Athenian public itself. There must have been literally hundreds of plays produced during the heyday of Athens, and most of them were probably not worth preserving. As with all human creations, there must have been the normally high proportion of mediocre trash.

But the forty-six dramas that have survived are masterpieces; and that judgment was made by time and posterity, which means the average intelligent and enthusiastic citizen playgoer——and not Plato's proposed board of censors.

Now let's jump 2,000 years to Shakespeare's London. In those 2,000 years the world had become either wiser or more practical; at any rate no philosopher of the time, such as Francis Bacon, came out for censorship. In fact, not many years after Shakespeare, one of the loudest blasts against censorship ever penned came from the great John Milton——himself an outstanding Puritan.

But the Puritans of Shakespeare's acquaintance were not so wise, and they took after the theater in no uncertain terms——sometimes in language so sulphurous it would probaby not be allowed on television today. As witness the following outburst of Philip Stubbs writing in 1583:

Do not they [the stage plays] maintain bawdry, insinuate foolery, and renew the remembrance of heathen idolatry? Do they not induce whoredom and uncleanness? Nay, are they not rather plain devourers of maidenly virginity and chastity?

For proof whereof but mark the flocking and running to Theaters daily and hourly, night and day, time and tide, to see plays and interludes, where such wanton gestures, such bawdy speeches, such laughing and fleering, such kissing and bussing, such clipping and culling . . . as is wonderful to behold. Then these goodly pageants being ended, every mate sorts to his mate, every one brings another homeward of their way, very friendly, and in their secret conclaves covertly they play the sodomites, or worse.

In 1597 the Lord Mayor of London demanded the closing of all theaters, averring "They are a special cause of corrupting the youth, containing nothing but unchaste matters, lascivious devices, . . . and other lewd and ungodly practices. . . . Neither in polity nor in religion are they to be suffered in a Christian commonwealth."

In the fourteen years between these two blasts, Marlowe had produced four masterpieces: *Tamburlaine, Dr. Faustus, The Jew of Malta, Edward II.* Shakespeare had written, among his other early plays: *Richard III, The Taming of the Shrew, Romeo and Juliet, Richard II, King John, The Merchant of Venice, A Midsummer Night's Dream.*

There is some good evidence that the Lord Mayor's charge was leveled in part at such plays as *Romeo and Juliet,* which Shakespeare had written and produced a couple of seasons earlier. We must remember that, to the average Elizabethan father Romeo and Juliet were juvenile delinquents of the most horrifying stripe. One thing above all that young men and women in those days were not supposed to do was to marry without their parents' full consent.

So the parents of today who worry whether *West Side Story* is fit for their teenagers to see, will understand how the Puritans of that other day felt about the swarms of young apprentices who crowded to cheer this play glorifying a couple of mutinous teenagers——the "rebels without a cause" of 1597.

Then, as today with the movies, the most enthusiastically vociferous supporters of the theater were the London apprentices——the teenagers of that era. When they heard of the Lord Mayor's threat, they promptly rioted. Queen Elizabeth loved the theater as much as did the apprentices. She intervened, and the ban was lifted. Shakespeare could now go on to write *Hamlet, King Lear,* and *The Tempest.*

The final decision was left to the Elizabethan public, which evidently did as good a job as did the Athenians in their day. The trash disappeared without any need for censorship. The public turned thumbs down on it. The great dramas survive.

Meanwhile, back in the U.S. matters were not going so well for the movies. By 1922 there were censor boards in nine states: New York, Ohio, Pennsylvania, Massachusetts, Maryland, Florida, Virginia, and Kansas——not to mention the granddaddy of them all, the Chicago Municipal Board which practically means adding Illinois to the roster. Also, at varying times, there were as many as ninety municipal censor boards, many of which, however, bloomed and faded as mayors and city councils came and went.

The situation continued pretty much unchanged until 1952, when the first direct challenge to the right of prior censorship was made. The film in question was an Italian import, the famous *Miracle* case. The New York State Board of Regents ruled the film sacrilegious. The distributor appealed all the way up to the Supreme Court, which held that sacrilege——particularly any one group's idea of sacrilege ——was not sufficient cause for the state to ban a film and ordered its reinstatement. Most important of all, the Supreme Court went on to state: "We have no doubt that moving pictures, like newspapers and radio, are included in the press whose freedom is guaranteed by the First Amendment."

This accolade supplied the movies with the necessary ammunition to launch a long-scale attack on the entrenchments of statutory censorship. The result: Censor boards have been disappearing from the landscape to the point where today they are active in only four states——New York, Maryland, Virginia, and Kansas——and (at latest count) 28 cities.

As indicated, since 1922——and that is 42 years——there have been no new state censor boards established. What kept them from spreading? The creation in that same year of the Motion Picture Association of America——in its early days nicknamed the "Hays Office"——as an organ of industry self-regulation. And of all its activities, the best known, most cussed and discussed, is the Association's Production Code. More than any other single factor, the code has been the industry's dam against the insidious seepage of statutory censorship in this country. It is the first and by far the best known case of a major industry——and an "art" industry at that——undertaking to regulate itself in such detail.

It has been paid the compliment of being adapted by three foreign countries. And the screen's young and vigorous nephew, television, has borrowed it almost bodily.

It was thirty-three years old last March. In these years, 26,000 films have been processed by it—12,500 of them full-length feature films. And these films have carried the stamp of America to the farthest shores.

The innate Americanism of the code operation is underlined by the act that the industry adopted it quite voluntarily, and out of its own innate sense of responsibility. It was not imposed on it by any outside force or agent. Like our Constitution, it exists by the will and consent of those governed.

It is in fact as near to a purely democratic system of industry control as can be found operating anywhere today. And unlike other forms of film control, such as state censorship, it is not likely to be declared unconstitutional. For this reason alone, it may outlast them all here in the United States.

The code is a set of self-regulations based on sound morals common to all peoples and all religions. To put it simply, it lays down the thesis that the screen should never be used to make what is basically wrong appear to be right. It assumes that the Ten Commandments are as applicable in the field of the imagination as they are in real life.

The code clearly defines the aim and objective of films. It states: "Theatrical motion pictures . . . are primarily to be regarded as entertainment."

It is well that the code recognizes this basic principle. Teaching and preaching are not the objective of movies; they are the prerogatives of the school and the church. Even in Elizabethan times, this distinction was understood and observed. Shakespeare was the actor and dramatist; Bacon, the philosopher and teacher. Neither poached on the other's preserve.

The code is a reasonable document. In dealing with stories of man's frailty and sin, it does not demand that the sinner be painted so black that we cease to be entertained. On the contrary, it states quite clearly that we may sympathize with the sinner though condemning his sin.

Nor does it insist on "an eye for an eye and a tooth for a tooth." Rather it inclines to the belief in a God who (as the Prayer Book puts it) "desireth not the death of a sinner, but rather that he may turn from his wickedness and live." A redeemed sinner should be a more positive incentive towards good living than a a dead gangster.

The code operation has one immeasureable advantage over such other forms of control as prerelease censorship. This latter can only delete material from an already finished film. By its very nature it can only act privatively and hence negatively.

The code on the contrary gets its licks in while the project is still in the script stage. And its approach is basically constructive. We are much happier when, instead of watering down a story, we direct our efforts towards adding something positive by way of moral emphasis and elucidation——what we call "compensating moral values." By insisting that all stories be told within a proper moral frame of reference, the code can help films take on added dimensions, explore deeper phases of life, and achieve genuine maturity. No man, and no art, can claim to be mature without an acute moral sense. This should be, and is, the code's primary contribution to picture making.

It should be made crystal clear that the code is not aimed at the censorship of ideas. It does not undertake to tell producers *what* material to choose for their films. All it undertakes is to outline *how* that material should be treated——in conformity with fundamental standards of morality and within the general limits of good taste.

In this connection I would like to quote the words of the distinguished Jesuit writer Fr. Harold Gardiner. In a recent book *Movies, Morals and Art,* without mentioning the code of course, he puts our case most trenchantly:

The *subject matter* of a film is not the area of prime moral concern of the films considered as an art form. This subject matter may indeed——and rightly——be a concern for parents and others charged with the guidance of youth. But to say this is not to throw the burden on the film industry; it is to throw the burden of responsibility where it belongs. You may not think that Johnny ought to be introduced to the existence of evil in the world by seeing a film on drug addiction, and you are most likely right. But that is not automatically to establish the fact that no such film ought to be made. The prime consideration is *how* almost any given subject matter is treated.

Seven years ago the Production Code was streamlined to permit the treatment of any story dealing with material generally considered acceptable for public discussion. This is as it should be; drama takes the whole of creation for its backdrop, and the proper study of mankind is man in all his manifestations. The only restraint on the artist is that the matter in hand be discussed with truth, intelligence, and taste.

The industry has now painfully come to admit that not all its films are suitable for all ages and audiences. Up to perhaps seven years or so ago we still dwelt in that Golden Age in which movies were the universal baby-sitter, hailed not only as your best entertainment, but also as the best possible way of securing peace and quiet for Ma on Saturday afternoon. The threatened loss of this handy refuge is at the root of a lot of current complaints.

Practically all other countries in this troubled world have met the problem head on by categorically forbidding by law the attendance of the immature at certain films which the authorities designate as suitable only for the mature adult. As stated earlier, the classifying is done by some central government body.

Lately there has arisen quite a clamor for this country to adopt the same procedure. But we have a special problem here. By reason of our federal set-up it would probably be impractical, as well as unconstitutional, for the federal government to undertake this licensing responsibility in lieu of each individual state. And to have fifty classification boards operating officially throughout this land would seem too cumbersome to tolerate.

Up to the present the quickest and quietest way out of the dilemma has been for the industry, not illogically, to follow Father Gardiner's suggestion and seek to put on the parents the responsibility for their offspring's movie mores. For the last couple of years our answer to unhappy and bewildered parents has been to urge them henceforward to undertake to supervise their children's movie-going as meticulously as they oversee the books they read and the dances they attend. And for their aid and comfort, we refer them to the increasing number of expert and detailed evaluations of films currently available wherever one turns.

PRESIDENT KENNEDY WAS ONCE ASKED, anent certain congressional investigations into juvenile delinquency, whether he had any thoughts as to the possibility of federal censorship of movies and television. He replied:

We are very much concerned in that area. We are also informed about what Congress is doing [referring to the then current investigation.] But this is a matter which goes to the responsibility of the private citizen. The federal government cannot protect the standards of young boys and girls. The parents have to do it, in the first place. We can only play a supplemental role. It rests with the families and the parents involved.

The experience of 2,000 years seems to suggest that President Kennedy was right. In ancient Athens, in Elizabethan England, as today, an alert, enthusiastic and violently opinionated public has always been the best censor.

WILBUR SCHRAMM

31 Who Is Responsible for the Quality of Mass Communications?

After all is said, then, the final question remains: How do we achieve a more responsible Press?

Among the many possible answers, Wilbur Schramm's reply seems to be the most practical of all: that the responsibility must be shared by (1) the media themselves, (2) the government and (3) the public ——with the public's responsibility to improve the media the necessary and most vital sparking force in our society.

Wilbur Schramm is the Director of the Institute for Communication Research at Stanford University. He is the author of Responsibility in Mass Communication, published by Harper & Brothers in 1957. The following essay forms the final chapter of that work.

THERE ARE only three great instruments which society may use to encourage or prod the mass media to responsible performance. These are government and its various regulatory bodies, national, state, and local; the media themselves, their individual personnel, and their formal and informal associations and administrative organizations; and the general public, with its formal and informal organizations and associations.

If we ask where, among these, responsibility lies for the kind of mass communication we have in this country, and for any change we want to bring about in mass communication, then quite clearly the answer is that responsibility is shared. Neither government, nor the media, nor the public can be counted on to do the job alone, and on the other hand, none of them is exempt from responsibility for doing it. What we are looking for . . . is a desirable balance of responsibility among them. . . .

Let us now consider the responsibility of the public.

The Commission on Freedom of the Press concluded that the more the media and the public are willing to do toward insuring a free and responsible communication system, the less the government will have to do; and that in general the "outside forces" of law and public opinion can check bad aspects of media performance, but only the media themselves can bring about good performance.

It is hard to disagree with these statements, but I depart somewhat from the Commission's emphasis. It seems to me quite clear that the media have the chief responsibility. If they do not assume it, if they do not voluntarily provide us with the public service on a high professional level which our society requires, then I do not see how our communication problem can be solved without to some extent going out of bounds, as we have defined the bounds of desirable action.

What the media do not do for us they invite the government to step in and do or cause to be done. This, in our view, is a dangerous, an ominous kind of action. For that reason, I have urged that the government "keep its hands off" wherever it can, that it put down the temptation to step in and set things right, that it set strict limits on the kind of actions it will take with reference to mass communication, and that these actions should be chiefly facilitating, rather than restrictive ones.

I have therefore tended to put somewhat more responsibility on both the media and the public than did the Commission. Whereas the media must assume the central responsibility and do the job, I envisage the public as being prime movers in the communication dynamic. It is my firm belief that the public can come pretty close to having whatever kind of mass communication system it wants. Of course, this requires that it know what it wants and say what it wants. I do not accept the old idea that the mass-media public is a vegetable. I think that the "great audience" can be active rather than passive, that it can assay its needs and be articulate in getting them. Granted those assumptions, then it seems to me that the people hold the balance of power in determining the shape of their system and the service it gives them.

The listening, viewing, reading public underestimates its power. The media heads do not underestimate it. I have seen very few media men who look on the public as a mass to be molded and say, "This year we shall teach them to like thus and so." Rather, they are deeply concerned with what the public will be interested in, what the public wants and *will* like, and one of their greatest problems is trying to find out these things.

Anyone who looks at mass communication as a social institution cannot fail to note the tremendous push and pull of public interests and tastes on the institution. The program pattern of the networks vibrates like a windharp to the breeze from the monthly program ratings. New films go out to "sneak" previews, sample public reaction, and go back to the cutting room. One hundred letters to a network will often bring a review of policy; even fewer letters to a station will lead it to review a program or a program structure. One visit of a serious committee to a newspaper editor will make him think hard about what he is doing, even though he will be crusty about making promises. The motion picture industry has been in greater fear of boycotts than of censorship. Its code is spotted throughout with "special legislation" intended to appease this or that group and avoid boycott or public criticism.

In an earlier part of the book we mentioned how a comparatively slight outpouring of public indignation forced a network to take a well-known personality off the air because he had offended the friends of "Silent Night." Letters to the Federal Communications Commission get into station files, and they have a way of turning up embarrassingly in hearings. Listeners' councils have been able in many cases to exert a real and salutary influence on the kind of programs a local station carries. And underneath all this is the great groundswell of audience and attention, which none of the media can ignore. A newspaper publisher, who may resist what he considers a special interest group or special pleading, will pay attention if his circulation begins to fall off. A network or a station will perk up when the ratings begin to drop. A film studio is keenly aware what kind of business its pictures are doing. A magazine is compelled to worry when its newsstand sales fall off, or its readership studies indicate little interest in a certain part of its content.

Ultimately, therefore, the audience calls the tune. The people hold the trumps. And the only question is whether they will play their cards.

Is it realistic to hope that the public, the great audience, will seize this opportunity? This, of course, is the fundamental problem posed by the coming of bigness and fewness to the media. When media were many and audiences were small; when only a small percentage of the population could read, and only a small elite group formed the reading audience for most newspapers, magazines, and books; when the entertainment media were small and intimate——then there was a close connection between the men who made the media and their audience. There was a quick and vigorous feedback of demands and judgments. The audiences themselves felt the closeness of their relationship and took a lively interest in what the media were doing. The readers knew the editors. The performers knew some of their audiences. But now that audiences have grown so large that they include almost the whole population, when a great anonymity has settled over them, and they become known to the media only in terms of program ratings or percentages of readership or circulation figures——is there a realistic hope that some of this liveness and intimacy can be recaptured?

Of course, CBS or Metro-Goldwyn-Mayer or the *Reader's Digest* is unlikely ever to recapture the relationship which the *Dial* maintained with its audience when that influential magazine had 200 subscribers, most of them known personally to the editor, Margaret Fuller. It is certainly unrealistic to expect that situation to recur except in the case of a little magazine subsidized to serve a coterie. But between that situation and the far end of the scale, at which audiences are a kind of anonymous mass, I think it is clearly realistic and possible for the audience of mass communication to move a long way up the scale from anonymity toward personality. It seems to me clearly possible for the great audience to become a live, responsive, discriminating audience, to make its opinions and wishes known to the media, and in its own quiet way to enforce those opinions and wishes on the media. And if it should appear that in this audience there are a number of levels of taste and kinds of need, then I think it is clearly possible for the audience to insist that the media serve those different tastes and needs, instead of ladling up an insipid common-denominator broth which appeals somewhat to each and satisfies none.

The basic responsibility of the public, therefore, is to make itself, as far as possible, an alert, discriminating audience. This may require a somewhat different habit of mind from the one we most commonly see on the part of many individuals who by virtue of position or education might be expected to be the leaders of and spokesmen for the public in their demands upon the media. This common attitude ——"Oh, I never watch television except when there's something like a political convention on——it's just trash!"——is fundamentally an irresponsible attitude. It neglects the fact that television doesn't *have* to be all trash, if indeed, it is. Television is potentially one of our greatest windows on the world. It is one of the best ways in which we could expand our horizons, bring a sense of reality to faraway events, make a more informed judgment on public figures, share the lectures and demonstrations at our greatest universities, see the kind of opera, ballet, drama, museums, and concert artists formerly available only to a few fortunate people, most of them in great cities. If television isn't being used that way, what a great social waste it is! What a loss we are suffering! And whose fault is it? Basically, it is the fault of the people who don't watch it and don't do anything about improving it.

The greatest newsgathering services man has ever devised are connected to our home-town newspapers. Through wire services these newspapers are connected to every corner of the world where news is being made. A statement by Nasser in Egypt is perhaps twenty minutes away from each of our newspapers. An incident beside the Iron or the Bamboo Curtain is, at the most, thirty minutes away from our newsrooms. A full interpretation of Mr. Dulles' latest statement is available if a few persons in Washington or New York or on a university campus are given a few hours to think about it. In that situation, have we any right to say, as so many of us do: "I can't get any picture of what's happening in the world, from our paper; it carries only six or seven foreign news stories a day"? Or, "I can't understand what's really going on in national politics or this international situation. We never get any background." Have we any right to say that, if we never complain to the editor? He has the space to put in more world news, more background, if he thinks his audience wants it. He is putting that space into sports, or features, or society, or some other news. If he thought there was a serious demand for more world news or background, he would carry it.

The first requisite, therefore, is an alert, interested audience. This implies that we pay some attention to our media. We read, view, listen. We find out what is in the media. We don't wash our hands of the media in the supposition that they are being patterned for somebody else.

Then we try to make ourselves a discriminating audience. We give some thought to what the media *might* be giving us. We talk about the media with our friends. Perhaps we organize listeners' councils or readers' groups to talk about what we find in the media. We try to see that our schools give some attention to the question how to use the media intelligently; there are good textbooks now on such subjects as "How to read a newspaper," and many schools are helping their students to make best use of the mass media, just as they prepare them to make use of other parts of human experience. After all, these young people will be giving perhaps five hours a day, or nearly a third of their waking time, to mass media. This is too large a segment of life to use wastefully. And so we try to see that our young people have a systematic introduction to the media. We try to read newspaper or magazine criticism of the other mass media, just as we read book reviews. And in every way we try to build into ourselves some standards for judgment of what we see, hear, and read.

Another way in which we can develop discrimination is by controlling our attendance upon the media. If we don't want all movies to be made as though for children, we can keep our children away from *some* movies. If we don't want all television to be filtered out so as not to be above the sensibilities and sensitivities of *any* member of the family, then let us exercise some discrimination about what members of the family watch television at a given time. This is partly our responsibility. We can't expect the media to serve the interests of all kinds of people and displease or offend none unless we do something about getting the right kind of people to the media at the right time.

Then the next step in our responsibility is to make our views known to the media. One way to do this is simply by reflecting in our patronage our discrimination in what we subscribe to, what we attend, what we view or listen to. If enough of us do this, it will have an effect. But this method sometimes cuts off our nose to spite our face. For example, if we stop buying our home-town newspaper because it carries only seven foreign news stories a day, that will lose us *all* the local news. The big stick is not the best way. A better way is to tell our media what we do and don't like about them, and what would make us like them better.

This we can do through letters———to the editor, to the station, to the network, to the theater, or to the studio. The more individual these letters are, the better. The media tend to fill their wastebaskets with letters which are all written in about the same words and therefore reveal that they are inspired by some pressure group. But individual letters are read and valued. So are individual contacts, when those are possible. These help to tell media employees, and especially media heads, what you think of their product. If you feel seriously enough about it, you can call on the editor or the station manager or the theater owner. You can certainly take advantage of meetings or social events or casual contacts to talk to media people. They appreciate these little feedbacks, and over the course of weeks such contacts add up to a picture of what the public wants and thinks.

Things like this you can do informally and individually. Or you can organize and go about it more formally. We have occasionally in this book said unkind things about pressure groups, but there is nothing in our political philosophy to keep audiences from organizing whenever and however they wish, to communicate more effectively with the media. Listeners' councils, where they have been organized, have been very effective in this way. Organizations like the League of Women Voters or the Association of University Women have some-times made the media their chief discussion topic and have sent delegations or resolutions to represent their opinions and needs to media heads. Sometimes community groups, or student groups, or church groups have arisen spontaneously because of dissatisfaction with some aspect of the media. Often these groups have asked newspapermen or broadcasters or theater operators, or magazine salesmen, to speak to their meetings, in order to get their side of the story and convey the feelings of the group.

There are already a number of well-organized groups active in the field, many of them with professional staffs watching the media, trying to keep out of them material offensive to the particular group. Such are, for example, the Legion of Decency, the Chamber of Commerce, the American Legion, et cetera. There is nothing wrong with this. Any group has a right to organize and tell the media what it thinks of them. But remember that our communication system is built on the theory of a free market place of ideas. It will not work right unless *all* viewpoints on a controversial question are freely presented.

Therefore, there is a kind of pressure-group activity which is as clearly out of bounds as is government interference with the media. I mean the kind of informal censorship which tries to remake the shape of the media in the image of one group's needs and sensitivities, at the cost of all other groups. The news about Christmas time, 1956, contained what may be an example of this kind of activity. Station WGN-TV, of Chicago, canceled the world première showing on television of the film *Martin Luther*. The station said the film was canceled because of the "emotional reaction" of the public to its plan to show the picture. This "emotional reaction," said the *Christian Century,* took the form of a telephone blitzkrieg "organized by Roman Catholics to keep WGN telephones humming with protests." The Chancellor of the Chicago archdiocese said that the Church had made no official representations to WGN-TV whatsoever, and that if any Catholics had protested it was an individual matter. It was claimed that the film was "down-right insulting" to Catholics.

Now I have neither investigated behind these facts nor seen the picture. It is a fact, however, that the film was shown in many theaters without any substantial opposition. If the facts are as suggested——an organized campaign by members of one religious sect to keep off the air a film about the founder of other religious sects——then this is a questionable kind of pressure-group activity. There could be no possible objection to one church exerting discipline over its own members and keeping them away from a theater or from watching a television program. But when such a group acts to deprive other groups of opportunities they very much desire in the mass media, and which are not obscene or otherwise clearly censorable, then it would seem that this is restricting the free market place, and should be resisted both by the media and the public.

As I say, the Chicago incident may or may not be an example of this kind of action; I have not thoroughly investigated it. And the particular religious group mentioned is by no means the only group, religious or political, which has been accused of such activity. But whoever does it, it doesn't fit into our system.

Pressure groups, like government, are usually on less dangerous ground when their activity is facilitating, rather than restrictive. That is, they are more helpful when they try to represent the needs of the public than when they speak for the sensitivities of particular groups. But even here caution is needed. We can't expect mass communication to meet all our needs if we depend on a few well-organized groups, each with a special interest, to speak for us. These groups may keep the media free of material which disturbs, and encourage the media to present material which pleases, the Legion, the Chamber, the Roman Catholic Church, or some other organization; but they will not necessarily be concerned that the media carry what the rest of the public wants or needs. The remedy for this situation is not to complain about "pressure groups," but to organize groups to represent our own interests, if these are not being represented. And when the media heads see the full spectrum of public needs and wishes, they will be better able to plan their product.

A further responsibility of the public, it seems to us, is to encourage intelligent criticism of the media. This is not an attack on the media; it is rather a service to media and public alike. Book reviews, for many years, have served not only to sharpen the standards of taste on the part of writer, reader, and editor, but also to call the attention of the public to new books of interest. It is amazing that so little criticism of broadcasting and newspapers has come into being. The influential daily critics of radio and television number less than a handful. No sustained regular criticism of newspapers has ever proved feasible. Yet criticism of this kind is surely a part of the professionalizing and general growing up of the media.

The Commission on Freedom of the Press recommended that "a new and independent agency" should be established to "appraise and report annually upon the performance of the press." By *press* the Commission meant all the mass media. This proposal was received with undisguised horror by the newspapers, and was equated with all sorts of dire threats to press freedom. Yet it is hard to see how such an agency, given a board of distinguished citizens and a competent staff, could really threaten freedom of the press. And it might do a great service, both in scrutinizing the media for the public and in representing to the media the dissatisfactions and unmet needs of the public. Such an agency would, of course, have no governmental connection and would represent the public in general rather than any segment of it. The Commission listed a long series of services such an agency might undertake, among which were the following:

> Helping the media "define workable standards of performance";
> "Pointing out the inadequacy" of media service in certain areas;
> Investigating areas and instances "where minority groups are excluded from reasonable access to the channels of communication";
> Examining the "picture of American life" presented abroad by the media;
> Investigating charges of "press lying," with particular reference to the persistent misrepresentation of the data required for judging public issues;
> Appraising "governmental action affecting communications";
> Appraising the "tendencies and characteristics of the various branches of the communications industry";
> Encouraging the "establishment of centers of advanced study, research, and criticism in the field of communications at universities";
> Encouraging projects which give hope of meeting the needs of special audiences;
> Giving "the widest possible publicity and public discussion" to all its findings.

For any one agency, this might be an overambitious assignment. Yet the objective of all of it is simple enough——an agency to represent the interest of the public as a whole, as distinguished from the special interest of groups; to speak for the whole public in a way that the public could never speak as individuals; to observe the work of the media and think about it in terms of the needs and interests of the American public; and finally to report both ways, to the media and to the public, and thus to serve as a valuable communication link between them. To choose the board and staff of such a public agency would be difficult. To outline and restrict its tasks to realistic goals and limits would take a great deal of thinking and some trial. But the result might be very salutary, might result in a much better mutual understanding between the media and their publics, and on the whole would be an excellent project on which a foundation might bet some money.

If such an agency of communication and observation is ever established, it is a responsibility of the public to do it. It should not be established by the government nor by the media, although it should counsel with both the media and government. It should represent public interest at the highest level. So far as the newspaper objection is concerned, it is a good guess that, after the first mechanical reaction of resistance, most of the newspapers and the other media would respect and welcome the new agency.

We said in the preceding chapter that it is a responsibility of the media to help in the establishment of adequate schools for prospective members of the profession, and also university research centers in mass communication. It is certainly a responsibility of the media to concern themselves with these problems and help with them, but the basic responsibility is the public's. The public has to found such organizations at universities, and send able young people to them. Over the next two or three decades the schools of journalism and their related training and research centers can make a profound difference in the level of media personnel. They can do so, that is, if they are used at their full potential which, as we tried to say in the last chapter, is not for vocational training, but for training of a breadth and depth which very few other occupations require.

Another way to say it is that journalism school and other mass communication curricula are not best used when they train students for the first six months of their employment; they should rather prepare their graduates for the years that follow the first six months: not in the skills which enable the young employee to do well at first, but rather in the understandings which enable him to do well throughout his career. There is no reason why he should not learn some skills, too; but, whenever there has to be a choice of time between learning the vocational skills and gaining the broad understanding of society and mass communication's place in it, the time should always be used for the broader and less immediately useful studies. The schools should aim for the long, not the short term; for on his job the new man can much more easily learn the skills of his job than he can learn to understand human beings, social organization, government, economics, and science.

Schools of journalism have been moving in this direction, but they are handicapped by a tradition which began in the land-grant colleges under the example of service to agriculture, and the early leadership of weekly newspapermen who wanted employees they would not have to train. Even now the schools of journalism are unlike other professional or quasi-professional schools in that *they* do not necessarily train the new members of the profession as do medical or law schools; their graduates have to compete on a level with graduates of every other curriculum in the university and with nongraduates of universities. Indeed, the fact that university graduates expect more salary gives an advantage to nongraduates on smaller papers and other media. Therefore, the school of journalism has felt some need to stress, by teaching journalistic techniques, its uniqueness in the university and its close relationship to the newspapers and the broadcasters. Even so, the best schools now build their curricula on a broad grounding of liberal studies in other departments, and this is a tendency which the public should certainly encourage.

Another healthy development is the establishment of research centers and programs in connection with a few schools of journalism and elsewhere in a few universities. This is a long step on the road to professionalization. Without strong research programs in connection with and feeding into schools of medicine, we should still be letting blood for various diseases and treating mental diseases with chains and dungeons. It should be pointed out that both the schools and the research centers in mass communication are essentially a public responsibility.

Another important way in which the public can demonstrate its discriminating concern with mass communication is in the encouragement of new ventures. It is increasingly hard to start anything new in mass communication because of the costs involved. Yet there is increasing need for new ventures, not only to provide a variety in viewpoint, but more important, to serve the needs of groups within the great audience who are not sufficiently served by "common denominator" media content. If the public, or segments of it, want these special services they must make their wants known, and be alert to support, or at least try out, new ventures when they come.

There could be more newspapers covering public affairs in somewhat the way *The New York Times* does, but in other parts of the country, if publishers thought people in sufficient numbers would buy them. There could be more and better community television stations, covering local public affairs and carrying the best in local entertainment and information, if audiences would give them a few dollars per viewer per year. The university radio and television stations would furnish a better service——indeed, they could give a very exciting service——if the public made known to administrations and legislatures that they wanted these activities adequately supported with budgets. There would be more theaters specializing in high-quality films, and more studios making such films for such theaters, if the public would patronize them. The possibility of endowed newspapers or broadcasting stations is a fascinating one, but it is not necessary to have financing from a foundation or a wealthy man in order to bring about superior communications. The thing most needed in order to have new ventures in mass communication is assurance that there is a discriminating public waiting for them, willing to support them.

In another way, too, the public has a peculiar responsibility in regard to mass communication. More nonprofessional members of the public must learn to use the media. There is no excuse for religious broadcasting being less skillful than entertainment broadcasting. There is no reason why the public should permit educational broadcasting to be any less skillful than entertainment broadcasting; yet the educational stations are starved for funds and are therefore unable to train and keep skilled performers. There is no reason why local broadcasting, radio or television, could not be more of a force than it is; for leaders in any community to acquire the basic skills of broadcasting would not be a great task. This implies also that more members of the nonprofessional public should come to understand the media——to learn what can be expected of the newspapers and the broadcasters especially, and how to work with them and make use of their media in the best way.

All this comes back to the question whether we can realistically expect to have a live, articulate, discriminating public concerning itself with mass communication. If so, great things are possible. If not, progress will be slow. For, as I have tried to indicate, responsibility in mass communication is a delicate balance between the media, the government, and the public. The chief responsibility for doing what needs to be done with mass communication is that of the media, but in a sense the basic obligation is with the public. The public's responsibility is to be an active, discriminating audience, to make its needs known to the media, to be helpful as the media try to meet these needs——in other words, to be full partner in the task of making the kind of communication society needs. To the extent that the public is less than a full partner, government and media will fill the gap, and we shall be less sure that we get what we want. For it is the public's own responsibility that is controlling in this case, and if we do not exercise it we deserve only what we get.

In a radio address to America in 1931, and in his usual salty, tongue-in-cheek manner, George Bernard Shaw startled some of his listeners with the following proposition: "Every person who owes his life to civilized society," he said, "and who has enjoyed since his childhood its very costly protections and advantages should appear at reasonable intervals before a properly qualified jury to justify his existence, which should be summarily and painlessly terminated if he fails to justify it."

I am not advocating such summary justice. But I should like to suggest that all of us who enjoy the protections and advantages of a free communication system do indeed have some obligation to justify our existence under it. I have been suggesting what that obligation consists of. And if we are not doing enough to justify such protections and advantages, then we certainly face the possibility in this fateful century of having our existence under them summarily but not painlessly terminated.

Appendix

Several sections of the Press have formulated their own codes of ethics. A sampling of these codes appears in the following order:

1. LIBRARY BILL OF RIGHTS

2. FREEDOM TO READ STATEMENT

3. HOW LIBRARIES AND SCHOOLS CAN RESIST CENSORSHIP (These three codes were formulated by the American Library Association)

4. ADVERTISING ACCEPTABILITY STANDARDS OF THE DETROIT NEWS (1961). Published by the Detroit *News;* published here in a slightly abridged format.

5. SELF-REGULATION IN ADVERTISING: A REPORT ON THE OPERATIONS OF PRIVATE ENTERPRISE IN AN IMPORTANT AREA OF PUBLIC RESPONSIBILITY: Submitted by the Advertising Advisory Committee to the Secretary of Commerce. A United States Department of Commerce publication. Reprinted here in an abridged format.

6. THE MOTION PICTURE PRODUCTION CODE: Issued by the Motion Picture Association of America, Inc. in 1956.

7. CODE OF ETHICS OR CANONS OF JOURNALISM: From the American Society of Newspaper Editors

8. CODE OF ETHICS OF THE INTERNATIONAL LABOR PRESS

*   *   *

A code of ethics is a kind of public "diary of conscience," a written record of the character of a profession. Like an individual's character, it is formed by the subtle and not-so-subtle pressures of governmental

362]

influence, personal integrity and societal demands. The code of ethics, then, is the sum total, or aggregate public statement, of that profession's sense of responsibility.

Many will claim that in some instances the standards have not been set high enough; in others too high to meet the realistic demands of the marketplace. There will always be criticism, of course; but the fact that codes of ethics are formulated at all indicate a basic premise of moral commitment to professional conscience and public good.

Obviously many more segments of the Press have issued Codes of Ethics——notably the radio and television industries——but the several presented here stand as a fair sampling of how the problems of interpreting the twentieth century have been tackled by some of the more influential creators of the ethos of twentieth century.

Adopted June 18, 1948
Amended February 1, 1961, by the A.L.A. Council

Library Bill of Rights

The Council of the American Library Association reaffirms its belief in the following basic policies which should govern the services of all libraries:

1. As a responsibility of library service, books and other reading matter selected should be chosen for values of interest, information, and enlightenment of all the people of the community. In no case should any book be excluded because of the race or nationality or the political or religious views of the writer.

2. There should be the fullest practicable provision of material presenting all points of view concerning the problems and issues of our times, international, national, and local; and books or other reading matter of sound factual authority should not be proscribed or removed from library shelves because of partisan or doctrinal disapproval.

3. Censorship of books, urged or practiced by volunteer arbiters of morals or political opinion or by organizations that would establish a coercive concept of Americanism, must be challenged by libraries in maintenance of their responsibility to provide public information and enlightenment through the printed word.

4. Libraries should enlist the cooperation of allied groups in the fields of science, of education, and of book publishing in resisting all abridgment of the free access to ideas and full freedom of expression that are the tradition and heritage of Americans.

5. The rights of an individual to the use of a library should not be denied or abridged because of his race, religion, national origins, or political views.

6. As an institution of education for democratic living, the library should welcome the use of its meeting rooms for socially useful and cultural activities and discussion of current public questions. Such meeting places should be available on equal terms to all groups in the community regardless of the beliefs and affiliations of their members.

By official action of the Council on February 3, 1951, the Library Bill of Rights shall be interpreted to apply to all materials and media of communication used or collected by libraries.

Freedom to Read Statement

Adopted June 25, 1953, by the ALA COUNCIL

The freedom to read is essential to our democracy. It is under attack. Private groups and public authorities in various parts of the country are working to remove books from sale, to censor textbooks, to label "controversial" books, to distribute lists of "objectionable" books or authors, and to purge libraries. These actions apparently rise from a view that our national tradition of free expression is no longer valid; that censorship and suppression are needed to avoid the subversion of politics and the corruption of morals. We, as citizens devoted to the use of books and as librarians and publishers responsible for disseminating them, wish to assert the public interest in the preservation of the freedom to read.

We are deeply concerned about these attempts at suppression. Most such attempts rest on a denial of the fundamental premise of democracy: that the ordinary citizen, by exercising his critical judgment, will accept the good and reject the bad. The censors, public and private, assume that they should determine what is good and what is bad for their fellow-citizens.

We trust Americans to recognize propaganda, and to reject obscenity. We do not believe they need the help of censors to assist them in this task. We do not believe they are prepared to sacrifice their heritage of a free press in order to be "protected" against what others think may be bad for them. We believe they still favor free enterprise in ideas and expression.

We are aware, of course, that books are not alone in being subjected to efforts at suppression. We are aware that these efforts are related to a larger pattern of pressures being brought against education, the press, films, radio, and television. The problem is not only one of actual censorship. The shadow of fear cast by these pressures leads, we suspect, to an even larger voluntary curtailment of expression by those who seek to avoid controversy.

Such pressure toward conformity is perhaps natural to a time of uneasy change and pervading fear. Especially when so many of our apprehensions are directed against an ideology, the expression of a dissident idea becomes a thing feared in itself, and we tend to move against it as against a hostile deed, with suppression.

And yet suppression is never more dangerous than in such a time of social tension. Freedom has given the United States the elasticity to endure strain. Freedom keeps open the path of novel and creative solutions, and enables change to come by choice. Every silencing of a heresy, every enforcement of an orthodoxy, diminishes the toughness and resilience of our society and leaves it the less able to deal with stress.

Now as always in our history, books are among our greatest instruments of freedom. They are almost the only means for making generally available ideas or manners of expression that can initially command only a small audience. They are the natural medium for the new idea and the untried voice from which come the original contributions to social growth. They are essential to the extended discussion which serious thought requires, and to the accumulation of knowledge and ideas into organized collections.

We believe that free communication is essential to the preservation of a free society and a creative culture. We believe that these pressures towards conformity present the danger of limiting the range and variety of inquiry and expression on which our democracy and our culture depend. We believe that every American community must jealously guard the freedom to publish and to circulate, in order to preserve its own freedom to read.

We believe that publishers and librarians have a profound responsibility to give validity to that freedom to read by making it possible for the readers to choose freely from a variety of offerings.

The freedom to read is guaranteed by the Constitution. Those with faith in free men will stand firm on these constitutional guarantees of essential rights and will exercise the responsibilities that accompany these rights.

We therefore affirm these propositions:

1. It is in the public interest for publishers and librarians to make available the widest diversity of views and expressions, including those which are unorthodox or unpopular with the majority.

Creative thought is by definition new, and what is new is different. The bearer of every new thought is a rebel until his idea is refined and tested. Totalitarian systems attempt to maintain themselves in power by the ruthless suppression of any concept which challenges the established orthodoxy. The power of a democratic system to adapt to change is vastly strengthened by the freedom of its citizens to choose widely from among conflicting opinions offered freely to them. To stifle every nonconformist idea at birth would mark the end of the democratic process. Furthermore, only through the constant activity of weighing and selecting can the democratic mind attain the strength demanded by times like these. We need to know not only what we believe but why we believe it.

2. Publishers and librarians do not need to endorse every idea or presentation contained in the books they make available. It would conflict with the public interest for them to establish their own political, moral, or aesthetic views as the sole standard for determining what books should be published or circulated.

Publishers and librarians serve the educational process by helping to make available knowledge and ideas required for the growth of the mind and the increase of learning. They do not foster education by imposing as mentors the patterns of their own thought. The people should have the freedom to read and consider a broader range of ideas than those that may be held by any single librarian or publisher or government or church. It is wrong that what one man can read should be conformed to what another thinks proper.

3. It is contrary to the public interest for publishers or librarians to determine the acceptability of a book solely on the basis of the personal history or political affiliations of the author.

A book should be judged as a book. No art or literature can flourish if it is to be measured by the political views or private lives of its creators. No society of free men can flourish which draws up lists of writers to whom it will not listen, whatever they may have to say.

4. The present laws dealing with obscenity should be vigorously enforced. Beyond that, there is no place in our society for extra-legal efforts to coerce the taste of others, to confine adults to the reading matter deemed suitable for adolescents, or to inhibit the efforts of writers to achieve artistic expression.

To some, much of modern literature is shocking. But is not much of life itself shocking? We cut off literature at the source if we prevent serious artists from dealing with the stuff of life. Parents and teachers have a responsibility to prepare the young to meet the diversity of experiences in life to which they will be exposed, as they have a responsibility to help them learn to think critically for themselves. These are affirmative responsibilities, not to be discharged simply by preventing them from reading works for which they are not yet prepared. In these matters taste differs, and taste cannot be legislated; nor can machinery be devised which will suit the demands of one group without limiting the freedom of others. We deplore the catering to the immature, the retarded, or the maladjusted taste. But those concerned with freedom have the responsibility of seeing to it that each individual book or publication, whatever its contents, price, or method of distribution, is dealt with in accordance with due process of law.

5. It is not in the public interest to force a reader to accept with any book the prejudgment of a label characterizing the book or author as subversive or dangerous.

The ideal of labeling presupposes the existence of individuals or groups with wisdom to determine by authority what is good or bad for the citizen. It presupposes that each individual must be directed in making up his mind about the ideas he examines. But Americans do not need others to do their thinking for them.

6. It is the responsibility of publishers and librarians, as guardians of the people's freedom to read, to contest encroachments upon that freedom by individuals or groups seeking to impose their own standard or tastes upon the community at large.

It is inevitable in the give and take of the democratic process that the political, the moral, or the aesthetic concepts of an individual or group will occasionally collide with those of another individual or group. In a free society each individual is free to determine for himself what he wishes to read, and each group is free to determine what it will recommend to its freely associated members. But no group has the right to take the law into its own hands, and to impose its own concept of politics or morality upon other members of a democratic society. Freedom is no freedom if it is accorded only to the accepted and the inoffensive.

7. It is the responsibility of publishers and librarians to give full meaning to the freedom to read by providing books that enrich the quality of thought and expression. By the exercise of this affirmative responsibility, bookmen can demonstrate that the answer to a bad book is a good one, the answer to a bad idea is a good one.

The freedom to read is of little consequence when expended on the trivial; it is frustrated when the reader cannot obtain matter fit for his purpose. What is needed is not only the absence of restraint, but the positive provision of opportunity for the people to read the best that has been thought and said. Books are the major channel by which the intellectual inheritance is handed down, and the principal means of its testing and growth. The defense of their freedom and integrity, and the enlargement of their service to society, requires of all bookmen the utmost of their faculties, and deserves of all citizens the fullest of their support.

We state these propositions neither lightly nor as easy generalizations. We here stake out a lofty claim for the value of books. We do so because we believe that they are good, possessed of enormous variety and usefulness, worthy of cherishing and keeping free. We realize that the application of these propositions may mean the dissemination of ideas and manners of expression that are repugnant to many persons. We do not state these propositions in the comfortable belief that what people read is unimportant. We believe rather that what people read is deeply important; that ideas can be dangerous; but that the suppression of ideas is fatal to a democratic society. Freedom itself is a dangerous way of life, but it is ours.

Endorsed by:

AMERICAN LIBRARY ASSOCIATION—*Council, June 25, 1953*

AMERICAN BOOK PUBLISHERS COUNCIL—*Board of Directors, June 18, 1953*

Subsequently Endorsed by:

AMERICAN BOOKSELLERS ASSOCIATION—*Board of Directors*

BOOK MANUFACTURERS' INSTITUTE—*Board of Directors*

NATIONAL EDUCATION ASSOCIATION—*Commission for the Defense of Democracy through Education*

How Libraries and Schools Can Resist Censorship

Adopted February 1, 1962 by the ALA Council

Libraries of all sizes and types have been under increasing pressures from persons who wish to use the library as an instrument of their own tastes and views. Such individuals and groups are demanding the exclusion or removal of books to which they object or the inclusion of a higher proportion of books that support their views. Similar attacks have been made on schools in connection with books used in their programs. In view of this fact, it seems desirable to set forth a few basic principles that may help librarians, trustees, and school administrators in preserving the freedom and professional integrity of their institutions.

The problem differs somewhat between the public library, with a responsibility to the public to present as wide a spectrum of significant reading matter as its budget can afford, and the school library, whose collections are designed to suport the educational objectives of the school. In both, however, there is involved the freedom of the school or the library to meet its professional responsibilities to the whole community.

Every library or school should take certain measures to clarify its policies and establish its community relations. These steps should be taken without regard to any attack or prospect of attack. They will put the institution in a firm and clearly defined position if its book policies are ever called into question.

As a normal operating procedure, every library, and the administration responsible for it, should establish certain principles.

1. There should be a definite book selection policy. This should be in written form and approved by the board of trustees, the school board, or other administrative authority. It should be stated clearly and should be understood by members of the staff. This policy should apply to other materials equally, i.e., films, records, magazines, and pamphlets.

2. A file recording the basis for decision should be kept for titles likely to be questioned or apt to be considered controversial.

3. There should be a clearly defined method for handling complaints. Any complaint should be required to be in writing, and the complainant should be identified properly before the complaint is considered. Action should be deferred until full consideration by appropriate administrative authority.

4. There should be continuing efforts to establish lines of communication to assure mutual understanding with civic, religious, educational, and political bodies.

5. Newspapers of the community should be informed of policies governing book selection and use. Purposes and services of the library should be interpreted through a continuing public relations program, as should the use of books in the school.

6. Participation in local civic organizations and in community affairs is desirable. The library and the school are key centers of the community; the librarian and school administrator should be known publicly as community leaders.

If an attack does come, remember the following:

1. Remain calm. Don't confuse noise with substance. Most attacks come from small groups of people who have little community backing. Time after time the American people have shown that, given the facts, they will back solidly the responsible exercise of professional freedom by teachers and librarians and that they will insist on protecting their own freedom to read. Insist on the deliberate handling of the complaint under previously established rules. Treat complainants with dignity, courtesy, and good humor.

2. Take immediate steps to assure that the full facts surrounding a complaint are known to the administration. The school librarian should go through the principal to the superintendent and the school board; the public librarian, to the board of trustees or to the appropriate community administration official; the college or university librarian, to the president and through him to the board of trustees. Full, written information should be presented, giving the nature of the problem or complaint and identifying the source.

3. Seek the support of the local press immediately. The freedom to read and the freedom of the press go hand in hand.

4. Inform local civic organizations of the facts and enlist their support where possible.

5. Defend the principles of the freedom to read and the professional responsibility of teachers and librarians rather than individual book. The laws governing obscenity, subversive material, and other questionable matter are subject to interpretation by the courts. The responsibility for removal of any book from public access should rest with this established process. The responsibility for the use of books in the schools must rest with those responsible for the educational objectives being served.

6. The ALA Intellectual Freedom Committee and other appropriate national and state committees concerned with intellectual freedom should be informed of the nature of the problem. Even though each effort at censorship must be met at the local level, there is often value in the support and assistance of agencies outside the area which have no personal involvement. They often can cite parallel cases and suggest methods of meeting an attack. Similar aid in cases affecting the use of books in the schools can be obtained from the Commission on Professional Rights and Responsibilities of the National Education Association.

Every librarian should be familiar with certain basic documents which have been prepared by the American Library Association and represent the position of this national organization of more than 26,000 librarians. Copies of each of these may be obtained by writing the American Library Association, 50 East Huron Street, Chicago 11, Illinois.

Library Bill of Rights (Adopted June 18, 1948, and amended February 1, 1961, by the ALA Council)

Statement on Labeling (Adopted July 13, 1951, by the ALA Council)

School Library Bill of Rights (Adopted July 8, 1955, by the ALA Council)

Freedom to Read Statement (Prepared by the Westchester Conference of ALA and the American Book Publishers Council, May 2–3, 1953)

Policies and Procedures for Selection of School Library Materials (Approved by the AASL, February 3, 1961)

Endorsed by: The Adult Education Association of the USA, Executive Committee, The American Book Publishers Council, The American Civil Liberties Union, The National Book Committee, The National Council of Teachers of English, The National Education Association Commission on Professional Rights and Responsibilities, The National Education Association Department of Classroom Teachers

Advertising Acceptability Standards

A STATEMENT OF ADVERTISING PRINCIPLES

Following is the creed of the American Federation of Advertising . . .
principles fully subscribed to by The Detroit News.

Good advertising aims to inform the consumer and help him to buy more intelligently.

Good advertising tells the truth, avoiding misstatement of facts as well as possible deception through implication or omission. It makes no claims which cannot be met in full and without further qualification. It uses only testimonials of competent witnesses.

Good advertising conforms to the generally accepted standards of good taste. It seeks public acceptance on the basis of the merits of the product or service advertised, rather than by the disparagement of competing goods. It tries to avoid practices that are offensive or annoying.

Good advertising recognizes both its economic responsibility to help reduce distribution costs and its social responsibility in serving the public interest.

PREFACE

Because advertising is carrying more of an economic burden than ever before, it is being watched as it never was before. Better Business Bureaus, the Federal Trade Commission, the U.S. Post Office, and state and municipal authorities have all become cognizant of the power of advertising and are, therefore, more determined to police it, to keep it truthful and healthful. The public, too, is taking a more sophisticated view of claims, descriptions, and statements, but aside from all this new emphasis on advertising practices, the advertiser himself must be aware of the rules that govern advertising and keep it truthful, in good taste, and productive. It is for this reason that this brochure has been published.

Advertising Changes with Economic Conditions

Advertising is constantly changing, and rules regarding it will change from time to time as laws and economic conditions alter our way of life. From time to time, therefore, the rules set forth in this brochure will be changed to meet new regulations and conditions.

The rules and suggestions published here pertain mainly to display advertising. A separate classified advertising manual covers the regulations governing that type of advertising.

Advertising Guide Posts

The Detroit News will be guided by the Fair Practice Code of The Detroit Better Business Bureau and the Federal Trade Commission's Guide

Against Deceptive Advertising as well as by the State of Michigan laws on advertising, special sales, etc., the Detroit Ordinance on Deceptive Advertising and U.S. Postal Regulations in all doubtful areas for advertising and selling, not specifically covered by other regulatory bodies.

Adherence to the principles stated here will produce better relationships between customer and seller and in general make advertising more effective.

Real Purpose of Advertising

Advertising under the free enterprise society in which we live performs an economic function of great magnitude and service. Without advertising, production would grind to a halt and warehouses could be clogged with merchandise for failure to effect distribution.

Advertising is also news in the true sense. It tells the reader about products new or old and tells where they may be had, under what circumstances, and at what price. It saves untold hours of searching for the busy buyer and brings together buyer and seller in an atmosphere of understanding. Advertising's function is therefore informative as well as economic.

The Climate for Effective Advertising

The effectiveness of advertising is dependent greatly on the reputation of the medium in which it is placed. To protect the public is the primary duty of the medium that accepts your advertising; indirectly this also protects the advertiser.

When the public places confidence in a certain medium, this confidence embraces the advertising in it. Therefore it is of the utmost importance that the advertising acceptability standards set forth in this manual be strictly followed.

HOW TO JUDGE ADVERTISING

"It has been suggested that an advertiser, judging the honesty of his sales message, need only ask himself a few direct questions:

Is it *really* honest?

Is it *clear* to the people who hear or look at it?

Can I *prove* all this?

Would I approve if my *competitor* used this copy?

Is this *straight* talk?

Would I want *my* wife to spend *my* money because of this ad?

Have I cut out *all* weaseling?

If the answer to *all* of these pointed questions is *YES*, then the advertising is legitimate, legal, truthful, meaningful, and also believable and productive."*

---

* Morton J. Simon, "The Advertising Truth Book," Advertising Federation of America, Inc., New York, 1960, p. 13.

A Judicial Definition

The principles which follow and which were set forth by the United States Supreme Court in affirming a postal fraud order in March, 1948, are indicative of what is meant by the paragraph above:

"Advertising as a whole must not create a misleading impression even though every statement separately considered is literally truthful.

"Advertising must be written for the probable effect it produces on ordinary and trusting minds, as well as for those intellectually capable of penetrating analysis.

"Advertising must not obscure or conceal material facts.

"Advertising must not be artfully contrived to distract and divert readers' attention from the true nature of the terms and conditions of an offer.

"Advertising must be free of fraudulent traps and stratagems which induce action which would not result from a forthright disclosure of the true nature of an offer."

The Advertiser's Responsibility

Statements which cause a person, institution, or group to be held up to ridicule or to be shunned or to be held in contempt are libelous, if false. Such material will not be accepted, and suspected material will only be accepted after a legal ruling by this newspaper's attorneys has been obtained. The advertiser agrees to assume sole responsibility for statements contained in his copy and to protect and indemnify The Detroit News against any and all liability, loss, or expense arising out of claims for libel, unfair trade practices, unfair competition, infringement of trade marks, names or patents, copyrights and proprietary rights, and all violations of the right of privacy resulting from the publication by this newspaper of the advertiser's copy.

Reservations and Exclusions

In the interest of the reader who is the mutual customer of The Detroit News and the advertiser, this newspaper makes every effort to exclude misleading, inaccurate, unethical, and fraudulent advertisements, as well as advertisements containing objectionable and unfair references to competitors. The Detroit News reserves the right to edit, revise, or reject any advertising copy.

UNACCEPTABLE ADVERTISING

The following classes of advertising are not accepted:
1. Fraudulent advertisements or those that contain statements of doubtful honesty.
2. Advertisements that make claims that can not be justified.
3. Ambiguous advertisements that can be misinterpreted by the reader to mean something other than the advertiser intends.
4. Attacks on a person or company or on the goods or services of another person or company.

5. Advertisements that promise exaggerated profits or extraordinary dividends.

6. Advertisements in bad taste or offensive to any group on moral, religious, or discriminatory grounds. Suggestive captions or illustrations are not permitted. No copy, headline, or illustration can be employed which states or implies conduct which by normal standards is considered morally or socially unacceptable.

7. Advertisements of motion pictures must conform to the Advertising Code For Motion Pictures adopted by the Board of Directors of the Motion Picture Association of America, Inc., as amended June 21, 1950. A copy of this code may be obtained from the Association.

8. Advertisements describing goods not available and not intended to be sold on request but used as bait to lure customers are not acceptable. Refusal to show, demonstrate, or deliver the advertised article within a reasonable period must be construed as an attempt at bait advertising.

9. Advertisements proposing marriage.

10. Advertisements that seek introductions to members of the opposite sex.

11. Medical advertisements of products containing dangerous or habit forming drugs or using unpleasant or offensive language. All medical advertising is accepted conditionally and is subject to censorship, review, or rejection by duly constituted authorities or by this newspaper. No mail order medical advertising is accepted.

12. Advertisements that offer free medical care or claim to cure certain diseases which are known to require a physician's care.

13. Advertisements that offer homework for pay.

14. Advertisements of fortune tellers and similar practitioners.

15. All advertising which makes dubious and exaggerated claims or is likely to cause injury to the health or morals of the reader or loss of confidence in the newspaper and its advertising.

16. Help wanted advertisements that make extravagant or misleading offers of salary or reward are not acceptable. It is illegal for an advertiser offering employment to advertise his own race, color, creed, or nationality or to indicate any such preference in his prospective employee. Employer requests for job applicants to send photographs are a violation of the Michigan Fair Employment Practice Commission's regulations, and such advertised requests are therefore unacceptable.

17. Advertisements asking the reader to send money to a Post Office box number or a Detroit News box number.

RULES AND DEFINITIONS

Limitation on the Word "Free"

Advertisements that use the word "free" must explicitly state what is involved and what obligations the buyer must meet to obtain the "free" article. A free trial or demonstration means a trial without obligation and that the merchandise so tried may be returned without cost or charge for its use during the trial period.

Contest Advertising Regulations

It is recommended that contest advertisers publish the names of the prize winners in this newspaper. In any case, a complete list of prize winners must be available for mailing to readers or contestants upon request. It must also meet the requirements of the U.S. Post Office Department for transmission through the mails and the laws against lotteries of the State of Michigan and that of the Federal Government.

Guarantees Must Be Defined

The use of the word "guarantee" must be explicitly qualified so that the reader may know the extent and duration of the guarantee and whether the dealer or manufacturer supports the guarantee. It must spell out just what is guaranteed; workmanship, durability, parts, appearance, etc. If the guarantee means an adjustment based on the advertisers' own judgment, this should be stated. A "money back guarantee" should state what portion of the money may be returned and under what circumstances. Guarantees of "money back" without stated qualifications should be honored with full refund in cash. Guarantees of "satisfaction or your money back" give the purchaser, not the advertiser, the sole right to judge whether he is satisfied. Terms such as "lifetime guarantee" may be construed as referring to the life of the purchaser. Otherwise "life" must be clearly defined.

Comparative Price Definitions

Comparisons of price must be confined to the advertiser's own prices, or to prices known to prevail in this area for the identical merchandise, as must comparisons of merchandise or service. Factory list and similar base prices do not make suitable grounds for comparison and can not be used. The use of savings claims or comparative prices in any form which is not provable, or which is based on an inflated price or a fictitious list price, or which is misleading in any respect is an unfair trade practice. Advertisers must adhere to terms and payment amounts specified in an advertisement. Duration of terms of purchase must be clearly stated.

Accuracy of Illustrations

Product illustrations must be accurate, must not exaggerate size, and must not create a false impression of the grade, quality, make, value, etc., of the product offered. If an illustration is not that of the advertised article, the price of this particularly illustrated article nor model must be given.

If accessories are illustrated or mentioned but not included in the price, the price of the accessories must be given separately or the advertisement must state that the accessories are not included in the price.

Financial and Mail Order Advertising

All investment advertising in businesses, new products, oil wells, etc., must have the approval of the Michigan Corporation and Securities Commission. Mail order speculative financial advertising is not accepted.

This newspaper reserves the right to examine merchandise offered in a mail order advertisement. Mail order advertising other than that of retailers must provide the reader with the option of purchasing the advertised item on a C.O.D. basis.

Mail order advertisements must carry a money back guarantee.

Meaning of Word "Wholesale"

The term "wholesale" means for resale and should not be used in retail advertising. This term should be deleted from advertising copy and the name of the advertiser when submitted.

Liquidation and Similar Sales

The term "liquidation" in any form such as "Liquidation Sale," "Inventory Liquidation," "Liquidating," "Stock in Hands of Liquidators," etc., shall be used only when the advertiser actually is in the process of liquidating his business preparatory to discontinuing business altogether. See Michigan statute on Going Out of Business and other special sales, page 13. The only exception to this rule shall be when stock is in the hands of a person or persons duly appointed by a court or other legal processes, or by licensed auctioneers offering for sale the stock of a concern which has discontinued or will discontinue business.

Advertising by Schools

Advertisements of trade schools can not be accepted unless the schools are duly licensed by the Michigan Department of Public Instruction, Division of Vocational Education.

Advertising of Correspondence Schools is subject to the laws contained in Part 124 of the U.S. Postal Regulations.

Advertisements Involving Mail Replies

All advertising which asks for mail replies is also subject to U.S. Postal Regulations, section 124 as is contest advertising.

Editorial Type Advertisements

Advertisements adopting a typographical style similar to editorial matter in this newspaper must be identified with the word "advertisement" prominently displayed at the top of each column of the advertisement. This type of copy must also conform to U.S. Postal Regulations.

LAWS, ORDINANCES, AND CODES

Following are The Better Business Bureau Fair Practice Code, texts of the State of Michigan Advertising Law and Special Sales Act and Detroit Ordinance, as well as information sources for a number of Federal Trade Commission rulings.

Fair Practice Code for Advertising and Selling (Recommended by the Association of Better Business Bureaus*)

---

* "A Guide for Retail Advertising and Selling," Association of Better Business Bureaus, Inc., New York, 1956, p. 4.

I. Serve the public with honest values.

II. Tell the truth about what is offered.

III. Tell the truth in a forthright manner so its significance may be understood by the trusting as well as the analytical.

IV. Tell the customers what they want to know——what they have a right to know and ought to know about what is offered so that they may buy wisely and obtain the maximum satisfaction from their purchases.

V. Be prepared and willing to make good as promised and without quibble on any guarantee offered.

VI. Be sure that the normal use of merchandise or services offered will not be hazardous to public health or life.

VII. Reveal material facts, the deceptive concealment of which might cause consumers to be misled.

VIII. Advertise and sell merchandise or service on its merit and refrain from attacking your competitors or reflecting unfairly upon their products, services, or methods of doing business.

IX. If testimonials are used, use only those of competent witnesses who are sincere and honest in what they say about what you sell.

X. Avoid all tricky devices and schemes such as deceitful trade-in allowances, fictitious list prices, false and exaggerated comparative prices, bait advertising, misleading free offers, fake sales and similar practices which prey upon human ignorance and gullibility.

Self-Regulation in Advertising

A Report on the Operations of Private Enterprise in an Important Area of Public Responsibility Submitted by the Advertising Advisory Committee to the Secretary of Commerce
U.S. Department of Commerce, Luther H. Hodges, Secretary

Self-Regulation by Advertising Trade Groups

In this chapter we shall be looking at the work of four major advertising associations, the *American Association of Advertising Agencies* (4A's), the *Association of National Advertisers* (A.N.A.), the *Advertising Federation of America* (AFA), and the *Better Business Bureaus* (BBB), as well as smaller advertising groups.

These organizations differ from the industry trade association discussed in the previous chapter in that their activities cover advertising in many different fields, rather than a single industry.

They also differ from many, if not most, industry associations in their size, structure, history, and breadth of experience.

All four of the larger associations, 4A's, A.N.A., AFA, and BBB, have been operating for more than 45 years, and their programs in the area of self-regulation represent a long history of development and refinement.

As we shall see, these programs differ considerably in method and technique, and even, to a degree, in philosophy. Such differences arise out of the fact that each of these organizations serves a particular area of advertising, and a particular kind or type of membership.

One other point to remember is that any national advertising organization, like an industry trade association, is subject to certain rigid limitations against "combining in restraint of trade" under the anti-trust laws.

(a) *The American Association of Advertising Agencies.*

In the structure of American advertising, the role of the advertising agency is essentially that of an outside firm of specialists, hired by an advertiser to plan, create, and place his advertisements and commercials.

As we have seen, some 40% of the country's advertising is handled by agencies, or $5.2 billion out of a total of $12.3 billion in 1962.

Of this amount, approximately $3.9 billion of advertising was handled in 1962 by agencies which are members of the American Association of Advertising Agencies (4A's).

The 4A's was organized in 1917, and there are today over 350 4A agencies, representing more than 770 agency offices in 180 cities and 33 other countries. The 4A program of self-regulation is built around the following:

(1) *Membership qualifications* for admission to the association.
(2) *Standards of Practice,* including a new, stronger Creative Code for 4A members.
(3) *Enforcement machinery,* through the operation (with A.N.A.) of the *Advertising Interchange* program.

In admitting new members the 4A's does not insist on any minimum size for an agency (except that an applicant must be able to render standard agency service) but it does investigate financial responsibility, ownership (agencies owned by advertisers and media are not eligible), character, and ethical and business standards.

The 4A qualification on this latter point reads as follows:

Ethical and Business Standards. While it is not important to know the applicant agency's form of organization in all details, or all of its operations, it is essential to know how it operates in relation to certain practices, declared by the Association to be unfair practices in the light of the obligation agencies have, not only to their clients, but to the media they employ, to the public, and to each other. These practices are stated in the 'Standards of Practice of the American Association of Advertising Agencies'.

4A Standards of Practice were first adopted by the Association in 1924, and have gone through a number of revisions since then, the latest dated April 28, 1962.

An interesting feature of 4A Standards, and one which reflects the character of the agency business, is the prominence which is given to advertising copy requirements.

Agencies, as the creators of advertising, are directly concerned with copy techniques, and 4A activities in self-regulation have, traditionally, been more involved with matters of copy treatment and taste than have those of other groups whose self-regulatory work is focused on securing obedience to the law.

Thus we find, in the most recent 4A Standards of Practice, a comprehensive Creative Code, which begins with a statement of Association beliefs:

1. That advertising bears a dual responsibility in the American economic system and way of life.

    To the public it is a primary way of knowing about the goods and services which are the products of American free enterprise, goods and services which can be freely chosen to suit the needs and desires of the individual. The public is entitled to expect that advertising will be reliable in content and honest in presentation.

    To the advertiser it is a primary way of persuading people to buy his goods or services within the framework of a highly competitive economic system. He is entitled to regard advertising as a dynamic means of building his business and his profits.

2. That advertising enjoys a particularly intimate relationship to the American family. It enters the home as an integral part of television and radio programs, to speak to the individual and often to the entire family. It shares the pages of favorite newspapers and magazines. It presents itself to travelers and to readers of the daily mails. In all these forms, it bears a special responsibility to respect the tastes and self-interest of the public.

3. That advertising is directed to sizable groups of the public at large, which is made up of many interests and many tastes. As is the case with all public enterprises, ranging from sports to education and even to religion, it is almost impossible to speak without finding

someone in disagreement. Nonetheless advertising people recognize their obligation to operate within the traditional American limitations: to serve the interests of the majority and respect the rights of the minority.

In backing these beliefs, 4A members not only agree to support and obey existing laws and legal regulations pertaining to advertising, but undertake to "extend and broaden the application of high ethical standards."

Specifically, they pledge in the 4A Creative Code that they will not knowingly produce advertising which contains:

(a) False or misleading statements or exaggerations, visual or verbal.
(b) Testimonials which do not reflect the real choice of a competent witness.
(c) Price claims which are misleading.
(d) Comparisons which unfairly disparage a competitive product or service.
(e) Claims insufficiently supported, or which distort the true meaning or practicable application of statements made by professional or scientific authority.
(f) Statements, suggestions or pictures offensive to public decency.

In the matter of good taste, the 4A Code goes on to say:

We recognize that there are areas which are subject to honestly different interpretations and judgment. Taste is subjective, and may even vary from time to time as well as from individual to individual. Frequency of seeing or hearing advertising messages will necessarily vary greatly from person to person.

However, we agree not to recommend to an advertiser, and to discourage the use of, advertising which is in poor or questionable taste, or which is deliberately irritating through content, presentation, or excessive repetition.

Finally, the 1962 version of the 4A Creative Code included for the first time a penalty clause:

Clear and willful violations of this Code shall be referred to the Board of Directors of the American Association of Advertising Agencies for appropriate action, including possible annulment of membership, as provided in Article IV, Section V, of the Constitution and By-Laws.

In looking back over previous 4A statements of advertising standards, including its first Copy Code in 1924, and its special Interpretation of the Copy Code with Respect to Television Commercials in 1960, it is clear that the Association has moved steadily ahead over the years toward the assumption of greater responsibility in matters of advertising ethics and taste.

Though it is too early to know how the "annulment of membership" provision in the present Code will be applied, there is a considerable body of evidence about the effectiveness of another type of 4A enforcement machinery, its so-called *Advertising Interchange* program.

Organized in 1946, and conducted independently by the 4A's until 1960, when it became a joint 4A–A.N.A. operation, the Interchange program ("Interchange of Opinion on Objectionable Advertising") is a reviewing procedure for dealing with matters of taste, opinion, and improper disparagement of competitors, rather than questions of fact, accuracy, or legal infractions.

It is administered by a Committee of twenty executives, ten representing agencies and ten representing advertisers, who review complaints about objectionable advertising and deal with them on a confidential basis.

Most of the complaints received come from people in advertising—— agencies, advertisers, advertising clubs, and media, though the Committee welcomes (but does not solicit) complaints from the public at large.

Under the Interchange machinery, complaints about specific advertisements are circulated to members of the Committee, together with a voting form and a copy of the print advertising, or script of the radio commercial, or photo-script of the TV commercial.

The entire procedure is confidential:

(a) Complainants are never identified to the Committee, the advertiser concerned, or the placing agency.

(b) The Committee's votes are never reported back to the Complainant.

(c) Committee members vote privately and individually by mail, so that no member is influenced by or even knows the opinions of the others.

(d) The Committee's votes and comments are given only to the advertiser and agency concerned.

(e) Cases are never publicly identified.

(f) The Committee has never yielded to pressure to divulge the names of advertisers or agencies from whom it requests action.

If a majority of the Committee considers the advertising either "objectionable" or "serious," the advertiser and agency involved are notified.

In cases which are voted "objectionable," a copy of the Committee's comments is sent along for information, but no reply is requested. In "serious" cases an answer is asked for.

Over the years the Interchange procedure has produced a surprisingly high degree of cooperation and corrective action on advertising voted "objectionable" or "serious."

Committee records for two years, 1961 and 1962, show:

	1962	1961
Criticisms received	88	88
Criticisms processed	53	41
Deemed questionable	11	20
Deemed serious	8*	9
Corrective action taken or presumed to be taken	7**	9
Non-compliance reported to A.N.A. and 4A Boards	1	0

* *Including one case carried over from previous year.*

** *Advertisement or campaign reported revised or withdrawn, 4. Advertisement not repeated, no further complaint, 3.*

Not all of the 88 criticisms received in 1962 could be handled by the Interchange——

10 were questions of fact or validity of claims outside the scope of Interchange work.

12 were screened out as trivial by the Co-Chairmen and Secretary.

3 were broadcast commercials which could not be identified by the description.

More than 65% of 1962 criticisms were on the score of "bad taste," including suggestiveness, semi-nudity, overdone physiological diagrams, or irreverent use of respected themes.

Other complaints involved misleading trickery in words, typography of illustration, "ridiculous" claims, derogatory statements, and scare copy.

The success of the Interchange program undoubtedly owes much to the high professional standing of individual Committee members. Their names are published regularly, and advertisers and agencies whose work has been cited by the Committee have frequently expressed gratitude for receiving the comments of experienced and respected advertising executives.

The weakness of the Interchange operation is clearly the small number of complaints received and processed.

Over the years this number has varied considerably (186 complaints were processed in 1953, 62 in 1955) and the Committee has tried in various ways to broaden the scope of its activities by publicizing its work among agencies, advertisers, advertising clubs, and media.

As it stands now, however, the Interchange program is a highly effective type of self-regulatory machinery which deserves much broader usage.

In addition to the Interchange, Creative Code, and Standards of Practice aspects of its self-regulation work, the 4A's also maintains an extensive and specialized library of information on Legal Restrictions on Advertising, and Legislation and Government Regulations, as well as an information service for its members on these subjects.

It also publishes and circulates widely each year a number of talks and speeches on matters of advertising taste and self-regulation given by agency executives at its meetings and conventions.

One final note on 4A operations is interesting for the light it throws on the restrictions inherent in association work.

In 1955 the Justice Department filed a civil anti-trust suit against the 4A's and five media associations. The suit was settled without trial through a consent decree signed by both the 4A's and the Department.

In the consent decree the 4A's denied the offenses charged, asserted its innocence but was enjoined from ever taking certain actions alleged in violation of the Sherman Anti-Trust Law.

Among these are two which have a direct bearing on self-regulation problems. The 4A's is "enjoined and restrained" from "entering into, adhering to, promoting or following any course of conduct, practice, or policy, or any agreement or understanding:

Establishing or formulating, or attempting to establish or formulate, any standards of conduct or other qualifications to be used by any media or any association of media, to determine whether media should or should not do business with, recognize or approve, any advertising agency.

Designed to cause any media not to do business with, not to recognize, or not to approve, any advertising agency.

Those who wonder why it is not possible for agencies, advertisers, associations and media to get together in some sort of "get tough" program to force higher standards of advertising taste and ethics will do well to study these provisions.

4A activities in self-regulation represent the most effective methods which a large, experienced, and influential association has been able to develop over the years, within the limitations under which it must operate.

(b) *The Association of National Advertisers.*

The second of the four major advertising organizations in our study, the Association of National Advertisers, has, like the 4A's, a long and influential record in advertising affairs.

A non-profit company membership organization, the A.N.A. was founded in 1910, and numbers today approximately 700 member companies. While figures are not available on the percentage of total national advertising represented in A.N.A., it is significant that all 10 of the largest national advertisers, and 86 of the top 100, are A.N.A. companies. (Among those not represented are Sears Roebuck, Montgomery Ward, and the Ford and Chevrolet Dealer Associations, which are not eligible for A.N.A. membership because their activities are primarily retail.)

A.N.A. philosophy and activities regarding self-regulation reflects to a very high degree the interests and needs of A.N.A. member companies, and for this reason a summary of their chief characteristics will help us to understand A.N.A. policy:

(1) *Larger Companies.* As national advertisers, A.N.A. companies are among the larger users of advertising, and in general represent larger corporate organizations.

(2) *Diversity of Products and Services.* The A.N.A. roster includes major companies in practically every product or service field—— automobiles, rubber, oil, liquor, food, drugs, cosmetics, etc.

(3) *Use of Agencies.* A majority of A.N.A. companies place their advertising through advertising agencies. A.N.A. involvement with agency activities is traditionally a close one.

(4) *Marketers rather than Advertising Craftsmen.* Unlike agency executives, however, A.N.A. members are managers of products and services, rather than specialists and craftsmen in advertising techniques and treatments.

(5) *Individual Codes and Standards.* Many, if not most, A.N.A. members maintain their own legal staffs to deal with problems of advertising regulation. A number have drafted their own standards of advertising ethics or support individual industry codes or associations.

Given this membership structure, it is not surprising that A.N.A. activities in the area of self-regulation should stand in marked contrast to those of other advertising organizations.

A.N.A. self-regulatory policies can be summarized as:

   i) *No formal A.N.A. code.* The association does not attempt to impose a code binding on all its members.

  ii) *Emphasis on individual rather than group self-regulation.* A.N.A. works to achieve higher individual standards on the part of its membership rather than group compliance.

 iii) *Cooperation with other associations.* A.N.A. executives and committees work closely with those of other advertising organizations on a variety of subjects and matters of advertising legislation and self-regulation.

 iv) *Leadership on major, overall advertising problems.* A.N.A. prestige and influence have often been used to bring together the various elements of the advertising (world) community to discuss and deal with major problems.

The fact that A.N.A. has no formal advertising code is wholly understandable in the light of A.N.A. membership. It should be pointed out, however, that the Association has formally endorsed the 4A Creative Code, which is binding on the agencies employed by many A.N.A. companies.

A.N.A.'s efforts to promote high ethical standards for individual advertisers are conducted, in the main, on an individual basis. We noted that A.N.A. backs the drafting of individual corporate codes, and the Association devotes a considerable amount of attention to alerting its members to new or complex matters of advertising legislation.

In this connection, one of A.N.A.'s most important efforts has been the publication of an authoritative booklet, *Legal Rules of the Road to Honest Advertising,* prepared by its general counsel Gilbert H. Weil.

Legal Rules of the Road goes far beyond the usual layman's explanation of advertising law. It is intended to help advertisers:

  (1) prepare advertising which satisfies legal fundamentals;

  (2) sense the possible existence of more subtle problems for reference to legal counsel;

  (3) comprehend more readily, when such advice has been sought, what legal counsel is concerned with; and through such better understanding, use his guidance more constructively.

Legal Rules of the Road does this through the statement and explanation of a fundamental legal concept which applies to all types of regulation or legislation, regardless of whether it comes from the FTC, Food and Drug Administration, Post Office, individual state statutes, or other sources.

The concept is contained in the following definition of honest advertising: "An advertisement is honest when *objective* facts which *bear upon* the product or service advertised fulfill in all *material* respects the *understanding* that is generated in *people* by the advertisement when observed in the way or ways that they *normally perceive it.*"

The explanation of this concept is given in a detailed discussion of the meanings of each of the italicized words——"objective," "bear upon," "material," etc.

It would not be proper to try to reproduce in this study the entire contents of *Legal Rules of the Road* (which is available from A.N.A.). However, one brief quote from the booklet on its use of the word "honesty" will indicate its depth and significance.

Honesty is referred to here in its objective rather than its moral sense. As will be pointed out later, the purpose of the law is to protect the public from being led to purchase by a misconception as to the true facts. The injury would be the same whether an advertiser misleads his audience intentionally, or through inadvertence, and the reprehensibility or purity of his subjective motivation is therefore irrelevant to the law's goal. Similarly, if factual error in an advertisement is not sufficiently consequential to affect the buying decision it does not amount to dishonesty in the legal sense.

Obviously, *Legal Rules of the Road* is intended to be used by advertising men whose knowledge, experience, and grasp of business fundamentals is well above average.

In the matter of cooperation with other advertising associations and groups, A.N.A. over the years has been active in practically all advertising areas, but has probably been closest to the 4A's, because of the advertiser-agency relationships involved.

As we have seen, A.N.A. and 4A's jointly operate the Interchange program and ten A.N.A. members sit on its Committee for the Improvement of Advertising Content, and vote on Interchange complaints.

The fact that A.N.A. companies are the largest clients of both advertising agencies and advertising media also gives the Association a uniquely influential position when it comes to exerting leadership on overall problems.

A good example of this occurred following the quiz show scandals in 1959. A.N.A. was not only the first advertising group to publish a statement admitting and detailing advertiser responsibilities, but it took the lead in calling a special meeting of advertiser, agency, and media executives to review ethical practices.

This meeting, held in New York in February, 1960, was addressed by the Chairman of the FTC, the Chairman of the 4A's, the Chairman of the NAB TV Code Review Board, the heads of the three TV networks, and representatives of the magazine and newspaper industries, as well as by A.N.A. members and officials.

It was, unquestionably, the most important and effective meeting held at the time on the subject of "Self-Regulation in Advertising," its success was due in large measure to the fact that it was held under A.N.A. auspices.

On the other hand, the very fact that A.N.A. membership includes nearly all of the country's (most potent and influential) largest advertisers also has a somewhat inhibiting effect on the Association's activities. Because of it, A.N.A. must conduct its affairs with extreme circumspection, and with no suspicion of power pressures.

A.N.A. remains, therefore, an important and active factor in advertising affairs, but one whose operations lack the news-making qualities of other organizations.

(c) The Advertising Federation of America

AFA, which was organized in 1905, is one of the oldest of the advertising associations, and at one time A.N.A., 4A's, and BBB were simply divisions of AFA activity. The Advertising Association of the West was formed in 1903 and today works closely with the AFA. AFA claims today a total of 50,000 members, drawn from three types of memberships:

(a) Local Advertising Clubs (more than 140, with membership of 22,000).

(b) Affiliated Associations (21 National associations representing media, advertisers, agencies' educational interests).

(c) Company members (800 companies or corporations concerned with the production, use, or sale of advertising).

Although more than 80% of AFA income is derived from company members and affiliated associations, AFA activities, particularly in the area of advertising self-regulation, are centered around the work of local advertising clubs.

This concentration on the problems of local advertising not only dovetails with the work of other associations, such as A.N.A. and 4A, which are generally concerned with the policing of national advertising, but has a long tradition at AFA.

AFA's active crusade for self-regulation began when it launched the vigorous "Truth in Advertising" movement in 1911, and "Truth in Advertising" remains both the slogan and basic concept of AFA self-regulatory work today. Indeed, the AFA/AAW were active in the "truth" effort much earlier.

Local advertising clubs which belong to AFA are organized to operate in five fields: Education in Advertising, Higher Standards for Advertising, Public Relations for Advertising, Legislative Service for Advertising, and Public Service Through Advertising.

Of these, there can be little doubt that most clubs devote a major share of their work to promoting Higher Standards for Advertising, through the Truth in Advertising program.

This program, which is primarily concerned with promoting greater compliance with federal, state, and local laws, rather than with matters of public taste or advertising techniques, is implemented by AFA with both educational and enforcement activities.

On the educational side, AFA has published and sold more than 10,000 copies of its *Advertising Truth Book*. This book, by former AFA Associate General Counsel Morton J. Simon, is not only a detailed explanation, for local club members, of various aspects of advertising law, but also a "how to" guide for setting up local Ethics Committees, Advertising Panels, and Better Business Bureau liaisons.

In this connection, it is interesting to contrast AFA's *Advertising Truth Book* with A.N.A.'s *Rules of the Road to Honest Advertising*.

The A.N.A. work, which is addressed to national advertising executives, is a tersely written, highly sophisticated exploration of legal principle and theory.

The AFA book, which is designed to aid local advertising club officials, spells out practical applications of the law under such chapter headings as "Seven General Rules," "A Catalog of Deception," "Price Advertising," "Use of the Word 'Free,' " "Bait Advertising," "Cooperative Advertising Under the Robinson-Patman Act," and "Sources of Guidance."

In its recommendations to, and work with, local clubs on the enforcement of ethical advertising standards, AFA stresses the machinery and procedures set up under the so-called *Cleveland Plan.*

This plan, developed in 1952 by the Advertising Club of Cleveland, Ohio, and prominent Cleveland advertisers and advertising agencies has these essential elements:

(1) *A local advertising code,* endorsed by advertisers, agencies, media, and suppliers in the area.

(2) *An advertising review panel,* composed of local businessmen, to consider complaints.

(3) *Code administration and enforcement* by the city's own Better Business Bureau.

The Cleveland advertising code was originally drafted by a committee named by the trustees of the Cleveland Better Business Bureau. The committee represented all major lines of advertising in Cleveland, and nearly all of its members belonged to the Cleveland Advertising Club (none was a BBB trustee).

The code itself was set up in three parts: general rules to apply to all Cleveland advertising, specific rules for specific types of advertising as necessary, and procedure under which code compliance would be sought.

These were then submitted for acceptance to various organizations and companies, including the Advertising Club, Chamber of Commerce, Retail Merchants' Board, newspapers, TV and radio stations, etc.

Companies and organizations accepting the code then recommended names for service on the Cleveland Advertising Panel. The total Panel now numbers fifty Cleveland citizens, who sit in groups of not less than five to review individual complaints.

Checking of local advertising for code infractions is done by the Cleveland Better Business Bureau. Advertisers thought to be violating the code are first notified of this by the Bureau, and are invited, if they wish, to bring up the problem before the Cleveland Panel.

If they disregard this invitation and persist in the code violation, they are sent a "Final Notice," and the matter is referred directly to the Panel.

A hearing is then scheduled, the advertiser is notified by registered mail, and a special panel of ten members (none may be a competitor of the advertiser summoned) is drawn up to pass on the case.

After reviewing all aspects of the complaint, the Panel may take one of four actions:

(1) accept assurance that future advertising will conform to the Code, and close the matter;

(2) request the advertiser to submit all future advertising to the BBB until he has given evidence of his desire to conform to the Code;

(3) recommend to advertising media that they require the advertiser to submit all future copy to the BBB;

(4) recommend to advertising media that advertising privileges be suspended indefinitely, or until the advertiser has presented satisfactory evidence of intention to conform to the Code.

The effectiveness of the Cleveland Plan has been due both to the thoroughness of this code machinery, and to the strong, continuing support given to the plan by Cleveland business.

The general provisions of the Cleveland Code follow closely the legal standards set up by the FTC and other bodies. Among special advertising subjects covered are guarantees, factory prices, claims of "wholesale," and liquidation and going-out-of-business sales.

The Cleveland Panel deals, of course, with local or regional advertising in the Cleveland area. Complaints involving national advertising are referred by the Panel to the A.N.A.–4A Interchange, and to the National Better Business Bureau.

AFA officials, commenting on the Cleveland Plan, report that it has been a powerful stimulant to the adoption of similar plans by AFA clubs in other cities. In a single year, 1960, for example, the Atlanta, Tulsa and Dayton Clubs established review panels patterned after the Cleveland approach. Ethics committees were set up that same year in Sioux City, Kansas City, Miaimi, Minneapolis, Akron, Indianapolis, Jacksonville, Knoxville, Topeka, Amarillo, and Abilene.

Today more than thirty other cities have similar programs, or are planning them. Exact details of local plans vary, of course, according to club size. Smaller groups, such as the Rio Grande Valley Ad Club, cannot operate in exactly the same way as clubs in cities which have a well-established Better Business Bureau. But the Cleveland principle is generally used.

AFA work is stimulating this type of local self-regulation, which is particularly important in the total advertising picture for two reasons:

(1) By far the greatest percentage of dishonest, illegal, and objectionable advertising occurs at the local rather than the national level.

(2) In many cases, such advertising is beyond the jurisdiction of the FTC or other federal agencies.

AFA, through its work with local advertising clubs, performs a service which is unduplicated by any other organization.

(d) *The Better Business Bureaus*

We now come to one of the most unusual and effective instruments of self-regulation ever developed by the private enterprise system.

The work of the Better Business Bureaus is so long established and highly respected that many people assume that a BBB is a semi-official agency.

They seldom realize that these Bureaus were started by advertising men and are, today, entirely supported by private business.

The origins of BBB go back to 1911, and the birth of the "Truth in Advertising" movement. To enforce the truth in advertising ideal, special Vigilance Committees were set up by AFA Clubs and members. These Committees were both national and local in scope, and were the immediate forerunners of the modern Better Business Bureaus. (The name was changed in 1916, and BBB became a separate organization in 1926.)

Today the BBB movement numbers 122 separate bureaus——108 local bureaus in major U.S. cities, nine in Canada, one each in Puerto Rico, Mexico, Venezuela, and Israel, and the National Better Business Bureau in New York City.

They are supported by more than 100,000 firms in all lines of business, whose membership dues or subscriptions total over $6½ million a year.

The Bureaus handle annually some 2½ million inquiries and complaints from business and the public, and in addition shop or investigate more than 40,000 advertisements each year for possible violations of truth or accuracy.

But such statistics, however impressive, do not begin to explain the purpose, scope, and techniques of BBB operations. For this we must look at the structure and work of a typical local Bureau.

Each of these Bureaus is organized as an independent, non-profit corporation. Each is usually supported by a diversity of business interests in the community, representing, especially, the fields of retailing, industry, and investment.

The Board of Directors of the local Bureau appoints a manager (generally a professional trained in BBB work) and authorizes the addition of staff and departments to fit the needs of a particular city. (Bureaus vary in size, and can seldom be established in communities of under 100,000.)

Typically, a local BBB is engaged in three main areas of activity:

(a) *Merchandise Division,* which is concerned with the advertising, selling, and delivery of goods and services.

(b) *Financial Division,* which deals with advertising and selling in the fields of investment and securities, real estate, business opportunities, schools, insurance, or any other type of business which involves investments by the public.

(c) *Solicitations Division,* which investigates campaigns aimed at securing contributions for charitable, philanthropic, propaganda, social, or economic causes, as well as advertising in or subscriptions to various types of magazines, publications of "puff sheets" with a charitable, civic, patriotic, or religious appeal.

In each of these areas a Bureau operates as an impartial "fact finding or fact dispensing" organization whose purpose, as stated in its charter, is to "protect business, investors, and consumers against unfair and fraudulent practices."

The Merchandise Division has, as its special function, to search out, both on its own initiative and as a result of consumer complaints, questionable advertising, selling, or delivery practices regarding goods and services, and to try to eliminate these practices by persuasion, education, public warning, or, if necessary, prosecution.

In its work the Division covers both general retailing and specific fields to which concentrated attention must be given. It meets with, and assists, local trade groups in setting up trade codes or standards of practice and with community groups in establishing and enforcing local advertising codes, as under the Cleveland Plan.

In addition it receives and reviews consumer complaints and operates a comprehensive system of "BBB shop-investigations."

Bureau shoppers follow up offerings in retail advertising with store visits, and they are carefully instructed that their role is not that of "detective, reformer, or merchandise expert."

Rather they are "representatives of the public," who investigate and then report to the merchant what they found when they answered his advertising.

They are concerned with three questions:
(a) What is the public reaction to the advertisement?
(b) Why is the public reaction favorable or unfavorable?
(c) How could the advertisement build more confidence and good will?

In BBB experience, infractions of advertising ethics fall into one of nine classifications, and Bureau shoppers are taught to recognize and understand each:
(1) Misdescription of Seconds, Irregulars, or Imperfects.
(1) Unsupported superlative statements.
(3) Misstatements of material content.
(4) Incorrect description.
(5) Misleading trade names.
(6) Misleading use of trade mark names.
(7) Not on sale (bait).
(8) Misstatement of sizes and colors.
(9) Abuse of comparative prices.

When a BBB shopper has completed a store check on the offerings of a specific advertisement, he or she then prepares a report, which is sent to the advertiser involved.

This report identifies the advertisement, states the shopping circumstances including the name of the sales person involved, and gives a brief summary of the shopper's opinion, as a "representative of the public."

Reports are of two kinds, favorable (blue sheet) and unfavorable (pink sheet). In the case of unfavorable reports, the Bureau asks an immediate reply from the advertiser if his investigation does not verify BBB findings. Otherwise, it is assumed to be correct, and the advertiser is urged to take corrective action.

BBB considers a case serious when it falls into one of these three classifications:
(a) *Fraudulent advertising*——designed to victimize those who respond to it. Clearly in violation of the existing laws.
(b) *Repeated misrepresentations*——by an advertiser who has had his errors called to his attention. BBB assumes that he usually intends to deceive the public, and will try to excuse his practices in the hope that the Bureau will not take drastic action.
(c) *Advertising by transient vendors*——who intend to sell their merchandise by any means and leave town.

The vast majority of cases, however, never reach the serious stage. BBB reports that 95% to 97% of all advertising which receives "Unfavorable" reports is corrected voluntarily by the advertiser, either on his own or after consultation with Bureau officials.

When voluntary compliance is not achieved, however, a Bureau is empowered to take up the case with local media (newspapers, TV, and radio stations) and with local law enforcement officials. In such instances, BBB's long experience with, and intimate knowledge of, advertising laws and regulations provides a safeguard which would be beyond the power of most business groups.

A local Bureau's *Financial* and *Solicitations Division* operates on the same principles as its *Merchandise Division,* but without the "shop investigation" machinery.

In these two areas BBB work concentrates on collection of complete factual material on all questionable advertising or offerings, investigations and direct interviews with promoters, close contacts with local law enforcement officials, bankers, investment houses, and other local officials or businessmen who can provide either information or special assistance.

BBB reports in all three areas are generally circulated, either in toto or in summary form, to local Bureau members, and are also sent to affiliate Bureaus in other cities. Communications between Bureaus provides important help in solving local problems or in spotting unethical operators who move from community to community.

Within the BBB structure, local Bureaus are concerned solely with matters of local advertising. All complaints or questions involving national advertising activities are forwarded by them to the National Better Business Bureau, an affiliated organization with offices in New York City.

The National Better Business Bureau deals with national advertisers according to the same principles as those employed in other BBB operations, but it has, in addition, certain broader functions.

As we have seen in the case of the American Seat Belt Council, the NBBB frequently assists new industries in developing industry codes and standards of practice, and it functions as administrator and enforcement agent for a number of these codes.

Another important NBBB activity is as a central source of information for advertisers, agencies, and media. It publishes an authoritative looseleaf service, "Dos and Don'ts of Advertising Copy," which summarizes legal restrictions, trade practice rules, industry codes, recent court or commission decisions, and other data for over thirty advertising fields. This service has more than 1,300 subscribers, and is unquestionably the standard reference work on the subject.

Finally, the NBBB publishes, as the need arises, service bulletins warning media, agencies, and advertisers of questionable practices and operators.

All of the bureaus, both national and local, are members of the Association of Better Business Bureaus, which operates as a service organization for the entire BBB movement.

ABBB engages in a great many educational and promotional activities directed toward advertisers, the public, and individual bureau operations.

For the latter field, ABBB publishes extensive operations and training manuals for BBB employees, aids in the formation of new bureaus, and acts as a consultant and advisor to BBB heads and directors.

For the public it brings out a succession of booklets, films, and other educational materials under such titles as "Safeguarding Your Savings" and "How to Invest Your Money," all aimed at forestalling questionable advertising and selling practices.

Among its advertiser-directed works are its highly regarded *Guide to Retail Advertising and Selling,* a fact-filled retail handbook now in its sixth edition.

Over the years, BBB has taken the lead in practically every crusade aimed at eliminating undesirable business practices. Following World War I it fought the stock swindler and bucket shop operators who sprang up during the period.

In the mid-1920's it exposed fraudulent promoters in the great Florida land boom. In recent years the Bureaus have waged notable campaigns against spurious charities, phony business proposition, and fake publications soliciting advertising.

Because of its long and wide experience, the BBB's judgments on the current scene are especially interesting. Even in the earliest days, the proportion of advertisers who used deliberately fraudulent practices was very small. But, say BBB officials, at one time the complaints received by the Bureaus far outnumbered simple inquiries.

Today the situation is completely reversed. Inquiries outnumber complaints by more than three to one, and a great deal of BBB work consists in dealing with minor exaggerations and inaccuracies. Questions of taste, rather than of outright deception and misrepresentation, are at the root of most current criticisms of advertising, and this change, in the opinion of BBB executives, reflects a gradual but steady improvement in business practices.

Traditionally, the BBBs have dealt with matters of fact and law rather than good taste, but a number of Bureaus are now forwarding such complaints to the A.N.A.–4A Interchange Committee.

Throughout its history the BBB's record and reputation for absolute fairness, impartiality, and complete independence, and its concern for the interests of both business and the public, have made it a uniquely powerful force in American life.

It is unquestionably the most significant single element in the entire structure of advertising self-regulation, and well deserves its accolade of "The conscience of responsible business, and the voice of the people in the marketplace."

(e) *Other Advertising Groups*

In addition to the four major associations, 4A, A.N.A., AFA, and BBB, there are a number of other advertising groups which participate in self-regulatory work.

Two of the largest of these are the Advertising Association of the West (AAW) and the Association of Industrial Advertisers (AIA).

AAW, which operates in twelve western states, unites 44 local advertising clubs, and maintains close relations with AFA (its clubs were once AFA members). Its self-regulatory program parallels that of AFA very closely——particularly in its emphasis on the Truth-in-Advertising theme, on Better Business Bureau cooperation, and on the enforcement machinery of AFA's Cleveland Plan.

One AAW feature not found in AFA are junior advertising clubs, paralleling senior clubs in a number of western cities.

AIA, whose members are defined generally as "those who advertise to industry," has chapters in 28 cities and a membership of 3,700, including advertising managers, agency men, and media representatives.

Applicants for AIA are required to subscribe to the Association's Standards of Practice, which include the following provisions:

To support unequivocally the principle of Truth in Advertising, avoiding all manner of misrepresentation and falsification.

To discourage the publication of industrial advertising that does not measure up to the highest standards.

AIA is one of the associations which belongs to AFA, and it supports AFA programs. Among its own activities are regular monthly Legal Letters to AIA members on legislative and regulatory problems.

Many other smaller advertising groups and clubs throughout the country maintain an active interest in self-regulation but, like AAW and AIA, their programs are usually patterned on, or allied with, those of the large trade organizations.

(f) *Summary*

Of the four main types of advertising self-regulation, that practiced by the advertising trade associations is probably the best known and most widely publicized.

As we have seen, these associations serve different phases of advertising and approach self-regulation in different ways.

Among the most significant differences between them are the amount of emphasis each places on individual rather than group self-regulation (most pronounced with A.N.A.) and the attention each devotes to matters of taste and ethics which are outside the scope of the law.

Though all four of the major associations are concerned with raising general advertising standards, it is fair to say that the programs of BBB and AFA are primarily directed toward securing obedience to existing laws, while those of 4A and A.N.A. are also aimed at improving advertising content in areas not covered by law.

To a certain extent the activities of 4A, A.N.A., AFA, and BBB overlap, and for obvious reasons there are close working relationships between 4A and A.N.A. and between BBB and the AFA clubs.

Each of the major associations (except BBB) engages, of course, in a number of activities not concerned with self-regulation, and each must exercise care to avoid anti-trust action.

Taken together, their self-regulatory programs present a broad pattern of coverage and effectiveness, and one which also provides a stimulant to the three other types of self-regulation——by individual advertisers, by individual industries, and by advertising media.

There are good reasons for both methods, and each can point to many successful accomplishments.

Motion Picture Association of America, Inc.
December, 1956

The Motion Picture Production Code

FOREWORD

Motion picture producers recognize the high trust and confidence which have been placed in them by the people of the world and which have made motion pictures a universal form of entertainment.

They recognize their responsibility to the public because of this trust and because entertainment and art are important influences in the life of a nation.

Hence, though regarding motion pictures primarily as entertainment without any explicit purpose of teaching or propaganda, they know that the motion picture within its own field of entertainment may be directly responsible for spiritual or moral progress, for higher types of social life and for much correct thinking.

On their part, they ask from the public and from public leaders a sympathetic understanding of the problems inherent in motion picture production and a spirit of cooperation that will allow the opportunity necessary to bring the motion picture to a still higher level of wholesome entertainment for all concerned.

THE PRODUCTION CODE

General Principles

1. No picture shall be produced which will lower the moral standards of those who see it. Hence the sympathy of the audience shall never be thrown to the side of crime, wrong-doing, evil or sin.

2. Correct standards of life, subject only to the requirements of drama and entertainment, shall be presented.

3. Law——divine, natural or human——shall not be ridiculed, nor shall sympathy be created for its violation.

Particular Applications

I. CRIME:

1. Crime shall never be presented in such a way as to throw sympathy with the crime as against law and justice, or to inspire others with a desire for imitation.
2. Methods of crime shall not be explicitly presented or detailed in a manner calculated to glamorize crime or inspire imitation.
3. Action showing the taking of human life is to be held to the minimum. Its frequent presentation tends to lessen regard for the sacredness of life.

4. Suicide, as a solution of problems occurring in the development of screen drama, is to be discouraged unless absolutely necessary for the development of the plot, and shall never be justified, or glorified, or used specifically to defeat the ends of justice.
5. Excessive flaunting of weapons by criminals shall not be permitted.
6. There shall be no scenes of law-enforcing officers dying at the hands of criminals, unless such scenes are absolutely necessary to the plot.
7. Pictures dealing with criminal activities in which minors participate, or to which minors are related, shall not be approved if they tend to incite demoralizing imitation on the part of youth.
8. Murder:
    (a) The technique of murder must not be presented in a way that will inspire imitation.
    (b) Brutal killings are not to be presented in detail.
    (c) Revenge in modern times shall not be justified.
    (d) Mercy killing shall never be made to seem right or permissible.
9. Drug addiction or the illicit traffic in addiction-producing drugs shall not be shown if the portrayal:
    (a) Tends in any manner to encourage, stimulate or justify the use of such drugs; or
    (b) Stresses, visually or by dialogue, their temporarily attractive effects; or
    (c) Suggests that the drug habit may be quickly or easily broken; or
    (d) Shows details of drug procurement or of the taking of drugs in any manner; or
    (e) Emphasizes the profits of the drug traffic; or
    (f) Involves children who are shown knowingly to use or traffic in drugs.
10. Stories on the kidnapping or illegal abduction of children are acceptable under the Code only (1) when the subject is handled with restraint and discretion and avoids details, gruesomeness and undue horror, and (2) the child is returned unharmed.

II. BRUTALITY:

Excessive and inhumane acts of cruelty and brutality shall not be presented. This includes all detailed and protracted presentation of physical violence, torture and abuse.

III. SEX:

The sanctity of the institution of marriage and the home shall be upheld. No film shall infer that casual or promiscuous sex relationships are the accepted or common thing.
1. Adultery and illicit sex, sometimes necessary plot material, shall not be explicitly treated, nor shall they be justified or made to seem right and permissible.

2. Scenes of passion:
    (a) These should not be introduced except where they are defi-
        finitely essential to the plot.
    (b) Lustful and open-mouth kissing, lustful embraces, sugges-
        tive posture and gestures are not to be shown.
    (c) In general, passion should be treated in such manner as not
        to stimulate the baser emotions.
3. Seduction or rape:
    (a) These should never be more than suggested, and then only
        when essential to the plot. They should never be shown
        explicitly.
    (b) They are never acceptable subject matter for comedy.
    (c) They should never be made to seem right and permissible.
4. The subject of abortion shall be discouraged, shall never be more
   than suggested, and when referred to shall be condemned. It
   must never be treated lightly or made the subject of comedy.
   Abortion shall never be shown explicitly or by inference, and a
   story must not indicate that an abortion has been performed. The
   word "abortion" shall not be used.
5. The methods and techniques of prostitution and white slavery shall
   never be presented in detail, nor shall the subjects be presented
   unless shown in contrast to right standards of behavior. Brothels
   in any clear identification as such may not be shown.
6. Sex perversion or any inference of it is forbidden.
7. Sex hygiene and venereal diseases are not acceptable subject
   matter for theatrical motion pictures.
8. Children's sex organs are never to be exposed. This provision shall
   not apply to infants.

IV. VULGARITY:

Vulgar expressions and double meanings having the same effect are
forbidden. This shall include but not be limited to such words and expressions as chippie, fairy, goose, nuts, pansy, S.O.B., son-of-a. The
treatment of low, disgusting, unpleasant, though not necessarily evil, subjects should be guided always by the dictates of good taste and a proper
regard for the sensibilities of the audience.

V. OBSCENITY:

1. Dances suggesting or representing sexual actions or emphasizing
   indecent movements are to be regarded as obscene.
2. Obscenity in words, gesture, reference, song, joke or by suggestion,
   even when likely to be understood by only part of the audience,
   is forbidden.

VI. BLASPHEMY AND PROFANITY:

1. Blasphemy is forbidden. Reference to the Deity, God, Lord, Jesus,
   Christ, shall not be irreverent.
2. Profanity is forbidden. The words "hell" and "damn," while
   sometimes dramatically valid, will if used without moderation be

considered offensive by many members of the audience. Their use shall be governed by the discretion and prudent advice of the Code Administration.

VII. COSTUMES:

1. Complete nudity, in fact or in silhouette, is never permitted, nor shall there be any licentious notice by characters in the film of suggested nudity.
2. Indecent or undue exposure is forbidden.
   (a) The foregoing shall not be interpreted to exclude actual scenes photographed in a foreign land of the natives of that land, showing native life, provided:
       (1) Such scenes are included in a documentary film or travelogue depicting exclusively such land, its customs and civilization; and
       (2) Such scenes are not in themselves intrinsically objectionable.

VIII. RELIGION:

1. No film or episode shall throw ridicule on any religious faith.
2. Ministers of religion, or persons posing as such, shall not be portrayed as comic characters or as villains so as to cast disrespect on religion.
3. Ceremonies of any definite religion shall be carefully and respectfully handled.

IX. SPECIAL SUBJECTS:

The following subjects must be treated with discretion and restraint and within the careful limits of good taste:
1. Bedroom scenes.
2. Hangings and electrocutions.
3. Liquor and drinking.
4. Surgical operations and childbirth.
5. Third degree methods.

X. NATIONAL FEELINGS:

1. The use of the flag shall be consistently respectful.
2. The history, institutions, prominent people and citizenry of all nations shall be represented fairly.
3. No picture shall be produced that tends to incite bigotry or hatred among peoples of differing races, religions or national origins. The use of such offensive words as Chink, Dago, Frog, Greaser, Hunkie, Kike, Nigger, Spic, Wop, Yid, should be avoided.

XI. TITLES:

The following titles shall not be used:
1. Titles which are salacious, indecent, obscene, profane or vulgar.
2. Titles which violate any other clause of this Code.

XII. CRUELTY TO ANIMALS:

In the production of motion pictures involving animals the producer shall consult with the authorized representative of the American Humane Association, and invite him to be present during the staging of such animal action. There shall be no use of any contrivance or apparatus for tripping or otherwise treating animals in any unacceptably harsh manner.

REASONS SUPPORTING THE CODE

I. Theatrical motion pictures, that is, pictures intended for the theatre as distinct from pictures intended for churches, schools, lecture halls, educational movements, social reform movements, etc., are primarily to be regarded as entertainment.

Mankind has always recognized the importance of entertainment and its value in rebuilding the bodies and souls of human beings.

But it has always recognized that entertainment can be of a character either helpful or harmful to the human race, and in consequence has clearly distinguished between:

a. Entertainment which tends to improve the race, or at least to re-create and rebuild human beings exhausted with the realities of life; and

b. Entertainment which tends to degrade human beings, or to lower their standards of life and living.

Hence the moral importance of entertainment is something which has been universally recognized. It enters intimately into the lives of men and women and affects them closely; it occupies their minds and affections during leisure hours; and ultimately touches the whole of their lives. A man may be judged by his standard of entertainment as easily as by the standard of his work.

So correct entertainment raises the whole standard of a nation.

Wrong entertainment lowers the whole living conditions and moral ideals of a race.

Note, for example, the healthy reactions to healthful sports, like baseball, golf; the unhealthy reactions to sports like cockfighting, bullfighting, bear baiting, etc.

Note, too, the effect on ancient nations of gladiatorial combats, the obscene plays of Roman times, etc.

II. Motion pictures are very important as art.

Though a new art, possibly a combination art, it has the same object as the other arts, the presentation of human thought, emotion and experience, in terms of an appeal to the soul through the senses.

Here, as in entertainment,

Art enters intimately into the lives of human beings.

Art can be morally good, lifting men to higher levels. This has been done through good music, great painting, authentic fiction, poetry, drama. Art can be morally evil in its effects. This is the case clearly enough with unclean art, indecent books, suggestive drama. The effect on the lives of men and women is obvious.

Note: It has often been argued that art in itself is unmoral, neither good nor bad. This is perhaps true of the thing which is music, painting, poetry, etc. But the thing is the product of some person's mind, and the intention of that mind was either good or bad morally when it produced the thing. Besides, the thing has its effect upon those who come into contact with it. In both these ways, that is, as a product of a mind and as the cause of definite effects, it has a deep moral significance and an unmistakable moral quality.

Hence: The motion pictures, which are the most popular of modern arts for the masses, have their moral quality from the intention of the minds which produce them and from their effects on the moral lives and reactions of their audiences. This gives them a most important morality.

1. They reproduce the morality of the men who use the pictures as a medium for the expression of their ideas and ideals.

2. They affect the moral standards of those who, through the screen, take in these ideas and ideals.

In the case of the motion picture, this effect may be particularly emphasized because no art has so quick and so widespread an appeal to the masses. It has become in an incredibly short period the art of the multitudes.

III. The motion picture, because of its importance as entertainment and because of the trust placed in it by the peoples of the world, has special moral obligations.

A. Most arts appeal to the mature. This art appeals at once to every class, mature, immature, developed, undeveloped, law abiding, criminal. Music has its grades for different classes; so have literature and drama. This art of the motion picture, combining as it does the two fundamental appeals of looking at a picture and listening to a story, at once reaches every class of society.

B. By reason of the mobility of a film and the ease of picture distribution, and because of the possibility of duplicating positives in large quantities, this art reaches places unpenetrated by other forms of art.

C. Because of these two facts, it is difficult to produce films intended for only certain classes of people. The exhibitors' theatres are built for the masses, for the cultivated and the rude, the mature and the immature, the self-respecting and the criminal. Films, unlike books and music, can with difficulty be confined to certain selected groups.

D. The latitude given to film material cannot, in consequence, be as wide as the latitude given to book material. In addition:

a. A book describes; a film vividly presents. One presents on a cold page; the other by apparently living people.

b. A book reaches the mind through words merely; a film reaches the eyes and ears through the reproduction of actual events.

c. The reaction of a reader to a book depends largely on the keenness of the reader's imagination; the reaction to a film depends on the vividness of presentation.

Hence many things which might be described or suggested in a book could not possibly be presented in a film.

E. This is also true when comparing the film with the newspaper.

a. Newspapers present by description, films by actual presentation.

b. Newspapers are after the fact and present things as having taken place; the film gives the events in the process of enactment and with the apparent reality of life.

F. Everything possible in a play is not possible in a film:

a. Because of the larger audience of the film, and its consequential mixed character. Psychologically, the larger the audience, the lower the moral mass resistance to suggestion.

b. Because through light, enlargement of character, presentation, scenic emphasis, etc., the screen story is brought closer to the audience than the play.

c. The enthusiasm for and interest in the film actors and actresses, developed beyond anything of the sort in history, makes the audience largely sympathetic toward the characters they portray and the stories in which they figure. Hence the audience is more ready to confuse actor and actress and the characters they portray, and it is most receptive of the emotions and ideals presented by its favorite stars.

G. Small communities, remote from sophistication and from the hardening process which often takes place in the ethical and moral standards of groups in larger cities, are easily and readily reached by any sort of film.

H. The grandeur of mass settings, large action, spectacular features, etc., affects and arouses more intensely the emotional side of the audience.

In general, the mobility, popularity, accessibility, emotional appeal, vividness, straight-forward presentation of fact in the film make for more intimate contact with a larger audience and for greater emotional appeal.

Hence the larger moral responsibilities of the motion pictures.

REASONS UNDERLYING THE GENERAL PRINCIPLES

I. No picture shall be produced which will lower the moral standards of those who see it. Hence the sympathy of the audience should never be thrown to the side of crime, wrong-doing, evil or sin.

This is done:

1. When evil is made to appear attractive or alluring, and good is made to appear unattractive.

2. When the sympathy of the audience is thrown on the side of crime, wrong-doing, evil, sin. The same thing is true of a film that would throw sympathy against goodness, honor, innocence, purity or honesty.

Note: Sympathy with a person who sins is not the same as sympathy with the sin or crime of which he is guilty. We may feel sorry for the plight of the murderer or even understand the circumstances which led him to his crime. We may not feel sympathy with the wrong which he has done.

The presentation of evil is often essential for art or fiction or drama.

This in itself is not wrong provided:

a. That evil is not presented alluringly. Even if later in the film the evil is condemned or punished, it must not be allowed to appear so attractive that the audience's emotions are drawn to desire or approve so strongly that later the condemnation is forgotten and only the apparent joy of the sin remembered.

b. That throughout, the audience feels sure that evil is wrong and good is right.

II. Correct standards of life shall, as far as possible, be presented.

A wide knowledge of life and of living is made possible through the film. When right standards are consistently presented, the motion picture exercises the most powerful influences. It builds character, develops right ideals, inculcates correct principles, and all this in attractive story form. If motion pictures consistently hold up for admiration high types of characters and present stories that will affect lives for the better, they can become the most powerful natural force for the improvement of mankind.

III. Law——divine, natural or human——shall not be ridiculed, nor shall sympathy be created for its violation.

By natural law is understood the law which is written in the hearts of all mankind, the great underlying principles of right and justice dictated by conscience.

By human law is understood the law written by civilized nations.

1. The presentation of crimes against the law is often necessary for the carrying out of the plot. But the presentation must not throw sympathy with the crime as against the law nor with the criminal as against those who punish him.

2. The courts of the land should not be presented as unjust. This does not mean that a single court may not be represented as unjust, much less that a single court official must not be presented this way. But the court system of the country must not suffer as a result of this presentation.

REASONS UNDERLYING PARTICULAR APPLICATIONS

I. Sin and evil enter into the story of human beings and hence in themselves are valid dramatic material.

II. In the use of this material, it must be distinguished between sins which repel by their very nature, and sins which often attract.

    a. In the first class come murder, most theft, many legal crimes, lying, hypocrisy, cruelty, etc.

    b. In the second class come sex sins, sins and crimes of apparent heroism, such as banditry, daring thefts, leadership in evil, organized crime, revenge, etc.

The first class needs less care in treatment, as sins and crimes of this class are naturally unattractive. The audience instinctively condemns all such and is repelled.

Hence the important objective must be to avoid the hardening of the audience, especially of those who are young and impressionable, to the thought and fact of crime. People can become accustomed even to murder, cruelty, brutality, and repellent crimes, if these are too frequently repeated.

The second class needs great care in handling, as the response of human nature to their appeal is obvious. This is treated more fully below.

III. A careful distinction can be made between films intended for general distribution, and films intended for use in theatres restricted to a limited audience. Themes and plots quite appropriate for the latter would be altogether out of place and dangerous in the former.

Note: The practice of using a general theatre and limiting its patronage during the showing of a certain film to "Adults Only" is not completely satisfactory and is only partially effective.

However, maturer minds may easily understand and accept without harm subject matter in plots which do younger people positive harm.

Hence: If there should be created a special type of theatre, catering exclusively to an adult audience, for plays of this character (plays with problem themes, difficult discussions and maturer treatment) it would seem to afford an outlet, which does not now exist, for pictures unsuitable for general distribution but permissible for exhibitions to a restricted audience.

I. CRIMES AGAINST THE LAW

The treatment of crimes against the law must not:

1. Teach methods of crime.
2. Inspire potential criminals with a desire for imitation.
3. Make criminals seem heroic and justified.

Revenge in modern times shall not be justified. In lands and ages of less developed civilization and moral principles, revenge may sometimes be presented. This would be the case especially in places where no law exists to cover the crime because of which revenge is committed.

Because of its evil consequences, the drug traffic should not be presented except under careful limitations.

II. BRUTALITY

Excessive and inhumane acts of cruelty and brutality have no proper place on the screen.

III. SEX

Out of regard for the sanctity of marriage and the home, the triangle, that is, the love of a third party for one already married, needs careful handling. The treatment should not throw sympathy against marriage as an institution.

Scenes of passion must be treated with an honest acknowledgment of human nature and its normal reactions. Many scenes cannot be presented without arousing dangerous emotions on the part of the immature, the young or the criminal classes.

Even within the limits of pure love, certain facts have been universally regarded by lawmakers as outside the limits of safe presentation.

In the case of impure love, the love which society has always regarded as wrong and which has been banned by divine law, the following are important:

1. Impure love must not be presented as attractive and beautiful.
2. It must not be the subject of comedy or farce, or treated as material for laughter.
3. It must not be presented in such a way as to arouse passion or morbid curiosity on the part of the audience.
4. It must not be made to seem right and permissible.
5. In general, it must not be detailed in method and manner.
6. Certain places are so closely and thoroughly associated with sexual life or with sexual sin that their use must be carefully limited.

IV. VULGARITY

This section is intended to prevent not only obviously vulgar expressions but also double meanings that have the same effect.

V. OBSCENITY

Dances which suggest or represent sexual actions, whether performed solo or with two or more; dances intended to excite the emotional reaction of an audience; dances with movement of the breasts, excessive body movements while the feet are stationary, violate decency and are wrong.

This section likewise applies to obscene words, gestures, references, songs, jokes and gags.

VI. BLASPHEMY AND PROFANITY

It is clear that neither blasphemy nor profanity should be permitted on the screen.

VII. COSTUMES

General principles:

1. The effect of nudity or semi-nudity upon the normal man or woman, and much more upon the young and upon immature persons, has been honestly recognized by all lawmakers and moralists.

2. Hence the fact that the nude or semi-nude body may be beautiful does not make its use in the films moral. For, in addition to its beauty, the effect of the nude or semi-nude body on the normal individual must be taken into consideration.

3. Nudity or semi-nudity used simply to put a "punch" into a picture comes under the head of immoral actions. It is immoral in its effect on the average audience.

4. Nudity can never be permitted as being necessary for the plot. Semi-nudity must not result in undue or indecent exposures.

5. Transparent or translucent materials and silhouettes are frequently more suggestive than actual exposure.

VIII. RELIGION

The reason why ministers of religion may not be portrayed as comic characters or as villains so as to cast disrespect on religion is simply because the attitude taken toward them may easily become the attitude taken toward religion in general. Religion is lowered in the minds of the audience because of the lowering of the audience's respect for a minister.

IX. SPECIAL SUBJECTS

Such subjects are occasionally necessary for the plot. Their treatment must never offend good taste nor injure the sensibilities of an audience.

The use of liquor should never be excessively presented. In scenes from American life, the necessities of plot and proper characterization alone justify its use. And in this case, it should be shown with moderation.

X. NATIONAL FEELINGS

The just rights, history and feelings of peoples and nations are entitled to most careful consideration and respectful treatment.

XI. TITLES

As the title of a picture is the brand on that particular type of goods, it must conform to the ethical practices of all such honest business.

XII. CRUELTY TO ANIMALS

The purpose of this provision is to prevent the treatment of animals in films in any unacceptably harsh manner.

Code of Ethics

or

Canons of Journalism

American Society

of Newspaper Editors

The primary function of newspapers is to communicate to the human race what its members do, feel and think. Journalism, therefore, demands of its practitioners the widest range of intelligence, or knowledge, and of experience, as well as natural and trained powers of observation and reasoning. To its opportunities as a chronicle are indissolubly linked its obligations as teacher and interpreter.

To the end of finding some means of codifying sound practice and just aspirations of American journalism, these canons are set forth:

I.

RESPONSIBILITY——The right of a newspaper to attract and hold readers is restricted by nothing but considerations of public welfare. The use a newspaper makes of the share of public attention it gains serves to determine its sense of responsibility, which it shares with every member of its staff. A journalist who uses his power for any selfish or otherwise unworthy purpose is faithless to a high trust.

II.

FREEDOM OF THE PRESS——Freedom of the press is to be guarded as a vital right of mankind. It is the unquestionable right to discuss whatever is not explicitly forbidden by law, including the wisdom of any restrictive statute.

III.

INDEPENDENCE——Freedom from all obligations except that of fidelity to the public interest is vital.

1. Promotion of any private interest contrary to the general welfare, for whatever reason, is not compatible with honest journalism. So-called news communications from private sources should not be published without public notice of their source or else substantiation of their claims to value as news, both in form and substance.

2. Partisanship, in editorial comment which knowingly departs from the truth, does violence to the best spirit of American journalism; in the news columns it is subversive of a fundamental principle of the profession.

IV.

SINCERITY, TRUTHFULNESS, ACCURACY——Good faith with the reader is the foundation of all journalism worthy of the name.

1. By every consideration of good faith a newspaper is constrained to

be truthful. It is not to be excused for lack of thoroughness or accuracy within its control, or failure to obtain command of these essential qualities.

2. Headlines should be fully warranted by the contents of the articles which they surmount.

V.

IMPARTIALITY——Sound practice makes clear distinction between news reports and expressions of opinion. News reports should be free from opinion or bias of any kind.

1. This rule does not apply to so-called special articles unmistakably devoted to advocacy or characterized by a signature authorizing the writer's own conclusions and interpretation.

VI.

FAIR PLAY——A newspaper should not publish unofficial charges affecting reputation or moral character without opportunity given to the accused to be heard; right practice demands the giving of such opportunity in all cases of serious accusation outside judicial proceedings.

1. A newspaper should not invade private rights or feeling without sure warrant of public right as distinguished from public curiosity.

2. It is the privilege, as it is the duty, of a newspaper to make prompt and complete correction of its own serious mistakes of fact or opinion, whatever their origin.

DECENCY——A newspaper cannot escape conviction of insincerity if while professing high moral purpose it supplies incentives to base conduct, such as are to be found in details of crime and vice, publication of which is not demonstrably for the general good. Lacking authority to enforce its canons the journalism here represented can but express the hope that deliberate pandering to vicious instincts will encounter effective public disapproval or yield to the influence of a preponderant professional condemnation.

Code of Ethics
of The International Labor Press

To serve better the members of the American Federation of Labor and Congress of Industrial Organizations, and to protect the good name of labor from exploitation by racket papers masquerading as union publications, the International Labor Press Association (AFL-CIO) and its member publications subscribe to and shall abide by this Code of Ethics:

1. Member publications will serve the best interests of the American Federation of Labor and Congress of Industrial Organizations, and uphold the high ideals of the AFL-CIO Constitution at all times.
2. Member publications will plainly and prominently publish in each issue an accurate statement of ownership and endorsement.
3. Member publications will not represent, either in their publications or in the promotion or sale of advertising, that they are endorsed by the national AFL-CIO.
4. Member publications will not knowingly solicit, accept, or publish advertising from any firm against which a strike or lockout is in progress, or from any firm on the unfair list of a central labor body.
5. Member publications shall refuse to accept advertising from any firm which is continuing to resist organization of its employees by the AFL-CIO.
6. Member publications will not solicit nor accept local advertising from outside their area of circulation. This does not apply to national advertising. The name of a publication should not be inconsistent with its actual area of circulation and endorsement.
7. Member publications shall not accept advertising which has no demonstrable value to the advertiser in his relations with the union members who read the paper.
8. Member publications will not employ high-pressure, long distance telephone solicitors, or accept or publish advertising obtained through such methods.
9. Member publications will make no claim or suggestion directly or through salesmen that the purchase of advertising space can accomplish anything for the advertiser beyond winning consumer acceptance or approval of the advertiser's product or service. All advertising in member publications, except that concerned with nationally advertised standard brands, must carry the name and location of the advertiser and, when pertinent, the identification of the product or service he sells.
10. Member publications will not associate themselves in any manner with the publication of any yearbook, directory, or program that

[407

has for its primary purpose the solicitation of donations under the guise of selling advertising.

Violations of this Code of Ethics by a member publication shall constitute cause for suspension and expulsion under procedures provided in the Constitution of the International Labor Press Association (AFL-CIO).

Index